FEELING SAFE IN SCHOOL

FEELING SAFE IN SCHOOL

**Bullying and Violence
Prevention Around the World**

EDITED BY
**JONATHAN COHEN
AND DOROTHY L. ESPELAGE**

Harvard Education Press
Cambridge, Massachusetts

Paperback ISBN 978-1-68253-449-6
Library Edition ISBN 978-1-68253-450-2

Library of Congress Cataloging-in-Publication Data
Names: Cohen, Jonathan, 1952- editor. | Espelage, Dorothy L. (Dorothy Lynn), editor.
Title: Feeling safe in school : bullying and violence prevention around the world / edited by Jonathan Cohen and Dorothy L. Espelage.
Description: Cambridge, Massachusetts : Harvard Education Press, [2020] | Includes index. | Summary: "Jonathan Cohen and Dorothy L. Espelage, two leading authorities in the fields of school climate and prevention science, have gathered experts from around the globe to highlight policy and practice recommendations for supporting children and adolescents to feel and be safe in school"-- Provided by publisher.
Identifiers: LCCN 2019054633 | ISBN 9781682534496 (paperback) | ISBN 9781682534502 (library binding)
Subjects: LCSH: Bullying in schools. | Bullying in schools--Prevention. | Microaggressions. | Cyberbullying. | Victims of bullying. | Classroom environment. | School improvement programs.
Classification: LCC LB3013.3 .F44 2020 | DDC 371.7/82—dc23
LC record available at https://lccn.loc.gov/2019054633

Published by Harvard Education Press,
an imprint of the Harvard Education Publishing Group

Harvard Education Press
8 Story Street
Cambridge, MA 02138

Cover Design: Ciano Design
Cover Image: beastfromeast/DigitalVision Vectors via Getty Images

The typefaces used in this book are Adobe Garamond Pro and Gotham

CONTENTS

PREFACE

THINK ABOUT A TIME when you were in middle school. Think about a time when you felt particularly safe and secure "in your own skin"—a time when you felt able to learn, to share what you were thinking and/or feelings, to be open about "feeling confused" and/or just not knowing something. And then remember another time when you were feeling shaky, insecure, afraid that you would be laughed at if you made a mistake. We can all remember painful moments when we did not feel safe and/or were not safe socially, emotionally, intellectually, physically. We know that feeling unsafe undermines children's ability to learn and that feeling or being unsafe as an ongoing experience undermines healthy development.[1]

But what does it mean to feel and be safe? Feeling and being safe are overlapping but different experiences. We can feel safe but, in fact, be in great danger. And vice versa. Most people are aware that safety refers to a range of experiences—social, emotional, and intellectual, as well as physical. Historically, educators have recognized physical dangers and fears about being physically hurt, but it is only in recent decades that practitioners and policy makers in countries around the world have begun to recognize and address social, emotional, and intellectual aspects of safety.

Over the last twenty years there has been an explosion of empirical research findings that underscore what many parents and teachers have known for decades: children learn best when we treat them as human beings with social, emotional, civic, and academic needs. We now know that there are a range of social, emotional, civic, and academic skills, knowledge, and dispositions that provide an essential foundation for school and life success. And we know that high-quality, intentional, and ongoing social, emotional, civic, and academic instruction needs to be paired with systemic efforts to ensure that every child feels safe, supported, and engaged in order to provide the optimal foundation to support the whole child.[2]

1

In tandem with these research findings, international organizations have begun tracking markers of student safety and well-being, including questions on major surveys designed to gauge trends in everything from the level of bullying students are experiencing to citizenship skills. Over the last twenty years, the independent International Educational Association (IEA) has studied academic achievement as well as students' knowledge and understanding, beliefs, and behaviors related to civics and citizenship in more than sixty countries and a hundred educational systems. In 2015 Trends in International Mathematics and Science Study (TIMSS), an international study of student proficiency in math and science, began to ask students whether they were bullied. And in 2017 the Programme for International Student Assessment (PISA), which randomly samples several thousand fifteen-year-olds every three years, began to ask questions about students' well-being, in addition to their reading, mathematical, and scientific literacies, in order to assess how well each country's educational system is preparing its young people for success. And the Organisation of Economic Co-operation and Development (OECD) is actively furthering international conversations and prosocial professional development support in their Future of Education and Skills 2030 efforts.[3]

As researchers and practitioners who have spent decades researching and working nationally and internationally on violence prevention and social, emotional, civic, and academic learning and improved school climates, we felt the time was ripe to undertake a survey of how different countries understand what factors lead students to feel unsafe and to highlight the types of policies and programs being putting in place as a result. We are very aware that there are terrible gaps between, on the one hand, research-based understandings about what children need to grow up in healthy ways and, on the other, current educational policy and practice guidelines. The eleven country chapters as well as the commentaries in this volume all highlight these terribly problematic gaps between current research and policy.

In an overlapping manner, this volume grows out of the work of the International Observatory for School Climate and Violence Prevention, a twenty-year-old international coalition of research, policy, and practice leaders who are invested in two goals: advancing the science of school climate and other prosocial (e.g., SEL, character education, mental health promotion, school climate) K–12 school improvement, as well as school safety efforts that support children's development, school, and life success; and supporting helpful research-policy-practice conversations that promote effective and sustainable school climate, social-emotional learning (SEL), and violence prevention efforts.[4] Many of the contributors to this volume have been active coleaders in the Observatory's learning and work. This volume honors and, we hope, supports the learning and work of many, including Ron Astor, Claire Beaumont, Rami Benbenishty, Eric Debarbieux and Catherine Blaya (who cofounded the Observatory), Veronica López, Mao Yaqing, Phillip Slee, Barbara Spears, Mitzura Taki, and Grace Skrzypiec.

There is a significant and growing interest in the prosocial, or nonacademic, aspects of K–12 education for two reasons. First, there is growing concern about how prevalent it is that students feel socially and emotionally unsafe, unsupported, and/or disengaged from school life and learning. Violence in schools is a major concern around the world. As we detail in chapter 1, this includes a growing appreciation that there is a spectrum of behaviors that undermine students feeling safe that range from normative moments of misunderstanding, to intentional acts of bullying and cruelty, to even more extreme forms of disrespect, like sexual harassment, date rape, and rape. Curiously, and tragically, there has been a deafening silence in K–12 education about how prevalent and toxic sexual harassment, date rape, and rape are. And we have not even begun to talk about the complicated set of "grey zone" sexual-social-emotional experiences that normatively color adolescent development. Yet, there is a growing appreciation that integrating SEL and school climate improvement efforts into K–12 school life and learning prevents school violence and also powerfully supports school and life success.

This volume will appeal to a wide range of interested readers focused on preventing and helpfully addressing bullying and school violence. This includes educators who are increasingly attuned to the importance of SEL, well-being, school climate, and mental health promotion efforts, including education policy and practice leaders around the world; education graduate students who are focused on bullying and school safety, international and cross-cultural studies, and prosocial educational efforts that include SEL, well-being/mental health, character education and peace education; members of the eighteen-nation International Observatory for Violence in Schools; and concerned citizens attuned to the foundational importance of our children feeling and being safe.[5]

This comparative study of eleven countries spanning five continents features chapters that assess the state of progress toward safety among students. We wanted to learn about a range of countries and continents and polled colleagues around the world to learn about possible countries we all could learn from. We thought it important to include a mix of countries, those that have been thinking about the issue of student safety for decades as well as those that are just beginning to focus on social and emotional as well as physical safety. We decided not to include low-income, or "developing," countries because these nations present their own unique sets of needs that differ considerably from those we focus on here.

The chapters in this volume evidence a growing appreciation, and early consensus, around the world that we can and need to recognize and promote the social, emotional, civic, and academic aspects of student learning and school life. Some countries have been leading the way in developing and evaluating innovative approaches to violence prevention and have seen reductions in bullying and other forms of school violence not seen in the US and elsewhere.

The volume begins with a chapter in which the editors explain the context that shaped our inquiry by introducing a spectrum of biopsychosocially informed experiences that contribute to children feeling and being safe. Part I contains the eleven country profiles. Authors of these chapters address a common set of questions designed to explain how their countries understand what it means for K–12 students to feel and be safe and how these understandings shaped educational policy and practice guidelines school improvement goals, strategies, and measures in their countries. These chapters also include recommendations for how teachers and educational administrators can make progress toward enhancing student safety. We asked the country case study authors to consider the following essential questions:

1. *understandings*: How does your country understand the nature and spectrum of mean, bullying, and/or disrespectful behavior, and how does this behavior manifest itself?
2. *goals*: How does this understanding shape bullying and/or school violence prevention policies and practice goals in your country?
3. *strategies*: What are the national trends that shape improvement strategies designed to actualize these goals?
4. *measures and measurements systems*: What measurement trends potentially help school leaders understand the extent to which their strategies have, or have not, helped school leaders actualize improvement goals?

5. *improvement trends*: How have educational policies and/or practice guidelines increased, or not, students feeling safe, prevented school violence, and/or promoted prosocial instruction and schoolwide efforts to create even safer, more supportive, and engaging climates for learning?

6. *recommendations for teachers, principals and superintendents/regional leaders*: What are the most important research, policy, and/or practice recommendations?

Part II offers four commentaries by international educators who have been involved with SEL, school climate, and/or violence prevention research policy and practice efforts. These chapters consider and comment on the trends in the eleven countries to further our learning and future international efforts. The editors' concluding chapter (written with the help of America J. El Sheikh) considers the significant themes emerging from each of the country chapters.

This volume highlights positive trends as well as gaps in research about effective educational, prevention, and intervention efforts on the one hand and current policy and practice on the other hand. Our hope is that this volume will further research, policy, and practice conversations that support children around the world in feeling and being safe—an essential foundation for healthy development and the ability to learn.

—Jonathan Cohen

CHAPTER 1

FEELING SAFE AND BEING SAFE

Individual and Systemic Considerations

JONATHAN COHEN
AND DOROTHY L. ESPELAGE

FEELING SAFE IS A BASIC NEED. Whether we use Maslow's understanding of our hierarchy of needs or more recent evolutionary biological, anthropological, and psychologically informed models, feeling safe is a foundational need for all people.[1] In fact, when we do not feel safe, we are all vulnerable to automatized, physiologically driven responses—fight-flight-freeze—that are designed to protect us from threat or danger. Think about what happens when you hear the words "Look out!" We are all surprised at how fast we move. To the extent that our children feel unsafe, these experiences undermine learning and healthy development.[2] In the short term, threats of physical violence or nonphysical harassment can undermine learning, school attendance, school engagement/connectedness, and academic achievement. Over time, feeling unsafe in schools seems to undermine life outcomes, including psychosocial and health issues that can impact a person's participation in the workforce, career status, and earnings.[3]

Until very recently, educational policy and practice leaders have only recognized how physical dangers (physical assault, murder, suicide) undermine feeling safe and being safe in schools. As this volume illuminates, it is only in the last three or four decades that the US and Japan have recognized social, emotional, and intellectual dangers. It is only in the last twenty years that other countries from Latin America, the EU, Australia, and the Middle East have recognized social, emotional, and intellectual aspects of safety. And some countries in Asia, the EU, and Canada have only recognized these sources of danger in the last decade.

The term *bullying* has been used for almost three hundred years. In the eighteenth and nineteenth centuries, bullying referred to physical or verbal harassment linked with death or severe isolation.[4] Most other forms of aggressive behavior were seen as "mischief" and a "normal" part of childhood. In fact, being physically aggressive has been "normal" in the sense that extreme forms of human aggression have been normative from an historical perspective.[5] War has shaped human evolution in a variety of ways.[6] Over the past 3,400 years, humans have been entirely at peace for only 268 of them, or just 8 percent of human history.[7] Although there are indications that this level of violence has been declining over time, violence against children continues to occur at staggering rates around the world, and suicide rates for youth are rising in many parts of the world.[8]

Dan Olweus's educational research on bullying in the 1970s contributed to an important shift in understanding and violence prevention goals.[9] He was the first to look closely at social and emotionally informed bullying among students and helped set in motion a growing series of empirical studies of the nature, prevalence, and impact of a person or group that has more power than the target, intentionally acting, verbally or otherwise, to be hurtful. Olweus suggested that the term *bullying* only be used when these behaviors happened more than once.

Interest in bullying, the bully-victim-bystander cycle, and bully prevention has grown in extraordinary ways around the world and is impacting policy and practice.[10] We suggest that while this growing focus on bullying has been importantly helpful, it has also been inadvertently problematic. It has raised awareness about the powerful social, emotional, and intellectual aspects of cruel and/or disrespectful behaviors and their short- and long-term consequences. Yet, it has focused on a narrow set of experiences that undermine children feeling safe and being safe. In addition, educators are too often concerned about the possible adverse effects of reporting instances of bullying; as a result, instances of mean and disrespectful behaviors are often unreported. We are concerned that this inadvertently contributes to educators paying less rather than more attention to the range of experiences that undermine children feeling safe. When educators are focused on the three research-based criteria of bullying (intent, repetitive, and power imbalance), they negate other forms of aggression that do not meet this criterion. We suggest that there is a spectrum of experiences that undermine children feeling safe, and bullying is certainly one important set of experiences that does contributes to that.[11] It is this spectrum that authors in this volume explore by addressing questions designed to uncover the opportunities and challenges for guaranteeing safety for children around the world.

There is a complex spectrum of biopsychosocially informed experiences—internal/intrapsychic, interpersonal/group, and societal—that undermines children and adolescents feeling safe, from normative moments of misunderstanding at one end to (literal or figurative) war and physical harm at the other end (see figure 1.1).

Intrapsychic or internal experiences—or mind-sets and the meanings we attribute to experience—color and shape how we perceive and understand experience. Human beings are meaning-making creatures.[12] There are several aspects of intrapsychic life that are relevant to understanding what supports children (and adults) feeling safe or not. On the one hand, our mind-sets are filters that shape our experiences throughout our lives. We have all had the experience of meeting someone for the first time and having an extremely positive or negative reaction to them. We know we do not really know how they are, yet, at a "gut level" we have the feeling that "I just do/don't like this person." In fact, as psychoanalysts have long noted, and more recently cognitive and other research have affirmed, we are not often fully present: our memories and/or expectations color and shape what we expect to hear, see,

FIGURE 1.1 The spectrum of biopsychosocially informed experiences that shape feeling safe

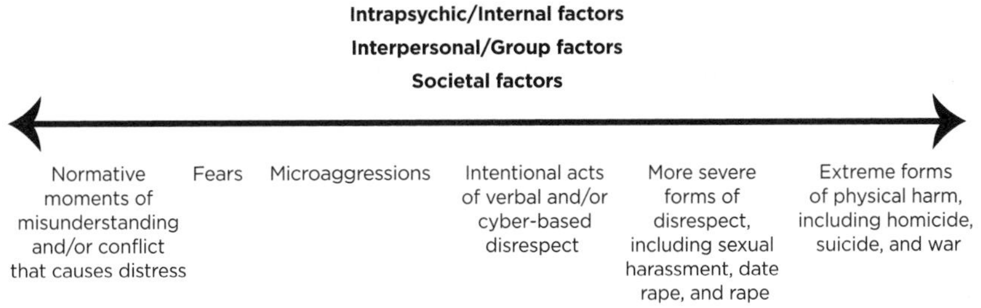

Intrapsychic/Internal factors
Interpersonal/Group factors
Societal factors

| Normative moments of misunderstanding and/or conflict that causes distress | Fears | Microaggressions | Intentional acts of verbal and/or cyber-based disrespect | More severe forms of disrespect, including sexual harassment, date rape, and rape | Extreme forms of physical harm, including homicide, suicide, and war |

and experience, and this can undermine our being "in the moment."[13] Conscious and unrecognized expectations color how safe we feel. For a variety of reasons, some people characteristically expect the best from others, others the worst. Typically, these expectations reflect the person's past experience, and these expectations can easily become self-fulfilling prophesies that color how safe we feel.[14]

Misunderstandings are a normal part of life. For example, you may say something to a friend with a given *intent* (e.g., to clarify an issue); yet, how your words "land" on the other person may have a profoundly different *impact*. Your friend may feel you were being critical rather than trying to clarify an issue. In fact, confusion and misunderstanding about intent and impact are the source of many relational problems, from individual romantic to international relations. Our capacity to recognize and address misunderstanding or confusion is a social-emotional skill that civic education has recognized and sought to address for decades.[15] Yet, even though the ability to have difficult and/or controversial conversations is fundamentally important, we do not routinely teach students the skills, knowledge, and dispositions that provide the foundation for these relational and civic abilities.[16]

Another important and relatively unexamined question is what meanings students attribute to making mistakes at school. A recent US survey reveals that a significant number of high school students are holding themselves back from getting the most out of their education because they are afraid of making mistakes.[17] The implicit belief or mind-set that making mistakes is in some way "bad" and/or shameful is important, because being confused and "failing" is, ideally, the foundation for learning. And the meanings people attribute to others who are different in any number of ways (e.g., racially, sexually) can also trigger anxiety and concerns that too often snowball in terribly problematic ways. From an evolutionary perspective, if we met someone who was not "like us" and/or "from our tribe," they may have been dangerous. But, again, educators do not tend to focus on how helpful it is to be aware of these anxieties and to then consider, "Do I really need to be anxious now?"

In fact, there are many ways in which confusion and ignorance can undermine feeling safe. An important and common example of this is psychiatric problems. One in five (if not more) adolescents struggle with a major psychiatric problem, like a bipolar, schizoaffective, or schizophrenic illness, as well as anxiety disorders.[18] These are biologically based diseases that are too often taboo topics. As a result, most children and many adults do not understand the nature of psychiatric illness. Although some countries (e.g., Australia, Canada, and New Zealand) have been involved with mental health/illness awareness in K–12 schools, until very recently there has been a deafening silence about these issues in most schools around the world. Just as diabetes is a medical illness that is colored by how the person and family (mis)understand the problem and respond, serious psychiatric problems represent other biological medical problems that undermine feeling safe in two important ways. First, struggling with anxiety, depression, and/or other serious psychiatric symptoms makes the person feel out of control. Second, it is scary for the people around the person who is struggling, their family, friends, and peers. Psychiatric illness is even more frightening to others when they do not understand the nature of the problems.

There are wide ranges of adverse experiences in childhood that commonly undermine K–12 students feeling safe.[19] Trauma is one example. Trauma and psychiatric illnesses overlap but are separate issues. Someone can be traumatized and not evidence an ongoing psychiatric illness. Yet people who are struggling with a psychiatric illness are more vulnerable to the complicating effects of trauma.[20] On average, every classroom has at least one student affected by trauma.[21] According to the National Child Traumatic Stress Network, close to 40 percent of students in the US have been exposed to some form of traumatic stressor in their lives, with sexual assault, physical assault, and witnessing domestic violence being the three most prevalent.[22]

Adverse experiences and how students and those around them recognize and address them is only one important set of intrapsychic and interpersonal factors that shapes how students feel and are safe.[23] Interpersonal and group factors constitute how we interact and the nature of our attachments and connections with others. Societal factors, including individual and organizational experiences, also importantly shape how safe or not we all feel. Well-being, mental health, and positive psychology provide an important foundation for feeling safe.[24]

Microaggressions are another phenomenon that can undermine children's feelings of safety. These verbal, behavioral, or environmental indignities, whether intentional or unintentional, communicate hostile, derogatory, or negative prejudicial slights and insults toward a group.[25] Microaggressions can include statements that repeat or affirm stereotypes about a minority group or subtly demean its members. Researchers are just beginning to study the impact of microaggressions.[26]

Verbal and cyberbullying are also a problem. Nearly 246 million children and adolescents worldwide suffer from bullying every year.27 Additionally, there is a growing awareness in many parts of the world that mean, cruel, disrespectful, and bullying behaviors overlap with sexual violence or sexual harassment, date rape, and rape.[28] Sexual violence—any unwanted sexual contact without consent—is an urgent public health issue.[29] Approximately 20 percent of all women have reported rape victimization, and about 6 percent of men have reported being made to sexually penetrate someone (forced or alcohol/drug facilitated, completed, or attempted).[30] Youth, in particular, are often victims of sexual violence; 41.3 percent of female rape victims were first raped before their eighteenth birthday, and 24.3 percent of male victims experienced it before age eighteen.[31] In addition to penetrative acts, the American Association for University Women's nationally representative online survey of students in grades 7–-12 found that an estimated 56 percent of girls and 48 percent of boys had been victimized by some form of in-person or online sexual harassment (e.g., unwelcome comments, touching, intimidation) during the school year.[32] In addition, a recent online study of ten- to twenty-one-year-olds found that 23 percent of male and 17 percent of female youth reported sexual harassment perpetration.[33] These data suggest that both sexual violence victimization and perpetration start early in life. Sexual violence is as prevalent in middle and high schools as it is on college campuses.[34]

However, despite the #MeToo movement that has helpfully focused on virtually every aspect of higher education and adult life, to a great extent there has been silence around the prevalence and toxicity of sexual violence in our K–12 schools. There are many reasons why this form of violence is so prevalent. Clearly one of the important reasons is that educators and parents tend to not talk about the inevitable complexity and conflict that is a normal part of navigating sexual-social-emotional experiences in youth. Even with the growing conversation about "sexual grey zones" in higher education, there is almost no conversation or educational effort focused on these important experiences in the K–12 years.[35]

Although K–12 schools are, in some countries, one of the safest places for students to be, extreme forms of violence color and shape way too many children's lives around the world. In the US, the youth suicide rate has been increasing, while homicide rates appear to be decreasing among youth.[36] The biggest increase can be seen among young girls aged ten to twenty-four, with the rate having doubled over the last twenty years.[37] Internationally, it is difficult to understand suicide as well as homicide rates, as they are not consistently documented, but suicide is the second leading cause of death among fifteen- to twenty-nine-year-olds around the world. And 79 percent of suicides occur in low- and middle-income countries.[38]

There are also important racist, sexist, homophobic, and other prejudicial societal trends that undermine students feeling safe and being safe. For instance, there is an overwhelming body of scientific evidence that racial minorities are disciplined more frequently and more harshly than is warranted by their behavior in US K–12 schools. Unnecessary suspensions and expulsions rooted in misunderstanding and implicit and explicit bias have damaging lifelong consequences for students, communities, and the entire country.[39] There is another body of research that underscores how prejudgments about people who are homosexual are pervasive and toxic.[40]

It is therefore important to consider the spectrum of experiences that undermine students feeling safe and being safe. Historically, educators have only focused on physical dangers that undermine feeling and/or being safe in schools. Over the last forty years, countries around the world have begun to recognize and address social and emotional as well as physical factors that undermine feeling safe and being safe in schools.

Today, educational researchers, policy and practice leaders in the US tend to focus on objective safety, or behaviors (e.g. bullying, fighting, sexual harassment, and gang violence) that can be operationally measured.[41] Subjective safety, or how we feel safe (or not), can be manipulated and is often reactive to transitory events and random events. Students in large schools, for example, feel less safe than students in small schools, even though there is no difference in the objective rate of violence. And there is always an understandable increase in fear after a school shooting, even though schools are one of the physically safest (if not the safest) places for children in some counties (e.g., the US). In fact, in the US, students are dramatically less safe in their homes or neighborhoods than they are in school.[42] This is not the case in many other parts of the world, depending on many factors.

There is a growing trend to use law enforcement tactics to make parents feel less anxious about school violence and mass shootings. Too often in the United States, and to some extent internationally, the response includes adding automatic lockdown systems, arming teachers with sidearms, and hiring additional police officers. Yet, research suggests that this approach has little to no effect on a school's safety.[43] In fact, these law enforcement–informed efforts tend to increase students' fear and diminish their feelings of safety.[44]

Feeling safe and being safe are foundational human needs. There is a spectrum of biopsychosocially informed experiences that shape how safe we feel and how safe we are. There are internal or intrapsychic as well as interpersonal and larger societal trends that interactively shape these experiences, and there is a series of experiences—from normative moments of misunderstandings and expectations (negative and/or positive) to micro-aggressions and intentional acts of cruel verbal or cyber behavior to even more extreme forms of hurtful behavior—that undermine people feeling and being safe.

PART I

COUNTRY PROFILES

CHAPTER 2

AUSTRALIA'S APPROACH TO ADDRESSING BULLYING AND WELL-BEING

A National Collective Response

BARBARA A. SPEARS AND PHILLIP T. SLEE

I have been impressed with the urgency of doing. Knowing is not enough; we must apply. Being willing is not enough; we must do.

—Leonardo da Vinci

THE MOVEMENT TOWARD the development of an Australian national policy outlining the requirements for safe school environments to support student learning and well-being and to address bullying behavior began with early research on bullying.[1] The landmark 1994 House of Representatives parliamentary inquiry, the *"Sticks and Stones" Report on Violence in Australian Schools*, reported that safe learning environments were being provided for all children, and while violence in Australian schools was not a significant issue, bullying was. The report also noted that as schools reflect the behavior patterns of the communities in which they are located, "schools alone could not provide solutions to a problem which largely finds it roots in society."[2]

The first National Safe Schools Framework (NSSF) emerged in 2003 largely in response to recommendations of the 1994 parliamentary report and provided a national approach to guide schools and their communities in how they support student well-being and address issues of bullying, harassment, violence, and child abuse and neglect.[3] To ensure the NSSF met the changing sociocultural and sociotechnical needs of Australian society, several revisions have since been made.[4]

Reflected in the latest iterations of the NSSF is a significant shift in how negative behaviors are viewed and dealt with in school settings—no longer as individual or school problems but increasingly as complex community and social relationship issues that require community partnerships to successfully bring about change. To this end, there is a convergence of various national initiatives—mental health, well-being, school climate, and bullying—so that a more integrated and holistic, transdisciplinary approach to preventing bullying and supporting well-being is adopted in Australia.[5]

Over the past twenty-five years, researchers, education policy makers, and governments have provided the platform for enabling Australia to be where it is now and the direction in which it is heading: where evidence-informed policy feeds the national debate about school safety, bringing with it strong bipartisan support for governments (state and federal) to work together to deliver nationally aligned responses. When viewed collectively, data and evidence gathered at the state and national levels provide a rich narrative about understanding bullying and well-being in Australian schools and form the basis of ongoing policy developments at both levels.

Uniquely, the Council of Australian Governments (COAG), through its Education Council (established in 2013), provides a national forum through which strategic policy on school education, early childhood and higher education, can be considered, shared, and coordinated.[6]

THE CONTEXT AND EDUCATIONAL LANDSCAPE IN AUSTRALIA

Global, commonly held views of education and its purposes hold that it is a universal human right, that it can have real and positive individual and societal effects, and that it is a contributor to productive economic growth and national development.[7] However, while schooling is ubiquitous, it has a unique quality and tone within its own national context. Although globally similar in theory and approach, schooling varies in practice as each nation locates education to maximize social, economic, and political benefits for its community. Efforts to support young people may therefore differ considerably due to the uniqueness of the national context.[8]

Australia's context draws heavily on the English schooling system, and its participation rates are among the highest in the world. Attendance is compulsory between the ages of six and sixteen (grades 1–10). Years of schooling consist of a preparatory year before grade 1 (not compulsory but commonly attended), primary school (generally grades 1–6), and secondary school (generally grades 7–12). Some schools operate entirely from kindergarten through grade 12, but most are separate primary or secondary settings.[9]

Demographics: Schools and Students

According to the Australian Bureau of Statistics, in 2017 there were 3,849,225 students enrolled in 9,444 schools in Australia: 19.9 percent were enrolled in Catholic schools, 14.5 percent in independent (nongovernment) schools, and 65.6 percent in government schools. There were 281,949 full-time equivalent teaching staff, and the Year 7–12 Apparent Retention Rate was 84.8 percent overall and 62.4 percent for Aboriginal and Torres Strait Islander (ATSI) students, a significant increase from 59.8 percent in 2016. New South Wales reported having the most students (1,209,307) and the Northern Territory the fewest (41,695), yet 40.2 percent of students in the Northern Territory identified as ATSI, compared to only 5.6 percent (215,453) of all students nationally identified as Indigenous.[10]

Students attend school from Monday to Friday each week for approximately 6.5 hours per day from late January/early February until December. Most states and territories have a four-term year consisting of approximately 9–10 weeks followed by a short break. There is a longer holiday in December and January.

Governance

Australia has a federated system of government, where each of the six states (New South Wales, Victoria, Queensland, South Australia, Western Australia, and Tasmania) has its own constitution but operates similarly to the federal government in terms of its parliament and judiciary. Two mainland territories (Canberra and the Northern Territory) have limited self-government rights. Education is primarily the responsibility of the six individual states and two mainland territories; however, the Australian Government Department of Education and the Commonwealth Minister of Education are responsible for national policies and programs to ensure quality educational access and equity for all young Australians.[11]

Each state and territory minister of education reports to the Education Council, a subcommittee of COAG, the top intergovernmental forum in

Australia.[12] This group coordinates strategic national education policy, shares information, and facilitates collaborative use of resources. The Australian Education Act outlines the principal legislation for the provision of government funding to both government and nongovernment schools and supports a model that is transparent, consistent, and needs based.[13]

Understandings

The empirical study of the phenomenon of bullying began in Australia around 1989–1990, following the first wave of studies in Europe and the UK, with the first Australian research subsequently linking bullying with well-being in 1993.[14] Australia's understanding of bullying and well-being is informed by international research but is uniquely contextualized by its schooling systems and multicultural contexts.

The Australian Commonwealth Senate inquiry into school violence in 1994 highlighted that, on the basis of early evidence, bullying was an issue for schools. The inquiry addressed significant questions regarding the frequency of violence in Australian culture, the impact of violence on the community, and, importantly, identified the need for intervention programs to reduce school violence, particularly that associated with bullying.[15]

Twenty-five years later, rich repositories of key terms and understandings, premised on internationally agreed definitions and contextualized to local settings, have formed the basis for all education and health policies and community information. Glossaries of terms are employed in government documents and on leading government-funded websites, and each serves a different purpose for the community. Three government-endorsed and -supported Australian websites related to bullying and well-being are:

- Bullying. No Way! focuses on supporting schools to deal with bullying and defines terms specifically relevant to schools, such as *school climate, relational bullying, school culture, school community, student voice, and social-emotional learning.*[16]
- The Student Wellbeing Hub is the central omnibus repository of information and resources for all schools on matters relating to student well-being, bullying, cyberbullying, and harassment. It offers a comprehensive suite of definitions of terms related to many other related areas, including *aggression, bystander behavior, conflict and covert bullying, homophobia, positive behavior support, racism and racial*

harassment, resilience, respectful relationships, restorative practices, and *student voice.*[17]

- The eSafety Commission focuses on online behaviors, so terms such as *sexting, cyberbullying, image-based abuse,* and *social networking* are prioritized and defined.[18]

All three websites crosslink to each other and utilize the same formal definitions.

The national definition of *bullying* for schools was revised in 2018 by the Safe and Supportive School Communities (SSSC) Working Group, a representative group of senior policy advisers and educators from all schooling sectors, states, and territories responsible for developing and promoting policy and programs at a national level.[19] The SSSC reports directly to each state/territory minister of education and is a working group of the COAG Education Council. It also manages the Bullying. No Way! website and hosts the National Day of Action Against Bullying held each year. *The new, revised national definition states:*

> *Bullying is an ongoing misuse of power in relationships through repeated verbal, physical and/or social behaviour that causes physical and/or psychological harm. It can involve an individual or a group misusing their power over one or more persons. Bullying can happen in person or online, and it can be obvious (overt) or hidden (covert). Bullying of any form or for any reason can have long-term effects on those involved, including bystanders. Single incidents and conflict or fights between equals, whether in person or online, are not defined as bullying. However, these conflicts still need to be addressed and resolved.*

The Australian Research Alliance for Children and Youth also established a conceptual definition of bullying for researchers.[20] It identified bullying as a systematic and repeated abuse of actual and perceived power that applied to relationships formed at school. This definition introduced the perspective of the legal notion of a "reasonable person" as the mechanism for determining intentionality. The objective test of a "reasonable person" measures the conduct of a hypothetical reasonable person placed in a similar position as the victim.[21]

Broadly speaking, understandings of bullying and prevention and intervention approaches are informed by both systems theory and social ecological theory.[22] Inherent within these understandings are strengths-based and development-focused perspectives which ensure that approaches are neither deficit in nature nor devoid of recognition of the role of maturation. Social ecological theory, commonly employed in education circles, emphasizes the nested contexts in which behavior occurs and acknowledges that risks emerge due to complex interactions between individuals and the settings in which they live, study, and socialize. Understanding the manifestation of bullying and cyberbullying and the sustainability of prevention and intervention strategies thus focuses on the need to target risk and protective factors across all levels, such as the individual (age and gender), family (attitudes toward aggression), and community (values and beliefs).[23]

Underpinning the view that bullying is collective in its nature and is based on peer and social relationships in the group is systemic theory, whose premise is that an identified problem such as bullying is not located solely within a particular individual.[24] From a systemic perspective, people are viewed in terms of their relationships with each other rather than simply being understood principally on the basis of their individual development. Importantly, interventions to reduce bullying may be understood in terms of two fundamentals of systematic thinking: first-order change and second-order change.[25] First-order change perspectives highlight a school identifying the issue of bullying and developing strategies to deal with it. The school system essentially remains the same but with a suite of strategies in place to address the problem. Second-order change occurs when the system itself changes. For example, the school may gain some insight through a review of policy and practice as to how current procedures maintain and even amplify or encourage bullying. Instead of focusing on changing the "bad" behavior of the bully and on helping the victim, consideration might be given to roles, relationships, and interactions and communication within the system that encourage or discourage bullying.

Understanding well-being is equally complex, as it is a commonly used term generally conceptualized as the quality of one's life, which could reflect economic aspects of well-being. It is now more broadly understood, however, that the concept encompasses noneconomic elements, such as happiness, health, the quality of family life.[26] Subjective well-being can be divided into two streams of research, "one that equates wellbeing with happiness and the other with human potential that, when realized, results in positive functioning in life." The "hedonic tradition" is typically followed in the first stream, and this relates to emotional well-being, while the second is associated with social and psychological well-being and "is the tradition of eudaimonia."[27]

That noted, the actual definition or description of the term is a contested one. In the last few decades a greater level of attention has been given to the well-being of children and a substantial amount of research has been undertaken on the well-being of students at school. In this realm, terms such as *social and emotional well-being* and *student well-being* are more commonly used, highlighting the emotional, social, and psychological components. Simply put, well-being encompasses an individual's personal evaluations of themselves and their life circumstances.

One factor impacting well-being at school is bullying, highlighting the idea that well-being and bullying are intertwined. However, in many western countries a great deal of published research has typically treated the two fields separately. It is argued in this chapter that in the Australian context there is a relatively long history in terms of psychological research and policy development of addressing the two fields as complexly interrelated.

Since the *"Sticks and Stones"* report on school violence in 1994, there has been a growing national understanding that bullying, more than a behavioral concern for schools, is also a well-being issue for all parties and the community, as it is a significantly damaging and impacting behavior, even potentially life altering, and one that needs a greater, more consistent, whole-country response.[28] The Roadmap for National Mental Health reform of 2012–22 endorsed by COAG, and based on a social determinants model, lists six priorities for improving national mental health, including developing mentally healthy workplaces free from bullying, harassment, and discrimination.[29]

POLICY CONTEXTS: SHAPING EDUCATION AND SOCIAL AND EMOTIONAL HEALTH AND WELL-BEING IN AUSTRALIA

Over the last decade, several significant national initiatives and policies endorsed by the COAG Education Council have underpinned Australia's approach to addressing bullying and supporting well-being.

The first, the Melbourne Declaration on Educational Goals for Young Australians, created in 2008, replaced the earlier Adelaide (1989) and Hobart declarations (1999) and is the key national statement articulating the vision for the education landscape in Australia.[30] The goals state: "(1) Australian schooling promotes equity and excellence" and "(2) All young Australians become successful learners; confident and creative individuals; and active and informed citizens."[31] All ministers of education unanimously commit to ensuring high-quality schools/schooling for all young Australians, upholding the vision that "schools play a vital role in promoting the intellectual, physical, social, emotional, moral, spiritual and aesthetic development and wellbeing of young Australians."[32]

Second, the development of the Australian Curriculum, managed by the Australian Curriculum Assessment and Reporting Authority (ACARA), an independent statutory body under the auspice of COAG's Education Council, unified and standardized curriculum content taught in Australian schools for the first time. Prior to 2008, each state and territory developed its own curriculum frameworks relative to their contexts. Importantly, with the national curriculum, a suite of general capabilities was also designed to develop knowledge, skills, behaviors, and dispositions over and above subject/content knowledge. One of these, personal and social capability, specifically targeted social and emotional development and learning.[33] Explicit references to bullying, inclusivity, diversity, and well-being subsequently appear within the health and physical education (HPE) curriculum content for all students across all grade levels.[34]

The third major education policy development was the Australian Institute for Teaching and School Leadership (AITSL), established in 2010 to determine the professional standards against which quality teaching and learning are measured: professional knowledge and practice and engagement. Under Professional Practice Standard #4, teachers, preservice teachers, and principals are expected to create and maintain supportive and safe environments and meet nationally agreed-on standards related to supporting student participation, managing classroom activities, managing challenging behavior, and maintaining student safety.[35]

Also released around the same time was a social policy, the National Strategy for Young Australians, which was designed to support youth participation for improved health and well-being.[36] The beginnings of cross-disciplinary, youth-oriented approaches to improving health and well-being are evident with this policy. A decade later, the Review to Achieve Excellence in Australian Schools continues to build and direct thinking concerned with improving educational outcomes for all Australian children.[37] Adjacent to these national policies and frameworks, are also each state's and territory's various and specific localized acts, initiatives, policies, and legislative frameworks.[38]

These national education, health, and well-being goals for young Australians highlight the recent and increasing interest in and shift toward aligning them so that schools and the community can work much more coherently and strategically in partnership to support children and youth. An example of this shift in thinking relates to the 2018 National Education Initiative Be You, which has been established "to promote mental health and wellbeing from early years to 18 years, offering educators and learning communities evidence-based, online professional learning, along with a range of tools and resources to turn learning into action."[39] This initiative brings together and integrates several existing, well-funded evidence-based programs that promote social and emotional health and well-being for children and youth in educational settings, such as Response Ability, KidsMatter Early Childhood, KidsMatter Primary, MindMatters, and headspace School Support. The resultant National Support for Child and Youth Mental Health Program has two components: the Mental Health in Education Program focused on the education and training of early learning, primary, secondary, and preservice educators and the National Workforce Support Program focused on providing education and training to clinicians and nonclinicians working with children ages birth to twelve outside of the education space.[40] Combined, they demonstrate the collective will of governments to support national approaches as well as resources that can be tailored to existing state-based requirements.

The education landscape is thus simultaneously complex and simple—complex in its federated structure and funding formulas (not described here) yet deceptively simple in its goals and aspirations to support and improve outcomes for all young Australians so that they realize their full learning and social and emotional potential (figure 2.1). State and federal initiatives are now strongly aligned in addressing bullying as a well-being issue and not simply as a behavioral or disciplinary problem for schools. For the first time, the new Australian Student Wellbeing Framework (ASWF) sits alongside the key initiatives directing education in Australia—the Australian Curriculum as directed by ACARA , the national teaching and leadership standards for schools as measured by AITSL, and all state and territory policies and acts—giving gravitas to it and its intent.

FIGURE 2.1 Education landscape for Australian schools

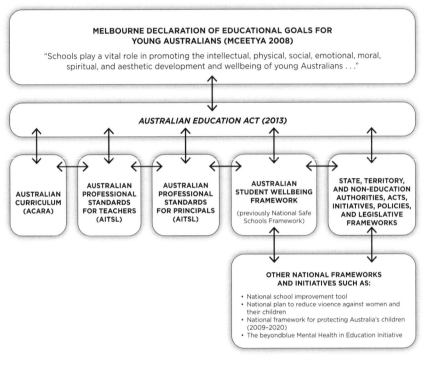

Source: Reproduced from Review and Update of the National Safe Schools Framework Summary Report, Education Services Australia as the legal entity for the Education Council, CC BY 4.0.

While the goals of schooling in Australia are to promote equity and excellence and to ensure that all young Australians become successful learners, confident and creative individuals, and active and informed citizens, there have been shifting policy emphases on *how* these goals and aspirations are to be achieved.

NATIONAL FRAMEWORKS TO SUPPORT SAFE SCHOOL ENVIRONMENTS

Australia is a signatory to the United Nations' Convention on the Rights of the Child, and together with the Sustainable Goals of the United Nations, these serve to safeguard children's quality of life and enable their rights to an education that is free from violence, harassment, exploitation, and neglect.[41]

The landmark *"Sticks and Stones"* report concerning violence in Australian schools specifically noted that bullying was "a significant emerging national problem." Importantly, it acknowledged that school violence consisted of overt *and* covert acts of bullying and that violence in schools was, by and large, "reflect[ive of] the behaviour patterns in the society in which [schools] are located," further stating that "it is unrealistic to expect that schools alone can provide solutions to a problem which largely finds its roots in the society."[42] With those understandings, the research and policy agenda was set for the next twenty-five-plus years.

The first National Safe Schools Framework emerged in 2003 and was one of the world's first integrated national policies. Its vision—that all Australian schools are safe and supportive environments—established it as the key national, strategic platform.[43] Endorsed by *all* Australian ministers of education, the NSSF is a collaborative, bipartisan effort presenting a way of achieving a shared vision. It is guided by principles that recognize the need for sustained, positive approaches and have an appreciation for the ways in which social attitudes and values impact the behavior of students in the school communities. NSSF suggested strategies include promotion of whole-school approaches, exploration of discriminatory behaviors, provision of professional training and development for staff, empowerment of students through authentic involvement in decision-making processes, and provision of specialist support staff (counselors, psychologists, school-based police).

In 2004, legislation required the NSSF to be implemented in all Australian schools by January 1, 2006. An accountability component, the Best Practice Grants Programme, was also funded to support schools in developing and evaluating effective ways of ensuring safe school environments. While there was considerable variation between schools in their approaches, many adopted a whole-school approach to establishing policies, procedures, and programs to address the concept of safety in their school contexts.[44]

In 2007, the government commissioned another landmark study: the Australian Covert Bullying Prevalence Study, which examined students' reports of bullying, teachers' perceptions of the extent of implementation of the NSSF, and teachers' capacity to address student bullying.[45] Cross-sectional data from 106 representative Australian schools revealed that there was a discrepancy between the rhetoric of providing safe and supportive schools and how the 2003 NSSF was being employed. Findings indicated that it was perceived by teachers as an overarching safety and well-being-oriented policy rather than as a specific bullying prevention framework. This study argued that greater implementation support was required for it to be utilized as a bullying prevention strategy and that legislation and compliance reporting were not sufficient.[46]

In 2011 and again in 2013, the NSSF was revised to address the increasing concerns about cyberbullying, a changing narrative shifting toward well-being and respectful relationships, and evidence-informed whole-school approaches that acknowledged the interconnections between student safety, well-being, and learning. The revised framework of 2011 thus reflected a largely positive school climate disposition: harassment, aggression, violence, and bullying were less likely to occur in a caring, respectful, and supportive teaching and learning community. A key difference between the 2011 version and the original from 2003 was the lack of legislation in 2011 mandating school use of the framework.[47] Schools were not required to report against it at the national level but were able to decide how and when they might employ it in relation to their state-based policies and initiatives. The decision to not make schools legally accountable to this version may have been an artifact of party politics at the time, or because of the timing of national agendas and elections, or due to recognition that state ministers of education wanted local impact through their own initiatives.

In 2013, the NSSF was again updated for online use within the Safe Schools Hub website, reflecting the exponential growth in online support and the shift away from print resources.[48] This site was subsequently reviewed, updated, and renamed the Student Wellbeing Hub, and the static *Resource Manual* was replaced with online, interactive displays and support materials for students, teachers, parents, and schools. The materials also clearly reflected the shift toward well-being as the global construct, as distinct from safety, as it had been previously interpreted.[49]

The review and update of the NSSF in 2018 was also driven by the need for a current, relevant, and contemporary framework that captured twenty-first-century sociocultural and sociotechnical aspects of schools and their wider communities.[50] This version was renamed the Australian Student Wellbeing Framework, and it is the central national reference point on student safety and well-being for all state and territory governments, government education authorities, and the Australian Government Department of Education.[51]

Designed to promote positive relationships and the well-being of students and educators, the ASWF aims to build a respectful, inclusive, and connected learning environment where all students can reach their potential. Comprised of five interconnected elements—leadership, inclusion, student voice, partnerships, and support—it provides the foundation for enhanced student well-being and learning outcomes in all Australian schools.

Importantly, this latest version of the framework closely aligns with and is guided by the key national curriculum and benchmarking documents linked to achieving the academic and social goals (see fig. 1). These provide the context for the ASWF and underscore the significant role schools and responsive and proactive, transformative, and visible leadership play in health-well-being-academic interrelationships. Important and critical aspects of this new ASWF are the emphases placed on authentic student voice and on connectedness to school, culture, family, and technology.

Critically, this new framework aligns with and supports existing state and territory well-being initiatives, local policies, and frameworks and is the go-to resource for creating inclusive and supportive school cultures within those local settings. The ASWF provides a connected, holistic approach to school safety and well-being that intersects with and across all existing educational curriculum and policy commitments.

Key messages or vision statements from each version demonstrate how Australia has grown its approach and strategies in line with the prevailing scientific evidence and languages of the time. The precursor *"Sticks and Stones"* report had as its vision that "schools provide a safe learning environment for most children."[52] The 2003 vision shifted toward a more holistic view that "all Australian schools are safe and supportive environments."[53] In 2011 student well-being and respect were highlighted, as "all Australian schools are safe, supportive and respectful teaching and learning communities that promote student wellbeing."[54] By 2013 the vision was inclusive and recognized diversity as a strength: "In a safe and supportive school, the risk from all types of harm is minimised, diversity is valued and all members of the school community feel respected and included and can be confident that they will receive support in the face of any threats to their safety or wellbeing."[55] Finally, the vision for the 2018 ASWF embraces positive relationships, well-being, and connectedness, noting that "all Australian schools promote positive relationships and the wellbeing of students and educators within safe, inclusive and connected learning communities."[56]

In 2019 the ASWF was distributed to all schools across Australia, providing a national strategic underpinning to improving well-being and decreasing negative behaviors like bullying, aggression, and violence. Critically, it supports a community approach to reducing these behaviors reflective of the original *"Sticks and Stones"* report, which articulated two important notions: (1) schools alone cannot resolve these issues, and (2) schools are reflections of the aggression and violence or, similarly, the wellbeing and health in their communities.[57]

Australia's approach to students' and educators' well-being and safety is national and strategic. It is a collaborative between and across the states and territories and is educative of the whole community concerning schools as safe places. It is enabling of student leadership and authentic voices and promotes visible, proactive, and transformative principal leadership. It engages in strong partnerships with community and provides support for positive student behavior. And this occurs in the context of vigorous debate at the highest level is unquestioned, with each state ministry of education bringing its own context to the COAG Education Council forum for consideration by the national minister, ensuring that what is agreed to by all is truly a national approach.

METHODS AND MEASUREMENTS

The challenges and opportunities that exist for creating safe, supportive, and engaging schools are many. Schools are nested systems, and the range of methodologies used to understand and measure student behavior, social networks, and school prevention and intervention approaches toward dealing with aggression, bullying, and well-being is increasingly diverse. Each methodological approach encompasses a worldview or paradigm that privileges how we understand *knowledge, information*, or *science*.[58]

A dominant force in social science research, and psychology in particular, is the empiricist or positivist paradigm, and this approach to understanding bullying and well-being in Australian schools has been significant, particularly in relation to determining prevalence over the past twenty-five years. Education and sociology, however, often employ qualitative/interpretivist approaches premised on the notion that we are active agents in our social worlds, constantly constructing meaning that is created, shaped, modified, and developed through interactions with others.[59] The advent of cyberbullying in the early 2000s saw challenges in understanding youth experiences within a changing sociotechnical environment. This has driven the emergence and increasing importance of qualitative/interpretivist inquiry for understanding bullying and well-being, where youth voice and participatory design are central to understanding the complexity of on- and offline interactions and behaviors. School bullying, cyberbullying, and student well-being operate through relationships in school communities, highlighting the need to converge methodologies and approaches for exploring these constructs. Reliance on any one method will not reflect the whole picture in documenting Australia's responses to addressing bullying and well-being.

We employed a historical method for this review that enabled consideration of three influential factors: history, culture, and the philosophy of science.[60] This approach facilitated the interrogation of records and policy documents, highlighting the changing sociocultural, technological, and political contexts related to schooling and demonstrating how concepts like bullying have changed over time in concert with new scientific understandings of the phenomena and changes in worldviews about children and their development. To simply report changes in prevalence data would not have captured the social, societal, and cultural shifts that are constantly occurring in and around school settings in Australia.

We considered how changes in government policy, worldviews, and new knowledges shaped how we understand the importance of creating a safe, supportive, and caring school climate. Spears and Kofoed, for example, articulated the importance of engaging youth as "knowledge brokers" and the need to transgress research binaries toward a more transdisciplinary approach.[61] Spears and Zeederberg also noted that engaging young people as coresearchers through participatory codesign methodologies could empower youth and direct youth-oriented messaging about cyberbullying. The postmodern contextual shift from early studies where young people were treated as "subjects" to be "studied" to a more participatory approach where they are engaged in a collaborative way to more fully understand the issue is an important way forward.[62]

This historical and contextual approach permits understanding of how national policy such as the National Safe Schools Framework, first introduced in 2003, evolved over time to become the Australian Student Wellbeing Framework.[63] Similarly, the first Australian national curriculum established and developed from 2008–14 introduced content explicitly focused on intercultural understanding, which shaped how schools have responded to bullying and the creation of safe and supportive school and classroom environments.[64]

Data Contexts

Australia does not participate in the comparative World Health Organization Health Behaviour in School-Aged Children study, a cross-cultural collaborative study conducted every four years in forty-eight countries to gain insight into young people's well-being, health behaviors, and social context.[65] It does, however, participate in the Organisation for Economic Co-operation and Development Programme for International Student Assessment, where, since 2015, student well-being has been explored.[66]

Nationally, several longitudinal studies provide insights into the health, mental health, well-being, and schooling experiences of Australia's youth, including *Building a New Life in Australia: The Longitudinal Study of Humanitarian Migrants*; *Footprints in Time: The Longitudinal Study of Indigenous Children*; *Growing Up in Australia: The Longitudinal Study of Australian Children*; *Longitudinal Surveys of Australian Youth*; and the *Household, Income and Labour Dynamics in Australia*.[67] Each explores various dimensions related to children/youth and their behavior and well-being.

Alongside these general national datasets sits the published, collective knowledge of the state-based and nationally funded cross-sectional, age-cohort, and short- and long-term longitudinal studies *specifically* about bullying and well-being. When triangulated and viewed holistically, these data provide a rich, rigorous, and reliable narrative about bullying over the last twenty-five years in Australian schools.

The empirical study of bullying began in Australia in 1989–90. Of more than 9,000 students aged 7–17 from various self-selected/opt-in schools around Australia 23 percent reported they were being victimized "on a weekly basis," and 7 percent indicated they could definitely join in bullying another child.[68] A decade later, in a large federally funded, representative, cross-sectional covert bullying study of more than 7,000 students aged 8–14, over 27 percent reported being bullied "every few weeks or more often," with 9 percent reportedly bullying others.[69] In 2015, a randomly selected, nationally representative sample of youth aged 11–17 (N=2967) completed the youth section of the Second Australian Child and Adolescent Survey of Mental Health and Wellbeing (Young Minds Matter), reporting that "in the previous twelve months," 83.2 percent of them were not involved in bullying

(N=2491); 13.3 percent experienced victimization only (N=374); 1.6 percent reported perpetration only (N=45); and 1.9 percent reported both victimization and perpetration (N=54).[70] Most students who were traditionally bullied also reported being cyberbullied.[71] A review of several studies involving over 50,000 students indicated that approximately 20 percent of Australian young people experienced cyberbullying each year.[72] While these studies reflect one of the common methodological tensions often found in this field, where different timeframes have been employed, collectively, across all studies over the past twenty-five years, they have provided the foundational evidence in Australia to inform school and government actions and policy directions.

One particular data context relates to a recent initiative by the government as part of its approach to ensuring the safety and well-being of children and young people online. The eSafety Commission gathers data under Section 15 of the Enhancing Online Safety Act (the Act) of 2015 to evaluate, interpret, and disseminate information relating to online safety, including cyerbullying, sexting, gaming, and image-based abuse, ensuring programs and resources are evidence based.[73] Recent nationally representative research involves young people and digital dangers, gaming, sexting, image-based abuse, social cohesion, and digital resilience, including online hate, bullying and violence, and online relationships. The Act established the world's first cyberbullying complaints scheme with legislated powers to investigate and quickly remove harmful cyberbullying material targeted at an Australian child. The eSafety Commission Annual Report (2017–18) revealed that over 95 percent of complaints were actioned within forty-eight hours, and over 75 percent of complaints were finalized within five working days; 2,500 individuals were referred to the Kidshelpline service. Young Australians aged thirteen to seventeen were the primary targets of reported cyberbullying material, accounting for approximately 79 percent of the complaints received.[74]

State-Based Initiatives

Education sectors in each state and territory also provide their schools with guidelines for developing localized bullying prevention policies in line with national policies, and these are informed by the work of the senior policy advisers to the ministers of education, thus ensuring that evidence underpins all advice and guidelines.[75] Several states have senior-level committees to support bullying prevention and well-being policy development: for example, the SA Bullying Prevention Coalition (formerly the Coalition to Decrease

Bullying, Harassment and Violence in SA Schools), the Queensland Schools Alliance Against Violence, and the Western Australian Cyber Safety for Children Working Party.[76] The education sectors in various states and the commonwealth are also informed by the policy advocacy of the Australian Universities Anti-Bullying Research Alliance (AUARA), an independent collaboration of key researchers invited to make submissions to such events as the Senate inquiry on the adequacy of existing offenses to capture cyberbullying.[77]

While the published evidence provides the foundation for policy and practices, the translation and mobilization of localized data and evidence is not as well utilized. A review of three states (South Australia, Western Australia, and Queensland) found that they employ in-house data collection mainly for accountability and performance measures related to truancy, attendance, enrollments, and critical incidents. Recently, however, a specially convened Queensland Anti-Cyberbullying Task Force undertook 59 consultation events with 650 attendees and received a total of 364 written submissions, with recommendations highlighting a need for a community approach to the problem.[78] Similarly, the New South Wales Department of Education employed evidence to support educators, parents and caregivers, and students at their major bullying prevention initiative in October 2018.[79] Resulting from the Cossey Report in South Australia, which specifically reviewed procedures and processes relating to bullying and violence in schools, all government schools were required to implement the recommendations and be accountable to them.[80] However, following a recent change in government, an internal audit in 2018 of 500 South Australian schools found that 12 percent of them did not have adequate policies, triggering a major policy review process.[81] South Australia has since reconvened its coalition of experts to work collaboratively across schooling and government sectors to devise a revised approach to addressing bullying in the schools, one that firmly places bullying in the context of community social relationships.

Unique to South Australia, and state-based initiatives, primary and secondary students in government schools have been specifically surveyed about well-being and engagement since 2013. In 2017, 96 percent of public schools in South Australia took part, with 88,703 students participating at least once from 2015 to 2017. Of those, 7.6 percent participated in all three years and 9.5 percent in two waves of the survey. Analysis shows that the majority of South Australian students report not being bullied; however, 18 percent report being bullied "at least once a week." Approximately 80 percent of these young people will still be bullied frequently (weekly/monthly) two years later.[82] School-specific data is then disseminated to participating schools to better inform their bullying prevention practices and well-being programs.

IMPROVEMENT TRENDS

Much has changed in the Australian education landscape since 1994 around the understanding and awareness of bullying prevention and intervention and student well-being. Australia has gathered sufficient and relevant state-based and national data over the last twenty-five years to identify and understand bullying as a well-being issue. Significantly, data continue to feed the national debate, to inform policy and practice, with strong bipartisan support from state and federal departments to work together to deliver nationally aligned responses to bullying and well-being.

Over the past quarter-century, there has been an explosion of strategies, programs, and interventions. Yet, the most important development has been the formation of the Education Council by the Council of Australian Governments. It has emerged as the top body driving a collective agenda for bullying prevention and well-being support, fueled by each state's minister and senior policy advisers. In February 2018, COAG tasked the Education Council to establish a Bullying and Cyberbullying Senior Officials Working Group to consider existing strategies and potential initiatives to help reduce bullying and cyberbullying and keep Australia's children safe. Endorsed at the twentieth meeting in September 2018 was an approach to enhance community responses to student bullying, including cyberbullying, through the Report and Work Program.[83] Four strategic gaps have been identified: a coordinated national action to create consistent messaging to the community; knowledge building through student voice; increased awareness of appropriate actions the community can take and the support available, particularly for parents; and the promotion of the need to model respectful behavior across the community as a way to prevent bullying and cyberbullying.

An example of this coordinated national action is the eSafety Commission's linking of their new guidelines for online safety directly to the Australian Student Wellbeing Framework, which is then directly linked to the national curriculum (ACARA) and the teaching and principal/leadership standards (AITSL). The ASWF, which aims to build a respectful, inclusive,

and connected learning environment where all students can reach their potential, was been approved by the COAG Education Council in 2018 as the
key national policy in this area, and it provides a backdrop against which the
senior officials working group can map its bullying prevention work.

There is significant recognition in Australia that bullying is a relationship and public health–related concern and that its prevalence in school settings reflects the communities in which they operate. As such, it requires a
community to come together to take action. For the first time, Australia is
in a position to take collective action across states and across governments.
While there are roles for all members of the community to play in modeling
respectful behaviors, there is a need for greater parental engagement and for
a focus on prevention. Continuing to treat bullying purely as a disciplinary
task in schools, or instigating legislation, as is often discussed following the
death by suicide of a young person, is insufficient to change attitudes or behaviors or to address community issues of aggression and violence. Rather, a
holistic, tiered approach to prevention and intervention is required: a community response led by bipartisan approaches from government which agree
that schools need to be safe and supportive, inclusive, and connected places
of learning.

The economic costs associated with bullying in Australia were recently
estimated at $AUD2.3 billion, noting that approximately 910,000 students
are victims of bullying each year. These costs are incurred not only while
the children are in school but also for twenty years after school completion
for each individual school year group.[84] The cost of doing the same or doing
nothing is significant. Gathering more data on particular and unique aspects
of the issues concerned with bullying and well-being will only keep driving
more of the same piecemeal approaches to an issue that clearly rests with the
whole community and how it engages and connects with itself and others.

RECOMMENDATIONS

Schools are complex organizations that pose significant challenges to the
delivery and evaluation of bullying prevention initiatives, such as a crowded
curriculum, multiple demands on a teacher's time, lack of professional learning opportunities, staffs' diminished confidence in their ability and capacity
to deliver programs, and considerations about whether bullying prevention
is indeed a teacher's "core business." If schools do reflect the violence found

in their communities, then there is a role for the community as a whole to step up and become part of the solution for there to be a national, collective action.

In light of these trends in the Australian context, we recommend that there be:

- recognition by the community that this is everyone's issue, that bullying remains a prevalent feature of a significant number of young people's school lives and requires community action to fully address it;
- full appreciation that bullying is physically harmful, socially isolating, and psychologically damaging for all involved, including bystanders;
- recognition of the integral links between bullying, well-being, and mental health; and
- identification and dissemination of evidence-based programs that reduce the incidence of bullying and promote the mental health and well-being of students through strengths-based approaches.

CHAPTER 3

CREATING SAFE, SUPPORTIVE, AND ENGAGING K-12 SCHOOLS

Challenges and Opportunities in Canada

CLAIRE BEAUMONT

THIS CHAPTER ADDRESSES the way many Canadians—researchers, decision makers, citizens, and education stakeholders—have tackled the issue of bullying and other types of disrespectful behavior that can harm the well-being and academic success of primary and secondary school students. It asks: How do Canadians perceive and define this phenomenon? What objectives has Canada's educational community established regarding the issue? And what methods, processes, or interventions have been put forth to face it?

The issue of bullying, which is primarily studied in school settings, could be addressed in a variety of different ways across the vast Canadian territory. Each of the country's ten provinces and three territories is home to a specific department of education that develops its own methods, based on its own values and sociocultural characteristics, to better respond to the needs of its students. Decision makers and educational stakeholders have therefore used their understanding of the phenomenon known as *bullying* when developing their educational policies and directing their actions to prevent school bullying.

Despite a measure of consensus across Canada regarding the necessity to create positive and secure school environments, it would be unrealistic to attempt a comprehensive portrait of the entire Canadian situation. Considering the difficulties surrounding this exercise, I provide an overview of the major points that have emerged across the country regarding these issues and then illustrate the situation as it applies to a specific province, Quebec. I conclude by offering a few recommendations to help Canadian education stakeholders direct their efforts in creating positive school environments, preventing school violence, and promoting student well-being.

To document, albeit inexhaustively, the way bullying is considered in Canada, I consulted the websites of various educational departments to understand the legal aspects involved, along with the measures that have been implemented by government authorities. I also visited Canadian university websites to collect a few scientific contributions from Canadian researchers regarding the issue and consulted a variety of other documents (scientific papers, legislation, programs, etc.), as well as a number of Canadian websites run by government and community organizations known for their involvement in bullying.

THE CANADIAN SITUATION: AN OVERVIEW

In Canada, school violence is not a new phenomenon for the students enrolled in public elementary and secondary schools.[1] Traditionally, the issue of school violence has been handled by assisting those students who manifest disruptive or physically aggressive behavior. However, today a very large number of Canadians consider that various forms of violence—physical, verbal, social, electronic, material, sexual—can cause harm to a person. In particular, sexual violence is now a source of increasing concern and is mobilizing the community. Our society continues to discuss such complex issues as online harassment, sexual expression, and violence against LGBT youth.

The Phenomenon of School Bullying

Despite the fact that international research has been focusing on school bullying since the 1970s, it wasn't until much later that Canadian authorities began addressing it as a specific concern. A 1995 study by the Auditor General of Canada revealed that several school communities had already begun taking steps to better understand the problem in an effort to improve their response.[2] After investigating the violence prevention policies and programs already in place across the country, the authors highlighted a series of worrisome practices within schools, most notably the pervasiveness of policy interventions based on the temporary or permanent suspension of those who had perpetrated violence, an absence of support measures for victims, a near-absence of early detection and educational methods to help perpetrators modify their behavior, and a lack of procedures designed to intervene in an emergency situation. Education staff members were found to be seldom asked to participate in policy-making committees or to take part in drafting action plans to prevent or mitigate the problem, and rare were the schools that kept records on the frequency of violent incidents within their establishment. Finally, official records from the school boards involved revealed very few measures intended to train staff members in matters of violence prevention.

At the time, the Auditor General gave the school violence report serious consideration and put forth a set of recommendations reminding all Canadian schools of the importance of fostering a positive school climate for everyone while at the same time reducing various forms of physical and verbal violence, intimidation, brutality, and threats, as well as the presence of firearms. Similarly, the Auditor General asked Canadian school boards to promote measures that would address the fundamental causes behind any form of violence that hinders sound student development. These multifaceted recommendations included family and community involvement and greater support for victims, along with measures intended to rehabilitate youth who perpetrate violence, as opposed to measures deemed strictly punitive, demoralizing, and rigid in nature. Recommendations also included a request for alternatives to school suspension. These recommendations are still relevant today, as punitive measures remain popular with the general public despite repeated attempts by researchers to demonstrate their ineffectiveness.[3]

Currently, each province's department of education is primarily responsible for ensuring that schools adopt measures to create positive and secure environments and to prevent school bullying. Overall, Canada's educational communities appear to grasp the importance of providing youth with school environments that promote respect, support, fairness, and dignity to help them develop their full potential. This philosophy agrees with that of the Organisation for Economic Co-operation and Development, which considers the quality of academic life as crucial to the "well-being" of today's youth, the psychological, cognitive, social, and physical qualities they will need for a happy life.[4]

Educational well-being, often linked to social adaptation and educational success, currently represents a primary concern for much of Canada's educational community. The Mental Health Commission of Canada, which focused on developing mental health among youths as a national priority in 2012, considered schools to be the best opportunity to reach children and their families.[5] As school bullying represents a threat to students' mental health due to its range of consequences, more and more Canadian schools are creating positive and secure school environments and implementing universal prevention measures focused on teaching socioemotional skills.[6]

Records from various provincial education departments in Canada reveal a measure of consensus regarding the importance of monitoring the well-being of students, though the steps taken to do so differ across the country. Some provinces emphasize the development of socioemotional skills in the students or promote their involvement in school life, while others encourage witnesses and friends to offer support for victims of school bullying. But long-held disciplinary traditions in Canada continue to ensure the ubiquity of punitive (school suspension, etc.) and legal (judicial proceedings, etc.) measures within the vast majority of the ministerial records consulted, despite the fact that research shows that such practices do little to help students learn and practice appropriate social behavior.

Since education policies and interventions rely on individual concepts of school bullying, it is interesting to note how such concepts and definitions vary from one province to another.[7] There are certain similarities and differences regarding the definitions used by educational authorities in various provinces. Generally, *school bullying* is defined as hostile behavior toward another. It involves an unequal power relationship and creates distress in victims who are unable to defend themselves. This negative behavior is primarily contextualized within a school setting. The notion of behavioral repetitiveness, as defined by Olweus, is only mentioned by a few provinces (e.g., Quebec, Nova Scotia), while other provinces state that the behavior has a "strong likelihood of recurrence" (e.g., New Brunswick), that it is "generally repetitive" (e.g., Ontario, Northwest Territories), or that it is "usually but not exclusively repetitive" (e.g., British Columbia).[8] Nor is there consensus around the idea of willfulness involved in aggressive behavior. Certain provinces state that school bullying is "intended to harm" (e.g., Alberta, Newfoundland and Labrador), while others offer less precision on the matter, or even a certain degree of ambiguity by referring to "behavior that is intended to cause, or should be known by the perpetrator to cause, fear in another" (e.g., Manitoba, Northwest Territories).

The documents describe the various forms of verbal, physical, social, or electronic aggression involved. Only a few provinces state that school bullying has an impact on the educational climate, whether or not the bullying occurs on school grounds (e.g., Northwest Territories, Ontario). Only Quebec provides two separate definitions for *violence* and *bullying* (*intimidation* in French). Within these definitions, a few ministerial documents list motives and vulnerabilities that can bring about school bullying, such as physical disability, sexual orientation, and/or ethnic origin (e.g., Alberta, Saskatchewan). Finally, cyberbullying appears sometimes within generalized definitions of school bullying, but it can also be described in a distinct manner.

Importantly, every document I consulted defines school bullying as a dynamic that involves an aggressor and a victim (and occasionally witnesses), but few consider the group dynamics that generate and aggravate most cases.[9] The contextual aspect, along with the influence of the group involved in school bullying, is seldom present in definitions used by government authorities tasked with directing measures used by educational communities.

The Scope of School Bullying

Several researchers have mentioned the methodological limitations that can hinder measurements regarding the actual scope of school bullying, including the definitions used, the age of respondents, the duration of the interview, the presence or lack of behavioral repetitiveness.[10] Data collected nationwide has nonetheless been helpful in documenting the phenomenon over the long term to help monitor the development of Canadian youth.[11] The data I used to document the prevalence of school bullying among these youth is from the study *Health Behaviour in School-Aged Children (HBSC) in Canada*, cross-national research conducted in collaboration with the World Health Organization internationally and the Public Health Agency of Canada nationally.[12] In 2015, the HBSC study distributed an electronic questionnaire to 29,784 adolescents (aged 11–15) from 377 schools across Canada. The issues primarily addressed by the questionnaire included support from family, community and friends, school climate, school bullying, and the use of social media, along with a variety of health-related matters (e.g., sleep, diet, physical activity). According to this study, the percentage of adolescent students who did not identify as either victims or perpetrators of school bullying rose from 65 percent in 2010 to 70 percent in 2014. Also, the percentage of students who identified as both perpetrators and victims of school bullying dropped from 8 percent to 5 percent, and fewer students reported having intimidated their peers in 2014 (from 8 percent to 3 percent). However, a slight increase in recurring victimization was reported by students (19 percent to 22 percent), with an emphasis on social exclusion and mockery, regardless of the form of aggression involved (verbal, physical, social, or electronic). The study also showed that Canadian youth who reported more positive perceptions of their school's climate were more likely to have never been victims or perpetrators of intimidation. Among students at higher levels (grades 8–10), those who had a more negative opinion of school also had less involvement in school life. Finally, a majority of students reported positive perceptions of their teachers' attitude and support, but these positive assessments diminished among older students.

Cyberbullying also represents a significant concern in Canada, with youth sexting emerging as one of its more worrisome aspects. While Canada, California, and the United Kingdom have seen fit to impose legal ramifications for nonconsensual sexting, little research has been done to determine the frequency and motivations behind the practice.[13] In an effort to document this phenomenon, an anonymous online survey of 800 Canadian youths aged sixteen to twenty was conducted in 2017.[14] Two-thirds of those who took part in the study reported having received sexts (13 percent "once or twice," 11 percent "more frequently," 4 percent "often"), half of which were unsolicited. Due to the far-reaching consequences involved, the authors of the survey recommended greater youth awareness regarding the dangers associated with nonconsensual sexting, along with greater awareness among parents, educators, and the wider public.

Objectives and Favored Approaches to Preventing School Bullying

Beyond their role in developing academic knowledge, schools are increasingly called on to help students build and practice the social and emotional skills that will help them thrive throughout their lives. In Canada, there are several approaches that can help prevent school bullying in a positive way (e.g., improving the school climate, improving the well-being of students, creating safe and caring schools). Currently, victims are receiving more support, and greater effort is being made to mobilize witnesses to prevent and reduce school bullying, along with the various types of bullying that can occur in any context (e.g., sports teams, leisure activities).[15]

Numerous Canadian researchers from fields like education, psychology, crime, law, and health care have contributed to an understanding of school bullying and its effects on the well-being and the mental health of young people. For example, Pepler and Craig have suggested interventions geared toward improving interpersonal relationships among youth, and Schonert-Reichl, Hanson-Peterson, and Hymel have recommended the development of socioemotional skills for students and teachers.[16] Paré and Collins have underscored the little attention the Bill of Rights for Children receives from programs and action plans designed to prevent and manage school violence, while Morrison and Vaandering have promoted the restorative approach.[17] Brière, Pascal, Dupéré, and Janosz have reported links between certain aspects of the education environment (e.g., school climate, educational practices) and school violence, and Beaumont, Frenette, and Leclerc have documented the reality of school staff violence toward students as an important component to consider in the complex problem of school violence.[18]

School Violence Prevention Strategies and National Trends

Over the last fifteen years, most provincial governments in Canada have either initiated or intensified their efforts to motivate schools in their bullying prevention and reduction measures.

Since 2004, most provinces have been progressively asking schools to develop specific action plans to halt the phenomenon. By 2018, eleven Canadian provinces and territories had adopted legislation or amended their education policies regarding violence and school bullying. Several ministerial departments now require that schools develop action plans detailing their prevention, management, assessment, and follow-up measures regarding violence and school bullying. In Quebec, for example, this action plan must be updated annually and submitted for approval from the school council (a committee composed of parents, management, and staff).[19]

At the legislative level, the Criminal Code of Canada governs many situations that involve bullying, including criminal harassment, child pornography, uttering threats and extortion, assault with intent, identity theft and fraud, and defamatory libel. Nevertheless, the public is ill-informed of these laws as it continues to demand new ones to address the issue of bullying.[20] Considering the growing public concern over cyberbullying, in 2015 the Canadian government passed Bill C-13, which addresses the nonconsensual posting of intimate photos online. However, according to Canadian researchers Coburn, Connolly, and Rosech, the specific criteria surrounding this piece of legislation risks criminalizing behavior that could be better resolved through age-appropriate educational approaches for young offenders.[21] Thus, teaching young people to better manage their interpersonal problems, promoting the disclosure of cyberbullying incidents to trusted adults, and referring violators to mediation with a view on restorative justice would do more to prevent the recurrence of aggressive behavior while supporting young victims in their healing process.[22]

In addition to the provincial departments of education involved, various government bodies and nonprofit organizations have shown greater interest in preventing violence, bullying, and cyberbullying. For example, Canada's Department of Public Safety has launched its National Crime Prevention Strategy (NCPC), which focuses on crime prevention through youth-related social development. Based on the declaration that all children have a right to feel safe in their homes, schools, and communities, the NCPC has spent the last twenty years providing support for the development and assessment of several antibullying school programs.[23] In a document titled *Building a Safe and Resilient Canada: Overview of Approaches to Address Bullying and Cyberbullying*, the Department of Public Safety provides a number of programs with various purposes, including the development of healthy relationships through socioemotional learning, the involvement of peers as trainers and helpers, the development of critical thinking and social responsibility, and the promotion of conflict resolution.[24]

There are many intervention programs that specifically target cyberbullying, but most programs have not yet been rigorously evaluated, despite their use within the school context. Some Canadian initiatives, however, are worth mentioning. Cybertip.ca, for example, provides information to help keep Canadians, adults and children alike, safe on the internet, while MediaSmarts, the Canadian Center for Digital and Media Literacy, advocates media and digital literacy and provides a variety of materials intended for families, schools, and communities.

THE CASE OF QUEBEC

Like all Canadian provinces, Quebec is home to its own, specific culture. Its main distinction is the French-language education it provides throughout most of its 2,675 primary and secondary schools. Its educational system is governed by 72 school boards, 60 of which are French, 9 of which are English, and 3 of which hold special nonlinguistic status (e.g., native communities).[25]

Understanding the Phenomenon of School Bullying

Over the last ten years, the Quebec government has been initiating and intensifying specific measures to prevent and reduce violence and school bullying. By acknowledging the link between the school climate, violence, and academic success, and by using an ecological approach to the phenomenon, a new paradigm has emerged and the fight against school bullying has begun intensifying its focus on "the creation of a positive and safe school climate."[26] Currently, positive approaches, such as support for positive behavior, continue to gain traction in schools.[27] Now, violence and bullying prevention is discussed primarily in terms of the overall well-being of students and staff, the teaching of socioemotional skills, the creation of caring schools, and the development of academic success in young people.[28] The phenomenon now extends beyond the school's jurisdiction, targeting every context of the young person's life, including cyberspace, sports teams, and leisure activities.[29]

Nevertheless, a common definition of *bullying* remains elusive in Quebec. The Education Act uses two distinct terms to describe acts of disrespect or aggression among primary and secondary school students:

> *Violence*: . . . any intentional demonstration of verbal, written, physical, psychological or sexual force which causes distress and injures, hurts or oppresses a person by attacking their psychological or physical integrity or well-being, or their rights or property.

> *Bullying*: . . . any repeated direct or indirect behavior, comment, act or gesture, whether deliberate or not, including in cyberspace, which occurs in a context where there is a power imbalance between the persons concerned and which causes distress and injures, hurts, oppresses, intimidates or ostracizes.[30]

As stated by Jacques Pain in his foreword to Olweus's book, French lacks any term that can properly illustrate school bullying as a concept.[31] While

France uses *harassment* to describe the issue as it relates to schools, Quebec has adopted *intimidation*, along with its inherent interpretive biases. This umbrella term is often used to describe any type of violent behavior, regardless of its repetitiveness or intentionality and regardless of any power imbalance involved. Different interpretations found within a single school can lead to approaches or interventions that fail to reach consensus within the same school team.

Quebec has a number of policies designed to manage such abuses of power toward vulnerable adults (e.g., policies against workplace harassment or the abuse of elderly people). In 2015, the Quebec government launched its Concerted Action Plan to Prevent and Counter Bullying in an effort to prevent disrespectful or abusive behavior between adults.[32] Since adults act as behavioral models for children, raising adults' awareness regarding the importance of maintaining respectful relationships at any age and in all contexts of life represents an important step forward.

The Scope of School Bullying in Quebec

Funded by the Ministère de l'Éducation et de l'Enseignement Supérieur (MEES), the longitudinal survey led by Beaumont, Leclerc, and Frenette aimed to document the phenomenon of violence in Quebec schools over the period 2013–19.[33] The research team collected data every other year from volunteer schools across the province using electronic questionnaires that surveyed students from primary grade 4 to secondary grade 5, as well as education staff, school principals, and parents. The surveys focused on various aspects of school and cyberspace violence (e.g., school victimization, school climate, the risk locations in and around school property, the observed violent and at-risk behaviors). Following each data collection, the team sent a confidential and customized profile covering the variables under study to the principal of each participating school, along with training material to help them analyze and use the data when developing their annual plan to combat violence and bullying, in accordance with legal requirements. School managers were encouraged to use these results when identifying their annual objectives. National reports issued one year after each data collection have provided the Government of Quebec with the information it needs to support schools in their efforts to prevent and reduce violence and bullying. Thus, a 2017 longitudinal follow-up conducted in eighty-six schools using three measurement times (respondents included thirty thousand students, staff members and parents) has served to establish a positive direction and has noted fewer cases of aggression within these schools, according to the views expressed by the respondents.[34]

Perceptions of the school climate have remained very positive over the years (more so at the primary level). Respondents have continued to report improvements in behaviors since 2013, particularly in terms of aggressive behavior in direct insult or threat forms, as well as in indirect social forms at the primary level. At the secondary level, 2017 saw a reduction in direct assaults, insults and threats, as well as in indirect social, material, and electronic forms of aggression. Another positive outcome shows fewer indirect/electronic assaults reported by secondary school students in 2017, despite a reported rise in teen use of electronic media. The survey also raised a number of concerns, including an increase in conflicts between ethnic groups, as reported by students at the primary and secondary levels and by staff at the primary level, and a higher percentage of primary school students (grades 4–6) receiving insults and humiliating comments via texting. Adult behavior, however, appears to have undergone the least amount of change since 2013, as adult aggression toward students remains steady, along with aggression between colleagues and even between parents and staff. Finally, in 2017, still almost 80 percent of teachers (primary and secondary) noted a lack of preservice training to prevent and manage school violence. Almost half of primary school teachers claimed they had not received in-service training on the issue, compared to almost 67 percent of secondary school teachers.

Objectives and Favored Approaches to Preventing School Bullying

In 2005, the Auditor General of Quebec issued a report indicating that acts of serious violence were rare in Quebec's secondary schools, but the phenomenon nonetheless deserved greater attention due to its impact on the school climate and academic success.[35] Despite noting ministerial and school board support for school measures to prevent and counter violence, the report also highlighted the education world's narrow and uncoordinated approach when attempting to correct the situation, along with an overall lack of available information that could help grasp the extent of the problem or assess follow-up measures regarding violent incidents.

In 2008, the Government of Quebec responded to these findings in its "2008–11 Action Plan to Prevent and Deal with Violence in the Schools," which defined a set of principles of action that schools could implement to prevent and reduce violence.[36] Support officers were hired in every region of Quebec to help school boards implement the action plan. In 2012, following the high-profile suicide of an adolescent who had been bullied, the province adopted Bill 56, An Act to Prevent and Stop Bullying and Violence in Schools, which was included in the 2012 Public Education Act.[37] According to Bowen and colleagues, this law represented a major turning point for Quebec schools, which were now obligated to produce an annual plan to combat violence and bullying.[38] One of the many indirect effects of the bill's adoption was the creation of the School Wellness and Violence Prevention Research Chair at the University of Laval, which provides training for pre-service and in-service education staff.

Today, one of the most important challenges is to help school principals and staff reflect on their practices so they can keep improving school climate and student well-being. It should also be noted that some schools still need help implementing their annual action plans.[39] To achieve this, since 2013 the School Wellness and Violence Prevention Research Chair organizes annual study days for the education community—including school principals, teachers, professionals, managers, government officials, unions, and parent committees—in an effort to address ongoing concerns while sharing scientific knowledge and field experiences.

In addition, a group of researchers and ministerial representatives have proposed four recommendations to help educational staff as well as government leaders in their decision-making on future policies:

- to design school interventions within an inclusive model that targets all levels of intervention, along with the school environment as a whole;
- to increase and consolidate the use of planning resources while implementing and monitoring control plans;
- to systematically and sustainably implement both universal and targeted/recommended prevention measures against violence in schools;
- to strengthen preservice and in-service training for teachers and school principals.[40]

These recommendations followed a series of observations made in recent years. Creating a positive school climate and responding appropriately to violence as it occurs should not be subject to improvisation; it requires a range of planned and calibrated interventions. This is why the crime prevention model proposed by Deklerck and adapted to Quebec's educational context by Beaumont has inspired the integrative model proposed to Quebec schools.[41] This model is interesting as it primarily focuses on the overall well-being of students by promoting healthy lifestyles that can turn school into a more pleasant experience and extends over a continuum of interventions calibrated to the problems that occur while at the same time considering the school climate. Comprehensive and structured measures implemented according to the severity of the situation can help schools respond properly to problems as they arise. Presented at Level 1 are fundamental prevention actions aimed at promoting healthy lifestyle habits (e.g., teaching social skills for all, designing captivating extracurricular activities, developing student talent). Level 1 does not target a specific problem but, rather, a variety of problems encountered by young people (e.g., mental health, school dropouts, substance abuse) to provide a foundation on which to build a better school climate. It encourages involvement and helps students develop a sense of belonging along with a desire to attend school. Level 2, general prevention, and Level 3, targeted prevention, also provide measures that specifically target violence prevention within a systemic vision that takes the climate and social context into account. These include measures that grow increasingly targeted and intensive. Finally, Level 4 provides curative measures for more severe problems that persist despite the measures implemented at Levels 1–3.

Annually, the Ministry of Education, working with school boards, and the School Wellness and Violence Prevention Research Chair, provides documents and teaching materials to support schools. In 2018–19, for example, following the year's theme of "Adults as Models of Kindness at School," the documents highlighted the role of school staff in modeling kindness and the impact it can have on creating a positive, healthy, caring, and safe school climate.

Also, in an important move, preservice and in-service teacher training offered in Quebec has been deemed insufficient in helping staff members prevent and manage violence and bullying.[42] Even at the bachelor's level of preschool/primary education, too little emphasis is placed on principles surrounding the child's social, cognitive, and emotional development or on strategies that can help educational staff teach and support students when developing these skills.[43]

School Violence Prevention Strategies

Even if the state does not require any uniform application of specific intervention programs throughout Quebec schools, a number of universal prevention programs designed and tested in Quebec have been implemented.[44] However, according to Bowen and colleagues, these programs, despite their positive results, are often abandoned after a time due to the lack of adequate and continuous training resources for staff.[45] Once again, staff training emerges as a major obstacle to the effectiveness and sustainability of interventions that seek to prevent and reduce school violence.

The teaching of socioemotional skills to promote student well-being and reduce violence has also increased in Quebec schools since 2014. Certain schools are currently developing this type of student activity, but, once again, only a tiny percentage provides these activities to the entire student body, as programs are often exclusively offered to students who have already exhibited aggressive behavior.

CONCLUSIONS AND RECOMMENDATIONS FOR THE SCHOOL COMMUNITY

This chapter documents how many Canadians understand, manage, and assess the school bullying phenomenon, along with other behaviors that can hinder the well-being and educational success of primary and secondary school students. Without claiming to provide any comprehensive portrait, I present both similarities and differences regarding the perceptions that surround the phenomenon, the objectives that seek to prevent it, and the approaches and methods chosen to achieve these objectives within the school environment. I also describe government measures and incentives, along with legislative articles, that can protect and guide the public toward the desired change. Today, fewer Canadian students aged eleven to fifteen claim to have been victims or perpetrators of school violence, while a slightly higher number claim to experience bullying on a repeated basis. Since the Auditors General of both Canada and Quebec issued their first reports in 1995 and 2005, respectively, Canada's educational community has been implementing a number of recommendations intended to create positive and secure school environments and to reduce violence and bullying in schools. However, some worrisome aspects continue to require specific attention.

Improvements Over the Years

For the last twenty years, Canada's educational community appears to have made progress on several fronts to improve its bullying prevention and management measures: the prevalence and nature of the phenomenon is now being measured, greater support is being offered to victims and perpetrators, more committees are seeking the input of staff members to create positive environments and prevent school bullying, laws are urging schools to document their actions, and community awareness continues to rise. Special attention is also being given to the witnesses involved, and more is being done to improve the school climate and develop students' socioemotional skills. These overall improvements are encouraging, but as Bowen and colleagues point out, certain schools are still in need of an annual action plan to support a positive school climate and prevent and manage violence and bullying.[46] Thus, more awareness is needed within the education community around action plans.

Recommendations to Further Efforts Toward Caring, Respectful, and Safe Schools

The problems involved in school bullying can only be resolved by mobilizing the entire community. In addition to the recommendations issued in 1995, which are still relevant, I offer five recommendations to help educational communities direct their efforts toward preventing and reducing school bullying as well as ensuring the well-being of a new generation.

DEVELOP A BROADER AND CONCERTED VISION THROUGHOUT THE EDUCATIONAL COMMUNITY. Despite the general use of positive and comprehensive methods in schools, more integration between educational stakeholders is required to develop a broader vision of this phenomenon. Parental and community involvement remains insufficient to prevent and manage the problem. Collaboration between schools and parents should not be limited to a mere transfer of bullying-related information or written notices outlining the school's handling of their child's victimization. A true partnership requires mutual effort: schools must be more creative when seeking regular parental participation in school life, just as parents must provide more time for their child's educational life, along with school life in general, using whatever means at their disposal. Furthermore, facilitating the presence of community organizations within schools could provide new resources and measures to help schools surpass their limitations and provide children with better overall care.

IMPROVE PRACTICES BEYOND THE PUNITIVE, DEMORALIZING, AND RIGID. Despite the greater availability of resources for young victims and perpetrators, the effectiveness of current methods deserves closer inspection: Do they truly provide better social skills to those who assault their peers? Do they provide young victims with the support they need to heal their emotional wounds? Do they help victims develop resilience through coping strategies that can help them better manage peer aggression in the future? Reflection is needed around the issues raised in 1995, when the Auditor General of Canada sought alternatives to suspension and expulsion, recognizing that the rehabilitation of aggressive youths was, at the time, all but uniquely focused on punitive, demoralizing, and rigid strategies.

The use of legislative measures targeting minors also raises a number of questions regarding their educational value and effectiveness at preventing the recurrence of inappropriate behavior. The entire population must reflect on this subject and become better informed of the actual impact of criminalizing certain behavior that could be better resolved through age-appropriate educational methods for young offenders.[47] A more informed population would be better equipped to choose the values it imparts to its youth: benevolence or intolerance. Do we wish to maintain a long and punitive disciplinary tradition that has been deemed ineffective when improving the behavior of children involved in an educational process? Schools remain the preferred avenue to disseminate this information to parents for the purpose of prevention.

Government authorities can also play a crucial role in transmitting the values underlying prevention and management interventions. While current laws seem better equipped to address the bullying in and out of schools, their content should be verified and shown to agree with the abundance of scientific literature that has dealt with the issue for more than forty years. Decision-makers should refer to scientific research results when drafting the documents that govern the school environment. Rising above politics and public pressure, evidence-based practices provide better guidance for the population as a whole and prevent the perpetuation of measures based on popular but counterproductive beliefs (e.g., expulsion or criminalization) both at school and at home.

INCREASE PEER-TO-PEER METHODS TO ADDRESS THE SCHOOL CLIMATE. The mobilization of all students is a necessary condition for creating a positive school climate and preventing violence. Despite the acknowledgment of the power of bystanders on the school climate, more concrete actions could be taken toward this direction. Students must be encouraged by school staff to get involved on an ongoing basis. In fact, this growing desire to increasingly involve students' school life is not always accompanied by concrete actions on the part of school staff. Moreover, according to the education laws, few specific actions are required of schools on this purpose. Promoting student engagement in school life through concrete means (e.g., system of peer support, peer mediators, peer tutoring) better prepares them for their future life as responsible citizens. Particularly through involvement in advisory committees, youth participation could provide a sensible new measure for any educational action plan regarding the prevention and reduction of school bullying. Moreover, since the group dynamics involved in peer aggression continue to receive little consideration, it would be worthwhile to deploy collective interventions that can influence institutional culture and create a climate of mutual aid and support. Massive intervention methods involving the entire class or student body could prove beneficial when several witnesses have been affected by incidents of school bullying or cyberbullying. In addition to the rehabilitation steps provided to victims and perpetrators, interventions that target the entire school could also help restore the school climate, which occasionally undergoes tremendous hardship.[48]

PAY GREATER ATTENTION TO THE INTERNATIONAL BILL OF RIGHTS FOR CHILDREN. As stated by Paré and Collins, children's rights are often neglected when preventing and managing school bullying.[49] The explicit inclusion of these rights within the educational legislation would provide a fundamental basis on which to build adult awareness around the duty to educate and protect minors, be they victims, perpetrators, or witnesses. It is up to the governments of each country signed on to the International Bill of Rights for Children, Canada among them, to steer public action and make this commitment a reality. It is conceivable that in recognizing this document, school adults would be more likely to provide support to the young victims involved than they would to the students who commit these acts, as many educational methods, including humiliation, public punishment, shouting, and ignorance, raise ethical questions regarding their use and impact on school climate and violence.[50]

STRENGTHEN PRESERVICE AND IN-SERVICE TEACHER TRAINING. For years, preservice and in-service teacher training has been deemed insufficient in guiding future educators toward practices and attitudes that can effectively prevent and manage school violence. The lack of training and support for school staff has also been identified as one factor behind the failure of certain violence prevention programs to achieve positive outcomes, despite the quality of the available tools.[51] A review of staff training would necessarily provide teachers with the support they need to perform their educational tasks.

According to Beaumont, to empower teachers and staff in supporting the social and emotional development of their students and prevent school violent, training should target knowledge (e.g., school climate, psychology of child development), skills (e.g., classroom management, active listening, own stress management), and attitude (e.g., benevolence, open-minded visions, collaboration).[52] Regarding the training content for teachers, the methods involved should be further based on research and reflective analysis to ensure that all staff interventions remain fully compliant with the ethical principles and responsibilities of their profession.[53]

Since teachers are primary participants in students' lives, we in society must take better care of their personal and professional well-being. For instance, teaching them strategies to manage their own socioemotional states as well as best research-based practices in school violence prevention should help them feel more confident and efficient in their interventions, thereby reducing their stress and increasing their well-being.

CHAPTER 4

SCHOOL VIOLENCE AND *CONVIVENCIA ESCOLAR* IN CHILE

VERÓNICA LÓPEZ

IN CHILE, as well as in all Latin American and Ibero-American countries, there is a term that is both commonly and scientifically used to study school life beyond academic achievement: *convivencia escolar*. Its direct translation is "school coexistence," and the closest term used in the anglosaxon literature is *school climate*. However, for many Ibero-American researchers, the terms are not synonyms. Although the concept of convivencia escolar is a sociohistorically situated construction in Spain and Latin America, it is also deeply connected with the changes and transformations in global educational research and intervention, especially those related to the guidelines of UNESCO for the development of a democratic, participatory, and inclusive education.[1] Roughly speaking, the term began to be coined as the construct for school climate policies during the 1990s in both Spain and Latin America. Nevertheless, this formative perspective toward school climate/coexistence is tensioned by accountability and high-stakes testing prioritized by many Latin American educational policies strongly pushed during the 2000s by the World Bank and the Inter-American Bank for Development. This seems to be a global political scenario.

For many Ibero-American researchers, the terms *school climate* and *convivencia escolar* are not synonyms; *school climate* is related more to school norms and developing a climate that allows school achievement, and *convivencia escolar* is linked more to cultural values of strengthening democracy and building capacities for citizenship. According to Jonathan Cohen, Catherine Blaya, and Verónica López, the transition from the use of *school violence* to *school climate* was due to a global transformation in school research and intervention, which recognized, first, that the reduction of school violence did not necessarily improve the quality of school life and, consequently, that it was necessary to invest resources in improving the conditions that make possible the construction of positive, preventive, and promotional forms of relationships.[2] From this perspective, the approaches of the World Health Organization (WHO) in relation to the development of primary and secondary prevention policies and how they could be incorporated in school through the promotion of enriched school climates became of great importance.

However, it is specifically the dimension of participation that connects with what in Ibero-American and Latin American literature is understood as convivencia escolar—a situated practice of interpersonal and group relationships between different social groups that generates the possibility of living together within contexts of social differences, whether socioeconomic, ethnic, gender, age, etc. From this perspective, several Latin American researchers have argued that *school climate* offers a static, "photographic" view of a specific moment (through cross-sectional studies) of the perception of students or the school community about the quality of the school environment.[3] In contrast, *convivencia escolar* refers to concrete, everyday, and locally situated practices that occur in a sustained manner over time. Moreover, school climate is understood either as a precondition or as an effect of school life and therefore does not describe the process of conforming to a way of life within the school community that leads to living with differences. Last, researchers argue that *school climate*, since it refers to the product and not the process, is less modifiable than *convivencia escolar*, which is essentially learnable—"to live together is something we all learn to do."

In fact, the spirit of the sense of convivencia escolar as a behavior and attitude to be learned in and through the school is present in the Delors Report, which set the tone in Latin American research during the late 1990s around the widespread adoption of the concept of convivencia by deepening the approach of the World Declaration on Education for All concerning the satisfaction of basic learning needs.[4] Together with the knowledges of learning to know and learning to do, the report integrated two more knowledges that are fundamental to this discussion: learning together and learning to live together.[5]

However, the conceptual differences between school climate and convivencia escolar have not been sufficiently documented, argued, or published in Latin American or Anglo-Saxon literature. Thus, the conceptual argumentation of the similarities and differences between the Anglo-Saxon concept of school climate and the Ibero-American concept of convivencia escolar remains a challenge. Also pending is an understanding of school safety within this general construct of convivencia escolar. For many practitioners, convivencia escolar highlights the need for democratic and peaceful coexistence of students, teachers, and staff. However, the need for safe coexistence is less stressed and is usually only understood within the construct of school violence. The need to advance understandings of the relationship between convivencia escolar and school safety is important because, as in the case of Chile, governments may argue for the need to improve students' safety linked to extreme forms of student violence on the school grounds but may limit the solutions by offering zero-tolerance punitive approaches that do not embrace a whole-school, formative approach more in line with convivencia escolar.

Although the concept of convivencia escolar is a sociohistorical construct in Latin America, it is also deeply connected with the changes and transformations in global educational research and intervention, especially those related to the guidelines of UNESCO for the development of a democratic, participatory, and inclusive education.[6] Yet, many of the current school-based policies of Latin American countries are also in compliance with guidelines issued by other international organizations, such as the World Bank and the OECD, which strongly pressure measurable, quantifiable, and therefore comparable results and situate the school community as a means to achieve the greater goal: to improve academic performance in standardized tests.[7]

The Latin American and the Caribbean Region faces two great challenges: low academic achievement and high educational segregation.[8] These challenges need to be considered if we want to understand how Latin America has dealt with the issue of creating safe and supportive schools. On one hand, systematic low academic achievements, as measured by standardized testing services, hinder students' opportunities for social mobility. On the other hand, highly segregated educational systems in which students from lower socioeconomic statuses (SES) attend low-achieving public schools that do not select students and students from higher SES backgrounds attend higher-achieving and highly selective private schools, with a mixed provision for medium SES families, have helped perpetrate social and geographical segregation, inequity, and social injustice. In this context, in a school system that segregates by social class, we end up concentrating problems of coexistence in sectors that are highly stigmatized.[9] This logic has not only generated the social exclusion of certain schools but has also reproduced it within the schools themselves, since students who are considered different from mainstream students, or different from what the school expects of them, do not participate equally in the learning spaces, are stigmatized, and are excluded by their peers as well as their teachers.[10] Therefore, the stratification of positive school climate by SES has become an issue of educational inclusion.

Given this, some academics, policy makers, and education stakeholders understand convivencia escolar as a means to improve all students' academic attainment by improving the conditions of the learning process both inside and outside the classroom.[11] Other researchers, policy makers, and stakeholders contend that convivencia escolar is an end in and of itself, since schools that create supportive and engaging environments foster students' social and emotional skills and allow them to have different means of civic and citizen participation.[12] When convivencia escolar is understood as an end to itself, the school is thought of as a space where children construct academic and socioemotional learning and learn to live together in a democratic way, becoming the protagonists of a more just and participatory society.[13]

RESEARCH, POLICIES, AND PRACTICES IN LATIN AMERICA

A unanimous finding derived from diverse investigations around the world is that the results of strategies dedicated exclusively to contain or attend the expressions of direct violence, although they might have an effect in the short term, are not lasting.[14] Moreover, punitive, zero-tolerance forms of addressing the issues of school violence and school safety are counterproductive, since they have been shown to create a school-to-prison pipeline that increases the number of students in the juvenile penal system, with consequential damage to their educational trajectories.[15] However, even though most of the countries in the Latin American and Caribbean Region have stated in their school curricula the importance of democratic forms of living together and citizen formation, this does not translate into concrete and/or effective practices for training citizens with civic knowledge and attitudes that justify forms of government democratic. Proof of this are the results of the 2009 International Civic and Citizenship Education Study (ICCS) *International Report on Civic Knowledge, Attitudes, and Engagement Among Lower Secondary School Students in 38 Countries.*[16] In five of the six Latin American countries that participated in the study, more than half of the high school students who answered performed comparatively at the lowest level of civic knowledge. For example, males presented forms of thinking that tended to justify authoritarian regimes (dictatorships), distrusting political parties, courts, and the police.

In addition, Latin American researchers emphasize the need to understand that there is no one type of school violence but multiple forms at different levels and historically instituted.[17] Toledo and colleagues propose a triadic view of school violence: (1) different forms of violence produced by the school itself, such as the symbolic violence that a given curriculum may produce by denying social differences, and included are forms of harassment and maltreatment from principals to teachers, teachers to students, students to teachers, and between students, such as bullying and other forms of peer aggression; (2) different forms of violence that are reproduced within the school, such as gender violence and other forms of heteronormative practices derived from sexism, classism, and racism; and (3) different forms of violence that pass through or across the school, such as political, urban, and intrafamilial violence.[18]

In 2011, the Inter-American Institute of Human Rights (IIDH) disseminated a study on legal protection and the political, institutional, and operational conditions for exercising human rights in education. Seventeen countries in the Americas participated, with a total of 136 documents analyzed. A follow-up study of the data reported that only half of the countries studied and/or collected statistical information on their policies.[19] Of the participating countries, thirteen had some kind of ministerial orientation regarding peaceful coexistence and prevention of school violence, evidencing the need to promote participatory action. While most countries had nationally available educational materials, budgets for working in the area were difficult to identify. Some collaborative but rather unsystematic links were observed with nongovernmental and local government entities to implement policies. Finally, most countries monitored school violence and/or school climate, but not consistently.

In 2011 PLAN International and UNICEF, after reviewing the legislation in thirty-three countries in Latin America and the Caribbean, warned that most countries (n=20) did not prohibit corporal punishment in school.[20] In the Caribbean it was still considered a corrective measure. In Central America and Mexico, although corporal punishment was prohibited by law, it continued to be practiced. In addition, repressive antidelinquency measures were implemented within schools, which placed students and communities at risk for stigmatizing processes.[21] There is also a progressive trend in Latin American countries toward policies of accountability that involve convivencia escolar through standardized tests, with consequences for schools and its administrators, and the installation of public devices to report acts of school violence, which the state investigates in a supervisory manner.

The last decade has witnessed great concern over the level of violence perpetrated in the schools in the region. In many countries it has led to the establishment of educational policies aimed at measuring school violence. Such is the situation in Chile, Peru, Mexico, and El Salvador, countries that have sought large-scale measurements of levels of school violence.[22] However, changes in elected governments have, at times, reduced the stability of evaluations. In addition, in most countries where assessments exist, the actual items are kept confidential by the governments, and it is unclear how the results of these evaluative efforts translate into improvements for schools.

CHILE: PUBLIC POLICIES ADDRESSING BULLYING, SCHOOL VIOLENCE, AND CONVIVENCIA ESCOLAR

Since 2002, Chile has designed and implemented various laws and educational policies aimed at improving, promoting, and developing school climate and reducing levels of school violence. However, paradigmatic tensions have been identified in the foundations of these policies and laws that create an ambivalent scenario for implementation.

In 1975, during the first years of the Pinochet military dictatorship, Chile began a radical design of a neoliberal educational reform following the principles of Milton Friedman.[23] This was achieved through the approval of the General Law on Education in 1980, whereby the administration of schools was transferred from the Ministry of Education to the municipalities (local government units) by incorporating private providers of educational services, who began to compete with each other and with public municipal schools for public resources under a voucher model, and establishing freedom of school choice as the foremost principle.[24] This education policy model was in alignment with the World Bank's subsequent recommendations that public services be carried out by private providers of public services, which would result in an expenditure effectiveness given that costs would only be paid for services provided.[25] The quality of the benefits can be regulated, according to this recommendation, through the use of standardized instruments that allow for an account of the results of the providers. In the case of education, this materializes in the fundamental recommendation to establish standardized tests for measuring learning outcomes, including but not limited to the areas of language and mathematics, and to evaluate and fund schools according to these results.[26] In Chile, this has been achieved through the System of Measurement of Educational Quality (SIMCE), which also measures other, noncognitive elements of educational quality, one of which is school climate.

The policies implemented in Chile are an extreme example of policies focused on the private provision of educational services financed by the state based on free choice and results-based accountability systems. Since these policies have been promoted by organizations such as the World Bank, OECD, and others, the Chilean policy implementation is far from being a national case study.[27]

In 2002 the Ministry of Education formulated the National Policy on Convivencia Escolar. In spite of changing governments, this policy remains in place and has been updated several times. For the latest update in 2019, the Ministry of Education formed focus groups to provide feedback on implementation. In general terms, this policy was designed from the view of democratic convivencia and has, more or less (depending on the government in office), been maintained as such.[28] However, this policy is not a law and therefore has no specific consequences for schools. Instead, the 2011 Law on School Violence, designed by the legislative power (not the Ministry of Education) to ensure social security, defines school violence as school harassment (*acoso escolar*, a term usually used in Spain for bullying):

> any act or omission constituting repeated aggression or harassment carried out outside or within the educational establishment by students who, individually or collectively, act against another student using a situation of superiority or defenselessness of the affected student and who cause in the latter abuse, humiliation, or well-founded fear of being exposed to serious ill, either by technological means or any other means, taking into account his/her age and condition.

In turn, the law defines a "good convivencia escolar" as "the harmonious co-existence of the members of the educational community, which implies a positive interrelation between them and allows the adequate fulfillment of the educational objectives in a climate that favors the integral development of the students."[29]

Underlying the 2011 Law on School Violence is a punitive logic based on legal punishments and reinforcement of controls, as opposed to a democratic logic based on teacher and student training.[30] This tension may provoke an ambivalent interpretation by the schools. The law mandates that schools provide all necessary means to prevent school violence and foster a safe and supporting school climate, which is translated as having updated protocols and school norms known by all members of the school community and having named a teacher or other adult the School Climate Coordinator. If a school is found not to have these norms in place, or not to follow them, then the school may receive a monetary fine that can be upward of several thousand US dollars.

Additionally, a new law that follows the logic of accountability was passed in 2011. Law No. 20.529 for the Assurance of the Quality of Education, or SAC, produced profound changes in the architecture of the Chilean educational system. Formerly there was one sole national unit in charge of education, the Ministry of Education. SAC created two additional independent bodies: the Superintendency of School Education, which deals with school audit processes and is in charge of overseeing that schools comply with the laws and regulations, and the Agency of Education Quality, which is in charge of evaluating the quality of schools in terms of student achievement in the standardized test SIMCE. Both regulatory bodies, by auditing and evaluating, respectively, implement agendas to deal with school climate. The Ministry for Education, through a small unit called the Transversal Unit (Unidad de Transversalidad), provides guidance to schools through the Policy on School Climate.[31] This national policy emphasizes a democratic, formative perspective on school climate. However, this perspective might not be at the center of school efforts to improve school climate, which are basically geared toward avoiding being fined by the Superintendency as the Law on School Violence mandates.

Whereas schools must comply with the 2011 Law on School Violence, hybrid as it is, they can translate school climate policies from a punitive and/or formative logic and design agendas based on the formative National Policy on School Climate to avoid the potential punishments of the Law on School

Violence that is audited by the Superintendency.[32] As David K. Cohen and Susan L. Moffitt indicate, it is precisely the ambiguity in the policies that generate various interpretations.[33]

The Law for the Assurance of Educational Quality, which created SAC, also redefined the concept of educational quality by incorporating "other, non-cognitive indicators of educational quality," now called "indicators of social and personal development." One of the eight indicators is *clima de convivencia escolar*. Conceptually, the term avoids taking sides in the historical dispute on whether to measure school climate or convivencia escolar by defining the concept as *"climate of* convivencia escolar." These eight indicators are now included in the total weighted score of the SIMCE rank that each school receives within a high-stakes testing scenario: 26.4 percent (3.3 percent for each indicator), with 73.6 percent for the core subject areas of language, mathematics, and science.[34] Therefore, as of 2011, school climate has become incorporated into the metrics of school quality within the logic of accountability. Moreover, SAC added an additional component, one with very high discursive strength: the threat of sanctions. As López and colleagues have posited, in terms of school climate, threat of sanctions can be explained by two complementary policies: the Law on School Violence, incorporated into the General Law of Education, and SAC.[35]

All of this legislation has added new actors to school climate policies and procedures. For example, schools must now designate a School Climate Coordinator and receive visits from officials from the Superintendency, who can ask to see any type of document they wish. A qualitative study performed by me and my colleagues to identify and analyze the tensions and critical nodes in the implementation of educational policies in convivencia escolar revealed that SAC officials at the center (Santiago) and at regional levels identified critical tensions and nodes at the conceptual (What is school climate?), methodological (How do we evaluate it?), and procedural (How do we improve it?) levels.[36] Conceptually, all participants from the three organizations within the SAC system agreed that while there is a formative approach that invites reflection and peaceful resolution of conflicts, there is also a punitive approach with parallel implementation. Methodologically, they visualized challenges in the measurement of convivencia escolar directly related to the conceptual construct. Participants also thought that the self-reported instruments used to measure convivencia escolar, since they are embedded in an accountability scheme, could encourage student training in terms of what should be answered, since the instruments are not in line with evaluating school practices. Finally, procedurally, regarding school management issues, the participants perceived a lack of clear job descriptions, roles, and guidelines for the School Climate Coordinator.

Although declaratively the 2002 National Policy on Convivencia Escolar and its updates highlight the responsibility of all educational actors in strengthening convivencia and the prevention of school violence, measurement and improvement trends have focused mainly on peer aggression and bullying. In 2005 the Ministry of Internal Affairs, working jointly with the Ministry of Education through third-party institutions in charge of fieldwork (Universidad Alberto Hurtado and Adimark GFK), conducted a biennial survey on school violence in the school environment known as ENVAE (Encuesta Nacional de Violencia en el Ámbito Escolar). This survey was carried out in three consecutive waves, in 2005, 2007, and 2009. In 2009, and with the aid of several researchers on school violence and school climate, questions regarding school climate were incorporated. However, for some unknown and officially undeclared reason, the ENVAE 2011 was not administered. After discontinuing it, in 2014 a new version of the survey was administered. Trends show that in the years 2007, 2009, and 2014, there was a slight drop in student-to-student harassment and a slight growth of teacher-to-student harassment (figure 4.1).

FIGURE 4.1 Trends in the national school violence survey (ENVAE) for years 2007, 2009, and 2014

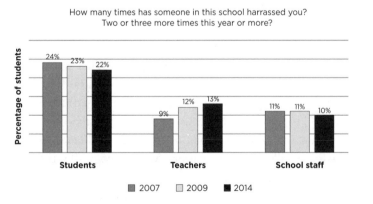

Source: Fundación Paz Ciudadana, Paz Educa, and Fundación Ibáñez Atkinson, Datos y estadísticas 2005–2016, https://pazeduca.cl/datos-y-estadisticas/.

Since 2012, the Agency for the Quality of Education has administered a national annual survey to fourth- and eighth-grade students who took the SIMCE test, which asks questions about bullying, school violence, school safety, and school climate. The establishment of this new agency, which is responsible for evaluating the quality of the school system, including social-emotional indicators, was probably the reason why the former ENVAE survey was dropped. Yet, while the agency presents scores on school climate in three categories (respectful climate, organized climate, and safe climate), it presents a composite score that includes students', teachers', and parents' perceptions in the "student score," where students' responses make up more than half of the total score. Specifically, the Decree 381, which operationalizes the SAC law, obliges the mandatory use of the following procedure for calculating the indicator of "clima de convivencia escolar":

For the calculation of the indicator of clima de convivencia escolar by grade, it is necessary to add the answers of students with those of teachers and parents/guardians weighed in a differentiated manner, as observed in formula no. 5, Aggregation of Student, Teacher, and Parent/Guardian Reports

$$Cj=0.5* Cej+=0.4* Caj+0.1* Cfj$$

Cj: Indicator of school coexistence climate by grade *j*, where *j* is the grade in which the questionnaire was applied

Cej: Score of the indicator in the questionnaires of students of grade *j*

Caj: Indicator score on questionnaires from parents and guardians of grade *j*

Cfj: Indicator score on questionnaires for grade *j* teachers

To ensure reliability, this indicator is only calculated when you have more than a certain percentage of the questionnaires answered by students taking the SIMCE test by grade or by their respective parents and guardians. This percentage is defined by the Agency according to technical criteria stipulated in a protocol.

Given previous analysis of the dataset which shows that the perception of the different actors might be negatively correlated, the "student total score" (formula no. 5), which is then aggregated at the school level to provide a school score of "clima de convivencia escolar," should be interpreted cautiously.[37]

This discussion, however, is not known to most schools, which interpret and use the school score as a valid and reliable information. Nevertheless, it is interesting to note how, in the agency's first administration of the survey in 2013, there were more students evaluating their school climate as "low" and "medium" than in the following surveys in 2014, 2015, and 2016 (figure 4.2). This might be due to the fact that the SIMCE results, including these social-emotional indicators, are part of the SAC national high-stakes accountability system. Based on the SIMCE scores, schools are ranked into four categories, and if a school ranked in the lower tier does not show signs of improvement in the same scores, the SAC law states that the school may

FIGURE 4.2 Percentage of fourth- and sixth-grade students evaluating their school climate, 2014–16

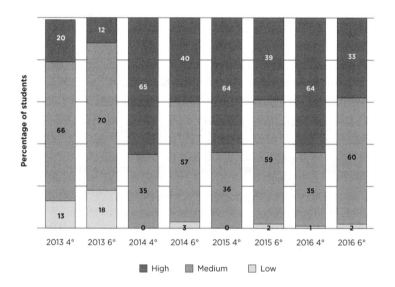

Source: Agencia de Calidad de la Educación de Chile, Entrega de resultados de aprendizaje 2014 (Santiago: Ministerio de Educación, 2014), http://archivos.agenciaeducacion.cl/resultados-2014 /Presentacion_Entrega_Resultados_2014.pdf; Agencia de Calidad de la Educación de Chile, Resultados educativos 2015 (Santiago: Ministerio de Educación, 2015), http://archivos.agencia educacion.cl/Presentacion_Resultados_Educativos_2015.pdf; Agencia de Calidad de la Educación de Chile, Resultados educativos 2016 (Santiago: Ministerio de Educación, 2016), http:// archivos.agenciaeducacion.cl/ResultadosNacionales2016_pdf.

be lose its official recognition as a school. Thus, after the first survey in 2013, and once schools became aware of the possible consequences of being ranked low, it is possible that students were prompted by teachers and school staff to evaluate their school climate as "high." A contending explanation is that schools made extra effort between 2013 and 2014 and actually improved on the school climate measures. However, beginning in 2014, trends among fourth- and sixth- grade students tended to stabilize, with the majority perceiving their school climate as "high," but with a greater number of fourth graders evaluating their school climate as "high" as compared to sixth graders.

Another part of the SAC system is the Superintendency of Education, which supervises public resources and the compliance of schools with current laws. Created in 2013, this office has a national complaint system that forms a very important part of its function. Any adult (aged eighteen or older) can file a complaint online or in person about any situation regarding a student's schooling that might affect their integrity and/or rights. Since the complaint system began in 2013, issues around violence toward students have constituted the largest number of complaints received each year (figure 4.3, on p. 70). The category "violence toward students" contains the following subcategories: "physical violence by adult(s) toward student(s)," "psychological violence by adult(s) toward student(s)," "physical violence between student(s)" (bullying), and "other forms of violence."

RECOMMENDATIONS FOR POLICY MAKERS, SCHOOL ADMINISTRATORS, AND SCHOOL STAFF

Research has shown that one approach that does not work to establish convivencia escolar are zero-tolerance policies that seek to "remove" the problem of bullying or school violence. School violence corresponds to the phenomenon of social violence; it goes far beyond what a school or a school system can do on its own. Violence is one of many ways to resolve a conflict, and conflict is part of daily life and school life, so it is about finding nonviolent ways of managing the conflicts.[38] In addition, bullying and other forms of violence at school are often the leaves indicating discrimination based on classism, racism, sexism, and other -isms, and the roots that reproduce new expressions of violence (e.g., cyberbullying) remain. Finally, zero-tolerance policies and methods generate zero knowledge because they do not develop in the school actors the ability to understand the origins of the conflicts or to make

FIGURE 4.3 Number of complaints received by the Superintendency of Education, 2013–17

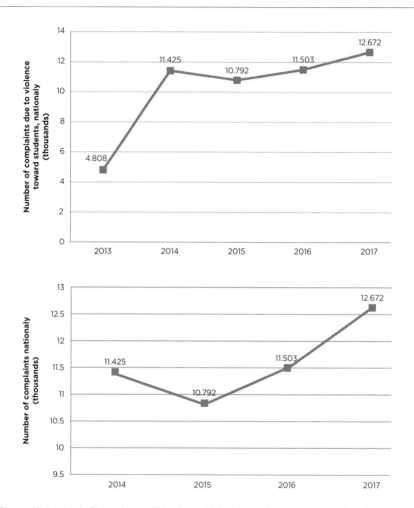

Source: Ministerio de Educación de Chile, Complaint Statistics by Complaint Subject, Superintendency of Education, 2014–17, https://www.supereduc.cl/categoria-estudios-estadisticas/estadisticas/.

decisions based on evidence—they remain unable to evaluate their impacts and learn from their experience.[39]

Another ineffective strategy is the hiring of psychologists, social workers, or other related professionals to attend to the problems of student behavior in the school through an individual approach in a clinical setting. The thinking is that if the problem is in children, then the solution is to "fix" these children. However, the pathologization of childhood is harmful because it leads to children's medicalization. This does not mean that some children cannot receive individualized care, or that they or others never require individual support. The problem is one of order and proportion: the strategy of individual care should be the last option.

In fact, what works in terms of convivencia escolar are systemic whole-school approaches that contemplate actions in the three levels indicated for psychosocial interventions: a level of primary promotion or prevention, a secondary level of prevention, and a tertiary level of prevention.[40] I offer a few suggestions and recommendations based on the experience of the PACES-PUCV research team, with which I have worked during the past ten years in examining public policies and day-to-day school practices on school violence and convivencia escolar and on teacher and school staff training and consultation.[41]

Strategic Orientations for Educational Policies and for Educational Actors

First, there is no single policy on convivencia escolar in Chile. Different convivencia escolar policies promote different objectives that come from distinguishable perspectives.[42] Morales and López have identified at least four: democratic coexistence, national security, school mental health, and new public management.[43] These perspectives have different consequences in relation to exclusion, inclusion, and citizen education.

In Chile, convivencia escolar policies have a hybrid logic because they stem from punitive and formative logics. The results of a four-year study for the National Commission of Science and Technology of Chile confirm that this vision of the hybridity of the policy of convivencia escolar is shared by those who design and implement these policies at the central, regional, and provincial levels.[44] A worrisome and urgent aspect is to improve the way in which Chile evaluates, reports, and makes schools accountable for the climate of convivencia escolar as part of the indicators of social and emotional development (Indicadores de Desarrollo Personal y Social, IDPS), whereby schools are invited to improve convivencia escolar through this indicator as part of the quality of education but lack a clear report of the specific issues in which they are doing well and poorly, and from whose perspective, since the indicator is a weighted, multiactor single score.

In the ambivalent scenario between punitive and formative policies, the forms of response from school administrators tend to be through administrative and judicial measures. Many schools adopt a "checklist" attitude just to avoid the penalties imposed by the Law on School Violence. This does not necessarily make it possible to move toward inclusive school coexistence, to improve opportunities for all students to access, stay, learn, participate, and be promoted. Especially worrisome is that the checklist administrative response is usually linked to the response of supervised, adult-centric participation of students and to the disciplinary and authoritarian response, which seeks to eliminate violence by removing "the rotten apple" (students with attitude problems and disciplinary issues). The results of the analysis of both educational policy and school practices showed a high predominance of the managerialist approach.

Second, the report shows that punitive practices are valued positively by students. There was a high correlation between democratic, inclusive, and peaceful school coexistence practices and punitive discipline practices. In effect, the ethnographic part of the report, carried out in three school establishments, showed just how deeply instilled some of the most historic devices for managing disruptive behaviors through punishment are: the registry of positive and negative annotations in the teacher's classroom log and the referral room (*inspectoría*).

The report makes the following recommendations:

- Review (and possibly modify) the IDPS of the climate of convivencia escolar—how it is defined, how it is measured, and how it is reported. At the same time, review the system of accountability associated with the climate of convivencia escolar.
- Review (and possibly modify) the devices within the schools, particularly the teacher's classroom log and the social function of the referral room as management devices for convivencia escolar. It is necessary to design and implement formative, not punitive, devices that promote dialogic conflict resolution between teachers and students.
- Avoid strategies from the perspective of zero-tolerance/national security policies, which correlate with the failure and desertion of the most unprotected. An example is a policy that promotes "expelling students who bring weapons," such as the 2018 Safe Classrooms bill.

- Reduce managerialist strategies that maximize and reinforce the use of accountability systems to improve convivencia escolar. The emphasis on accountability generates a school culture that tends to respond to standards but does not necessarily produce the cultural changes needed to sustain improvements. As a consequence, most schools tend to be current regarding school regulations but lack participation or development of citizen and democratic competences.

- Engage teachers, especially classroom teachers, in the promotion of convivencia escolar by strengthening their pedagogical leadership and competencies for conflict resolution. In order to do this, the definition of the role of the School Climate Coordinator and the training of the people who work in convivencia escolar become particularly important.

- Enhance collaborative work through the development of strategies that strengthen teams of convivencia escolar through interdisciplinary and collaborative work rather than actions aimed at individual attention in a clinical setting. In this sense, the latest guidelines from the Ministry of Education, which incorporate roles and functions of the school convivencia teams, are relevant and consistent with the results of this report.

- Address the management of convivencia escolar from a systemic and integral perspective, which allows for coordinating and establishing dialogues between the different plans and projects promoted by the Ministry of Education.

THE NEED TO CLOSE THE GAP BETWEEN RESEARCH AND POLICY

Coincidentally, on the same day the final report of the FONDECYT research grant was submitted, September 20, 2018, the president of Chile, Sebastián Piñera, and his Minister of Education, Marcela Cubillos, proposed the Safe Classrooms (Aula Segura) bill to "strengthen the faculties of school principals to expel and cancel enrollment in cases of violence indicated."[45] The "cases" referenced were related to episodes of violence by students enrolled in academically selective public high schools in the municipality of Santiago, located in downtown Santiago, who, supposedly as part of student protests, dressed in white overalls and masks and threw gasoline at teachers and school staff. These episodes were widely covered in the media and were used by the president and his ministers to justify this bill. The argument was that "these students are not students, they are delinquents" and that "teachers and students need to study in a safe environment."[46]

The executive branch proposed the Safe Classrooms bill to the legislative branch with extreme urgency. Chilean researchers on school violence and convivencia escolar, myself among them, joined forces to protest the bill, signing two public declarations and participating as experts in the Chamber of Deputies in the Senate and appearing on more than thirty TV, radio, and newspaper forums to speak out against the bill.[47] Our argument was that punitive, zero-tolerance measures to address school violence and school safety have been shown to not only be ineffective but cause more harm to an already highly segregated and exclusionary school system. Despite the protest, the Senate passed the bill on November 12, 2018, just fifty-four days after it was introduced, with some amendments, which mainly incorporated guaranteeing students due process, included actors other than students as possible perpetrators, added both "serious" and "very serious" faults to the physical and mental integrity of any school member, and incorporated suspensions as part of the due process. The Chamber of Deputies did not add further amendments and approved the version modified by the Senate.

Although there is no one-size-fits-all view among those who signed the public declaration with respect to the role of researchers in public policies, we all agree that it is necessary to close the gap between research, policy, and practice. I think it is necessary to join forces as researchers in order to participate as social actors in influencing public policies on school violence, school safety, and their relation to school climate and convivencia escolar. By sharing our experiences, we help other researchers around the world who also see the need to react against zero-tolerance policies and act toward building policies that may help schools become safe and supportive havens for all students.

CHAPTER 5

THE UNDERSTANDING, CURRENT SITUATION, AND COPING STRATEGIES OF SCHOOL BULLYING IN CHINA

MAO YAQING AND ER'LIN HE

THE NUMBER OF STUDENTS in China's schools is larger than most any other education system in the world. A detailed survey of China's youth population in 2007, conducted by the China Youth and Children Research Center, showed that the total number of K–12 students was about 235,276,800 (primary school, 105.64 million; middle school, 57.36 million; high school, 45.27 million).[1] In 2010, the number of students in K–12 was 198,847,700; in 2013, 181,595,300; in 2015, 180,352,300; and in 2017, 185,028,000. The large number of students has led to serious concern about safety in China's schools.[2]

In response, "Measures for the Safety Management of Kindergartens, Primary and Secondary Schools" were issued by the Ministry of Education, the Ministry of Public Security and ten other ministries on September 1, 2006, marking the first regulatory document in China dedicated to the safety management of kindergarten, primary, and secondary schools. Then, in 2007, the Ministry of Education gathered experts and scholars to formulate the "Guidelines for Public Safety Education in Primary and Secondary Schools." In 2010, the National Medium- and Long-Term Education Reform and Development Plan (2010–2020) proposed that safety education, life education, national defense education, and sustainable development education should be paid greater attention. In March 2013, the Ministry of Education issued the "Guidebook for Post Safety Work in Primary and Secondary Schools" and the "Guidelines for Post Safety Work in Primary and Secondary Schools."[3] In February 2014, the General Office of the Ministry of Education issued "Guidelines for Emergency Evacuation Exercises for Kindergartens, Primary and Secondary Schools" to assist schools in dealing with safety incidents.[4] These guidelines and manuals clearly define the responsibility of safety work and have played an important role in the safety management practice of primary and secondary schools. School safety measures not only protect teachers and students from any external dangers and injuries in teaching and learning activities, but, more importantly, they encourage students to achieve a healthy, comfortable, harmonious state while at school.

In China, the school security environment can be divided into "hard environment," the material conditions and infrastructure in the school, and "soft environment," the educational atmosphere and interpersonal relationships between teachers and students. Both hard and soft environments have an impact on the safety of students; it is no longer just about the facility's safety but about the safe, warm, and healthy atmosphere of mutual respect created by teachers and students. Early policy documents focused on the bodily safety of students and the construction of a hard environment. It wasn't until 2014 that the Ministry of Education began considering the soft environment. The "Compulsory Education School Management Standards (Trial)" named fourteen requirements for improving schools' safety and health infrastructures; for building a school culture with tolerance and respect as the core; for carrying out safety and health knowledge education, with life skills as a primary focus; for establishing a sound, and parallel, safety and health management system; and for constructing a safe and warm campus atmosphere for primary and secondary school students.[5]

School management is charged with attending to the overall development of children by providing a healthy, safe, psychologically supportive, and protective school environment. A supportive learning environment in which all students can feel safe is a basic function of all schools, and this must be a basic understanding of school administrators. Improving the care of children in the school environment can greatly promote the establishment and maintenance of their mental health. School should provide a positive experience for children in a happy learning environment to promote mental and emotional health and well-being and help children develop healthy self-esteem and self-confidence. In a safe school environment, children are protected from physical harm as well as from verbal, emotional, and sexual abuse.

China's new focus on human development aims to improve people's material living standards as well as their characters, emotions, sense of responsibility, and quality of life, which all contribute to social civilization and harmony. But this requires enrichment beginning in primary education and is the foundation of a quality education—the expansion of the concept of quality, the promotion of the active and healthy development of students in a coordinated way, attention to the development of students' personalities and emotions, and cultivation of students' social-emotional knowledge and skills. These elements of improvement respond to the requirements of the new era for comprehensive primary education in China.

BULLYING ON SCHOOL CAMPUSES

Bullying at school is a worldwide problem. On January 17, 2017, the United Nations Educational, Scientific and Cultural Organization (UNESCO) released a report which showed that nearly 246 million children and adolescents worldwide suffer from bullying at school every year.

In China, bullying has become all too common in recent years, and the situation is getting worse. It is now an issue of great concern to the Chinese people and government. According to a 2015 survey conducted by the China Youth Research Center of 5,864 primary and secondary school students in 10 provinces and municipalities, 32.5 percent of the respondents said they were occasionally bullied, and 6.1 percent said they were often bullied by senior students.[6] According to the 2017 China Education Development Report, a survey of 1,003 students in 12 schools in Beijing (4 primary, 4 middle, and 4 high schools) showed that 46.2 percent of primary school and middle school students had experienced intentional conflict, 6.1 percent of them suffering physical bullying almost every day and 40.7 percent being called unpleasant nicknames. Of the respondents, 11.6 percent experienced verbal bullying almost every day, 18.6 percent endured group bullying by many students, and 2.7 percent faced relational bullying almost every day.[7] In 2015 the Supreme People's Court reported reviewing sixty-seven cases of school crimes, including thirty-eight cases of intentional injury.[8] That same year, the Beijing Higher People's Court reviewed eight local bullying incidents, including infliction of intentional injury, gang fighting, and instigating quarrels.[9]

In response to growing public concern, the Chinese government is actively strengthening its management of bullying on school campuses. In April 2016, the Education Supervision Committee under the State Council issued the "Notice on the Special Administration of School Bullying," which called for the rectification of school bullying, the first time the government raised the problem of school bullying to a "state action."[10] In November 2016, the Ministry of Education issued "Guidelines on Prevention and Management of Bullying and Violence in Primary and Secondary Schools" in conjunction with the Comprehensive Administration Office of the Central Committee, the Supreme People's Court, the Supreme People's Procuratorate, the Ministry of Public Security, the Ministry of Civil Affairs, the Ministry of Justice, the Central Committee of the Communist Youth League, and the National Women's Federation.[11] In November 2017, the Ministry of Education, together with ten other departments, released the Plan to Strengthen the Comprehensive Management of Bullying in Primary and Secondary Schools.

UNDERSTANDING SCHOOL BULLYING IN CHINA

School bullying in China is best understood by examining the definition of the term in government documents, by consulting domestic research, by considering the type of bullying and the reasons for it, and by acknowledging its impact. Legal documents variously use "campus security," "campus violence," "school bullying," and "student bullying" when referring to school bullying. For example, the "Safety Management Measures for Kindergartens, Primary and Secondary Schools" and the Juvenile Protection Act of 2006 and the Compulsory Education Law reenactment of 2006 all use "campus safety" to refer to school bullying.[12] "Campus violence" appears in important instructions Premier Li Keqiang made on June 12, 2016, regarding the frequency of school violence. "School bullying" appears in the 2016 "Notice on the Special Governance of School Bullying." "Student bullying" appears in "Guidelines on Prevention and Management of Bullying and Violence in Primary and Secondary Schools" of November 2016 and in the Plan for Strengthening the Comprehensive Management Plan for Bullying of Primary and Middle School Students of November 2017.

There is a gradual, clear process of clarifying the definition of *school bullying* in China's legal, government-issued documents. In April 2016, in order to strengthen the prevention and management of bullying incidents on school campuses, the Education Supervision Committee carried out special governance and issued the "Notice on the Special Governance of School Bullying," which states: "In recent years, the school bullying incidents, which happened among students deliberately or maliciously through physical, language, and network means, caused harm by bullying or insulting, which have damaged the physical and mental health of students and caused great concern in society." In the document, the term *school bullying* is used and the manifestation of school bullying pointed out, but the connotation of school bullying is not clearly stated. The 2017 Plan to Strengthen the Comprehensive Management of Bullying in Primary and Secondary Schools, however, did clearly define *student bullying* at the national level for the first time: "Incidents occurring on or outside the campus (including primary and secondary schools and secondary vocational schools), between students, one party (individual or group) intentionally or maliciously bullying or insulting the other party (individual or group) through physical, linguistic and network means, resulting in physical injury, property loss or mental damage, etc."[13]

As for domestic research on the definition of school bullying in China, we found that the number of studies on school bullying has grown rapidly. We searched for the key word *school bullying* in online libraries like CNKI.net and Baidu Scholar to sort out research on school bullying conducted between 2000 and 2017 (figure 5.1).

In research on the connotation of school bullying, Chinese scholars define school bullying differently based on place, object, influence, characteristics, and means. In examining the *place* where the bullying occurred, scholars consider "inside and around the school," "inside and outside the school," and "inside the school" theories. In studying the *object*, or target, of the bullying, they determine whether the behavior is directed against students, teachers and staff, or people from outside the school.[14] Leijun Ma, for example, asserts that school bullying is an act of violence, destruction, and abuse committed against students, teachers, schools, and off-campus intruders.[15] In investigating *influence*, scholars look at the impact of school bullying, not only the physical and mental injury but also its effect on property. For instance, Linmei Sun and Ling Lin found that school bullying has an impact on students' physical and mental health, causing bodily injury and mental

FIGURE 5.1 Statistics on the number of research articles on school bullying

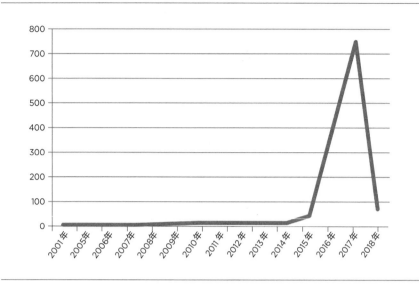

anguish.[16] Based on these examinations, most scholars believe that school bullying has two *characteristics*: concealment and repeatability.[17]

In terms of *means*, or how school bullying is enacted, research shows that it is not only through physical violence but also through abusive language, sexual violence, isolation, discrimination, and now cyberbullying.[18] School bullying has many forms. Weiyue Yu claims that it includes physical bullying, verbal bullying, social bullying, cyberbullying, and sexual bullying.[19] Jincai Lin contends that school bullying includes physical bullying, verbal bullying, relational bullying, sexual bullying, and retaliatory bullying.[20] In general, scholars agree that the main types of school bullying are physical bullying, verbal bullying, and sexual bullying.

The first reason for school bullying identified by Chinese researchers is the family environment, including inconsistent and indulgent parenting; an unhealthy family environment and/or parental relationship (e.g., an unhappy intimate relationship, a single-parent family, divorced parents, a reconstituted family, a poor parent-child relationship); parents' absence from children for an extended period; the lack of parent-to-child education; and the backwardness of educational views due to ideas of uneducated grandparents living in the home.[21]

The second reason researchers give for bullying is the school environment, which includes lax school management; aggressive disciplinary behaviors, such as corporal punishment; disharmony between teachers and students; a results-oriented concept of running a school; and the lack of student education on the legal system.[22] The third reason behind bullying behavior is a student's social environment, including the anomie of social culture, changing social structures, the absence of cultural rules and thought, the disorder of social behavior, and violent acts communicated through film, television, and books.[23]

A fourth reason is personal factors, including the psychological immaturity of students, the imitation of school bullying, rebellion and escape psychology, contrastive psychology, imitation of peer behavior, misunderstanding of teasing, and negative personally traits, such as jealousy.[24] The fifth, and final, reason given by Chinese researchers for school bullying behavior is the absence of a legal means to punish it.[25] The main laws used to regulate school bullying in China are criminal, juvenile protection, and juvenile delinquency laws.

School bullying impacts the bullies, the victims, and the bystanders. The impact on bullies cannot be ignored; it affects their psychological well-being, academics, and behavior.[26] School bullying can cause lasting psychological harm to the victims, who can show depression, loneliness, low self-esteem, and even suicidal tendencies. The victims of bullying can also develop negative personalities, find it difficult to adapt to school, and face social barriers. The main influence of bullying on bystanders is its effect on their attitudes toward both the victim and the bully. Some bystanders will even imitate the bully's behavior.[27]

COPING STRATEGIES

Policy on School Bullying

At present, there is no specific legislation on school bullying in China, and the governance of school bullying is one of administrative restraint, which cannot fundamentally solve the problem of school bullying.[28] The issue is managed in accordance with other existing laws or bills, such as the Law of the People's Republic of China on the Protection of Minors, Law of the People's Republic of China on Administrative Penalties for Public Security, "General Principles of the Civil Law of the People's Republic of China," "Notice on the Special Management of School Bullying," and Plan for Strengthening the Comprehensive Management of Bullying in Primary and Secondary Schools. These legal documents provide the basic principles for governing school bullying cases: protect the legitimate rights and interests of students and uphold the principles of education and protection. For example, the Plan for Strengthening the Comprehensive Management of Bullying in Primary and Secondary Schools points out the basic principles of school bullying governance as persist in educating, adhere to prevention practices, insist on protection, and uphold the rule of law.

In the existing legal documents of China, the measures the government is taking to address issues of school bullying include relying on cooperation among family, school, and society; improving the mechanism of governing school bullying; strengthening legal education in schools; and strengthening special governance. The 2016 issuance of the "Notice on the Special Management of School Bullying" marked the launch of the special management of school bullying in China. The special governance consists of two main stages of implementation. The first stage (April–July 2016) was completed through education, improvement of the system, strengthening prevention, timely handling, supervision and guidance, and organizational deployment. The second stage (September–December 2016) mainly involved conducting a comprehensive self-examination, supervision, and summary according to the situation of special education and the improvement of rules and regulations set out in the first stage.

"Guidelines on Prevention and Management of Bullying and Violence in Primary and Secondary Schools," issued in November 2016, put forward specific guidance for schools: actively and effectively prevent bullying and violence among students, deal with student bullying and violence incidents according to laws and regulations, and make a coordinated and collaborative effort to prevent bullying and violence among students.[29] To actively and effectively prevent bullying and violence, the document recommends effectively strengthening ideological and moral education, legal education, and psychological education in primary and secondary schools; carrying out special education on the prevention of bullying and violence; strictly enforcing daily safety management of schools; and strengthening comprehensive management around schools. To deal with the bullying and violence according to the laws and regulations, it calls for protecting the physical and mental safety of students who are victims of bullying and violence; strengthening the role of education in disciplinary deterrence; and implementing scientific and effective follow-up counseling. To effectively form a joint effort to prevent and control bullying and violence among students, it calls for strengthening the overall coordination of departments, implementing the responsibility of parental guardianship in accordance with the laws, strengthening the construction of a safe campus, and jointly protecting the healthy growth of minors.

In the Plan for Strengthening the Comprehensive Management of Bullying in Primary and Secondary Schools, some measures include clarifying the definition of *school bullying*, establishing and improving the coordination mechanism of prevention and management of student bullying actively and effectively prevent it, and dealing with school bullying according to laws and regulations. The measures for active and effective prevention include instructing schools to effectively strengthen education, organizing parent training, strict daily management of schools, and conducting regular investigations.

These measures to control school bullying mainly involve prevention and comprehensive management. As such, without post-supervision and feedback mechanisms, the governance of school bullying lacks long-term effectiveness. And since there is no special legislation on school bullying and/or its concealment, punishment is mainly handled administratively.

In 1987 the "General Principles of the Civil Law of the People's Republic of China" was issued, which could be considered the legal provisions around school bullying. Section IV suggests ways of assuming civil liability: stopping infringement, removing obstacle, eliminating danger, returning property, restoring original condition, repairing and replacing, compensating loss, paying liquidated damages, eliminating influence, restoring reputation, and apologizing.[30]

The Law of the People's Republic of China on Penalties for Administration of Public Security, implemented in 2006, is the basis for punishing school bullying. The categories of punishments include warning, fine, administrative detention, and suspension of licenses. Among them, those who have reached the age of 14 and are under the age of 18 and who violate the administration of public security shall be given a lighter or mitigated punishment; those who haven't reached the age of 14 but who violate the administration of public security shall not be punished, but their guardian shall be ordered to exercise strict discipline (as stipulated in Article 12). Those who beat others or intentionally injure another's body shall be sentenced to not less than 5 days but not more than 10 days of detention and fined 200–500 yuan; if the circumstances are relatively minor, a detention of less than 5 days or a fine of less than 500 yuan shall be imposed (as stipulated in Article 43).

The 2016 "Notice on the Special Management of School Bullying" states that if school bullying incidents occur during the period of special management, resulting in adverse effects, the offender will be notified, held accountable, and supervised. Punishment stipulated in the Law of the People's Republic of China on Penalties for Administration of Public Security is lighter for minors who break the law. Punishment indicated in the "Notice on the Special Administration of School Bullying" only addresses reporting bullying in school. Although these legal documents define punishment measures for school bullying to varying degrees, they are more based on administrative punishments, such as education, fines, and scolding.

Although the general provisions of the legal documents can provide some reference for the governance of school bullying, they are not targeted. For example, the Law on the Protection of Minors of the People's Republic of China stipulates the protection of the legitimate rights and interests of minors but does not include any specific principles against school bullying. Therefore, the law is insufficient to handle bullying, and the definition of bullying is not clear.

Also, the governance of school bullying in legal documents is more of macro-level guiding measure. The measures at the specific operational level are not clear, and the legal effect is not significant. Furthermore, there is no special law to define the connotation of school bullying in China. We can only refer to the definition cited in the Plan for Strengthening the Comprehensive Management of Bullying in Primary and Secondary Schools, which is just an administrative restriction, not a law.

Finally, the punishment of school bullying lacks a deterrence component. For example, only some regulations of the Law of the People's Republic of China on Administrative Penalties for Public Security involve the punishment of school bullying (e.g., the provisions in Articles 42 and 43). Furthermore, the punishments for school bullying laid out in the Law of the People's Republic of China on Penalties for Administration of Public Security are warnings, penalties, and detention. Without a legal deterrent, it is hard to prevent the occurrence of school bullying.

Prevention Measures

Prevention measures directed against school bullying in China need to be improved through special legislation around school bullying coming from the top levels of government.

The first step is to establish special legislation. At present, there is no special legislation against school bullying in China.[31] Due to the concealment and ambiguity of school bullying, it is very difficult for many laws to determine the penalty for school bullying, and the administrative penalty of the law does not have a deterrent effect on school bullying. Also, legislation around school bullying should define the term itself. At present, there is no law that clearly defines *school bullying*. Legislation should define the behavior, location, participants, means, and types of school bullying.[32]

In addition, new legislation needs to strengthen both prevention measures and trial mechanisms. Juveniles' legal awareness should be raised, and their knowledge of crime prevention and self-defense measures should be strengthened.[33] It needs to further improve and standardize the trial mechanisms of juvenile courts and protect the legitimate rights and interests of minors. The legal liability of perpetrators of school bullying should include civil liability and criminal liability and involve investigating the legal liability of perpetrators, quantifying their responsibility, and strengthening the trial mechanisms.[34]

At present, most of the punishments for school bullying are administrative penalties, such as education and fines. Some local governments have begun trying school bullying cases and quantifying the crime, which may serve as a practical foundation for the governance of school bullying nationwide. For instance, on December 13, 2016, the People's Court of Lucheng District, Wenzhou, Zhejiang Province, tried a case of juvenile bullying. The number of youth found guilty was as high as seven, with the highest prison sentence of six and a half years and the lightest sentence of nine months. This case has served as a clear standard of conviction and sentencing and has also provided the platform for a law against school bullying. Similarly, on November 2, 2017, the People's Court of Xicheng District of Beijing sentenced five people under the age of eighteen in a school bullying case. One defendant was sentenced to one year in prison for picking quarrels and provoking troubles; the others were sentenced to eleven months for the same crimes.[35] Of course, the verdict on school bullying is not just these two cases, but they do demonstrate an increased role of the Chinese government in the punishment of school bullying. It's no longer as simple as just educating and fining the principal offenders of school bullying.

In addition, in April 2016, China issued the "Notice on the Special Management of School Bullying," which addresses the special management of school bullying. Under the guidance of this document, the Supreme People's Procuratorate and the Ministry of Education jointly launched a three-year nationwide lecture tour to introduce the rule of law to school campuses. The Supreme People's Procuratorate selected 24 top prosecutors to form a lecture tour, invited experts to conduct training, and developed a number of high-quality courses on resistance to campus violence, crime prevention, self-care education, and classes for parents, to name a few initiatives. By November 2016, the tour group had traveled through 14 provinces, conducted 97 tours of 63 schools, met more than 90,000 students, and distributed more than 8,000 pieces of publicity materials.

In addition, each province has strengthened the daily management of its school campuses based on the current situation. For example, Shanghai oversight agencies analyzed the occurrence of campus violence and bullying in recent years and found that the lack of family education and improper measures were the main causes of school bullying. They explored the establishment of a long-term mechanism of parental education, which included identifying the root causes of the problem, formulating education programs, coordinating with judicial measures, regulating the system, and leveraging resources from various ways to improve education effectiveness. This response has gained wide public recognition.

Schools also need to improve education and carry out special activities on bullying. Therefore, it is necessary to strengthen the rules, psychological education, and legal education in schools to control school bullying with the lowest cost and the speediest outcome.

To strengthen the rules, schools should clarify the content and optimize educational behavior, balance the proportion of rule education and consider the combination of heteronomy and self-discipline education, and strengthen education guidance and supervision to help each student grow. Prevention and control measures can be carried out from a psychological perspective. Specific efforts can be made to introduce role-playing to let students experience what it is like to be bullied, to enter into a contract with the bully so that both sides have to determine goals and measurements, and to provide counseling for the victims so that they can express and affirm themselves in front of others through gradual training.[36]

Strengthening legal education in schools can also alleviate certain school bullying behaviors. Legal education activities include using blackboard newspapers, radio publicity, and training programs to cultivate student awareness of safety, rules, and the law.[37]

Families need to be involved in transforming the way of educating and cultivating students' positive characteristics and personalities. Because many parents in China are busy with their work, they don't have much contact with their children; thus, the parent-child relationship is not close, and children are vulnerable to being bullied and becoming bullies.[38] As such, legislation should include family education and clarify the responsibilities of parents in their children's education. Family and society should work together to make education more effective and reduce school bullying.

The establishment of parent schools would provide regular training and relevant knowledge to help parents understand the law and encourage parent-child communication. Schools could regularly carry out special education programs to help parents identify school bullying problems and to intervene to help solve the issues early.[39] A parent committee would involve parents in the management of schools, allowing them to provide advice for schools on school bullying issues and with addressing some difficult incidents. Innovation is needed around family-school communication mechanisms and sharing of information. Parent meetings, home visits, and telephone interviews are some other ways to regularly provide feedback to parents on problems.

Schools certainly play an important role in the prevention and control of school bullying. Schools conduct investigations into and evaluate incidents. Schools can also provide counseling services for families and establish a home-school communication mechanism. Schools should provide counseling services for families to help parents understand the serious consequences of bullying.[40]

There should be a cross-departmental coordination mechanism for school bullying at the government level to clarify the division of tasks, strengthen work responsibilities, improve prevention and control measures, strengthen assessment and inspection, and improve working mechanisms.[41]

Measurement and Research

Presently, the research tools for quantitative research on school bullying in China are questionnaires, including the Positive Psychological Capital Scale and the Bullying Behavior of Middle School Students. Researchers could, however, design appropriate questionnaires according to the actual research needs. The analysis methods of the questionnaires in use mainly include structural models (e.g., Chi-square tests, logistic regressions) to analyze the impact of positive psychological capital on bullying behavior.[42] The questionnaire data is processed and analyzed by Chi-square tests, logistic regression analysis, and correlation analysis, and then a logistic regression model is established. The results show that there are significant differences in the psychological status of adolescents in different age groups.[43]

The results of school bullying research will provide some reference for teachers, principals, and policy makers. Intervention on school bullying, however, mainly relies on practitioners, especially teachers; the school atmosphere and the overall environment affect any intervention around school bullying.

SUGGESTIONS

Legislation: Defining *School Bullying*

Legislation is key to preventing school bullying in China. The first step is to clarify the meaning of *school bullying*. Although the Plan for Strengthening the Comprehensive Management of Bullying in Primary and Middle Schools defines the concept of school bullying, there is no specific legal document that explicitly states the meaning of the term.

To assist in new legislation, the Chinese education system should strictly enforce school discipline, create a law-based school management approach to eliminate violence, and include schools, families, and society in the deterrence and prevention of school bullying.[44]

Prevention: Strengthening Multiparty Cooperation in School Bullying Governance

The comprehensive governance of school bullying in China requires government, schools, and families to join forces to strengthen prevention and oversight efforts.

The government should formulate relevant laws and regulations and implement them at all levels. Effective governance should include formulating a special anti–school bullying law as soon as possible and establishing a national mechanism around bullying that includes warning, notification, investigation, and psychological intervention.

Schools at all levels should attach great importance to the management of school bullying and establish special mechanisms for addressing it. Schools should conduct research on school bullying, actively carry out legal education, life education, and mental health education to prevent school bullying. Principals should strengthen the formulation of campus safety programs and guidance documents so that the school's school bullying governance and prevention can be supported by documents. Principals should also crack down on school bullying to combat bullies and provide psychological and physical assistance to the victims.[45] Teachers should pay attention to the needs of students and their interpersonal dynamics. Teachers improve students' consciousness to safeguard their rights by carrying out rules education, psychological education, and legal education.

Family is the foundation of prevention and control of school bullying. Parenting style, home environment, and the relationship between parents and parents and child are all factors that influence bullying behaviors. Parents should respect their children and guide them in establishing correct values and attitudes and developing a healthy, positive character. To reinforce this important role, the government should legislate on family education to clarify parents' responsibilities in their children's education.

Society also plays a role in the prevention of school bullying. School bullying governance should involve a collaboration of various agencies and departments at different levels of government around the mechanisms of school bullying work to better understand school bullying and then prevent it.

Adjudication: Quantifying the Crime of School Bullying

The management of school bullying needs to include improvements to the trial system, where the court clarifies how to punish students guilty of bullying. Students must bear the legal responsibility for their behavior, and teachers must also assume the legal responsibility for not managing school bullying well.

Many scholars insist on pursuing the legal responsibility of school bullying, using the law to safeguard victims' legitimate rights and calling for special laws. The "Notice of the Office of the Education Supervision Committee Under the State Council on the Special Management of School Bullying" and the "Guidelines on Prevention and Management of Bullying and Violence in Primary and Secondary Schools" both provide guidance on the prevention and control of school bullying, but there are no specific legal provisions. Therefore, the improvement of the legal system around the issue of school bullying should be based on establishing a school bullying governance committee to lead the special reform work; determining the legal punishments for school bullying; clarifying the definition of school bullying; and improving the assistance system around bullying.[46]

CHAPTER 6

DEMO-CRITICAL CLASSROOMS

An Alternative to Promote Safe Schools in Colombia at a Postconflict Juncture

SANJAY K. NANWANI

También es cierto que apenas me has pegado alguna vez, de verdad. Pero aquellas voces, aquél rostro encendido, los tirantes que te quitabas apresuradamente y colocabas en el respaldo de la silla, todo eso era casi peor para mí.

It is also true that you have hardly hit me, really. But those voices, that burning face, the suspenders that you would take off hurriedly and place on the backrest of the chair, all that was almost worse for me.

—Franz Kafka, *Carta al padre* (my translation)

THIS CHAPTER PROVIDES insights into the challenges and opportunities around creating safe, supportive, and engaging schools in Colombia. While great advances have been made, further efforts are needed to integrate a broader notion of safety in Colombian schools to ensure environments that support and engage students in their learning.

I focus on how, in broad terms, the nature of mean, bullying, and disrespectful behavior has been conceived in Colombia and how this type of behavior manifests itself in educational contexts. I also look at the country's violence prevention and practice goals in the educational domain and discuss national trends that shape improvement strategies designed to actualize these goals. I focus my attention on measurements and measurement trends that potentially help school leaders, and those responsible for policy design and implementation, to understand the extent to which their strategies have (and have not) helped actualize improvement goals. I close by outlining recommendations and possible paths forward for educators and policy makers in Colombia and potentially in other countries.

For my research, I reviewed a variety of sources on educational policy related to the prevention of school violence and the promotion of citizenship competencies, including legislative measures and policy strategies undertaken in the last fifteen years to support educational policy; policy guideline documents published by the Colombian Ministry of Education; a review of national policy trends focused on strategy implementation affecting school violence and peaceful coexistence; global policy initiatives and reports published by organizations informing school violence prevention in the Caribbean and Latin America; and an appraisal of research trends, including studies carried out by government entities in Colombia and academia-informed school violence prevention and promotion of citizenship skills in Colombia. This empirical research was also part of my doctoral work: a qualitative, multiple case study conducted in marginalized school contexts in Cali, Colombia, where there are high levels of community violence and fragile social fabrics. I focused on teachers' conceptions and practices at the classroom level to cultivate democratic skills and dispositions and whether, and how, they succeeded in constructing safe and democratic classroom climates. This work has direct implications for school violence prevention and promotion of democratic citizenship and informs how to create safe, supportive, and engaging schools in Colombia. I also drew on my own experience with the Swedish International Development Agency, where I worked on educational projects focused on children's rights and school and classroom management across Latin and Central America.

UNDERSTANDINGS

The Political Constitution of Colombia, ratified in 1991 and replacing the Constitution of 1886, provides a comprehensive political and legal framework with implications for guaranteeing the rights of children and promotion of safe schools and classrooms. It declares Colombia to be an "Estado social de derecho," a state guided by the rule of law. Article 44 of the Constitution outlines fundamental rights of children, stating that they "shall be protected against all forms of abandonment, physical or moral violence, kidnapping, sale, sexual abuse, economic exploitation, and risk-related work.[1] It adds that children will also enjoy the other rights enshrined in the Constitution, in laws, and in international treaties ratified by the state. Similarly, Article 45 outlines that adolescents have "rights to protection and integral development" and that the responsibility of the state and society is to guarantee the active participation of youth in public and private entities in charge of their protection, education, and progress.[2]

The nature and spirit of the Constitution of 1991 has influenced Colombian educational policy: the very idea of citizenship, which is central to understanding how violence in educational settings is understood and countered, as well as some of the core constructs in educational policy, spring from the political commitments articulated in the Constitution. In 1994, Law 115 (General Law of Education) was passed with a decree that operationalized some of the elements within the Constitution. This law emphasized an education that respects life, human rights, peace, democracy, coexistence, pluralism, justice, solidarity, equity, tolerance, and freedom. The framework of Colombian education policy prioritizes the concepts of citizenship, human rights, and participatory democracy, which has implications for creating safe, supportive, and engaging K–12 schools.

At the Colombian education policy level, the term *violence* is understood as conduct (action or omission) that provokes harm and/or suffering of a physical, psychological, or sexual nature, including death. This conception stems from a power imbalance in relations and/or interactions between the involved parties. The power imbalance may be real or perceived, and it can manifest itself in multiple ways, including physical, psychological, sexual, or economic mechanisms, leading to different degrees and types of violence. In recent years, there has been increasing focus on gender violence and cultural violence, particularly given Colombia's deeply rooted patriarchal social structures and the lack of recognition of the Indigenous and Afro-descendant communities.

The National Ministry of Education, in its *Guide to School Environment and Improvement of Learning*, refers to *school environment*, *school climate*, and *positive school environment*.[3] It distinguishes between *school environment* and *school climate*, despite overlapping elements. *School environment* is understood as the set of relations among members of the educational community. It is determined by structural, personal, and operational factors that define relationships among members of an educational community. It includes factors related to the physical atmosphere, school infrastructure, school organization, and social and cultural environment surrounding the school. *School climate* is understood as being "based on patterns of people's experiences of school life and reflects norms, goals, values, interpersonal relationships, teaching and learning practices, and organizational structures."[4] It also integrates teachers' and students' personal experiences into their school life, as well as norms and values that condition their interactions in the different school spaces. The guide cites the five components of a positive school climate as safety, relationships, teaching and learning, institutional environment, and institutional improvement processes.[5] Characteristics of a positive school climate are democratic leadership exercised by directors and senior managers, with the shared responsibility of all actors in the school; effective and dialogical communication within the school, expanding the capacity to listen among directors, teachers, and students; relationships and teaching styles at the classroom level based on respect and warmth, avoiding extremes of permissiveness and authoritarianism; norms and limits agreed on by the educational community and practiced in daily living, supporting social self-regulation of groups; and collaborative learning among students to encourage inclusion.

Law 1620 (Ley de Convivencia Escolar) of 2013 aimed at ensuring safe and supportive school settings.[6] *Coexistence* is my translation of *convivencia*, which is a concept that is referred to in Colombian (and Latin American) educational policy and connotes living together in peace. (I use *convivencia* in some discussions in this chapter.) Through the Decree of 1965, Law 1620 led to the creation of the National System of School Coexistence and Development for the Exercise of Human Rights, Education for Sexuality, and the Prevention and Mitigation of School Violence.[7] Article 39 of this decree introduces definitions of *conflict, inadequately managed conflicts,* and *school aggression. Conflict* is understood as a situation characterized by real or perceived incompatibility between persons in relation to their interests. *Inadequately managed conflicts* are situations where conflicts are not resolved in a constructive manner, leading to events that affect school coexistence. These events may be altercations, confrontations, or quarrels between two or more members of the school community, of which at least one member is a student. Inadequately managed conflicts do not include bodily harm to (or jeopardize the health of) any of the parties involved.

The Decree of 1965 defines *school aggression* as action committed by one or more members of the school community that intends to negatively affect other members of the community, of which at least one is a student. It outlines different forms of school aggression (physical, verbal, gestural, relational, electronic) and includes bullying, cyberbullying, sexual violence, violation of children's and adolescents' rights, and restitution of children's and adolescents' rights.

This legal framework is complemented by Article 40 of Decree 1965, which classifies three types of situations that affect harmonious school coexistence. Type 1 situations refer to inadequately managed conflicts and sporadic situations that affect school climate but do not include bodily harm. Type 2 situations refer to aggression, bullying, and cyberbullying that do *not* possess the characteristics of a crime or criminal offense but that occur repeatedly or systematically or that inflict bodily harm but do not disable any of the parties. Type 3 situations refer to school aggression that includes alleged crimes or offenses against the freedom and/or integrity of the victim, including sexual violence. These include crimes listed in Colombian penal law.

The political and legal framework around children's and adolescents' rights, with implications on safe schools and classrooms, is complemented by Law 1098 of 2006, known as the Code of Childhood and Adolescence (Código de la Infancia y la Adolescencia).[8] Law 1098 provides a comprehensive framework aimed at the integral protection of children and adolescents, who are "subjects of rights." Child mistreatment is understood as all forms of harm, punishment, physical or psychological abuse, neglect, negligence, omission, ill-treatment, and sexual exploitation, including abusive sexual acts and rape. Article 2 of Law 1098 establishes substantive and procedural norms to protect children and adolescents and to guarantee their rights and liberties enshrined in international human rights treaties, both in the Political Constitution of Colombia as well as in Colombian legislation.

The fact that there is a comprehensive educational policy framework in place in Colombia that is rights based and accounts for addressing school violence in its different forms is commendable. However, there is much work to be done, not only to *prevent* and counter abusive and/or disrespectful behavior but also to *promote* democratic participation in schools in its broadest sense. This needs to be complemented by a positive conception of peace that accounts for individuals' dignity and is rights centered, not just in theory but in practical terms, rather than a negative conception of peace characterized by the absence of war or open violence. The practical conception of peace should consider not only what conditions are necessary to counteract school violence but also what conditions are necessary to promote and implement healthy school environments.

It is important that legislative gaps are not only identified but acted against. In this regard, while the Global Initiative to Put an End to All Corporal Punishment of Children refers to legal prohibition of punishment as a key element of compliance to the Convention on the Rights of the Child, only nine countries in the Caribbean and Latin America have laws in place prohibiting it unequivocally in all settings, including the home. Colombia is *not* one of them. The Latin America Progress Briefing 2015 by the Global Initiative states the following on Colombia: "[The] 1994 Constitutional Court judgment ruled against violence in child rearing and [the] Code on Children and Adolescents includes 'punishment' in [its] definition of 'abuse,' but [the] Civil Code confirms [the] right to 'correct' children and 'sanction them moderately.'"[9]

Similarly, a report published in 2011 by UNICEF and PLAN International on school violence in the Caribbean and Latin America pointed out that Colombian legislation only prohibits corporal punishment that causes injury.[10] More recently, however, Colombia's Constitutional Court noted that schools are prohibited from imposing sanctions that are cruel, humiliating, or degrading and that lead to physical or psychological violence.[11] Despite this, humiliating forms of punishment, including corporal punishment, persist and are socially accepted, often considered an appropriate "corrective" and a way of "disciplining."

What is important is that understandings of violence in its different forms are not only outlined on paper but are effectively acted on in school contexts. It is also essential that gaps in the legislative system, including ambiguity, are effectively addressed. Moreover, the emphasis on "prohibition" should translate into practice through effective and complete elimination of all forms of violence, including corporal punishment.

GOALS

Research That Informs Violence Prevention Goals

The goals related to school violence and prevention policies seek to counter not only bullying but other forms of violence as well. These goals are closely related to how violence is understood in Colombian education policy specifically and Colombian legislation more broadly. The goals are also shaped by the country's history, marked until recently by an armed conflict between the state and the Revolutionary Armed Forces of Colombia (FARC), a guerilla movement that funded its operations through kidnapping, drug trafficking, and other illegal forms of economic activity. The effects of this armed conflict and the effects of violence at the macro level, connected in complex ways, have been documented in various studies. In this chapter I am interested in those findings that may have implications for the Colombian education context. Much of this research has likely shaped the goals aimed at creating safe schools and classrooms through violence prevention.

Important bodies of research underlie Colombia's current school violence prevention goals and school climate improvement efforts. Education policy, particularly regarding violence prevention, relates to evidence that documents Colombia's high levels of family violence, school-related violence, and gang-related and community violence.[12] Studies also document criminal activity not linked directly to the armed conflict.[13] Studies also indicate that children who are exposed to violence have a greater likelihood of developing higher levels of aggression, replicating violent behavior and becoming perpetrators of violence themselves.[14] This phenomenon has been referred to as the "cycle of violence" and "intergenerational transmission of violence." Other effects of exposure to violence include emotion dysregulation, aggressive fantasies, and normative beliefs reinforcing aggressive behavior.[15]

Furthermore, contexts experiencing, or emerging from, violent conflict often exhibit a normalization (or naturalization) of violence that is reproduced in schools. This is complemented by a body of research on the negative effects of aggression and violent attitudes on the well-being of individuals and social groups. This normalization is linked to a higher risk of experiencing interpersonal conflicts, engaging in school violence, dating and domestic violence, and gun violence.[16] These factors increase the vulnerability of those already at risk of being targeted. Studies also show that a student's use of violence in schools places them at higher risk of dropping out and of having problems with the criminal justice system.[17] At a societal level, this undermines a positive community climate, which, in turn, undermines the social fabric and affects school climate, creating a vicious cycle.

Core Elements of the National Standards of Citizenship Competencies

Colombia's pioneering educational approach to countering violence in the Latin American region has, since 2003, been to develop citizenship competencies through the National Standards of Citizenship Competencies (NSCC).

These competencies are conceived around ideas relating to living together peacefully, participation and democratic responsibility, and pluralism, identity, and respect for differences.[18] These three central elements seek to develop individuals equipped to exercise their citizenship holistically and to live in a society characterized by peace, democracy, and pluralism. Perhaps the most pressing challenge lies in unlearning certain mind-sets, dispositions, and behaviors to allow for learning and internalizing new ways of interacting with each other while cultivating more democratic mind-sets, skills, dispositions, and behaviors. In a country marked by decades of armed conflict, this is a challenge that requires deliberate strategies which combine both violence prevention and democracy promotion models.

The NSCC are part of a larger effort to look for alternatives to resolve conflicts peacefully, overcome social exclusion, open new spaces for citizen participation, address high levels of corruption, and contribute to healthier schools, workplaces, public spaces, and homes. The standards also outline "genuine democratic communication" based on Habermasian principles; their underlying philosophy is closely linked to moral development.[19]

The fact that the NSCC have emerged as a sustainable policy goal cannot be ignored. They combine, at least in theory, both prevention- and promotion-based models with their respective goals: preventing school and community violence while promoting convivencia based on a human rights framework. The prevention-based model seeks to reduce different forms of violence and abuse in schools. The promotion-based model (beyond intending to cultivate citizenship competencies) is based on institutional policies that focus on harmonious school coexistence and school climate improvement.[20] These are aimed at generating an environment for the genuine and effective exercise of human, sexual, and reproductive rights in the school setting, among other elements.

While part of a larger effort to contribute to a well-functioning democratic nation guided by the rule of law, the standards themselves intend to accomplish nine specific goals at the primary and secondary school levels:

- promote knowledge of civics;
- promote communicative competencies;
- promote cognitive competencies;
- promote emotional competencies;

- promote integrative competencies (where the communicative, cognitive, and emotional converge);
- support moral development;
- contribute to establishing convivencia and peace;
- promote participation and democratic responsibility; and
- promote pluralism, identity construction, and the valuing of difference.

In essence, the NSCC represent a national policy initiative to advance knowledge, skills, and dispositions that provide a foundation for democracy.

Complementary Legislative Measures

This citizenship competency-based approach at the school level has been complemented by a number of legislative measures since 2003, all aimed at building a more inclusive, peaceful, rights-based, democratic nation. Examples of these legislative measures, and their underlying converging goals, are the Code of Children and Adolescents (2006), the Prevention of Sexual Violence and Integral Care of Child Victims of Sexual Abuse (2007), the Convention on the Rights of Persons with Disabilities (2011), and the International Convention for the Protection of All Persons from Enforced Disappearance (2012). Other institutional and policy measures include the Public Policy on Gender Equality (2012); the Strategic Plan to Eliminate HIV/AIDS Mother-to-Child Transmission (2011); the Policy and Strategy on Early Childhood, known as From Zero to Always (De Cero a Siempre, 2010), aimed at ensuring adequate integral development of infants beginning before birth; and the National Action Plan for Children and Adolescents (2009–19). These are all part of a comprehensive policy focus with the goal of not only building a more inclusive nation but also accounting for sectors of the population affected by violence direct or indirectly and recognizing communities that have been neglected.

STRATEGIES

Beyond the Ministry of Education, there are other entities whose work contributes to providing safe, supportive, and engaging schools, including the Ministry of Health and Social Protection; the Ministry of Culture; the Ministry of Information and Communication Technologies; the Colombian Family Welfare Institute; and circa ninety-five Secretarías de Educación (education secretariats) nationwide. It is important to note that Colombia is divided into thirty-two departments in addition to the District Capital of Bogota. Each department is divided into municipalities, and these into districts.

National Committee of School Coexistence and the Route to Integral Care for School Coexistence

In addition to the National Committee of School Coexistence, there are committees of school coexistence at the department, municipality, district, and school levels. They all comprise a prevention and promotion framework based on concrete protocols (based on different types of violence) that are implemented through the Route to Integral Care for School Coexistence (RICSC), a system established in Law 1620 to guarantee students' human, sexual and reproductive rights and a healthy "convivencia" in both schools and the community.[21] The RICSC also supports schools in mitigating risks, managing situations that affect convivencia, and following up on particular cases.

The RICSC has four aims: *promotion* of school climate improvement and convivencia; *prevention* based on timely intervention that could affect the exercise of human, sexual, and reproductive rights; *care* based on providing timely support to schools in specific situations affecting the exercise of human, sexual, and reproductive rights; and *follow-up* and evaluation of strategies and actions undertaken by other actors and other bodies comprising the NSSC.

The three types of violence situations outlined in Article 40 of Decree 1965 affecting harmonious school coexistence have specific protocols.[22] Protocols for Type 1 situations (inadequately managed conflicts that do not include bodily harm or jeopardize health) are based on prolonged mediation with those involved in a conflict. They seek solutions impartially, equitably, and in a just manner, including actions seeking reparation for harm caused and restitution of rights and reconciliation. They also establish compromises and follow-up.

Protocols for Type 2 situations (aggression, bullying, and cyberbullying not possessing the characteristics of a crime or criminal offense but occurring repeatedly or systematically or inflicting bodily harm not involving any form of disability of any of the parties) include providing physical and mental health care; contacting administrative authorities if necessary; providing protection measures for those involved to avoid recurring actions against them;

informing parents or caregivers; providing spaces to listen to what actually happened from those involved; specifying restorative actions to be taken for reparation of harm caused, restitution of rights, and reconciliation; registering incidents in a single national database, the Sistema de Información Unificado, to report cases of violence, analyze them, and provide follow-up and solutions on the part of the respective school committee.

Protocols for Type 3 situations (school aggression that includes alleged crimes or offenses against the freedom and/or integrity of the victim, such as sexual violence and crimes listed in Colombian penal law) include providing physical and mental health care; informing parents or caregivers; registering cases with the Childhood and Adolescence Police authorities and the School Committee; providing protection to the victim(s), the perpetrator(s), and those involved in the incident; and registering incidents in the Sistema de Información Unificado. The respective school committee and other pertinent committees at the municipal, district, or department levels are responsible for providing follow-up on these cases.

A Decentralized School System

The organizational framework, including committees of school coexistence at the national, department, municipal, district, and school levels, provides a strategic system for implementing relevant goals established in Law 115 of 1994 (General Law of Education) and Law 1620 of 2013 (Law of School Coexistence). However, a decentralized school structure means that each school defines its curricula, pedagogical orientation, or Proyecto Educativo Institucional (PEI) and school-level strategies to reach the goals established in the laws. While the Ministry of Education provides a comprehensive framework in relation to safe, supportive, and engaging schools, what strategies are implemented largely depends on individual schools.

This decentralized system has both advantages and disadvantages. One advantage is the autonomy that it provides schools. Schools can potentially foster greater engagement insofar as school leaders, and teachers can support and work in partnership with parents and students. In contrast, a disadvantage is that the success of strategy implementation may largely depend on each school's capacity and resources (human and other) as well as the challenges arising from parent involvement. Parent involvement in school affairs may be less in the case of working parents in marginalized communities who are trying to make ends meet.

This decentralized system also pertains to the implementation of the NSCC, which are a policy strategy in themselves to advance safer, supportive, and more engaging schools. Each school decides what strategies to employ and how to best implement the NSCC. It is noteworthy that through the standards, citizenship education has been given the same level of priority as other traditional academic subjects. This is complemented by the construction of democratic and peaceful climates, a citizenship education that is transversal, and specific spaces for citizenship development. The NSCC are also focused on developing emotional, cognitive, communicative, and integrative competencies.

Evaluation of Citizenship Competencies

A further policy strategy is the assessment component of the NSCC through the standardized Pruebas Saber tests administered in the third, fifth, seventh, ninth, and eleventh grades in civics, mathematics, science, and Spanish classes. These tests evaluate if and to what degree the national standards are being met. Chaux and Velasquez contend that, given the strongly decentralized system, the standards and tests are almost the only control mechanism the Ministry of Education has to make sense of the quality of education schools deliver.[23]

Cátedra de Paz

Another important policy strategy implemented is the Peace Chair, or Cátedra de Paz. This 2015 initiative for all schools in the country seeks to promote peace in schools. It is a program designed to be implemented through different school subjects to provide students with knowledge and competencies relating to relevant themes in the Colombian context, including themes around territory, culture, social and economic contexts, and historical memory, each of which seeks to develop a broader understanding of the unique structural dynamics at play, particularly in light of the country's violent history. Researchers at Universidad de Los Andes have published pedagogical material to support teachers in implementing the Cátedra de Paz. *Secuencias Didácticas para la Educación para la Paz* and *Orientaciones Generales para la Implementacion de la Catedra de Paz* focus on pedagogical peacebuilding strategies that broadly support the reconstruction of Colombia's social fabric.[24]

Colombian educational policy includes a commendable strategic framework that combines both prevention- and promotion-based mechanisms to actualize goals aimed at making schools safer. The articulation of specific protocols depending on different types of violence is also commendable, reflecting a system based on restorative action, reparation of harm caused, and restitution of rights and reconciliation. The Sistema de Información Unificado is also an appropriate measure, particularly in contexts of displacement. Moreover, this system also provides mental health care to children and families who have been psychologically affected as a result of an armed conflict.

MEASURES AND MEASUREMENTS SYSTEMS

Limited Data

Instruments to measure school climate and bullying are scarce in Colombia as compared, for example, to the US context.[25] Challenges emerge around what exactly is to be measured and how. The National Institute of Legal Medicine and Forensic Sciences (Instituto Nacional de Medicina Legal y Ciencias Forenses, INMLCF) contends that there is limited data on the "real" violence against children. In the 2017 report relating to violence, the INMLCF suggested the need for a unified epidemiological surveillance system to provide precise numbers and details of specific cases to support decision-making and adoption of public policy.[26]

While measurement systems are scarce, the most recent Demography and Health National Survey, which conducted every five years by the the INMLCF, indicates (beyond the percentages) what aspects are actually measured. The survey revealed that only 10.9 percent of women and 14.9 percent of men reported that no one in their households punishes children; taking care of children is a responsibility mostly undertaken by women; 26.2 percent of women and 15.8 percent of men reported that they punished children (boys and girls) by hitting them or hitting them with objects; 14.7 percent of women and 7.3 percent of men punished by slapping (*palmada*, which refers to slaps of different intensities). The survey findings also revealed that 0.6 percent of women and 0.4 percent of men punished by pushing children.[27]

In regard to nonphysical punishment of boys and girls, the survey findings also indicated that 54.6 percent of women and 34.8 percent of men punished children by withholding or prohibiting something they liked; 48.6 percent of women and 38 percent of men punished by verbal reprimand. Other forms of punishment were ignoring children (1.5 percent of women and 0.5 percent of men); locking them up (0.9 percent of women and 0.7 percent of men); enforcing other forms of deprivation (0.9 percent of women and 0.5 percent of men); taking away financial support (0.3 percent of women and 0.2 percent of men); giving them inappropriate chores or work (0.2 percent of women and 0.1 percent of men); and other forms of punishment (3.2 percent of women and 1.8 percent of men).[28]

Government Entity Surveys

At the regional government level, school climate reform and violence prevention have also been the focus of three surveys focusing on Bogotá, and its neighboring municipalities These were conducted in 2006, 2011, and 2013 by the Secretaría de Gobierno de Bogota and the Secretaría de Educación de Cundinamarca, respectively. Broadly, the results showed different manifestations of violence and aggression and their prevalence in schools in the Bogota region, including verbal aggression and exclusion; physical aggression, fights, and intimidation; and more severe forms of aggression, including the use of weapons. They also showed the frequency of robberies in school compounds, the perception of insecurity in schools, and aggression on the part of teachers.

The 2013 survey sample was made up of nearly 120,000 students in grades 6–11 who responded to 120 questions mainly focused on school climate and victimization. It sought to track the evolution of indicators of violence and aggression in schools across the preceding surveys and to characterize the presence of gangs and the sale and consumption of psychoactive substances, among other illicit drugs.

Other measurements conducted by individual researchers in academia reflect a diversity of approaches to define and make sense of school climate, denoting a lack of consensus in how school climate and related concepts are understood. This is associated with abundant methodologies that are evaluation focused, narrative, and context based. These seek to evaluate the emotional impact, incidence, prevalence, and seriousness of phenomena relating to safety in schools; make sense of individuals' written words, spoken words, and/or visual representations; study specific elements in school contexts.[29]

The multiple instruments designed to measure or make sense of school climate include observation techniques, interviews, discussion groups, and questionnaires or scales. In the Colombian context, various instruments have been used, among them the School Social Climate Scale; the questionnaire for the detection of bullying; the Family APGAR to measure family functioning; the MOS social support survey; Cisneros's scale to assess bullying ; and the California School Climate and Safety Survey.[30] What predominates among these studies is a focus on bullying (including the roles of aggressor, victim, and observer/witness) and the types of violence manifested. While important, they suggest an approach that does not address safety and school and classroom climate holistically.

Other studies conducted in Colombia have focused on the prevalence of bullying, aggression, or abuse, but these have employed different instruments, with psychometric limitations, which impede comparing results.[31] Studies conducted in Medellín have indicated that 68.3 percent of rectors reported cases of bullying in their instutions.[32] Yet, Higuita-Gutiérrez and Cardona-Arias contend that studies which address bullying, school safety, and school climate holistically, from a student perspective, are scarce and also present psychometric limitations.[33] Among studies that account for student perspectives, Chaux and colleagues conducted a two-year quasi-experimental evaluation with 1,154 students from 55 classrooms in 7 public schools in 2 Colombian cities.[34] This particular study focused on evaluating a specific multicomponent citizenship development program, Aulas en Paz, in high-violence neighborhoods, with findings showing positive results in prosocial behavior, a reduction of aggressive behavior based on teacher reports, and a reduction of verbal victimization based on student reports. A second study used a database with more than 1 million students from various regions of Colombia, and it showed higher levels of aggression among children and adolescents living in municipalities with high levels of violent conflict, including homicide.[35] A third comparative study in 2008 by Chaux and Velásquez based on findings of the 2006 survey found that 1 in 3 students in Bogota reported having been subject to physical aggression at school in the last month; and 1 in 4 reported that a school friend/acquaintance had brought a knife to school in the last year.[36]

The Synthetic Index of Quality Education

There are no known nationwide or regional measures actually mandated to schools by the government that have a direct bearing on mean and/or disrespectful behavior and/or bullying. However, in 2015 the Ministry of Education introduced the Synthetic Index of Quality Education (SIQE) to measure the educational quality of Colombia's primary and secondary schools. With a range from 1 to 10, it measures *progress*, based on scores of the Pruebas Saber tests; *performance*, based on Pruebas Saber school scores in comparison to other regions; *efficiency*, based on the number of students who pass the academic year; and *school environment*, which aims to evaluate adequate conditions for learning in the classroom.[37]

There are several limitations with the SIQE. First, climate is considered one of four constitutive elements of quality education and not a central element in itself with its respective constitutive parts, thereby arguably underestimating the importance of climate. Cohen and colleagues suggest that measuring and working to improve school climate "is the single most powerful K–12 educational strategy that supports schools intentionally creating democratically informed communities which foster the skills, knowledge and dispositions that support students' healthy development and capacity to learn and become engaged and effective citizens."[38] Second, from a quality education perspective, the SIQE relies on standardized test scores to measure "progress" and "performance." I argue that high-stakes standardized tests are sometimes insufficient to make sense of quality education and are used inappropriately to evaluate students, educators and schools. They also lead to a focus on test-taking skills at the expense of subject mastery and divert resources from poor-performing schools, labeling them as "failures." Moreover, such testing indirectly excludes students who may not perform well under excessive pressure, thereby restricting their opportunities to access tertiary education.From a school safety perspective, school environment is considered the total sum of the climate of classrooms within the school, and "to improve the learning level of students, we must think of the school environment of each of our classrooms."[39]

However, concrete strategies for school climate and classroom climate improvement need to be clearly delimited: school climate is composed of school-level variables (e.g., relations between school director and teachers, school governance), while classroom climate is composed of classroom-level variables (e.g., teacher-student relations, teaching and learning processes, teacher practices). While both have implications for safe, supportive, and engaging schools, they are distinct. Classroom climate measurement systems focus on manifestations of violence from teachers to students/students to teachers and among students, with perhaps a greater focus on symbolic, or discursive, violence. In contrast, school climate measurement systems focus on broader relations between different management levels, including teachers, and interinstitutional relations. From a student safety perspective, school climate may also include school spaces where there may be limited, or no, adult supervision (e.g., corridors, bathrooms, lockerroom, dining rooms, restrooms) and thus a greater likelihood of physical abuse, bullying, and violence in general.

Measures and measurement systems need to integrate more holistic measurement models that include relevant elements relating to safe, supportive, and engaging schools comprehensively. These need to account for what data are collected and how, how data are shared among different stakeholders, and how that data are used to contribute to safer, more supportive, and more engaging communities, schools, and classrooms.

RECOMMENDATIONS

The following recommendations are aimed at supporting educators, researchers, policy makers, policy implementers, school personnel, and the community at large in integrating a broader conception of safety in Colombia, thus providing safer, more supportive, more engaging, and healthier learning environments and communities. These recommendations underpin the importance of both violence prevention *and* promotion of democratic citizenship. In order to internalize specific skills and dispositions, other "skills" and dispositions may have to be unlearned. While these recommendations focus on the Colombian context, they may also inform other contexts.

Policy-Level Recommendations
- Secure political will and commitment at all levels.
- Advance strategic interministry, state entity, and public-private sector collaboration relating to school safety and data sharing.
- Include children and adolescents in policy design and implementation.
- Evaluate feasibility of a three-tiered public health approach comprised of universal programs to promote health, second-level programs to reduce risk factors, and third-level early interventions. Include gender-affirming mental health services and interventions to support transgender youth.

- Advance legislation relating to technology mediated violence.
- Scale good practices.

Research-Related Recommendations

- Devise measures and measurement systems to evaluate school and classroom climates holistically.
- Focus on what is to be measured and how to measure it.
- Advance research on complex spectrum of experiences undermining children feeling safe, including psychopathology cases contributing to chronic anxiety, depression, and suicidal behavior.
- Advance research to identify successful drivers pertaining to school safety, violence prevention, and positive school and classroom climates.

School-Level and Classroom-Level Recommendations

- Focus on constructing democratic classroom climates, particularly in marginalized regions.[40]
- Support teacher development around restorative discipline management strategies.
- Support teacher development to integrate multiple mediums for children to express experiences relating to violence through art forms. Support teacher development to identify signs of violence and abuse.
- Implement strategies to address teacher care and well-being. Teachers who are cared for will be better able to provide care to their students.
- Support community-parent-school alliances.
- Implement inclusion-based strategies aimed at children from displaced families and/or rural contexts and with different abilities and disabilities.
- Scale and systematize good practice.
- Avoid pathologizing childhood, the notion that if the "problem" is in children, then the solution is to "fix" these children.[41]

Community-Level Recommendations

- Provide socioemotional learning to students, teachers, school personnel, parents, and caregivers.

CONCLUDING REMARKS

Education in Colombia has enormous potential to pave paths toward peace and a robust democracy. At a macro level, how Colombia's robust political framework and sound education policy are implemented to achieve this at this complex postconflict juncture becomes critically important. At the school level, how education is conceived and subsequently practiced can make important contributions to unlearning violence and promoting a culture of peace that strengthens democracy and the *estado social de derecho* (social rule of law) that the Principle Constitution of Colombia outlines. Design and implementation of education policy should thus effectively guarantee safe and supportive educational contexts.

Despite notable advances in the Colombian educational sphere over the past years, a more definitive shift needs to happen, one that moves from a reactive stance in addressing violence and aggression to a much more preventive and proactive promotion-based stance around peace construction and democracy in schools.

CHAPTER 7

THE FRENCH POLICY TO UNDERSTAND AND ADDRESS VIOLENT, MEAN, BULLYING, AND/OR DISRESPECTFUL BEHAVIORS IN K-12 SCHOOLS

ERIC DEBARBIEUX

AS IT IS IN MANY OTHER COUNTRIES, the prevention of school bullying and any form of violence within the school environment is a key priority for French policy makers and the Ministry of Education. Although school bullying has been at the heart of education research since the 1970s in Northern Europe, the interest in violence in schools and bullying is rather recent in France, with the first studies dating back only to the early 1990s.

In France, violence in schools became a permanent part of the political and media agenda in November 1990 following a demonstration in Paris by upper-secondary-school students that drew some 35,000 people.[1] The protesters' banners demanded "More security in high schools" and "More supervisors." At that moment the media discovered a phenomenon that would dictate the action of the politicians in power, particularly the education ministers, who were requested to "react," to propose a "damage control plan," to "restore authority," and, in short, "to eradicate violence" in the schools. At the National Assembly, during the session dedicated to the representatives' questions, Minister of Education Lionel Jospin referred to events that had taken place in several colleges in the Paris region in the weeks following that first demonstration: "We wish for schools to remain immune from violence, that they be places of education and knowledge, where young people are protected as much as possible from the disturbances of the outside world."

Thus, from 1991 to 2011, no fewer than thirteen series of measures were proposed, often approved in the French legislature in the form of a national "plan" for combating violence in schools. These plans placed the courts and/or the Gendarmerie (military police) and the national police force at the center of the process. Indeed, most of these policies held onto a conception of school violence as a phenomenon related to external intrusions. This denied any internal causality on the part of schools and placed blame on paroxysmal violence from the outside, such as gang intrusions or school shootings, even though school shootings are very rare in France.

It is only since 2011 that there has been an expanded understanding of school safety and violence. There has been a growing appreciation for a wider spectrum of behaviors— social, emotional, and intellectual factors—that undermine students feeling safe. It was not until 2011 that it was considered helpful to think in a more ecological or school climate way when approaching school safety and violence. The question of well-being at school became an important concern. The main transformation was the consideration of minor victimizations, and their repetition, and the gradual rise in the importance of school climate in the prevention of violence in schools.

In writing this chapter, I relied on my own experience with the issue of school bullying in France. In 1991 I created the first French school climate and victimization survey, which, together with Catherine Blaya, was carried out several times with the support of the International Observatory on Violence in Schools (the latest survey dates from 2018). Beginning in 2011, adapted versions of these survey were conducted in secondary schools by the Ministry of Education. Also, as the first Ministerial Delegate with responsibility for preventing and fighting against violence in schools, I have become an actor in the public policies around school violence. While my roles may raise questions about "distance from the object," they allow me to provide an inside look at how national policies are constructed around school safety in France.

HOW PUBLIC THOUGHT BEGAN TO CHANGE

It may seem strange that for years France ignored such a well-known and common phenomenon as school bullying. Instead, the government's focus was on delinquency, violence from the outside, and intrusions. In the French public opinion, schools were to be fortresses, cut off from their communities, which were considered dangerous. Schools were to be isolated from the buzz of the city and focused on dispensing a universal knowledge. There are historical reasons for this. The French state school, from the early twentieth century, has been considered a school of the republic, one against religious particularisms and a base of French secularism. As such, what happens outside the schools should not interfere with the teaching and learning going on inside.

The Antiviolence Plans, 1991–2011

The antiviolence plans developed since 1991 have been aimed at dealing with the problems that are outside the schools.[2] A striking summary of this approach was President Nicolas Sarkozy's speech on May 28, 2009, in which he called for "turning the school into a sanctuary."[3] Similarly, at a meeting with the principal actors in security, the criminal justice system, and national education, the president declared:

> Schools must be turned into sanctuaries, sheltered from all forms of violence. This is an absolute priority for the State authorities . . . Turning schools into sanctuaries, here are the principal measures announced:
>
> - undertake a diagnostic safety survey of 184 at-risk schools;
> - provide accreditation for educational staff to check bags and satchels;
> - install on a case-by-case basis, where necessary, security gates;
> - set up a mobile team for each Rector, able to intervene as reinforcement for head teachers;
> - make Police officers as points of contact for schools more generally available, implement mechanisms making possible almost instantaneous intervention in schools by the Police;
> - opening recruitment for voluntary reservists in the national Police force to reinforce the securing of schools.

This succession of plans also had roots in politics and the media. Violence in schools became an ideological topic, often influenced by xenophobia and a high electoral risk. It made its appearance in a period marked by the electoral success of the extreme Right in France and remained prominent with the conservatives who made the topic of insecurity in the country their main

electoral argument. The pressure of public opinion was strong. Whether outbreaks of violence were or were not the result of a build-up of tension over the
long term was not considered important; it was the immediate reaction that
was important for reassuring people and for securing political positions. Under such conditions, the need to react to the crisis was a demand for intervention rather than long-term policy. Thus, the plans rapidly became discredited
one by one and were sometimes considered merely lip service.

Recent Developments

In January 2010, the death of an eighteen-year-old student changed public
opinion. The young man succumbed to his injuries after being stabbed by a
classmate in a corridor of his upper-secondary school in Le Kremlin Bicêtre
(near Paris). The immediate response of legislators was to recite the measures taken, in particular "managing the school as a sanctuary." However,
it seems that there was a recognition of the insufficiency, indeed the useless-
ness, of these types of measures: the drama took place between students and
in a rather peaceful school in which video surveillance equipment had been
installed. The public realized that the "technical" response had been insufficient and that that it had not been a "gang problem" and that it had not been
linked to drug trafficking, as the ministers who visited the school declared
several times.

A response to the public anxiety was the General Conference on School
Safety held at the Sorbonne University April 7–8, 2010. Counterintuitively,
the presidency of the General Conference on School Safety was entrusted to
me. I had publicly published results of my research demonstrating the ineffi-
ciency of repressive measures and the global ineffectiveness of technical measures that restrict "situational prevention" to the positioning of closed-circuit
television (CCTV) cameras, installation of security gates, or searching of
school bags.[4] The conference was well attended by the media, and a presentation by Russel Skiba, an expert in zero tolerance, demonstrated not only the
lack of effectiveness of such measures but also their potential negative side effects. On the whole, the discussion during this event went against the dominant ideology.

The subsequent period was marked by strategic and ideological inflections
that led to a change in perspective, especially with the emergence of the topic
of school bullying, which emphasized the need to deal with violence both
pedagogically and from inside the school (without, however, denying the im-

portance of outside partnerships). This ideological swing was the direct result of academic research supported by and relying on mobilization from the
community and the media. The General Assembly Against School Bullying,
held in Paris in March 2011, gathered government officials (ministers of education, interior, justice), administrators, academics, and representatives from
nongovernmental organizations (NGOs), teacher unions, and parent associations to address the issue. Several things led to this. First, the publication
of a nationwide victimization survey that involved research teams from eight
different universities.[5] Second, the publication of an open letter written by
NGOs and mental health professionals in favor of developing national public policies against school bullying. And third, the meeting of the education
minister with victims and their parents away from any media presence.

The conclusions of the General Assembly on School Bullying can be summarized as: (1) the acknowledgment of the academic and psychological consequences of school bullying; (2) the association between bullying and other
outbreaks of violence (in particular school shootings); (3) the recognition that
school bullying does not happen in socially underprivileged schools only;
and (4) the understanding that most violence issue in schools are not from
outsiders only and thus cannot be dealt with by simply securing the premises
from the surrounding neighborhood.[6] Taking an interest in school bullying
means not dealing with public safety only but considering the importance
of student well-being as a whole. Effective violence and bully prevention efforts need to include an individual and systemic focus on well-being, with a
range of instructional, schoolwide, and relational efforts to foster proactive
and positive school improvement. The conclusions were supported by findings from international research on the subject.

The General Assembly on School Bullying was held in an electorally troubled period, when the issues of public safety were central in the minds of the
legislators and the public. It fostered a national consensus across all opinion
groups about the importance of taking school bullying seriously.

In January 2012 the first website with videos devoted to the subject, the
first helpline, and the first training courses for school staff were launched.
There was a risk that the newly appointed education minister, Vincent Peillon, would not share similar views and would put an end to the undertaken
reform. Fortunately, this was not the case. In fact, an interesting sign of continuity despite partisan differences was the creation by Peillon of a ministerial delegation in charge of the prevention and reduction of violence in

school policies, which he charged me with heading, despite having worked with "the previous political party." It was a display of a political will to rely on long-term research and intervention rather than be guided by ideology in the short term.

In a February 2013 press conference, Peillon delivered an update on the work of the delegation responsible for preventing and reducing violence in schools. In terms of intervention, providing a positive school climate and improving daily life in schools to tackle "ordinary violence" was at the heart of the strategy.[7] It was obvious that the facts of paroxysmic violence were not disregarded and that the delegation was also working to help with serious crisis management. The gradual implementation of specific training courses for school staff at the Training Center for Gendarmerie was one of the delegation's achievements.

PUBLIC POLICIES AND PRACTICE IN FRANCE

On July 9, 2013, the Law of Orientation and Programming for the Refoundation of School in the Republic was published in the *Official Journal*.[8] In terms of violence in schools, it specifies:

> Safety and, more precisely, the conditions for a peaceful climate must be established in schools to promote learning, the well-being, and personal development of the students as well as good working conditions for everyone. Violence in schools, which has many sources, requires in fact a global treatment and long-term action and not a simply security-based approach, which is not sufficiently effective. The fight against all forms of bullying shall be a priority for each school. Each school will design intervention strategies in collaboration with the whole school community.

This law is quite clear on the fact that risk prevention and/or health/mental health promotion are important goals.

In 2014, Minister of Women's Rights Najat Vallaud-Belkacem introduced legislation addressing "real equity between women and men," which was passed by the parliament. In this law bullying and mobbing are recognized as criminal offenses. The penal code under the Article 222-33-2-2 considers the bullying of a minor under the age of fifteen to be an aggravating circumstance; as such, this law is applicable to the school context. The law recognizes that it is not the common behavioral difficulties that are so targeted but, rather, repeated behaviors aimed at harming another student.

Since the enactment of these laws, the prevention of bullying is considered in a systemic way in guidelines and recommendations. It is based on specific actions by and legal obligations for schools and their staff, who must inform and raise awareness among children and parents, and on indirect prevention by improving school climate and social learning. In a country like France, where power is politically centralized, this national framework is supposed to be relevant and implemented everywhere. It is, however, an ideal scheme, one that is far from perfectly implemented.

STRATEGIES, NATIONAL TRENDS, AND CONTRADICTIONS

The Ministry of National Education suggested a series of measures to implement an ambitious action against violence and school bullying. In January 2012, a helpline, the first videos addressing "Le harcèlement à l'école," and a website with specific pedagogical material for teachers, students, and parents were made available publicly.[9] The first trainings were given to educational managers (mainly inspectors and administrators) and then expanded with the creation of the Ministerial Delegation in Charge of Violence in Schools in October 2012. These trainings included a theoretical section that defined the terms *school bullying* and *violence*, established the links with school climate, and discussed the causes and consequences of these two issues. Some more practical workshops were also offered to participants (educational managers and school health staff, including nurses and counselors) that introduced care for the victims and presented various intervention programs, such as nonviolent communication, restorative justice, and positive discipline.

Approximately 100 people have been trained each year since 2012—or 700 out of 1 million.[10] This is a small number, and, as a consequence, effects of the training program are limited. And while there are also training programs at the school district level, there is no visibility around what is done in the training. There are very few training programs to help non–mental health staff deal with emotional and behavioral difficulties.

In a November 26, 2013, press conference, Minister of Education Vincent Peillon launched a "Plan for the Prevention of Bullying in Schools," which was organized around four points of action: awareness raising, prevention, training, and taking responsibility. The Higher School of National Education would provide in-service training, to spread across several years, for school senior executives, the person in charge of bullying in the school district, and, in the initial training, school principals and inspectors.[11]

Also, the "No to Bullying" competition was launched. The purpose of this was to give students and young people aged eight to eighteen the opportunity to voice their experience and design a poster or video to communicate the antibullying policy in their school. This competition was directly inspired by research on school climate, which showed the necessity of making "the witnesses react."[12] The program was funded by the Mutuelle Assurance Elèves (a private insurance company), and every year since 2013 the announcement of the winners became an occasion for a speech by the education minister. While there has been no formal evaluation of the impact of this program, each year between 2014 and 2018 saw 900–1,300 submitted projects, making it the most popular competition in French national education.

After the September 2014 appointment of Najat Vallaud Belkacem as Minister of Education, whih reinforced the nation's determination to act against bullying, continuity was sought, which included occasional such announcements as the National Day Against Harassment, scheduled to be held every year. Following the shocking *Charlie Hebdo* terrorist attacks on January 7, 2015, the number of crisis management training programs grew, with the opening of five training centers by the Ministry of the Interior for school principals and education decision-makers. Four-day training sessions are provided each year to about 800 staff managers who work in priority education zone schools. The major goal is to train staff in crisis management, such as terrorist attacks or gang intrusions. The training is organized around theoretical inputs and workshops on the detection of crisis mechanisms, collaboration with the police and justice services, the prevention and crisis management protocols, and the prevention of violence through school climate improvements.

French public policies are extremely centralized, with a very strong bureaucracy and hierarchical decision-making processes. But French centralist logic is not conducive to a localized and contextualized "program"; it is, instead, better suited to a global logic for a nationally implemented "plan." Therefore, these laws, guidelines, and regulations *should*, in principle, be applied uniformly top to bottom. This is not the case, however; a national directive is not always accepted locally, in every school. The reactions of school staff can cover a very wide spectrum, from adherence to the national plan to a refusal to implement it.

Reluctance to implement such a plan against school bullying is largely due to the perception of many teachers that their responsibility lies in transmitting knowledge only. These teachers consider dedicating time to other tasks, such as caring for the students' well-being, as detrimental to learning and a loss of precious teaching time. A widespread ideology in France is the antipedagogy, which is based on the belief that only academic knowledge matters and that the rest is a waste of time. This is reinforced by teachers' initial training, which is predominantly academic and focuses very little on other educational matters. It is therefore mainly nonteaching staff that are asked to deal with bullying, and this is not adequate.

The current situation in France is complex, with many initiatives that are short term and temporary or barely known outside of the school. These initiatives often depend on the goodwill of individuals or mandates from the immediate hierarchy. They can be supported by NGOs that specialize in intervention programs—peer mediation, the KiVa program, positive discipline, nonviolent communication, drama, restorative justice, to name a few—but these organizations are financially fragile, because public subsidies are diminishing, and France is a country where private sponsorship is not well developed. In general, French authorities do not recommend ready-made "programs," even if there is a growing interest in them. For instance, no lists of evidence-based programs are provided to schools. And even if there is an interest in the latest intervention scheme, the logic of the French national plan remains strongly rooted. In schools, the allocation by the government of additional teachers and school staff is usually considered to be the only solution. Strategy remains directive and national.

Yet, gradually school leaders are able to better identify students in trouble, students at risk, and students who are troubled. Local victimization surveys tend to be more frequent to assess schools' situations. And school nurses and education counselors are often solicited and trained to help these victims, though their training sessions are often too brief to be effective.

As for aggressors, it is the repressive and punitive approach that is still widely used. Official guidelines certainly recommend restorative justice, but no training is provided on it. The lack of training also reflects the contradictions in representations of what the teaching profession is, as well as the anthropological status of childhood.

MEASURES AND MEASUREMENT SYSTEMS

In France there are several systems for measuring violence and school bully-ing: a daily report by the school principal (secondary school) or the district inspector (primary school), a national survey by the Statistics Directorate of the Ministry of National Education (SIVIS), and national and local school climate and victimization surveys.[13]

Daily, the principal (or their representative) must report via a dedicated website any incident that has occurred during the course of the school day, including any acts of violence, bullying, reprehensible behavior, suicide at-tempts. These reports are intended to inform the administration and may prompt outside help. However, they rarely give rise to systematic treatment. They are essential to informing the administration in case of serious events that might get media coverage.

The SIVIS survey is conducted annually using a randomized sample of secondary schools across the country. It focuses on the most serious acts of violence, those incidents brought to the attention of the police or justice sys-tem and that are likely to lead to a formal complaint or a disciplinary hear-ing or that require medical care. The SIVIS results show that there are 13.8 incidents per 1,000 students each year. The data have been stable since 2007. In 2017, the survey has included a questionnaire to better understand the cli-mate in the school and its evolution. SIVIS is useful but presents some seri-ous limitations, namely: reporting is done by the school principal, who could sometimes minimize the problems; many schools (40–60 percent) never complete the questionnaires; the overall school climate is assessed by just three questions; and the survey is only for secondary schools.

The first school climate and victimization surveys were developed in 1991 to help schools at the local level.[14] From the beginning, the link between school climate and school violence was established in these surveys. With the national extension of these surveys, a comparative method has emerged: each participating organization can be compared with others of the same social profile. This enables better identification of the challenges the school meets as well as its positive achievements around school climate.

School climate surveys include the evaluation of a range of indicators of school life. Students and staff complete the surveys. Staff are also asked about the quality of teamwork and spirit in the school as well as the quality of re-lationships with management and potential conflicts between adults in the school. More rarely parents are asked to complete a similar questionnaire, though this presents problems with representation, as underprivileged or immigrant parents are not as responsive. This method is now used in various and sometimes contradictory ways. It can be implemented by university teams but is also used by safety teams and local education authorities.

In the various existing surveys, questions and indicators are largely the same. This is also the case for randomized national surveys conducted by the National Education Statistical Services. The indicators are:

- perception of quality of relationships within the school (between students, students-teachers, students principal, etc.);
- perception of the quality of school premises;
- feeling of insecurity;
- sense of justice, with questions on the types and frequency of sanctions;
- sense of well-being;
- quality of academic achievement and perception of the quality of learning;
- support from teachers and other school staff;
- sense of belonging;
- sense of fear;
- truancy;
- perception of the quality of the school neighborhood; and
- victimization, from nasty nicknames to physical injury with weapons, including a range of verbal, physical, and symbolic (ostracism) victimizations.

Data are collected by either research teams or the education board departments, and analyzed with statistical procedures that may seem similar, though the logic of action is different. In conducting the surveys, researchers, experts outside the school, are not caught in team conflicts, which are very common in schools that face trouble. Researchers make a school climate and victimization assessment and submit the results to the management teams as well as to all school staff members and often to the parent representatives. They often also present the survey findings to the upper-secondary students.

In surveys carried out by education authorities, the statistical analyses are made by an office of the Ministry of National Education and then sent to the local school safety teams in charge of introducing them to the school management team. The principal disseminates these findings to the school staff. However, since surveys often reveal some conflict, principals, who cannot take a position of neutrality, may feel it best not to report the results. So for a serious analysis of the data, and to be able to answer the more specific questions that the team may have to ask during the findings presentation, it would be better for those who hand in the survey findings to have access to the original databases so that they can answer questions from school staff. However, this is not the case with the official, centralized, bureaucratic approach that is currently implemented in France. The bureaucratization of the tools for intervention and analysis—even though inspired by scientific research—has significant negative side effects and to be of a very limited effectiveness.[15] There are very few evaluations of the impact of innovation, intervention, and prevention schemes. There is very little, or no, research funding dedicated to these issues. Evidence-based policies remain a wish more than a reality.

However, the national measurement systems that are implemented in randomized surveys show important trends. These trends are present in local surveys, and it is precisely the differences from average and most common situations that often give the most interesting and useful information on the way a school is managed. The results of the French surveys are consistent with the leading international surveys.

The local surveys indicate that French students feel pretty good at school, both primary and secondary.[16] For instance, in the 2017 survey conducted by the ministerial office among a large randomized sample of 18,000 middle school students, 92.5 percent reported feeling good or very good in their school.[17] The vast majority (87 percent) reported that they got along well with their teachers, and 90 percent had a positive image of their relationships with management teams and about school life. The results were similar in surveys I conducted in secondary or primary schools, even in very socially deprived areas, where 88 percent of the respondents stated they felt good at school.[18] However, a minority of students (12 percent in primary schools, 10 percent in middle schools, and 5 percent in upper-secondary schools) reported being victims of school bullying. These surveys clearly highlight the association between climate of schools and bullying, as do other surveys conducted on cyberviolence and cyberbullying.[19]

A growing problem in France is the feeling that sanctions are unfair. One-third (33 percent) of middle school students consider the discipline management to be unfair, but the percentage rises to 44 percent in priority education zones and up to 80 percent in the schools most in trouble.[20] There is a link between this feeling of unfairness and bullying. However, this is not only a case of "too many sanctions." More than one-third of the students who reported unfairness considered the discipline to be not strict enough to protect them well enough from bullying or violence. Recent surveys have found strong evidence that in some areas on the outskirts of Paris, the temporary exclusion rate is very high, sometimes as high as 30 percent of students each year.[21]

This raises major issues around public safety, dropout, and mental health. Punitive inflation does not solve the problem. Instead, it creates a feeling of disaffiliation from school and, later, alienation from society. Research has long shown in France and elsewhere that discipline has a color and is ethnically based.[22] It contributes to a reactive ethnicization that fragments communities. It is even more pernicious that harassment and bullying are most often practices of ostracism that a group exercises against an individual thought to be outside the in-group norms. I often summarize bullying as a conformist oppression through which the peer group identifies against an individual who is judged as "different." Indeed, racism, homophobia, LGBTQphobia, and xenophobia are all associated with bullying. When politicians express negative views against migrants for election purposes, which colors the issues around ethnic identity that emerge in schools, students hear this intolerance and rejection and then reproduce it. This is true for France and elsewhere.

RECOMMENDATIONS FOR TEACHERS, PRINCIPALS, AND SUPERINTENDENTS/REGIONAL LEADERS

Intervention strategies against school bullying in France tend to focus on the improvement of school well-being, and outcomes are encouraging but limited. There is a real national mobilization around the issue, and public awareness campaigns have been developed. However, nationally designed strategies have limitations, as neither rules nor laws are sufficient to improve the situation. Most important are local and contextualized interventions. Moreover, the commitment of school staff is one of the major ingredients, but, unfortunately, it is not assumed. Also, school bullying prevention and the promotion of student and staff well-being can be part of the positive climate strategies, but they depend on the overall school policy. School policy must draw on the cooperation among all members of the school community—parents, local authorities, neighborhoods, and school professionals.

Eight fundamental findings from research on violence in French schools and school bullying are the basis for my recommendations to improve the fight against school violence at the class, school, regional, and national levels.

- *Finding 1* shows that the personal experience of victimization is, for both pupils and teachers, linked to minor incidents; serious victimizations are very rare.[23] The true problem tends to be a high frequency of incidents of minor victimization and a lack of respect (indignities), rather than hard-core delinquency.

- *Finding 2* suggests that violence in schools is very rarely caused by intrusion of outsiders or outside events. Even statistics from the Ministry of National Education show that these constitute just 2.3 percent of incidents brought to the notice of the administration in secondary education and 2.1 percent in primary education. Of course, this does not mean that it is not necessary to deal with and prevent incidents of intrusion, however rare they may be. It means that the vision of the fortress school, fortified against violence from outside, is obsolete.

- *Finding 3* notes that "repeated incidents" must be studied and considered in regard to their effects on both the schools and the people involved, especially when they reach the level of bullying.[24] The consequences may be academic (dropping out, poor results) and/or physical (suicide attempts, depression) and may even affect security.[25] After all, 75 percent of perpetrators of school shootings said they were bullied. Isolated incidents of micro-violence must not be underestimated, as their effect is cumulative.

- *Finding 4* suggests that repeated victimization, which can be as serious as bullying, concerns a minority of students, though these students may be suffering acutely. Also, these students are not necessarily in deprived areas or in priority education zones, though there is a very strong link between bullying and discrimination.[26]

- *Finding 5* indicates that school violence is a sociology of social exclusion, though not necessarily exclusion based on socioeconomic factors (e.g., homophobia). However, socioeconomic factors remain an additional risk factor in the bullying of students and, more significantly, the victimization of staff.[27]

- *Finding 6* suggests that the multiplicity of factors explaining violence in schools is recognized within a complex system. Among these factors there are certain determining academic factors. Many studies show that there are very strong links between violence observed in schools and the quality of the academic climate. Protection facts linked to collaborative work by the adults; the presence of a clear, unambiguous disciplinary system; the stability of the teaching teams; activities offered by the community and taken up by the school; and the involvement and collaboration of parents are often cited as promoting the maintenance of a stable, safe school climate.[28]

- *Finding 7* notes that the feeling of injustice connected with excessive sanctions is one of the surest predictors of violence. The literature is very consistent on this and clearly lays the blame on zero-tolerance policies and repressive management.[29] Marked inequality of gender and ethnicity is also noted in the application of these repressive policies.[30]

- *Finding 8* suggests that with the build-up of aggressive behavior, early prevention is the preferred course of action.[31]

Recommendations for Classroom Teachers

Students' well-being and the prevention of school bullying are key elements for successful learning. Bullying is a strong predictor of truancy and school dropout. It can affect the best students. We should systematically be alerted by a drop in academic achievement, by students being isolated from a group of peers, and by students who suddenly exhibit outbursts of anger that can be linked to repeated mockery or aggression. In that respect, a teacher is in the best place to identify signals that reveal bullying. Giving care and attention to students is one of the first steps, well before thinking of designing intervention programs. That means that teachers should not neglect petty aggressions that may seem ordinary and that they should not advise students who believe they are being bullied that they should "toughen up" and "stand up for themselves."

Nevertheless, teachers should not expect to be able to solve a bullying situation on their own. Classrooms are one part of the school community. A victim might be bullied in class but also, and even more often, in the common spaces of their schools, on the stairs, on the playground, at club meetings, in locker rooms. Teamwork is another condition for the promotion of a safe and peaceful school climate. It is also the best protection for the teachers; an isolated individual is more at risk of becoming a victim. Genuine situational crime prevention is rooted in a network of professional and collegial solidarity.

In terms of pedagogical attitudes, it is difficult to summarize in a few lines the skills that require months, even years, of training. However, there is sound evidence that inappropriate behaviors should not be dealt with through either repressive authoritarianism or a laissez-faire attitude hidden under the veil of a cooperative educational style.[32] Most of experts agree that respectful authority should enable young people exhibiting difficult behaviors to find a positive role within their peer group, that excessive authority strengthens negative and undesirable behaviors that often grow into power conflicts, and that laissez-faire attitudes generate anxiety among students.

A cooperative approach is demanding because it involves taking on concrete responsibilities. For a child or a teenager to behave in a responsible way, it is necessary for them to consider responsibility as the result of a process and not as an intrinsic psychological characteristic. As emphasized by Lanaris, the most common mistake is to reproach youth for "discharg[ing] their responsibility without having tried to empower them previously": "Youth learn how to behave in a responsible way through experiences that enable them to learn the meaning of being responsible."[33] Glasser's choice theory and positive discipline are now being promoted in France.[34] These approaches have in common their insistence on the empowerment and responsibility of youth through cooperative meetings that aim to set up rules of communal life in a way that includes consequences for infringements. These are concrete rules of life and not abstract and moral considerations. They enable action around concrete projects and for daily life.

There is no existing miracle solution that would eradicate school bullying or inappropriate behaviors once and for all. As stressed by Roland and Galloway, the problem is that many programs that try to change behaviors, including antibullying programs, tend to consider that behavior is the main issue—"sort it out and it will be okay!"[35] However, evidence suggests that school effectiveness needs much more complex intervention than just calls to reduce or eradicate behavior problems. It cannot be approached without considering the overall structure and organization of the school as a whole as well as its discipline management and the quality of learning. In other words, a whole-school approach is necessary.

Recommendations for Principals and Superintendents

The role of the principal is paramount. All the existing meta-analyses on the effectiveness of intervention programs against violence and bullying and for the promotion of a positive school climate show evidence of the importance of the school management team.[36] Yet, the principal's role is not to deal with challenging behaviors on their own. Research strongly suggests that the effectiveness of prevention programs depends heavily on the quality of their implementation, but this also depends on the quality of leadership in the school. Prevention programs should take place in an organizational environment free of any abuse of power.

Showing evidence of the effectiveness of an intervention program is not enough. It is crucial to think about the ways to implement it with the least effort on the part of the staff. Effective intervention requires the consent of the whole school community. To be effective, the promotion of student well-being must go along with the fostering of the adult well-being. In that respect, various practices can be implemented, from commonsense, basic actions to sophisticated interventions: induction days, new teacher mentoring by more experienced colleagues, organization of social events, etc. A survey in Quebec of new teachers showed that those who felt welcomed by their colleagues and beneficiated from genuine support from the school's principal reported fewer victimizations and that students were also less bullied.[37] As a consequence, the principal should focus on fostering a positive, democratic community spirit that is based on shared responsibility for a positive daily atmosphere.

The main change that is needed is to not implement anymore new programs but to instead improve routine prevention so that behavior problems do not escalate into more severe and violent situations. Behavior problems are not an extra task to be dealt with in the teaching life of school professionals; they are events that are likely to happen, and management of them is one of the routine professional duties of teaching. Asking an already overtasked teacher to take on extra work, attend training sessions, and go to more meetings, as well as learn new approaches, is unrealistic, and trade unions would fight such requests, or demands. As Hargreaves states, the challenge is not to work more but to work better.[38]

CONCLUSION

Violence in French schools is a very complex issue that cannot be solved through simplistic, often demagogic measures. It is an issue that is too often seen through the lenses of either extreme violence or violence imported from the outside. While this can be the case, school violence more commonly takes the form of petty violence, deviant behaviors that cannot be considered crimes, though their repetition is a problem for victims in the school environment. As with any deviant or delinquent behaviors, violence in schools is rooted in multiple causes; no single factor can explain such behaviors. Nevertheless, violence in schools presents specific characteristics because it comes out of group dynamics and the school environment. This is not to say that the schools and teachers are solely responsible for violent behaviors, but they are accountable for the quality of the school climate. Research has shown evidence that the influence of school factors, such as the quality of teaching, the structure and strength of school teams, and a positive school climate, are key ingredients for the effective and successful implementation of intervention programs.[39]

Since violence in schools is not the consequence of the intrusion from outsiders on the school premises, and because it is influenced by the quality of the relationships among all the members of the school community, it will not be possible to eradicate it through the intervention of external agencies. Although they can be of great help and a valuable resource, such as social workers or the police, schools must think in terms of school-based prevention.

Improving intervention against school violence need not be restricted to simply tackling the problem or instituting some "magical" program (even if well evaluated). The addressing of school violence and bullying must focus on a whole-school approach for global change in the quality of relationships within the school and between the school and its local community. A school cannot solve the problem alone. And while there are effective programs, they work only if the professionals in the school are really mobilized and committed. In short, without an internal policy to improve the school climate, it is impossible to fully address violence in the schools.

CHAPTER 8

THE ISRAELI MODEL

A Centralized National and Local System Designed to Achieve Optimal School Climate Driven by Monitoring on Multiple Levels

RAMI BENBENISHTY, RON AVI ASTOR, HANNA SHADMI,
HAGIT GLICKMAN, EINAV LUKE, DAVID RATNER,
HILA SEGAL-ZADVIL, AND TAL RAZ

THIS CHAPTER PRESENTS the Israeli model of developing and maintaining an optimal educational climate that promotes safety and well-being. This is a unique model, as it is integrated into the infrastructure of the educational system and aims to be a way of life, part of the school mission, organization, and practice rather than a set of disjointed evidence-based programs imposed from the top down or selected by individual schools. It is a combination of clear and binding national principles and directives and a wide latitude for school and district discretion and practices that reflect the local context. The system is proactive and is part of everyday practices in all Israeli schools. It also has components that are designed for schools that require more intensive focus on improving climate and school safety. Climate and safety standards are woven into the academic accountability system and are driven by a monitoring system on multiple levels to help inform continuous school improvement.

The chapter is based on the experience and knowledge of its authors, some of whom are in key positions in the Israeli Ministry of Education division in charge of improving and monitoring school climate and other scholars who have been studying the system for the last two decades. In preparing this chapter, we examined relevant literature assessing school climate in Israel and reviewed academic papers describing the Israeli system, based on a wide range of methods, analyses of archival data, and interviews with policy makers.[1] Our theoretical framework was influenced to a large degree by the model provided in *Bullying, School Violence, and Climate in Evolving Contexts*.[2]

THE ISRAELI CONTEXT

The Israeli society is a complex and dynamic tapestry of diverse social, cultural, and religious groups. This complexity is reflected in the organization of the education system, which has several educational streams based on cultural, religious, and ethnic affiliations. There are Jewish secular, religious, and ultra-orthodox schools with Hebrew as the teaching language; these schools educate students from very different socioeconomic and cultural backgrounds. Religious and secular schools that teach in Arabic also include students from multiple religions and cultural groups, including Muslim and Christian Arabs, Druze, Bedouin, and Cherkistani. Within each of these groups there are shared interests and values, but also a considerable degree of cultural and religious differences.

A large majority of these schools are part of the formal system; as such, they receive resources from the central or local educational administration and are expected to follow regulations, policies, and practices originating from the Ministry of Education. The educational system is centralized to a large extent, with some built-in variations that reflect local context. Schools belong to local authorities (e.g., cities and regional associations of smaller localities) and to eight regional districts staffed with Ministry of Education personnel (e.g., school supervisors). Thus, what is presented in this chapter is relevant for a very large majority of the approximately 1.7 million students, 150,000 staff members, and 5,000 schools in the K–12 system in Israel.

From time and historical perspectives, concern with school violence and students' unruly behaviors has existed in Israel for many years. This concern has focused on serious physical violence as well as on unruly and undisciplined behavior in class that interferes with academic achievement. However, the public interest in this issue has been inconsistent, and the press has addressed school violence only periodically, mostly in response to severeviolent events.

Yet, in the last two decades, issues of school climate, violence, and safety have undergone major changes. These changes are reflected in shifts in awareness, norms, organizational structures, and policies. The turning point could be traced to the end of 1990s, when a series of violent events drew heightened public and political interest and prompted the formation of a blue-ribbon committee, the Vilnay Committee, and a series of research reports on monitoring school violence in 1999, 2000, 2003, and 2005, and it coincided with (and probably precipitated and reinforced) organizational changes in the Ministry of Education.[3] The most significant change was the redefinition of the role of the ministry's Psychological and Counseling Service (SHEFFI), which took on the role of addressing the challenge of school violence in Israel. While there had been only a part-time position dedicated to dealing with school violence, the system now includes about six thousand counselors and three thousand psychologists who see issues of school climate and violence prevention as important components of their professional role.

Over time, there seems to have been an associated shift in the public norms surrounding school violence. There is far less tolerance of behaviors that were once seen as indications of "normal male" behaviors and less acceptance of emotional and sexual victimization. While there have been significant reductions in almost all aspects of school violence, the press and the public have heightened expectations and still feel that "violence in schools is rising."

UNDERSTANDING SCHOOL VIOLENCE AND BULLYING

The basic premise of the Israeli model is that there are multiple individual and ecological factors that may underlie violent and bullying behavior, such as personal (biological, personality traits), family, interpersonal, school, community, culture, and societal influences. The model follows, to a large extent, the ecological approach in *School Violence in Evolving Contexts*, with the school at the center.[4] In this model, the Archimedean point for leveraging change is the school as a whole. The importance of personal, family, and community factors is not overlooked, but the focus is on creating a school environment that can buffer multiple outside influences and promote safety and well-being.

By creating a basic sense of safety, belonging, and trust that adults are present and supportive, individual students can cope better with bullying incidents. Furthermore, a school with optimal climate may be able to create a positive change in its surrounding community. Accordingly, the main idea underlying the understanding of, and the response to, bullying and school violence is that an optimal and safe school climate facilitates instruction and learning and prevents violence, bullying, and risk behaviors. A safe and respectful environment is essential to students' school adaptation, sense of safety, emotional and moral growth, and social-emotional skill and character development. Furthermore, positive climate is seen as making a unique contribution to academic learning and as being an effective means toward reducing inequality in the education system.

The goal of creating optimal climate and reducing school violence is therefore a major priority of the Israeli Ministry of Education, especially since 2005. Therefore, the ministry defined a set of standards for optimal climate and positive climate that is now part of the educational accountability standards, alongside students' academic achievement. The standards that underlie SHEFFI's work cover seven areas, and promoting safety is only one aspect of the holistic approach to school culture and climate. The standards communicate the expectation that schools create an academic and social environment that is safe, is supportive, promotes equality, and is aesthetically pleasing. These expectations reflect underlying values, such as respect for human dignity, interpersonal caring, tolerance, mutual responsibility, and love for country. Each of the standards is accompanied by assessment criteria. For instance, the safety standard presents a series of criteria that include the development and dissemination of a school treaty that describes the school vision, expectations of all members of the school community, mechanisms to impose discipline, enhanced supervision in certain areas and times, and ongoing monitoring of school climate and violence.

UNDERLYING PRINCIPLES OF THE MODEL

In general, SHEFFI does not offer packaged evidence-based program for each type of challenge facing schools and described in the circular. Instead, their aim is to empower the school community to tailor its responses to the unique context of the school and the students involved, following the guidelines provided. School counselors working with the school leadership are key to achieving this goal.

SHEFFI trains and supervises school counselors. These counselors, most of whom hold teaching credentials and a master's degree in educational counseling, are responsible for working with school leadership to initiate and coordinate efforts to provide an optimal climate in the school. The counselors are expected to work very closely with the school leadership and educational staff to help them become aware of the importance of school climate and respond accordingly. Over the years there is a marked shift in their focus, and they now work more to guide and support school principals and leadership teams than work directly with students. The role of an expert counselor- has emerged. These professionals receive extensive training and supervision to help them lead efforts of school improvement and supervise the school counselor. They guide intensive school-level improvement programs, namely the Intensive Schoolwide Intervention to Promote Optimal Social Climate (ACHAM).

Much of the counselors' work is preventive in nature, to help build a caring and disciplined environment that promotes mental health and wellbeing. One of the important steps in doing this is building schoolwide consensus on a school covenant or treaty. This written document is created by students, educators, and parents and reflects an agreement among the various school constituents around the school vision and value priorities; the expectations of students, staff, and parents; and the rules of conduct and how they are enforced.

Based on the national guidelines and the school-level treaty, when incidents do occur, the responses combine both disciplinary actions that aim to communicating boundaries and the importance of following rules and educational (and sometimes psychosocial) interventions that aim to help students be aware of expectations and develop the skills to carry out expected normative behaviors. When appropriate, the school psychologist and counselor provide the consultation, referral, or psychological intervention aimed at supporting individual victims and changing inappropriate behaviors of repeating perpetrators. Further, when the school team assesses that the student's behavior reflects major difficulties at home (e.g., abuse, neglect, domestic violence), they approach the local social work department and ask for consultation and collaboration. In some areas, mainly in regions that experience major psychosocial challenges, social workers are added to the school student-personnel team.

Prevention and intervention target the school as a whole, including students, staff, and parents. Furthermore, responses to violent incidents target all involved—perpetrators, victims, bystanders, the whole school student body, as well as all staff members, parents, and others in the community who may be alarmed by such violent incident or who could provide services and supports.

In the Israeli model, the school has wide-ranging responsibilities that are not limited to school grounds and class time. Schools address incidents that occur in the community, on the way to and from school, and during school events, such as sport events offsite and field trips.

While the model attempts to use the same principles to address all age groups, the whole range of students' abilities and needs and all cultural streams in the education system, adaptations are made for each of the particular groups. For instance, the same directives and rules apply to all students, but the specific responses take into account the differences in needs and abilities, including special needs. Similarly, responses to kindergarteners take into account the unique needs and developing skills of very young students.

In much the same way, efforts to build optimal climate and effective responses to violent incidents are sensitive to the cultural context of the school. The many cultural differences among Jewish religious, secular, and ultra-orthodox schools and the many different groups within the Arab population, Muslims, Christians, Druze, and Bedouin groups in the north and in the south of Israel require careful planning to take into account the unique cultural aspects of each school. For instance, in religious schools there are many references to how peaceful and emphatic behaviors are condoned by the sages and the holy scriptures. Similarly, some Arab schools use the cultural ritual *Sulcha* as a ceremonial way of encouraging mutual forgiveness following conflicts between students, students and teachers, and parents of students involved in violent incidents that could erupt into major conflicts among clans.[5]

STRATEGIES

To meet the standards and help schools become accountable for their climate and their prevention of school violence, SHEFFI has been developing strategies and practices that help schools reach their goals. Ongoing monitoring of school climate as part of the educational accountability system is integrated into these strategies and practices.

The Ministry of Education and the Counseling and SHEFFI have developed an integrated series of strategies and practices employed to communicate the importance of optimal school climate, explicate policy guidelines, and provide guidance, support, and supervision to schools. This strategy is based on interdepartmental processes within the Ministry of Education that integrate academics, counseling and psychological services, supervision, and administration.

Intensive Schoolwide Intervention to Promote Optimal Social Climate (ACHAM)

All schools and counselors are expected to conduct ongoing prevention and intervention activities to promote positive school climate. Some of the schools are also engaged in more intensive schoolwide (systemic) intervention that is supported by a designated counselor-guide expert provided by SHEFFI. This process is initiated in two main ways. For most schools, the school leaders decide that their school needs a more intensive engagement in climate improvement and ask for support from the ministry through their school counselor or the regional ministry supervisors. Other schools are designated by the national accountability system, the MEITZAV Aklim, as schools in need of improvement, or "schools in focus." (The central accountability mechanism is called MEITZAV, the Hebrew acronym for Indices of School Effectiveness and Growth).

The engagement in this program is voluntary. Even schools that were officially identified as needing improvement may resist engaging in the program. School leaders may decide, for instance, that because the principal is new to the school and has not established authority yet, or because the school underwent a major crisis, a program would not be effective at that time. Because the ideology is that school improvement is an internal process driven by the school leadership, schools are not officially "forced" to engage. Nonetheless, county supervisors may exert pressure on schools to enter the ACHAM process when they are concerned about a school's climate.

The heart of the ACHAM is an internal process of building awareness, engagement, and self-study as a basis for a school plan of continuous improvement. The principal is in charge of leading the process with the aid of the school counselor and the support of an external SHEFFI-provided expert (a guide, *madrich*), who is most often a counselor in another school who has significant training and experience in leading such programs. SHEFFI is in charge of these expert resources and allocates them according to needs and availability.

A structured questionnaire designed by SHEFFI is the self-assessment and monitoring instrument. Along with other means, such as focus groups and dialogue circles, it provides the school with pertinent information on how its students and staff experience the current climate and is used to identify areas in need of improvement. And since engagement in this intensive process lasts two to three years, the survey provides feedback on how successful the process is in addressing the school climate challenges.

This self-assessment has added value beyond the national climate survey, because it can be conducted by the school at any time, and it also provides classroom-level information not available in the reports produced based on the national survey. The ACHAM instrument is also more flexible in its content and administration (e.g., online instead of paper and pencil) and includes the views of staff members regarding their own safety and their perceived abilities to improve school safety and needs for training and support. And because this is an internal tool, the school does not have to share the findings with anyone outside the school, including ministry supervisors.

Many schools have adopted this tool, and it has become an integral part of their school improvement practices. There are concerns, however, that in some schools the processes are not systemic enough and are not sustained. There are also indications that not all schools are able to use effectively the information provided by the questionnaire.

Policy Circulars and Directives

Israel does not have a law that focuses on bullying or school violence. Instead, the general manager of the Ministry of Education issues policy circulars and directives that serve as the binding guidelines for all schools. These documents inform the education system what the priorities of the ministry are and what the principles are that should underlie school responses to educational challenges, including developing and maintaining optimal school climate. These guidelines delineate the areas in which schools can use discretion and internal processes and under which circumstances they are required to follow set procedures, such as reporting certain events to the police. Schools are expected to follow these mandates based on existing resources. There are no mechanisms for submitting grant proposals to the ministry to address a specific challenge.

The process of policy formation involves many partners—the Ministry of Welfare, the police, youth corrections, the public defender's office, the teachers union, the national PTA, representatives of local educational departments, the Council for the Child (an influential children's rights advocacy nongovernmental organization), and focus groups comprised of supervisors, principals, and teachers. And the policy statements are quite detailed. Table 8.1 presents the structure of the 2015 circular relevant to these issues.[6]

These policy guidelines address the whole spectrum of violence in schools—physical, emotional, sexual, and cyber victimization. They cover the severity continuum, from incidents of incivility and common disagreements to the most severe cases of victimization. They describe both proactive school practices that help create a positive climate and prevent violence and guidelines for responding to violent incidents. The policy outlines the boundaries of discretion—what schools *must* do under certain circumstances and what they *could* decide to do on their own, based on school internal processes. Discretion is not unlimited, however, and is expected to follow the guidelines.

TABLE 8.1   A Circular from the General Manager of the Ministry of Education Regarding Optimal School Climate and Coping with Incidences of Risk and Violence (2015)

Section	Content
The foundations of proactive system-wide organization and procedures	Presents the overall system model, its goals and components. It emphasizes the proactive nature of developing and maintaining optimal school climate.
Norms and expectations regarding daily conduct and behaviors in schools	Presents what is expected of students in issues such as attendance, tardiness, and class behavior. It outlines the range of educational and disciplinary responses to rule breaking and explains the rationale underlying the discretionary application of various responses, such as suspension.
Responses to violence incidences	Detailed instructions on how to respond to violence and risk behaviors in school. The chapter presents the principles that determine how responses should be tailored to the specific characteristics of the incidents and the students involved. This includes special references to incidents that occur off school grounds (e.g., during a field trip or in the community) and online bullying incidents.
Climate and conduct in Kindergarten	Focuses on the beginning stages of formal education, emphasizes the impact of positive climate on young children development, and provides guidelines on responses to non-normative behaviors, including excessive aggression and age-inappropriate sexual behaviors.
Special needs	Addresses children with special needs who are mainstreamed, as well as students in special education classes and schools. It provides guidelines and indicated responses to deal with behavioral difficulties expressed in risky and aggressive behaviors.

For instance, disciplinary responses need to correspond with the severity of the incident.

SHEFFI is in charge of disseminating the circular and building capacity to implement the policy. As an example of dissemination material, SHEFFI created a PowerPoint presentation and accompanying links to "interactive training workshops" that present the main points of the guidelines and demonstrate the implementation process through a series of case examples.[7] These examples include violent incidents among students, violent incidents off school grounds (e.g., substance abuse, violent incidents, weapon carrying, sexual assault), cyberbullying (e.g., shaming and dissemination of nude pictures of a student), and alcohol and tobacco consumption on and off school grounds. The training materials provide insight to the ways SHEFFI addresses issues of bullying and school violence.

To illustrate, to help schools implement the guidelines on the appropriate responses to violent incidents, a detailed case example is provided of a spat between two female students in a special education class who argue over who "snitched" to the teacher about their smoking on school grounds. The incident became much more physically violent when a male friend of one of the students, known for his involvement in previous violent incidents, kicked the other student in the head as a "payback," sending her to emergency room with a concussion. The training material details the appropriate decision-making process and the school response to the incident through a series of steps guided by the policy directive.

As a first step the document presents the detailed criteria to establish the severity of the incident and reviews criteria, including the physical and mental consequences, whether it is a repetitive act, degree of power imbalance, and the number of victims. Based on the detailed criteria provided in the guidelines, it can be concluded that in the example the incident met the criterion of severity that requires reporting. The training material then leads the school staff through the steps of who should be informed and what information they are required to provide and what they should not do or say under the circumstances. In the example, the school staff needed to report the incident to the police, protective services, parents of the students involved, and the Ministry of Education.

The training material reviews the series of educational and disciplinary responses as they relate to all involved and to the whole school and suggests possible educational and disciplinary responses. In the example, the male student was suspended for eight days (the maximum number of days permitted by the guidelines). In considering the response to the female student who incited the student's physical attack, the fact that she was a student with special needs was an important factor. The decision was to create an individualized program to help her self-regulate negative emotions. Her much shorter *in-school* suspension reflected the concern that this student would be at enhanced risk if suspended and left unsupervised in the community. Such a response reflects the emphasis on relying on school-level responses to the unique local context and the specific individual characteristics, rather than preset zero-tolerance responses (e.g., automatic suspension or expulsion) that do not consider the uniqueness of each incidence.

Social and Emotional Learning, Violence Prevention, and Climate Improvement

The Israeli model sees strong connections between students' social and emotional skills and their involvement and responses to violence. The development of social and emotional learning (SEL) skills is seen as part of the overall efforts to create a safe and supportive school climate. The acquisition of SEL skills is expected, among other outcomes, to help students empathize with others, understand their point of view, and deal peacefully with conflict. The underlying model of psychological well-being, based to a large extent on the Eudaimonic approach, identifies five dimensions that are interrelated and reinforce each other to create a holistic approach to addressing life tasks:

- me, my personal identity;
- regulating and directing myself;
- managing myself in everyday tasks (school, work, leisure);
- between you and me, interpersonal competencies;
- I can cope with stress, risk, and crises.[8]

In Hebrew, the acronym of the five foci is *On Be*, meaning "the power [is] in me."

Based on this model, SHEFFI has developed a "Life Skills" curriculum that is implemented in all K–12 schools. The lesson plans use the same principles across all age and cultural groups with developmental and cultural adaptations. For instance, while in first grade the focus is on entering a new world of school and meeting new peers, in the twelfth grades an important focus is on graduating and entering the compulsory military service. Here, similar tasks of entering a new environment that require reassessing one's identity are addressed using different developmentally appropriate methods. Also, the curriculum for the religious schools was developed in collaboration with religious educators and scholars and integrates content and examples particularly relevant to issues addressed in the religious stream. The curriculum for Arab schools is in Arabic and integrates examples familiar to the Arab student, from their families and communities.

An illustration of this process is the curricular module "Super (Don't Be) Heroes" (in Hebrew the word *super* can be easily altered to *don't*, and the name of the program is a play on this double meaning), which addresses the goal of "developing personal and social responsibility to cope with bullying." This classroom-level intervention aims to encourage students and the class as whole to develop a sense of social responsibility, empowerment, mastery, and control over their lives. The aim is to help students develop three main "superpowers," or strengths, presented as *don'ts*—Don't hurt (Do not become a bully); Don't keep silent (When you are a victim, do not give up and share what you are experiencing); and Don't just stand by (When you are a bystander, get involved and find help for the victim). The aim is to enhance the sense of responsibility and empowerment of both the individual student and the class as a community. The training material presents the review of the academic literature on victims, bullies, and bystanders. It incorporates multiple class activities and assessments of attitudes and skills. There are distinct modules in Hebrew and Arabic as well as for primary schools, middle schools, and high schools.

Currently, the ministry is studying lessons learned around the world with regard to disseminating SEL skills in all aspects of the Israeli educational system.[9] This includes examining the range of curricula to develop concrete skills and the interface of these skills with concepts like internal motivation, self-regulation, character development, and moral education.[10] As with other aspects of the system, the aim is to integrate these ideas into the everyday practices, organization, and climate of schools and to support ground-up solutions rather than count on outside providers to help students acquire discrete skills.

Supporting Training Materials

In general, the focus of training is on providing schools and local communities with guidance and supports, rather than prepackaged intervention curricula.

An illustration of this is a document addressing the issue of social exclusion in school and ways to deal with it. First, the document notes the inclusion of this type of victimization in the range of issues being targeted and contains a review of the professional and empirical literature on the issue, the origins of social exclusion, its consequences for all involved, and programs that have been developed to address it. The training material includes examples of activities directed toward the excluded students, the excluding peers, and the parents. It brings case examples and describes examples of effective responses. And it also includes methods to help train and support educational staff who face the challenges of excluded students in their school. Further, a module to help "train" students deal with exclusion presents detailed instructions for adults who support these students, including their parents. A final module of the training material targets specifically parents of students experiencing social exclusion and provides guidance to help them cope with and change the situation.

Another example of training material is a set of eleven experiential sessions intended to foster healthy dating and intimate relationships among high school students. This material was developed in cooperation with the Ministry of Welfare, which is in charge of preventing adult intimate violence. The aim is to address both healthy behaviors and the more extreme and pathological intimate relationships. Typically, the training materials provide methodical principles and multiple training exercises and ideas, and the group leader (a counselor or a trained teacher) is expected to tailor the program to the unique circumstance of each group of students.

Schools' Collaborations with External Providers

The main focus of the Israeli model is empowering school staff and providing internal supports to address the challenges. Nonetheless, there is a recognition that there may be external programs that schools may want to implement as part of their overall strategy of addressing a range of educational challenges. The Ministry of Education has created a database of programs delivered by external providers, categorizing them as Green, programs that the ministry is involved with in a range of ways (e.g., initiating the program, evaluating it); Blue, programs with no involvement on the part of the ministry; and Red, programs that schools are not allowed to implement. Under the rubric of improving school climate, there is a listing of 179 external programs. Schools need to find their own sources of funding to pay for such external programs, often through the municipality or parent support.

For each of the external programs, the ministry's database provides several pieces of information to help schools consider the relevance of the program to their needs. A program abstract describes the aims and content of the intervention and any information on program evaluation. Additional information provides details on the external organization that offers the program (so that its reliability can be assessed) and elaborates on the program's target audience, the resources (e.g., time, money, personnel) the school would need to implement it, testimonials from schools that have implemented the program (including their contact information), and assessments or evaluations made by supervisors from the Ministry of Education. Examples of external programs include:

- The Golden Bridge, a program to help kindergarteners resolve interpersonal conflicts;
- Paths to Empathy, a program designed to enhance empathy through experiential training;
- coaching for principals and leadership teams to help improve their leadership and management skills;
- Afikim (a Hebrew word meaning riverbeds, paths), a program intended for religious schools to help them develop a value-laden ethos for the students and the school that goes beyond academic achievement; and
- Providing a Voice, a program designed to help religious schools address issues of sexual victimization.

A review of programs included in the ministry database indicates that only a very small number of programs have been empirically evaluated, and the few evaluations presented are mostly post hoc client-satisfaction surveys. Further, the part the Ministry of Education staff's assessments of the program quality are missing from almost all the program records. This may reflect the deemphasis on implementing programs from external providers.

MEASURES AND MEASUREMENTS SYSTEMS

One of the hallmarks of the Israeli model is that it is based on the integration of policy, practice, and measurement. This is achieved in a partnership between SHEFFI and the Israeli National Authority for Measurement and

Assessment in Education (RAMA). RAMA was established in 2006 as an independent professional body associated with the Ministry of Education. Its motto is "evaluation in the service of learning." As such, it conducts all major and periodic evaluations of educational issues, including academic achievements, pedagogical issues, and school climate.

The MEITZAV is a system of school-based measures that cover student academic achievement tests in four subject matters, as well as surveys that focus on school climate and pedagogical processes. The academic tests are administered to fifth and eighth graders, and the climate questionnaires are administered to students in grades 5–11, as well as to teachers and principals. Each school participates every third year in both the academic achievement tests and in the school climate surveys. On a national level, the schools participating in a given year are a representative sample of all Israeli schools. More recently, RAMA has launched a school climate survey for parents.

The core content of the climate surveys is stable across the years to allow for comparisons over time. Nonetheless, some items have been added and others deleted based on lessons learned and emerging needs (e.g., the advent of cyberbullying). The climate survey contains items on various pedagogical and climate issues. The survey's sections dealing with violence and violence prevention are related mainly to student verbal-emotional, social, physical, sexual, and cyber victimization; students' feelings of (in)security at school; student victimization by staff; students' and teachers' perceptions of school policies and efforts to prevent violence; and teacher victimization by students.

A few months after the MEITZAV is administered, every school principal receives a report that includes both the academic achievement results and the school social and pedagogical climate data. Climate reports present both summative indices and item-level distributions and include text, tables of numbers, and color charts. These reports present the schools' overall results in each of the areas and by grade level. They also compare with results from previous years and with results from all other schools with similar socioeconomic characteristics. In addition to school-based reports, RAMA generates county-, city-, and national-level reports, which are submitted to policy makers and educational leaders at each level. All MEITZAV reports are open to the public and are available on the internet for each participating school.[11] Special attention is given to providing a friendly interface to help schools and the general public access the information.

School leadership teams are expected to examine the detailed reports provided by the school and to discuss their implications for school improvement. These reports are also examined by supervisory bodies on the district and city levels. In most cases, schools prepare reports that delineate what they have learned from these reports and what they intend to do to improve their climate. These reports serve as an agenda for work sessions involving education ministry supervisors, local education department leaders, and the school leadership team. On a national and regional level, the MEITZAV data help identify those schools that are doing well and are making progress and those schools that may need additional help, those that are "in focus" and encouraged to initiate an ACHAM improvement process.

For many years, the Ministry of Education resisted releasing this school-based data to the general public out of fear of the detrimental impact of "league tables" that make simplistic comparisons between schools, put schools to shame, and encourage fierce competition among schools that do not contribute to the educational processes, as well as parental pressures. However, in 2012 the Supreme Court forced the ministry to make the information public. One of the implications of this being made public is that real estate companies embed this information in their analyses of residential neighborhoods and make the information available on the internet.

Participation in the MEITZAV every three years is compulsory for all schools, except of ultra-orthodox schools, which are exempt. Additionally, schools are encouraged to conduct internal academic tests and climate surveys in the years between surveys to help monitor their progress and support their school improvement efforts. The national climate questionnaire is not available in a ready-made form (mostly due to a concern of overexposure of the questionnaire that might jeopardize its validity when administered by RAMA), but schools are encouraged to join the ACHAM process. The data from the internal processes are not open to the public.

Systemwide Monitoring of School Violence

In addition to the MEITZAV, RAMA conducts a large-scale biannual representative national monitoring study that addresses issues of climate, violence, and risky behaviors (e.g., alcohol and other substances) in much more detail.

The sampling method is a two-stage nonproportional stratified cluster sample. Fifteen strata are used: three school levels (primary 4–6, middle 7–9, and high 10 and 11) divided into five ethnic groups (secular Jewish, religious

Jewish, Arab, Druze, and Bedouin). In the first stage, schools are randomly sampled to represent schools (including school-level socioeconomic status and school size) and students within those schools. In the second stage, two classes in different grade levels are randomly selected from each of the sampled schools, and all students present in class on the day of the data collection are surveyed anonymously by professional proctors. These biannual surveys typically collect data on more than 470 schools and 24,000 students. Student response rates range between 82 percent among Jewish boys to 90 percent among Arab girls. Sampling weights are computed and used in all analyses to ensure representativeness of the sample.

Reports on the national monitoring studies are presented to the policy makers and the general public and are made available on the internet. These reports provide information on the educational system as a whole by grade, gender, and the study strata. Comparisons over time are conducted to assess changes for the educational system as a whole as well as for particular subgroups. Data are available to researchers after all school-level identifying information is removed. Additional sophisticated multilevel statistical analyses are conducted on the large number of schools and students to identify school-level, student-level, and cross-level interaction effects. Theoretical models and issues of interest are also studied.[12]

Citywide Monitoring

There are a few cities that conduct their own climate monitoring to support their school improvement efforts. These efforts are in addition to the state-required MEITZAV process. These cities identify issues that they consider central to their local educational mission and not covered well by the national MEITZAV. They are responsible for developing the instrument, data analysis, report generation, and dissemination and utilization of the reports and for conducting annual monitoring.

These initiatives have several advantages, key among them is the ability to tailor the monitoring to the local concerns, policies, and resources. The annual surveys also provide richer and more immediately relevant information than the three-year cycle of the MEITZAV. Yet, there are also disadvantages associated with these local surveys, given the additional administrative burden they place on schools each year. Further, these surveys attract enhanced attention by parents as well as the city leaders, which some principals experience as unwelcome pressure and overinvolvement in school practices.

Indications of Improvement

Israel conducts a systemwide monitoring study every other year. RAMA has conducted far five waves (2009–17) of data collection. These studies indicate a gradual reduction in almost all forms of victimization among most of the population groups. For instance, verbal-emotional victimization went down in grades 4–6, from 52 percent in 2009 to 42 percent in 2017, and in grades 10–11, from 27 percent in 2009 to 22 percent in 2017. Moderate physical victimization went down drastically from 2009 to 2013 in grades 4–6, from 35 percent to 24 percent and then stabilizing at 25 percent). Among high school students the rate dropped from 12 percent to 9 percent. Severe victimization has also gone down. For instance, in grades 4–6 it declined from 28 percent to 19 percent among Arab students and 15 percent to 11 percent among Jewish students. Similar patterns are seen in social (indirect) and sexual victimization and in the numbers bringing knives to schools. Only cyber victimization has been stable over the years, hovering between 8 percent and 10 percent.

Every year a third of all schools participate in the MEITZAV climate survey. These surveys provide support for the improvement trends reported in the biannual national monitoring surveys. For instance, while in 2009 19 percent of Arab students reported involvement in violence, the prevalence decreased to 7 percent in 2018; and among Jewish students the drop was from 16 percent to 9 percent. Cyber violence was stable in both Arab (7 percent) and Jewish (4 percent) high schools. The percent of elementary school students feeling unsafe in schools dropped from 19 percent to 6 percent in Arab schools and from 7 percent to 4 percent in Jewish schools. Similar trends were observed in middle schools. In Jewish high schools, however, the percentages were quite stable, hovering between 3 percent and 4 percent, though they increased slightly in Arab high schools, from 8 percent in 2010 to 11 percent in 2018.

FINAL COMMENTS

Education systems around the world are engaged in efforts to prevent school violence and promote positive school climates. They face many challenges associated with inherit tensions between competing demands. These challenges include the need to find a balance between an emphasis on accountability and a focus on school improvement, between a centralized one-size-fits-all program and an unlimited array of programs, between using only programs that are evidence based and allowing ground-up innovations, between emphasizing supervision and inspection and focusing on support, and between extensive reliance on outside experts and sole dependence on internal resources.

We think that the Israeli model is striking a good balance between these competing demands. It is a centralized system that provides a unifying conceptual framework, directives, and guidelines while providing a comprehensive infrastructure designed to support and promote school-level innovation and localized solutions. An underlying driving force of this system is an accountability and monitoring system that is integrated into the school academic and social mission, one that helps direct schools to improve their social climate, reduce school violence and bullying, and promote the well-being of students and educational staff as part of their core educational mission.

CHAPTER 9

LIGHTS AND SHADOWS OF THE ITALIAN CONTEXT

ANTONELLA BRIGHI

VIOLENCE AT SCHOOL impacts not only the mental health of those who suffer from or witness it but also the whole school environment and society at large. It creates a sense of insecurity and fear that undermines the educational and academic aims of the school; it violates the rights of young people to live free from fear and intimidation while they are at school.[1] This chapter illustrates the way Italian educational leaders, in accordance with European recommendations and guidelines, have come to understand and address through policy and practice guidelines the two phenomena that make children feel the most unsafe in school: bullying and cyberbullying. It chapter analyzes the actions of the Ministry of Education in the face of increased school violence, physical as well as psychological. The Italian strategy against bullying dates back to 2007, and since then it has been developing a strong preventive approach. I outline this as well as discuss some prevention programs implemented in Italian schools based on international and national research.

In defining terms, it's important to differentiate between *direct* forms of bullying, where the bully openly acts against the victim with verbal and physical attacks and/or by taking or breaking someone's things, and *indirect* forms, where the bully induces other peers in the social network of the victim to isolate or humiliate the victim. Bullying can also occur online, which constitutes cyberbullying, which is carried out through the use of information and communication technology tools (e.g., mobile phones, smartphones, computers) and content (e.g., instant messaging, social network, web channels, emails).[2]

In Italy, research on bullying at school began to appear in the 1990s, following a worrisome proliferation of incidents among children and adolescents.[3] Studies undertaken by the European Commission showed that Italy scored higher for incidents of indirect bullying than did the other EU countries in the study.[4] My analysis of the Italian policy for confronting the issue of violence in schools and promoting student safety is grounded in in an examination of the documents issued by the Ministry of Education and Research (MIUR), the Ministry of Equal Opportunities, and the Italian Parliament, which include laws, decrees, guidelines, official newsletters, and institutional websites, as well as some commentaries available in literature.

A challenge in this study concerns the statistical analysis of incidents of school violence, since in Italy the statistics on school violence are generated through a variety of instruments, and, in general, there is no systematic data gathered on a large scale and regularly across time. Many surveys provide indirect or partial information on the phenomena, focusing, for example, only on bullying (rather than violence), while other official statistics focus on juvenile violence in general or on juvenile delinquency and vandalism but not on the school context. For this reason, and considering the strong interest Italian legislators have in combating school bullying and cyberbullying, I focus my analysis on the prevalence and incidents of these phenomena gathered by public research institutes like CENSIS (Centre for Social Studies and Investments) and ISTAT (Italian Statistical Service). I also considered large-scale surveys carried out internationally, and on a regular basis in Italy, by the World Health Organization, the Organisation for Economic Co-operation and Development (OECD), and the Program for International Student Assessment (PISA), which provided reliable trends about the diffusion of the school bullying and cyberbullying phenomena.

THE ITALIAN SCHOOL SYSTEM

In Italy, the education and training system is organized according to the principles of subsidiarity and autonomy of educational institutions. With the principle of subsidiarity, introduced in the Italian Constitution, the state, together with regions and the schools, supports the education of its citizens.[5] The state has the exclusive legislative power with regard to the "general rules on education," the fundamental principles, and the determination of the essential levels of achievement that must be guaranteed throughout the nation. The regions have concurrent legislative power around general education and exclusive authority with regard to vocational education and training. The schools, too, have their own didactic, organizational, and research autonomy; they are free to develop their own education plans within the framework of the national and regional requirements. However, state, or public, schools abide by government policy that all children will be afforded educational opportunities that are substantially equal, though programs may vary among regions and districts. Therefore, these school provide free and secular education.

In addition to the state schools, there is a growing number of private schools, approved independent schools (*parificata*) and recognized schools (*privata*). Approved independent school are included in the national education system once they meet specific standards. Although they are not run by the state and have full autonomy from the point of view of cultural and educational orientation, contrary to private recognized schools, they can issue degrees that are equivalent to those of state schools. These schools generally charge tuition. Moreover, they can be run by both secular and religious organizations and do not have to fulfill the obligation of secularism, as do state schools. Many of the approved independent schools are Catholic schools. Recognized schools are those private schools that cannot issue degrees with legal value, but attendance allows students to fulfill their educational obligations. These schools are wholly private: students pay tuition and also pay fees to take final qualification exams in either approved independent or state schools.

Compulsory education lasts 10 years, for children from ages 6 to 16, and includes 5 years of primary school, 3 years of lower-secondary school (first cycle), and the first 2 years of either upper-secondary school (second cycle) under state authority (high schools, technical institutes, and vocational schools) or vocational training and training pathways under regional authority (see table 9.1). The last 3 years of the second cycle are not compulsory. However, all young people are expected to pursue education and training for at least 12 years, until age 18, or until they achieve a 3-year professional qualification. The final state examination of upper-secondary school enables students to access tertiary education courses (universities).

In the 2017–18 school year, 8,422,419 pupils attended all grades of both Italian state and approved independent schools; of that number, about 10 percent did not have Italian citizenship, and they were distributed with high

TABLE 9.1 Student population in the Italian school system, 2017–18

Type of school	Number of schools	Number of students	Number of students with non-Italian citizenship
Preschool	22.797	1.420.639	347.461
Primary school	17.369	2.690.006	300.928
Lower-secondary school	8.797	1.689.229	170.032
Upper-secondary school	8.868	2.622.075	125.497
Vocational education training school	NA	512.633	64.112
TOTAL	57.831	8.422.419	818.421

Source: MIUR, http://dati.istruzione.it/espscu/index.html?area=anagScu.
Note: The data include students enrolled in state schools and in approved independent schools.

variability among the twenty-one Italian regions, with a prevalence in northern regions. An increase in the number of students without Italian citizenship attending Italian schools was reported in the 2015 PISA survey: in 2006, 9.4 percent of students in Italian schools had an immigrant background, compared to 12.5 percent in 2015, although the trend has stabilized.[6]

According to the MIUR ***statistics, in 2018 the number of second-generation children (not Italian citizens but born in Italy) increased (+5.7 percent) compared to the data collected in 2013–14 (4.7 percent).[7] Of the total of the students population with non-Italian citizenship, second-generation students represent 63 percent; of the total student population, the percentage of second-generation students reached 6.1 percent. There was also a significant increase in the presence of unaccompanied migrant minors; however, only a small number of these adolescents attend education/training courses, and they do not fully figure into the MIUR statistics because, in large part, once they get to Italy they become untraceable. Despite a law enacted in 2010 that sets a maximum of 30 percent for the portion of students with non-Italian citizenship in each class, the reality is different. In Lombardy (northern Italy), 789 of the schools (10.5 percent of schools in the region) have greater than 30 percent of non-Italian citizens in their classes, while Emilia Romagna (north-central Italy) has 434 schools that exceed the state maximum.[8]

Important in any discussion of the Italian school system is the value attributed by the Ministry of Education to policies of inclusion, which are considered fundamental to the Italian educational system. This has been affirmed through the acknowledgment of the value of socialization and peer learning in daily confrontation with diversity and the appreciation of the biographical and relational uniqueness of every child. This is the reason why children with any form of disability have, since 1977, been included in mainstream classes, tutored by a special education expert who complements the teaching staff. Inclusion also informs the policies enacted for children with a migrant background and/or unaccompanied foreign minors, as well as actions and recommendations for affirming equal opportunities between genders.[9]

Yet, despite the priority placed on inclusion, the Italian education system faces high levels of student dropout, among the highest in Europe, especially in the transition between lower- and upper-secondary schools (the highest rates are among students aged fourteen to fifteen).[10] Moreover, the percentage of children who report a delay in their academic career (because they fail to pass a grade or because they are enrolled in lower-age grade) is almost double among non–Italian citizen children (32.9 percent) as compared with Italian citizen children (10.5 percent) in upper-secondary school.

The issue of immigration is a highly contested one in Italy and the subject of ongoing political debate, and schools often serve as the battlefield where different views on immigration policy face off. This poses further challenges for immigrant students' integration in the schools. Thus, despite the appreciation of diversity and an orientation toward inclusion, stated as core values in the Italian education system, the day-to-day reality for some children is quite different and too often results in an exclusive rather than inclusive scholastic experience.

THE SAFETY ISSUE

The term *safety* in the Italian school context means something quite different from what is discussed in the international literature on school climate. The MIUR website uses "safety" in reference to the structural improvement of school buildings, as a response to the recent earthquakes and to some unexpected collapses of parts of some school buildings, many of which are old and often inadequate. Despite a large plan of investment since 2013, the Convention on the Rights of the Child's (CRC) "Report on Children' Rights in Italy" affirms that "the situation regarding the safety of Italian schools is quite dramatic: 15% of schools are structurally damaged, maintenance is totally inadequate in 1 in 6 schools and only 5% are in an excellent state of repair."[11] It wasn't until 2015 that the word *safety* was used in the MIUR's guidelines in reference to the psychological and behavioral dimensions of bullying and cyberbullying: "'Safety' has to do with the behaviors that students have to take online, being aware of the pitfalls and risks that the online experience may hide."[12] Promoting safe use of the internet thus became one of the aims of several actions that the MIUR recommended schools undertake, including fostering activities on media education and developing awareness about online risks.

Safety is integral to another important concept in Italian public administration—organizational well-being, which addresses the relationship between social climate in the workplace and the psychological health of the workers. Physical safety in the workplace, which concerns threats to the physical integrity of all workers, must be assured; but the psychological safety of workers, their right to be respected, motivated, and acknowledged for their contribution to the organization, is equally important. In this frame, "well-being in relationships" is a focal point for the promotion of organizational well-being.[13]

ITALIAN LAWS AND GUIDELINES FOR ADDRESSING BULLYING

Bullying and cyberbullying are the two main threats to safety and psychological well-being in the Italian schools. However, compared to other EU countries, like the UK, Spain, and Germany, Italy was late in adopting a national preventive strategy that addressed the various levels of school antibullying initiatives. It wasn't until the ministerial decree of February 2007, "General Guidelines and Actions at a National Level for the Prevention and Combating of Bullying," that national policies aimed at directly combating the phenomenon of bullying and other forms of violent behaviors, such as micro-criminality and discrimination.[14] Previous measures targeting violence were focused on improving the climate in schools, promoting school performance, and reducing dropouts and only indirectly addressed the prevention of violent behavior. Then in 2015 a legislation outlawing cyberbullying was approved, and in 2017 the ministry guidelines on bullying and cyberbullying were updated.

In the 2007 decree, the Ministry of Education relied on the definition of *bullying* proposed by Olweus and further developed by Whitney and Smith that addresses the underlying elements of aggression (physical, verbal, or indirect), the intentionality of the act, its repetition, and an imbalance of power between peers.[15] This definition has been commonly used in international comparative research. In the Italian ministry's definition, bullying is seen as being embedded in group dynamics in society and as displaying distinctive features of other forms of violence, such as property damage, discrimination, and theft, which are criminal offenses. The decree stressed the responsibility of each school to determine the best strategy to raise awareness around bullying and affirmed the importance of involving students and families in establishing a "culture of legality" and in promoting active citizenship in the schools.

When it published the guidelines, the ministry launched a web page aimed at raising awareness among students and schools and providing possible intervention strategies, a national toll-free hotline, and a nationwide awareness-raising campaign against bullying.[16] It also established Permanent Regional Observatories against bullying to create a network among local associations, schools, and institutions for collecting and sharing best practices and responding in a coordinated way to the local needs. A key task of the Permanent Regional Observatories is to monitor and to prevent bullying and to provide training for teachers. Each Observatory has promoted, coordinated, and supervised the antibullying initiatives at schools and in the community in its respective region, which has helped spread more systematic and successful initiatives.

In its guidelines, the ministry recommended that schools adopt disciplinary measures aimed at making the bully take responsibility for their action, delegating to each school the application of disciplinary sanctions. At the same time, the decree reaffirmed a commitment to restorative justice practices over rigid traditional sanctions, such as suspension or expulsion from school. In response to several cases involving school bullying, the ministry guidelines included more severe disciplinary measures in cases of offenses against the dignity of another human being or actions that could endanger others' safety. The document also indicated that parents and student should, upon enrollment in school, sign a joint Responsibility Pact with the school aimed at defining the rights and duties of the school, student, and family.[17] In 2009 the Minister of Education and the Minister of Equal Opportunities signed a joint protocol establishing the Week Against Violence in Schools to promote information and training for students, parents, and teachers on the prevention of physical and psychological violence.

A further step in Italy's national policy against bullying and cyberbully-ing in the schools has been the MIUR's enactment of the 2015 "Guidelines on Action to Combat Bullying and Cyberbullying."[18] In this document, the emphasis shifts from bullying to cyberbullying as a growing and worrisome phenomenon. And while it underscores the group dimension of cyberbully-ing and the need to consider all the actors involved, it reaffirms that "bully-ing arises from intolerance and stereotypes that lead to prejudice" and targets especially those who are different for reasons of ethnic origin, religion, gen-der, gender identity, or sexual orientation or because of psychophysical char-acteristics, such as students with special education needs.

The ministry defines a new organizational structure configured around a network of schools, local institutions, and the provincial offices of the MIUR. These networks, CTSs (Territorial Support Centers), have become the focal points for the promotion and evaluation of the interventions against bullying and cyberbullying at the local level. They are also responsible for implement-ing the new policies addressed at national and supranational (e.g., EU initia-tives) levels. This was the case with the Safer Internet Programme established by the European Parliament and the European Union Council and which led to the creation of Italy's Safe Internet Center, Generazioni Connesse (Con-nected Generations), a national educational campaign aimed at promoting the safe use of the internet that included the roll-out of two online helplines for reporting cyberbullying and other negative online experiences, including pedo-pornographic content. Within this new organizational structure, the MIUR served as a "control room" at national level and as an interface for ex-ternal (pan-European) initiatives. Institutions, with respect to the actions for awareness raising, prevention, and combating bullying and cyberbullying, as well as monitoring the actions promoted in Italy by various institutions. This happened through the creation of an advisory board for the promotion of a synergistic and effective collaboration around the prevention and combating of cyberbullying and every illegal online communication.

Another important point in the 2015 guidelines concerned the necessity of involving all the school constituents—students, teachers, families, and nonteaching personnel—in the antibullying programs. It also pointed out the need to provide a theoretically sound training for all school principals, teachers, and personnel in order to empower them in this work. The train-ing was to be focused on the acquisition of an interdisciplinary knowledge (sociological, psychological, juridical, educational, technological) that could improve teachers' skills in detecting bullying and cyberbullying and in dealing with conflicts.

Building on this, the 2016–17 "National Plan for the Prevention of Bullying and Cyberbullying at School" asked schools to organize awareness-raising campaigns and to promote good "digital citizenship."[19] In addition, it set out an ambitious plan for teacher training involving a large number of teachers across Italy, which has been implemented through the online platform ELISA developed by the MIUR in collaboration with the University of Florence.[20] It also aimed to establish and strengthen the interinstitutional alliance with Italian universities, police, nongovernmental organizations, associations, and internet providers to prevent and combat school bullying and cyberbullying. The MIUR guidelines "Educating Toward Respectfulness" were proposed as cultural tools to combat gender-based prejudice and violence and online hate speech.[21]

These initiatives promoted a set of educational and formative actions in schools aimed at ensuring the acquisition and development of social and civic competencies, which are part of the broader concept of "education for active and global citizenship." Moreover, through a dedicated platform, Noisiamopari, the schools can send and share the initiatives and best practices carried out around the themes of equal opportunity and the fight against discrimination.[22]

A further improvement by the Italian government in promoting safety in school is the enactment of the Law for the Prevention and Combating of Cyberbullying, which is specifically focused on children and adolescents involved as both victims and perpetrators in cyberbullying.[23] In the Italian legal and penal systems, bullying and cyberbullying do not constitute specific instances of crime but are conducts that materially involve crimes regulated by specific laws (e.g., injuries, threats, defamation, private violence, instigation to suicide). This new law acknowledges that minors over age fourteen who commit an act of cyberbullying have a "right to oblivion" and can ask the manager of a website or social media platform to obscure, remove, or block the malicious content. If removal does not happen within forty-eight hours, the youth can contact the Guarantor of Privacy, who will then intervene. With this, the law introduces a "warning" of possible sanctions in an action of cyberbullying, where the police commissioner summons the child and at least one parent/guardian for a discussion of the action and possible consequences, which is then noted on the student's record. Another feature of the law is the placement in every school of an "antibully teacher" who handles all issues around bullying. This person handles initiatives aimed at preventing and combating bullying as well as all cases of bullying and cyberbullying, in coordination with law enforcement. The head of the school has the important job of informing the parents of the children involved and then implementing appropriate educational actions and sanctions. In line with previous actions, the schools have a fundamental role in detecting and addressing bullying and cyberbullying; therefore, the legislation emphasizes the duty of the schools to be trained and skilled in handling these situations. The indications and actions suggested to schools for the application of the law are contained in the updated guidelines issued by the MIUR in October 2017.[24]

The actions by the MIUR over the last decade delineate a global and coherent strategy:

- to prioritize a preventive rather than repressive approach toward bullying and cyberbullying by promoting actions such as dissemination of best practices and scientific knowledge aimed at fostering responsible citizenship in both the real world and the virtual domain;
- to combat bullying and cyberbullying through the establishment and/ or strengthening of networks of educational institutions, as well as the coordination with the Safer Internet Center, adopting a bottom-up rather than top-down approach around the coordination and evaluation (and funding) of initiatives;[25]
- to centralize the school's role in promoting positive and responsible citizenship using an ecological framework where students' education is linked to the resources and the needs of the sociocultural context, thus sharing the common goals of promoting such universal values as respect, dignity, tolerance, responsibility, and equal opportunity, making real the idea of "educative communities."[26]

Despite the initiatives undertaken by the MIUR, the implementation of bullying and cyberbullying prevention programs still varies greatly among Italian regions and among schools within the same locality.[27] Schools have autonomy in applying all these suggestions, and there is no formal mechanism for control over their implementation. For these reasons, it is difficult to evaluate the extent and the effectiveness of the measures implemented through the different guidelines and laws developed over the years. For example, despite the recommendation of monitoring bullying and cyberbullying consistently and regularly by the 2007 guidelines, the Italian government carries out only a very limited number of national surveys, and there are no nationwide surveys aimed at evaluating students' perceptions of the school climate and their safety at school.

NATIONAL SURVEYS ON BULLYING AND CYBERBULLYING IN ITALY

Following the publication of the "General Guidelines and Actions at a National Level for the Prevention and Combating of Bullying" in 2007, the MIUR indicated the need to have statistical data shared at national and more local levels. To do this, the ministry decided to carry out in 2008 the CENSIS, the first national survey on bullying, to analyze the characteristics and extent of the phenomenon.[28] The report on the survey data involved a stratified representative sample of two thousand families across Italy and examined the parents' perception of bullying. The percentage of families that reported bullying of some type (verbal, physical, psychological) in their children's classes was very high (49.9 percent in upper secondary and 59 percent in lower secondary). But in terms of repeated acts, the proportion of families that reported bullying in the classes was reduced to 22.3 percent of the total. The frequency of reports was the same in the four major geographical areas and in the different population centers. Parents reported that bullies combined different forms of bullying and that the action usually took place in the school: 51.8 percent reported episodes occurring in the classroom; 52.8 percent stated that the episodes took place in other closed and less supervised places in the school, such as gyms, corridors, etc.; and 29.2 percent of parents said bullying happened on the way to/from school (often on public transportation).

A further updated and reliable source of information about the diffusion of bullying and cyberbullying is the national survey carried in 2014 by ISTAT with 24,000 participating families, with a representative sample of adolescents aged 11–17 years.[29] More than 50 percent of the adolescents claimed to have been a victim of offensive, disrespectful, and/or violent incidents in the twelve months before the interview/survey. A significant 19.8 percent claimed to have experienced "typical" bullying actions one or more times per month; and for almost half of these students (9.1 percent), the acts occurred one or more times a week. Girls had a higher percentage of victimization than boys: 9.9 percent of females experienced bullying one or more times a week, as compared with 8.5 percent of males. The percentage of adolescents who claimed to have suffered bullying behaviors decreased as the age of the participant increased: 22.5 percent of males aged 11–13 experienced harassment by peers one or more times during the month, compared to 17.9 percent of teens in the age range 14–17.

The most common form of bullying was the use of offensive nicknames, profanity, or insults (12.1 percent); derision of physical appearance and/or the way of speaking (6.3 percent); defamation (5.1 percent); exclusion for opinions expressed (4.7 percent); and incidents involving jostling, thrashing, kicking, and punching (3.8 percent). In general, 16.9 percent of the males aged 11–17 were victims of acts of direct bullying, and 10.8 percent of indirect acts. Among females, the results show a slight difference between direct and indirect bullying (16.7 percent and 14 percent, respectively).

Alarming evidence from the survey concerns the overlapping of different forms of aggression, often both direct and indirect, against the same person. Of the 19.8 percent of participants who suffered bullying repeatedly, 7.8 percent suffered as many direct as indirect actions. In other words, about 72 percent of those who complained of defamation and/or exclusion were also victims of verbal offenses and/or vulgar insults and/or threats. Moreover, 22.2 percent claimed to have suffered some aggression through technology, such as mobile phones, the internet, or email. Among the entire adolescent population of internet users (about the 90 percent of the sample), 5.9 percent complained of having repeatedly suffered bullying through SMS, email, chat, or social networks. Females were more often victims of cyberbullying (7.1 percent) than males (4.6 percent). Around age differences, the data show a higher risk for younger adolescents than for older adolescents; 7 percent of students aged 11–13 said they were repeatedly cyberbullied, compared to 5.2 percent of students aged 14–17.

Among the reported widespread offenses and verbal injuries both at school and online, violent verbal (and sometimes physical) acts are categorized as "discriminatory bullying": behaviors aimed at discriminating against someone for reasons of religion/belief, disability, age, sexual orientation, gender, or ethnic origin.[30] The prevalence of this kind of bullying is easily underestimated in the statistical surveys because it is often buried in the broader categories of direct and indirect bullying. Discriminatory bullying, thus, may be specifically directed against those students who do not fit into the "normative expectations" of the community. For example, in a recent study by Caravita and colleagues of 711 immigrant and native Italian students enrolled in primary and lower-secondary schools, immigrant children were found to experience more bullying than their nonimmigrant peers, 17.9 percent versus 11.4 percent.[31] Moreover, adolescents with a homosexual or bisexual orientation or minority gender identity were also found to be bullied more frequently, as homophobia and other sexual prejudices are still widespread in Italian society.[32]

Taken together, these data depict a situation of pervasive victimization in the schools, where violence is exerted by peers through different channels, places, and actors and persists beyond school hours.

INTERNATIONAL COMPARATIVE STUDIES AND TREND ANALYSIS OF VIOLENCE IN SCHOOLS

Every four years, the World Health Organization's Health Behaviour in School-Aged Children (HBSC) study collects information on adolescents' health behavior and their relationships with their school, parents, and peers, as well as general information concerning their cultural and social backgrounds. This has provided descriptions of health behaviors of children, and their perceptions of health and well-being, from thirty-three countries.[33] As with other HBSC surveys, the 2014 survey included 65,000 students aged 11, 13, and 15 and attending public schools in all of the Italian regions.

HBSC surveys carried out in Italy from 2002 to 2010 reported a decreasing trend in bullying behavior, particularly after 2006, when the Italian government became more invested in bullying prevention.[34] The frequency of victimization was above 50 percent from 2002 to 2010. More specifically, there was a consistent decrease after 2006. A similar trend emerged for occasional victimization, occasional bullying, and frequent bullying, with no differences across genders. This trend was confirmed in a comparative perspective, with thirty-three countries also showing a decreasing trend in chronic victimization for both genders from 2001 to 2009.[35]

Unfortunately, the 2014 HBSC survey showed a drop in the encouraging trend; the percentage of males and females who were victims of bullying at least twice in the two months prior to the survey interview increased in all age groups.[36] The increase was particularly significant for 11-year-olds, both males (from +6 percent to +10 percent) and females (from +3 percent to +5 percent). Among 13-year-olds this trend seemed to point to an increase in the diffusion of bullying, especially among females (from +3 percent to +6 percent). The trend among the 15-year-olds was consistent with the other age groups. The phenomenon tended to reduce with age. Also, the involvement in bullying was more common among males: about 17 percent of the males reported that they had experienced bullying, compared with 13 percent of females. Of the respondents, 7 percent said they were victims of cyberbullying, with some differences for age and gender among the 10 percent of students. They declared to said they were victimized through SMS, chat forums, online videogames, and social media. Thirteen-year-old females reported this kind of behavior the most (13 percent), while reporting among males and other age groups ranged from 5 percent to 9 percent.

Besides bullying, about one-third of the students reported having been involved in other violent actions at least once during the last year, 35 percent among 11- and 13-year-olds and 27 percent among 15-year-olds. Those who said they were involved in violent actions four or more times in the last year were 3.6 percent of the 15-year-olds and 6.6 percent of 11-year-olds. Males were more involved in such violent behaviors than girls; about half of the male sample (46.1 percent) said they participated in a violent fight in the last year, compared to the 18.2 percent of the females. The frequency of violent incidents seemed to decrease with age. A possible explanation for this tendency is the information about the enactment of antibullying prevention programs in Italian schools. Around 60 percent of lower-secondary schools put in place measures to prevent bullying, compared to the 50 percent of upper-secondary schools. Furthermore, these trends are characterized by a variability among regions.

An evaluation of the overall school experience expressed by students in the 2014 HBSC survey points out some relevant risk factors: almost a third of the students perceived unfair treatment by the teachers; they did not feel accepted by them or did not trust them. Also, the students' appreciation for their school experience was worse than it was in the 2010 survey. The 2014 survey reported lower satisfaction for the school, with more than one-third of the students indicating they did not appreciate the school and a similar portion reporting that school as a stressful experience. This perception, to which bullying may contribute, was reinforced by the presence of psychosomatic and psychological symptoms among Italian adolescents: the data from the 2014 survey pointed out an increase in the number of males and females who said they suffered from two or more of the symptoms investigated (headache, stomachache, backache, depression, irritability, nervousness, dizziness, insomnia) from 2010. A PISA survey also showed that Italian students scored higher than average for stress, anxiety, and psychosomatic symptoms and were less satisfied about their school experience.[37] This feeling was even stronger among special educational needs students, who were also among the preferred targets of discriminatory bullying.

DEVELOPING ACTIONS FOR IMPROVING SAFETY AND WELL-BEING IN ITALIAN SCHOOLS

The international prevention of violence and promotion of well-being are the complementary aims, as acknowledged by international policies and action plans endorsed by the member states of the World Health Organization. As such, global policies call on the Italian government to implement evidence-based prevention programs, such as those that promote positive parenting, nonviolent discipline in all settings, antibullying programs in schools, life-skills training, and restricted access to alcohol and weapons.[38]

Accordingly, the underlying idea of many actions undertaken (and yet to be undertaken) in Italy is that in order to combat bullying, it is necessary to improve the school climate by creating supportive and empathic relations both inside and outside the classroom. This goal is pursued through the adoption of a systemic approach wherein the school is an active subject of intervention and not a passive recipient of expertise from outside. Therefore, it is crucial that schools take full responsibility for developing the potential of all their components by enacting an appropriate training plan. The training of teachers is key, an idea that is underscored not only by research but also by ministerial guidelines. Training is mainly focused on the need of raising teacher awareness on the spread of bullying and cyberbullying and the negative effects for the well-being of the victims, the bullies, and the whole class. Teachers also have to emphasize group dynamics; a positive change in dynamic can lead to beneficial effects on the school climate.

The climate of the classroom is related to the ability of the teachers to manage conflicts and to guide pupils to choose nonaggressive strategies as their solutions. This suggestion is conveyed in the P.E.A.C.E. Pack project by Slee and validated for the Italian context by Brighi and colleagues.[39] This intervention project developed in Australia combines the prevention of bullying with the promotion of coping skills related to well-being. In this program, teachers acquire specific skills for working with secondary school students on styles of conflict management and alternative solutions to aggression.

In terms of teachers fostering the development of prosocial behaviors among their students, some interventions are inspired to the model of socio-affective competence: knowledge and management of emotions of self and others, social problem solving, and promoting responsible social behaviors. For example, the SEEDS project is based on learning through group work, a range of sociocognitive competencies (self-awareness, emotional literacy, empathy, assertiveness, and effective communication and conflict management) that can help regulate aggressiveness, thereby preventing situations of abuse among students and fostering pleasant, safe, inclusive, and respectful class relations that value individual differences.[40]

Teacher training also needs to be concerned with the possibility of having to carry out actions for the mobilization of bystanders (onlookers, passive spectators) toward becoming upstanders (active spectators, reactive). The "Relations for Growing" ("Relazioni per crescere") intervention aims to train teachers so they can sensitize adolescents in secondary school to taking active roles in stopping bullying.[41] Teacher training should also be focused on cooperative learning, since this teaching methodology fosters group cohesion and promotes prosocial behaviors as deterrents against bullying. Forms of peer support do come into play in some Italian programs aimed at preventing bullying and cyberbullying, such as No Trap! ("Non cadiamo in trappola!"), where students trained by experts act as mediators between adults and students in distress. Peer support uses young people's knowledge, skills, and experience in a planned and structured way to reduce or prevent bullying.[42]

In light of the multicentric and bottom-up vision endorsed by the Ministry of Education, it is difficult to highlight one prevalent model for the prevention and contrast of bullying in Italy's schools. These approaches have fostered many local initiatives tailored to the culture and specific needs of each context. Nevertheless, at the national level, an important piece of the puzzle is still missing: the incorporation of bullying-prevention models into teacher training. Such a measure would ensure that all teachers, even the newest, have basic skills in detecting and reacting to different types of bullying, thereby making school a safe and pleasant place that nurtures all of Italy's children.

CHAPTER 10

UNDERSTANDING AND ADDRESSING MEAN, BULLYING, AND HATEFUL BEHAVIORS IN JAPAN

MITSURU TAKI

AT THE END OF THE 1970S, some Japanese in the education field began to notice a new kind of problem threatening student safety.[1] This new problem, *ijime*, a traditional Japanese word describing mean behaviors and/or attitudes with some kind of discrimination, looked different from more common violence, *bouryoku*, because it was not always accompanied with explicit physical force and did not cause students bodily harm but instead hurt them mentally.

In the early 1980s, researchers began conducting research on ijime. At the time, they believed that such aggression without physical violence was unique to a homogeneous society like Japan and did not exist in the West because of those countries' diversity. By the middle of the 1980s, most Japanese people knew of the fear of ijime that was driving students to mental crises and sometimes even suicide and recognized it as being different from bouryoku. Since then, both ijime, which I translate as *harassment*, and bouryoku, *violence*, have been main issues threatening student safety in Japan's schools.

In 1990s, when many English-language books and articles on bullying were being published, Japanese ijime researchers began to exchange information with Western researchers and share the knowledge around ijime and bully-ing. Some Japanese researchers, however, see a difference between ijime and bullying.[2] The overlap between ijime and bouryoku in Japan is smaller than between bullying and violence in Western countries. Japanese ijime research focuses strongly on aggression without physical force and on trying to distin-guish it from bouryoku, the more common kinds of physical violence. This Japanese perspective on determining problems as either mental suffering or physical suffering can contribute to research on bullying in other countries. Thus, throughout this chapter I use *ijime* and *bouryoku* and not *bullying* and *violence*. I also discuss the difference between the Japanese perspective on ijime and the Western perspective on bullying.

In my analysis I utilize evidence from longitudinal surveys in Japan that show the differences between ijime and bouryoku clearly.[3] The data also show what strategies are effective in addressing these problems.

PROBLEM BEHAVIORS IN JAPANESE SCHOOLS

In Japan there are approximately 20,000 primary schools, 10,000 junior high schools, and 5,000 senior high schools. The six years of primary school and three years of junior high school are compulsory, while the three years of senior high school are not, though most students (over 98 percent) attend se-nior high school. Close to 1 million students are in each grade. Most schools in the primary and junior high levels are called "municipal" schools, as they are established and overseen by the local government. At the senior high level, 25 percent of the schools are not municipal but private, and 30 percent of all students attend private schools.

The school system, like other Japanese administrative systems, has a cen-tralized structure but not a federal structure. Most of schools are managed on the basis of national standards. Teachers in municipal schools are employed as civil servants and are assigned to each school by prefectures, or big cit-ies. They are transferred to another school within the prefecture every three to six years. Some are promoted and become principals, and they, too, are transferred about every three years. This transfer system in municipal schools works to establish equality among the schools within each prefecture.

In Japanese schools, bouryoku and ijime are problematic behaviors and issues of much research and discussion. Typical bouryoku behaviors are as-sault, threat, property destruction, and so on. Such behaviors are not only wrong but illegal. In the late 1970s, *kounai bouryoku* (school violence) was rampant all over Japan, not calming down until the middle of 1980s, when, to control school violence, the police began playing an important role. Students and teachers understood then that any violence could be punished by law, even if it had been perpetrated inside school by students or teachers. After that, violence rates in Japanese school were low, until the present.

Typical ijime behaviors involve excluding, ignoring, spreading rumors, calling names, teasing, and so on. At the end of 1970s, teachers warned that this kind of harassment or mischief was dangerous. However, at that time, most people were preoccupied by the growing fear of kounai bouryoku, and few paid attention to "bad" behavior that did not involve physical force.[4] It wasn't until the early 1980s, as kounai bouryoku was on the decline, that more teachers and researchers took notice of serious incidents of harassment and mischief. Although mean behavior and/or negative attitudes without physical force looked to be merely trivial daily relationship troubles among students, they could lead to death. Such behavior and/or attitudes applied to someone repeatedly by a few or cumulatively by many can cause serious harm to its victims. It was at this point that researchers began referring to this sort of serious harassment and mischief as *ijime* and called for a strategy to combat it.

Recognition of the distinction the Japanese make between ijime and bouryoku is supported by longitudinal research. In the Western bullying research, by contrast, there is no distinction between bullying and violence; bullying is viewed as an extension of violence. This difference in perspectives between Japan and the West is important not only in the discussion of academic definitions but also in the actual practice of preventing these behaviors.

The lack of awareness in distinguishing bullying from violence came out of the history of research on bullying. European bullying research started with a focus on violence. Heinemann examined Swedish *mobbning* (mobbing) and focused on violence among young males.[5] Olweus also wrote about mobbning in Norway and used *bullying* instead of *mobbing* to characterize this behavior in a revised English-language edition of the book.[6] Now, the widely recognized concept of bullying includes not only physical but also other forms of abusive behavior, such as psychological, social, and verbal, as well as cyberbullying. However, physical abuse is still seen as the main form of bullying. As such, in Western research it is hard to distinguish between bullying and violence.

Japanese ijime research was undertaken independent from European research in 1980s. The concept does not come from any Western word, concept, or research. *Ijime* means behaviors and/or attitudes based on discrimination of and contempt for the weak and/or mentally challenged. Japanese researchers chose *ijime* to describe this type of aggression without physical force that was different from *bouryoku*, which involved physical force.

Further underscoring the distinction between ijime and bouryoku are results of the longitudinal survey by the National Institute for Educational Policy (NIER), which has been conducted twice a year since 1998 in all primary and junior high schools within the same city. The sample is made up of all students in grades 4–9, with approximately 700–800 in each grade. Students are requested to answer an anonymous self-reported questionnaire and then tracked for 6 years, also anonymously. The questionnaire includes 6 questions about their victimization by others and 6 questions about their victimizing of others. In those questions, the word *ijime* is intentionally absent.

Figure 10.1 shows that most students experienced ijime as victims; 87 percent had some experience of being "victimized socially" in grades 4–9 (2010–15). The number of incidents ranged from "none" to "12 times" almost equally, and almost half of victims said they experienced ijime more than 6 times in 6 years. Figure 10.2 shows that most of the students surveyed had been involved in ijime as perpetrators of the behavior; 87 percent of students reported having some experience of "victimizing socially" in grades 4–9. Furthermore, the number of experiences also ranged from "none" to "12 times" almost equally, and almost half of the perpetrators had victimized someone more than 6 times in 6 years. Figures 10.1 and 10.2 show that ijime is not a problem experienced only by some students but, instead, by all students. As such, any strategy to address and prevent ijime must be based on this evidence, for a strategy focused only on some students will not reduce or prevent the behavior.

Figure 10.3 shows that a considerable number of students also experienced bouryoku; 62 percent reported having been "victimized physically on purpose, harshly," in grades 4–9. However, the number of experiences was not as wide-ranging as with ijime incidents; almost half of the victims said they experienced bouryoku only once or twice, and only 11 percent of students experienced it more than six times in six years. Figure 10.4 shows that many students were involved in bouryoku as perpetrators; 45 percent reported having some experience "victimizing physically on purpose, harshly," in grades 4–9,

FIGURE 10.1   Number of reports of students being "victimized socially" (ijime)

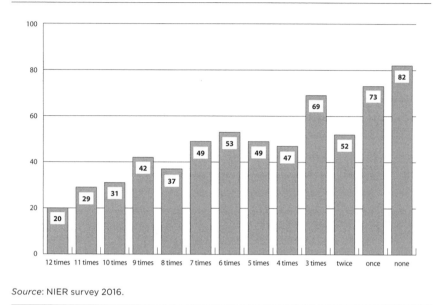

Source: NIER survey 2016.

FIGURE 10.2   Number of reports of students "victimizing socially" (ijime)

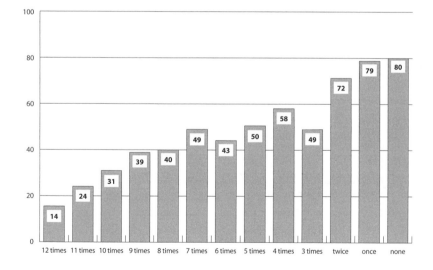

Source: NIER survey 2016.

FIGURE 10.3 Number of reports of students being "victimized physically on purpose, harshly" (bouryoku)

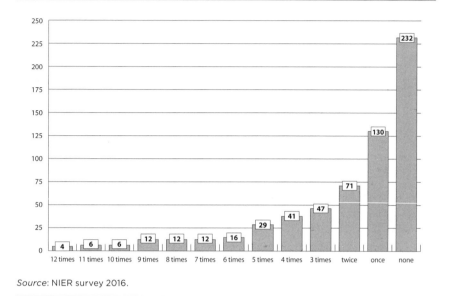

Source: NIER survey 2016.

FIGURE 10.4 Number of reports of students "victimizing physically on purpose, harshly" (bouryoku)

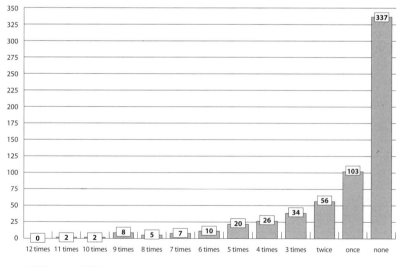

Source: NIER survey 2016.

with almost half doing so only once or twice and only 6 percent more than six times in six years. Figures 10.3 and 10.4 show that bouryoku is a problem mainly with some students, and any strategy used to prevent bouryoku should be different from one used to prevent ijime.

WHAT JAPAN WILL ACCOMPLISH BY ADDRESSING IJIME AND BOURYOKU

The Act to Promote Intervention Against Ijime

In 2013, the Act to Promote Intervention Against Ijime (Ijime Boushi Taisaku Suishin Hou) was authorized, marking the first law against ijime. The reason for this delay was that ijime was seemingly not suited to the Japanese legal process. Any behaviors classified as bouryoku, such as hitting or kicking, could be judged as "bad" regardless of situation or context and were therefore better suited to the legal process and were already restricted by criminal law. However, ijime behaviors are not always judged as "bad"; it depends on the situation, the context, and/or the feeling of individuals (e.g., teasing or joking makes people happy in some cases and unhappy in others). Most Japanese felt that ijime was not subject to criminal law; as a result, the Act executed measures to reduce ijime, not criminalize it.

For the forty or so years before the Act, the centralized school regulation system played the major role in the prevention of ijime and bouryoku in schools. The Ministry of Education guided and supervised the boards of education of the forty-seven prefectures by giving administrative officials notification about what prefectures should do and gathering reports from them every year. The prefecture boards of education also guided and supervised the boards of education in their cities and towns. And, in turn, the boards of education of prefectures, cities, and towns guided and supervised the schools. This meant that the Ministry of Education was only very indirectly guiding and supervising all schools in Japan. The 2013 Act reinforced this regulation system.

Among other actions, the Act defined the term *ijime*; determined the responsibilities of the national government, local governments (prefecture, city, town, village), and schools around the issue of ijime; established basic measures against ijime; and advised on ways of coping with serious incidents of ijime. It also assigned two new responsibilities to schools: to develop a basic policy against ijime (Gakkou Ijime Boushi Kihon Houshin) that includes prevention, coping, and aftercare; and to form a committee to effectuate this policy. The Act expects schools to work as a unified organization.

To this time, Japanese teachers traditionally had two roles: to teach academic subjects and to support children's social development. They were expected to have enough skill and knowledge to teach subjects and manage classrooms and to demonstrate professionalism and leadership in a classroom. Such expectations led to teachers working independently and not always sharing common recognition with their colleagues. Thus, the expectation of the Act to encourage teamwork at the school level has been, for many teachers, a new experience.

The National Basic Policy Against Ijime

In response to the Act, the Ministry of Education formulated the National Basic Policy Against Ijime (Kuni No Kihon Houshin). This policy detailed how local governments and schools are to design their basic policy in accordance with the Act and then carry it out. Especially to schools, the policy suggested a cyclical intervention process, thereby ensuring the implementation of a basic school policy.

NIER published two handbooks explaining how to set a basic school policy and make it effective. The first handbook emphasizes three key processes for each school: (1) decide its own policy actively, not simply copy-and-paste a sample from the board of education; (2) determine the policy based on some objective indicators reflected in its actual situation; and (3) involve teachers in the policy-making process and encourage them to come to a common understanding of and recognition of strategies to prevent ijime.[7] The second handbook shows schools how to achieve a cyclical intervention process.[8] Namely, each school should implement its own policy and, at the end of each term, make an objective survey for measuring the effectiveness of teachers' activities around the policy, and then have teachers review the results of the survey to improve their activities for the next term.

Ijime is not the problem of just some students but, instead, the whole student body. This means that while personal factors (e.g., temperament, characteristics and/or disorders associated with birth or growth processes) increase the possibility of exhibiting ijime, they are not its main cause. Any student has potential to become both of a victim and a perpetrator of ijime in their school life. So the strategy against ijime should not be to treat some students but, rather, to tend to all the students.

This strategy offered in the handbooks takes a pedagogical approach to promoting the development of all students. This is not a manual for how to change students; instead, it relies on in-service training to make teachers better able to identify and address ijime. The two handbooks lay out the tactics to make a teacher's role more active and collaborative for the development of all students.

HOW TEACHERS CAN IMPROVE THEIR CLASSROOMS AND SCHOOLS

Most bouryoku behaviors come out of students' personal and/or family problems. Therefore, strategies against bouryoku should be considered from the standpoint of criminal law or psychological/medical care. Most ijime behaviors, however, arise from trivial daily relationship troubles of the sort all students experience. These kinds of troubles usually disappear in a short period of time, though some continue and become serious issues. The escalation depends greatly on the relationships among students and the climate of the classroom and/or school. The strategy against ijime should therefore focus on all the students and take a pedagogical/developmental approach.

Approaches to Classroom Management and Improving the School

In Japan, two approaches to classroom management are emphasized: *ibasyo-zukuri* is the building of a belonging space as well as team building by the teacher; *kizuna-zukuri* is team building by the students themselves. Both of these approaches contribute to not only keeping the classroom order but also promoting the social and emotional development of students and, as a result, reducing ijime.

Following ibasyo-zukuri, schools and teachers should keep the classroom environment clean and healthy, maintain safe and secure conditions, and create a calm and cheerful atmosphere. If students feel unsafe and unsecure, they become uneasy and/or angry and are prone to escalating even trivial troubles to serious ijime. Each teacher is responsible for structuring their lessons so that students are able to participate actively and to understand the content. Teachers are also responsible for monitoring relationships among students and watching for signs of trouble.

Following kizuna-zukuri, schools and teachers should encourage students to communicate with each other and to accept and respect each other. If students have no experience being respected by others and no social bonds to connect them with others, they easily become displeased with and/or aggressive toward other students' behavior and/or attitudes. These students take offense with trivial daily relationship troubles as victims, but they also direct their angry or aggressive feelings toward others and become perpetrators of ijime.

Kizuna-zukuri came out of findings from research on fostering *syakaisei*, social-emotional competencies, conducted by NIER in 2001–04.[9] This research showed that a foundation of syakaisei is the feeling of social self-efficacy, or *jiko-yuuyou-kan*, and that jiko-yuuyou-kan can reduce ijime. Jiko-yuuyou-kan is the positive feeling that comes from being accepted and respected by others—"I am useful to others," "I have something to contribute to others," "I am accepted by others," and so on. Since jiko-yuuyou-kan cannot be taught, teachers can only prepare students for opportunities to experience jiko-yuuyou-kan for themselves. One example of an activity for fostering jiko-yuuyou-kan is *osewa-katsudou*, which is designed to give older students a role in caring for younger students. Also, while students who excel are more often accepted and respected by teachers and their fellow students, other, less talented students are not; osewa-katsudou is a means to give all students such attention and appreciation. Osewa-katsudou requires teachers to offer multiple chances during lessons and daily school life for each student to play an active role and experience the approval and respect of other students.

CYCLICAL INTERVENTION FOR IMPROVING CLASSROOMS AND SCHOOLS

NIER research conducted in 2013–16 showed the extent to which schools can reduce ijime by improving the relationships among students and the climates of the classroom and school and by stopping the escalation of trivial daily relationship troubles. The study of school districts' interventions in accordance with the 2013 National Basic Policy Against Ijime found that the cyclical execution of the teacher interventions ibasyo-zukuri and kizuna-zukuri over two years was effective.[10]

What follows is a summary of findings around the cyclical intervention process executed by the cooperating schools.

1. On the basis of the results of the survey at the end of the academic year, all teachers together decided on the plan and activities for the school's basic policy on ijime for the next academic year.

2. All teachers implemented their activities according to the plan through the first term.
3. On the basis of results from a survey teachers gave to their students at the end of the first term, all teachers in the junior high school district gathered together and discussed the results. If the value of the survey did not show improvement across the term, they reevaluated their plans and revised them for the second term. They repeated this evaluation process at the end of every term.

This process was repeated during each academic year under study (2014–16). NIER helped with simple data aggregation but did none of the analysis.

In the study, NIER asked the junior high school district teachers to do three things as part of their cyclical intervention process:

- implement cyclical execution over two years according to each school's basic policy on ijime;
- meet with all teachers in the junior high school district to discuss the change in students from the end of previous term; and
- use a common questionnaire for discussing and evaluating their policies and activities.

These steps were designed to control the academic research process. Teachers were given the research framework but not any advice on implementation practices aimed at reducing ijime, such as a special tool or program. The intervention process in this research was chosen and executed by teachers themselves.

To help make the discussions among teachers more fruitful, NIER also offered a checklist:

- ☐ Did they make it clear to students at the beginning of the term that the survey would be about the problems of the previous term?
- ☐ Were the goals of the previous term appropriate to the students' actual state, as shown by that term's survey?
- ☐ Was the action plan for the previous term appropriate to the goals?
- ☐ Were activities in the action plan for the previous term executed according to the plan?

☐ Did teachers execute the activities with the goals in mind?

☐ Did teachers share the purpose of the activities?

☐ Did students actually work on the activities?

The Verification of Cyclical Intervention

The verification was executed by comparison between an experimental group and a control group. The experimental group was made up of the cooperating schools, which consisted of two junior high school districts in a city. Each district had one junior high school and two elementary schools, so six schools were in the experimental group. At the end of each term, the schools made a common questionnaire survey that they distributed to their students for measuring the effectiveness of teachers' activities during the term, not to diagnose problems or issues in the classroom or school. The survey results were used in teacher discussions that took place during each holiday period.[11]

In contrast, the control group did not execute cyclical intervention. The control group was sampled to be similar in size to the experimental group in terms of the number of respondents to the 2013–15 NIER longitudinal survey on ijime. The purpose of the longitudinal survey from 1998 was to measure the ijime experience precisely, and the questionnaire was reliable. NIER issued an extra survey with same questionnaire to students in the experimental group schools for comparison to the control group, to indicate whether cyclical implementation of plans over two years reduced ijime or not.

The figures for each grade show the experimental group and the control group and include the change in the experience rate of students who reported being "victimized socially" from 2013 to 2015 and the results of McNemar test. Each school in the experimental group started implementing its intervention plan in 2014, so the test compared the results of four periods after the implementation (June 2014, November 2014, June 2015, and November 2015) and one (November 2013) before the implementation. The control group did not implement cyclical intervention plans, but the survey compared the same periods as the experimental group.

Figure 10.5 shows the results of the grade 5 cohort in 2014 (grade 4 in 2013 and grade 6 in 2015). The experimental group showed a significant decrease in the rate of victimization in the latter half of the first year (2014) and also in the second year (2015), whereas the cohort grade 5 in the control group saw an increased rate of victimization in the first half of the first year, which did not decrease significantly. Figure 10.6 shows the result of the

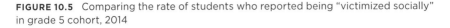

FIGURE 10.5 Comparing the rate of students who reported being "victimized socially" in grade 5 cohort, 2014

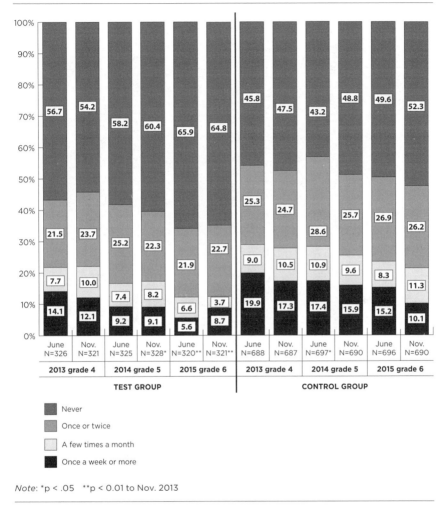

Note: *p < .05   **p < 0.01 to Nov. 2013

grade 6 cohort in 2014 (grade 5 in 2013 and grade 7 in 2015). Both the experimental group and the control group showed significant decreases in the rates of victimization in the second (2015), however, the drop was clearer in the experimental group.

Figure 10.7 shows the result of the grade 7 cohort in 2014 (grade 6 in 2013 and grade 8 in 2015). The experimental group showed a significant decrease in the rate of victimization in the second year (2015), while the control group

FIGURE 10.6 Comparing the rates of students who reported being "victimized socially" grade 6 cohort, 2014

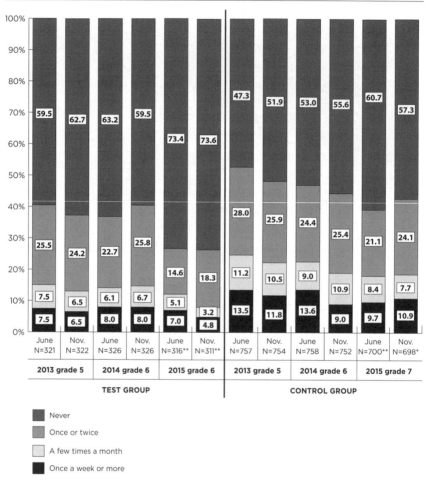

Note: *p < .05   **p < 0.01 to Nov. 2013

did not show a decrease in either the second (2015) or third (2016) year. Figure 10.8 shows the results of the grade 8 cohort in 2014 (grade 7 in 2013 and grade 9 in 2015). Both the experimental and control groups showed a significant decrease in the rate of victimization in the second year (2015) likely because it was their final year of compulsory education, and troubles among Japanese students typically decrease in the final year of school.

FIGURE 10.7 Comparing the rates of students who reported being "victimized socially" from the grade 7 cohort, 2014

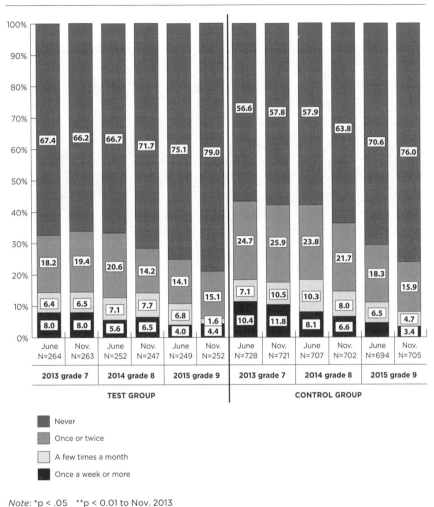

Note: *p < .05   **p < 0.01 to Nov. 2013

These figures suggest that the cyclical intervention by all teachers based on a school's basic policy on ijime can indeed reduce ijime. However, it took almost one year for all junior high school district teachers to understand the meaning of their collaboration. Through discussions involving all teachers, they came to recognize ijime and devise interventions to reduce or prevent it.

FIGURE 10.8   Comparing the rates of students who reported being "'victimized socially" from the grade 8 cohort, 2014

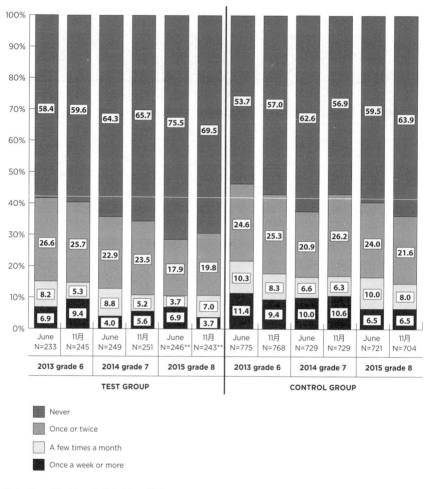

Note: *p < .05   **p < 0.01 to Nov. 2013

MEASUREMENTS

NIER uses two sets of measurements: the longitudinal surveys, which are geared more toward research, and the simple objective surveys issued by schools, which are for general use.

The Core Questions on the NIER Longitudinal Surveys

This measurement does not use the word *ijime* directly because the notion of ijime is very different among students. Instead, the explanation preceding a set of questions frames the targeted behaviors, and students respond to each question with "never," "once or twice," "a few times a month," "once a week," and "several times a week."

> Students can be very mean to one another at school. Mean and negative behavior can be especially upsetting and embarrassing when it happens over and over again, either by one person or by many different people in the group. We want to know about the times when students use mean behavior and take advantage of other students who cannot defend themselves easily.

> *First some questions about what others might have done to you.*
> There are many different ways that students can be mean and use negative behaviors against others in the group who cannot defend themselves easily. We are interested in *how often this term* other students have been mean/negative to you:
>
> - physically (for example, hitting, kicking, spitting, slapping, pushing you or doing other physical harm, on purpose, jokingly)
> - physically (for example, hitting, kicking, spitting, slapping, pushing you or doing other physical harm, on purpose, harshly)
> - by taking things from you or damaging your property
> - verbally (for example, teasing, calling you names, threatening, or saying mean things to you)
> - socially (for example, excluding or ignoring you, spreading rumors or saying mean things about you to others or getting others not to like you)
> - by using computer, email or phone text messages to threaten you or make you look bad.

> *Now some questions about what you might have done to others.*
> There are many different ways that students can be mean and use negative behaviors against others in the group who cannot defend themselves easily. We are interested in *how often this term* you have taken part in being mean/negative to others:
>
> - physically (for example, hitting, kicking, spitting, slapping, pushing them or doing other physical harm on purpose, jokingly)
> - physically (for example, hitting, kicking, spitting, slapping, pushing them or doing other physical harm on purpose, harshly)

- by taking things from them or damaging their property
- verbally (for example, teasing, calling them names, threatening them, or saying mean things to them)
- socially (for example, excluding or ignoring them, spreading rumors or saying mean things about them to others or getting others not to like them)
- by using computer, email, or phone text messages to threaten them or make them look bad.

The Common Questionnaire Issued in the Schools

The Common Questionnaire, which came out of NIER research conducted in 2001–03 on fostering syakaisei, presents twelve statements that are used in teacher discussions.[12] Students respond "a lot like me," "a little like me," "neither," "not much like me," and "not at all like me" to statements a–h and "never," "once or twice," "a few times a month," "once a week," and "several times a week" to statements i–l.

a. School is enjoyable.
b. It is enjoyable doing something with friends.
c. I study well in the classroom.
d. I understand what I learn in class.
e. I like myself.
f. I make some good points in class.
g. I have something to contribute to my classmates.
h. I have something to contribute to students in other grades.
i. I was struck, kicked, or pushed strongly. I have been the victim of violence.
j. Although it is not violence, I was treated unfairly or harassed.
k. I struck, kicked, or pushed someone with force. I have acted violently toward another person.
l. Although it is not violence, I have treated someone unfairly or have harassed someone.

The responses to statements a–h are used by teachers as indicators for checking their activities for improving their classroom and/or school. The responses to items i–l are used for checking the cyclical implementation process to reduce ijime and bouryoku. Teachers try to improve the relationship of students and the climate of the classroom and/or school but not reduce ijime and bouryoku directly. They do not use any special tools or programs in their work to reduce or prevent ijime and bouryoku. The improvement of classrooms and schools is expected to decrease these behaviors.

RECOMMENDATIONS FOR TEACHERS, PRINCIPALS, AND SUPERINTENDENTS OR REGIONAL LEADERS

Ijime issues in Japan can be prevented by intentional cyclical intervention, not through special tools or programs. Because ijime issues are the problem of all students, it is necessary for teachers in the same junior high school district, for example, to share information and discuss their interventions using common objective measurements. This type of collaboration, as well as a shared sense of understanding and purpose, is key.

Teachers in Japan are knowledgeable and skilled, but too often they lack awareness of school policy or school district policy. Reducing and preventing ijime requires targeting all students and the efforts of all teachers working together.

CHAPTER 11

ABUSIVE BEHAVIOR IN SWEDISH SCHOOLS

Setting Limits and Building Citizenship

ANTOINETTE HETZLER

AS THE WORLD LEARNS of the tragedies of repeated school shootings in the United States, Swedish society worries about how to avoid a similar situation. The Swedish government maintains that the importance of school climate in curbing extreme violence in its schools is not dependent on the use of metal detectors or armed guards. Sweden continues to emphasize that a positive school climate free from extreme violence relies on inclusion—the right of all students to a free and equal education absent abusive behavior—and the social and emotional well-being of each student.

It was more than sixty years ago, in 1958, that all forms of corporal punishment were abolished in Swedish schools, fifty years ago that Sweden started its fight against bullying in its schools, and forty years ago that Sweden made history by being the first country in the world to outlaw parental practice of physical punishment. In this chapter I focus on how Sweden, today, manages to contain extreme violent behavior and promote good emotional health in its schools. Research material on Swedish school violence shows that nonverbal violence is more common than minor physical violence, which is much more common than extreme physical violence.[1] I center my examination of abusive behavior in schools around the policies, rules, and regulations in compulsory schooling in Sweden.

Compulsory schooling in Sweden consists of four stages: a *förskoleklass* (preschool) for all children aged six followed by *lågstadiet* (grades 1–3), *mellanstadiet* (grades 4–6), and *högstadiet* (grades 7–9). All schooling after grade 9 is optional and thus not part of my discussion. In 2018–19 there were 1,068,274 students enrolled in Sweden's 4,834 compulsory schools, of which 822 were charter schools. The ratio of teachers to students is 12.1 students per teacher.[2]

Although school personnel are responsible for seeing that preschool children and students in their care are not harmed or injured, there is no direct regulation of the responsibility in Swedish law. There is, however, an indirect referral to responsibility when students are given the right to a secure and peaceful working environment while at school through both the Education Act (Skollag) of 2010 and the national curriculum (Läroplan).[3] In addition, as employers, municipalities governing public schools and owners of charter schools are required to follow work environment regulations regarding safety and security at school.

In 2007 the Swedish National Council for Crime Prevention (Bröttsförebyggande rådet, Brå) was commissioned by the Ministry of Education and Research to map the extent of extreme violence in Swedish schools. The report, published in 2009, concluded that extreme violence in Swedish schools is very uncommon and emphasized that much of what is currently being discussed in international research to avoid extreme violence (e.g., school shootings) is already in place and functioning in the schools. At the same time, the report pointed out that because schools take in new students every year, it is important to maintain trust and to keep prevention programs from losing their relevance.[4]

Today, Sweden has a zero-tolerance policy regarding abusive behavior in its schools.[5] According to the Education Act of 2010, *abusive behavior* is any behavior that, without being legally defined as discriminatory, violates a child's or student's dignity. In addition, the law abandoned the earlier concept of "student health care" (*elevhälsovård*) and adopted instead the idea of "student health" (*elevhälsa*), which encompasses a variety of competencies among personnel to promote good health and prevent ill health. As such, Sweden has gone further than any other country in defining and fighting not only bullying in schools but all behavior that can be considered abusive and that can negatively affect the emotional well-being of students. This decisive action begs two questions. First, why did Sweden legally expand the concept of "unacceptable behavior" at school to include "abusive behavior"? And second, why was this step taken during the 1990s at a time when the Swedish government went from a system of detailed regulation of compulsory schools to regulation by frame laws emphasizing the goals that should guide schools and the results that should be attained?

METHODOLOGY

My analysis of Swedish educational policy and goals across fifty years of policy documents includes extensive empirical work gathered in two different studies in the period 2010–18 for which I was the principal investigator. The first study, based on conflict at school, targeted eight upper-level schools in two Swedish cities over a four-year period, 2010–14.[6] The research team conducted ethnographic work over a two-year period at every participating school. Sixteen-year-old students completing grade 9 at the eight targeted schools responded to a survey on conflict at school.[7] In addition, data included five hundred national cases of alleged abuses of school rights that had been reported by parents on behalf of their children to the Swedish School Inspectorate (Statens Skolinspektion, SSI) before and after the changes in the Education Act of 2010 were analyzed. Also, the team conducted focus group interviews with teachers at all of the participating schools.

The second study took place in 2014–18. Six of the eight upper-level schools that participated in the first study, plus two new schools, joined the study. The research team administered the survey again to the current student body and analyzed results with those from the first study and continued the ethnographic work started in 2012. In addition, forty teachers, five from each school, participated in three different individual interviews lasting over an hour each and taking place across a two-year period. The team also analyzed all complaints submitted by compulsory school employees in Sweden to the Swedish Working Environment Authority (Arbetsmiljöverket) regarding threats and violence at schools resulting in injuries or sickness to school employees.

THE CONCEPT OF "ABUSIVE BEHAVIOR" IN SWEDISH SCHOOLS

Sweden, a country with approximately ten million people, is known for its politics of neutrality in international affairs and also for its asylum procedures for refugees. Currently, almost 20 percent of Swedish residents have a non-Swedish background. Sweden, with a high general level of income among its residents, is a social democratic model of the welfare state: basic social securities of health, education, and welfare are available to all legal residents.

The Legal Structure of Swedish Schools

The legal foundation of the current Swedish school system is the Education Act of 2010, adopted by the Swedish Parliament to replace the Education Act of 1985. The Education Act of 2010 specifies the national goals of education. The national curriculum, also a legal ordinance, states the fundamental goals and guidelines for the schools. It includes norms and values, knowledge goals, and pupils' responsibility and influence and requires syllabi that set up the goals for teaching in each subject. These two laws are joined by a variety of rules, regulations, and guidelines issued by the National Agency for Education (Skolverket), which also produces a Code of Statues (Skolverkets författningssamling) regulating daily procedures in the schools.

When Sweden municipalized its compulsory school system in 1991, it abolished two earlier supervising authorities, replacing them with the National Agency for Education. Then, in 2008, the government charged the SSI with ensuring, through inspections and audits, that municipal and independent schools comply with national educational goals. The Office of the Children and School Student Representative (Barn- och Elevombudet, BEO), created in 2006, became part of the SSI in 2008.

Regulation of Swedish schools changed with municipalization in 1991. The government's goal was to decentralize and deregulate the schools, arguing that the Swedish state should govern using the goals specified in law and determined by each school. By the middle of the 1990s, a new curriculum for the compulsory school system was introduced (Läroplan för det obligatoriska skolväsendet förekoleklassen och fritidshemmet) that described the goals and the results that should be reached by the schools. This curriculum allowed for substantial leeway on the part of the local municipalities to implement national goals for schools.

This radical change in the organization of Swedish schools was accompanied by a parallel development to increase rights of participation and choice for parents and pupils. The 1992 Independent School reform introduced the use of a voucher system that allowed a student who chose an independent school to take with them the amount of money his education cost the taxpayer from the municipal budget. The thinking was that this would promote the free choice of the citizenry.

Today, the Swedish central government is responsible for the development of the curriculum through its determination of national objectives and its provision of guidelines. The management of directing compulsory schools toward accomplishing national objectives is shared among the Ministry of Education and Research, National Agency for Education, SSI, National Agency of Special Needs Education, and Swedish Institute for Education Research.[8] The National Agency for Education and the Ministry of Education and Research coordinate setting national goals and devising curriculum and manage the collection, analysis, and dissemination of quantitative data regarding the school system through publishing educational statistics in two publicly available databases. SSI, through five regional units, performs inspections of schools. These agencies provide feedback to the schools and the municipality or school owners through both oral and written reports.

Policy, Law, Bullying, and Abusive Behavior

Views on bullying, its causes, and how it can be addressed in schools can be found as early as 1969 in Sweden's national curriculum. The problem identified at that time was defined in terms of certain students being isolated from others and was seen as best handled by the school's health personnel.

A more developed concept of bullying showed up first in the rules presented in the curriculum introduced in 1980, which legislated that schools were to create a school environment free from violence and harassment. Problems of bullying among students were to be managed in the classroom through such approaches as collective work forms, such as small collaborative group work projects, where students would rotate between different groups; greater student democracy, where students had more influence in the decision-making processes on issues that affected them; and improved teacher training. Curative work, or work with students with special developmental needs, was still considered within the province of the school's student health personnel or the school's "antibullying team," a select group of school administrators (including the principal or vice principal), teacher representatives, and a student representative who worked with the health personnel to deal with bullying incidents.

The Education Act of 1985 was amended several times to increase clarity around the promotion of antibullying behavior and the curtailing of all abusive behavior. In 1993 it was amended and formally introduced the concept of "abusive behavior." The law stated that "especially, those employed within the school shall endeavor to obstruct every attempt from students to expose another for abusive behavior."[9] The 1994 curriculum stated that it was the school's responsibility to work actively to counteract bullying, harassment, and discrimination. At this time, the problematic behavior of bullying was included within the broader concept of "abusive behavior." In 1999 the law was amended once again by adding that school employees should "actively obstruct" all types of abusive behavior, such as bullying and racism.

In 2006 Sweden went one step further and introduced the Children and Student Protection Law, which prohibited discrimination and other abusive treatment of children and students. At this time, most schools only had an action plan against bullying. The 2006 law demanded that every school also have an Equal Treatment Plan that stated the school's systematic work against discrimination, harassment, and other abusive behavior. This law was replaced by the 2008 passage of the Discrimination Act, which also established the Discrimination Ombudsman (Diskrimineringsombudsman, DO). Now the protection of student rights against discrimination, harassment, and other abusive behavior was divided among the BEO, the DO, the Education Act of 1985, and the Discrimination Act, depending on whether an action was caused by discrimination or by another abusive behavior. Often the actions were intertwined, and procedures around the resolution of cases were discussed by the BEO and the DO.

The most recent legal steps regulating schools were the Education Act of 2010 (effective July 2011) and the national curriculum in place since 2011.[10] The Education Act of 2010 specifies that if a teacher or other employee receives information that a student believes themselves to be a victim of harassment or other abusive behavior, the school employee is obligated to report this to the principal. The principal is then obligated to send the information to the municipality (or, for independent schools, to the school owner).

Models Used to Prevent Bullying and Abusive Behavior

Another way to understand the changes in national legislation is to look at how the general ideas around preventing bullying and abusive behavior have changed over time. Sweden has advanced from simply blaming the victim and using school health personnel to understanding that the problem of discrimination and other abusive behavior cannot be solved through laws alone, recognizing that it involves more than the incorrect behavior of a person and points instead to the workings of the school and the larger community.

These changes demonstrate that the Swedish school system's difficulties in combating abusive behavior arise not from its failure to treat an individual, to find the right way to organize a classroom, or to properly construct teaching teams. They show the shift from blaming the individual student to questioning the democracy within schools, the school system, and, finally, the organization of the local level of Swedish society: the community. To address this, national legislation introduced expanding students' and parents' participation in how the school is operated as well as increasing school accountability as measures to ensure the end of abusive behavior. The measures Sweden has taken to stop abusive behavior and strengthen student well-being include:

- establishing anti–abusive behavior teams at all schools;
- increasing democratic student participation in all aspects of school activities;
- changing the organization of the traditional classroom to promote more group work;
- increasing individual education plans for all students with special needs;
- expanding the role of teachers as mentors to students;
- organizing teachers into work teams around student needs;
- increasing school inspections and publication of results;
- instituting a formal student/parent complaint system under the SSI and the BEO;
- making mandatory at each school the reporting and documenting of each incident of abusive behavior, an action plan against abusive behavior, and an Equal Treatment Plan to prevent abusive behavior, with the plans evaluated and revised annually; and
- amending the Discrimination Act in 2017 and replacing Equal Treatment Plans with a general requirement that work with preventive measures against all types of discrimination should be documented and evaluated at every school annually (specific methods for doing this can be chosen by schools), with the SSI in charge of seeing that plans are in place and, if not working, revised.

All of these measures are used in Swedish schools today.

With the 1991 decentralization of Swedish state authority through the municipalization of Swedish schools and the transferring of financing and organizing schools to local authorities, it was difficult for the government to ensure that schools were meeting the goals stipulated in the Education Act of 1985 and to be certain that schools had resources to cope with both students' needs and instances of abusive behavior. Schools are funded at the municipal level, with the central government redistributing financing from better-off municipalities to those not so well off through a system of state grants designed to produce a structural financial equality among municipalities. Independent schools are allocated funds on the same principles as the public schools within the relevant municipality. Although the Swedish government has attempted to align school financing, equal management of schools in addressing abusive behavior or school quality is harder to guarantee. The Swedish government is currently increasing the use of legal instruments and the monitoring work of the SSI to better manage a decentralized school system.

In sum, Sweden expanded the concept of inappropriate behavior at school from "bullying" to include all "abusive behavior" to alleviate the necessity of continually redefining what behavior at school is unacceptable. "Abusive behavior" is seen as addressing the dignity and rights of the individual student.[11] It is a general concept, one that is flexible enough to allow for expansion according to changing times and changing situations. It is the student who experiences a behavior as unacceptable and who decides if the behavior was unwanted, and thus for that person the behavior is identified and experienced as being abusive.

The reforms around the municipalization of schools and the introduction of public funding for charter schools had a tremendous impact on how teachers, students, and parents experience schools. Hanberger and colleagues have noted that the decades of school reforms in Sweden—"decentralization," "recentralization" (through strengthening of school inspections), and "marketization" (allowing nonpublic school providers)—have made "the governing of schools complex and the division of responsibility unclear."[12] What they and others do not point out is that along with decentralization through municipalization, Sweden's schools also entered into a period of deregulation.[13] The Swedish government lost control over implementation of school policy. Yet, while the organization and management of schools are matters of continual political dissension, the main values of inclusion and equity, together with a commitment to zero tolerance of discrimination and other abusive behavior, remain intact in the Swedish school system.

GOALS

The Education Act of 2010 stipulates that the goal of education in the Swedish school system is having students acquire and develop knowledge and values. It also stipulates that education provided in each school level and in the afterschool centers should be equivalent, regardless of where in the country it is provided. Moreover, education should be organized in such a manner that all students are assured a safe and peaceful school environment.

In the national curriculum, the government determines the core educational objectives, while the National Agency for Education issues guidelines in the Code of Statutes, as well as commentaries that explain the purpose and motives of national goals and give examples of how they can be reached. There are two types of goals: a general value goal to aim for and specific step goals to be attained. For example, around the value goal of knowledge, a school's aim is to organize activity in terms of the knowledge to be attained within the selected subject areas. The goals to be attained represent minimum levels of knowledge in a subject that all students should be able to demonstrate in national tests at the end of, for example, grades 6 and 9 of compulsory schooling. In addition to being related to goals of produced knowledge, these national goals also concern norms and values to be demonstrated by students:

- develop and express ethical views based on knowledge of human rights and basic democratic values, as well as personal experiences;
- respect the intrinsic value of other people;
- reject the subjection of people to oppression and abusive treatment and help other people;
- empathize with and understand the situation other people are in and also develop the will to act in their best interests; and
- show respect and care for both the immediate environment and the broader environment.

The Education Act of 2010 stipulates measures to be taken against abusive behavior. A legal overlap between both this law and the Discrimination

Act have resulted in a shared goal of protecting students from discrimination, harassment, and abusive behavior. The SSI supervises adherence to the Education Act, and the DO supervises the adherence to the provisions of the Discrimination Act.[14]

Changes proposed in Education Act of 2010 and the Discrimination Act require schools to work actively against discrimination following a framework that outlines four stages in the prevention of discrimination: investigation, analysis, measures applied, and evaluation and follow-up. In addition to working actively to avoid discrimination, schools are obligated to have guidelines and routines in place to help in the prevention of discrimination, harassment, and sexual harassment. Enactment of the prevention stages are to be documented jointly by representatives of students and school employees. The work of documentation can be incorporated into schools' action plans. The SSI has the authority to see that schools are continually working against discrimination, thus raising the importance of documentation work for the schools. Also, in the Education Act of 2010 the work of school health services, special student care, and special pedagogical measures are coordinated into a student-welfare team, which provides students access to medical, psychological, social-psychological, and special pedagogical competencies.

NATIONAL TRENDS SHAPING IMPROVEMENT STRATEGIES

An important trend in Sweden since the 1990s is the increased recognition that the country's educational system is based on the principle of inclusion, that all pupils have the same right to personal development and learning experiences. The current national curriculum does not separate students into special classes. The burden is on the school to argue why an individual student cannot be included in the regular classroom and why a school is not able to supply the necessary support for the student so that they are able to function in the regular classroom.

Indeed, the curriculum gives the municipality (or independent schools) a high degree of discretion on how it uses staff and how it groups students. The municipality also has discretion over the content of knowledge subjects being taught. The long-term trend in the organization of Swedish schooling has been to make compulsory education even more oriented toward the individual student, and also more goal oriented. Though each pupil is supposed to achieve the minimum knowledge goals of a certain subject, ways to reach the goal and the time involved can vary. Thus, there are a variety of options available for municipalities in dealing with special support and special needs, as well as issues of discrimination or other abusive behavior.

Critical reports from the Swedish School Commission, special investigators, monitoring agencies, government agencies, and international cooperative organizations usually conclude with recommendations and improvement strategies. Often critical reports are taken with a grain of salt. After the 2015 Organisation of Economic Co-operation and Development (OECD) report criticized the failure of local school authorities to meet national goals to improve educational quality, the chairman of the School Leaders Union stated that he thought the most important question was how to ensure an equal education for all students, no matter where in Sweden they reside, and that faults within the Swedish school system were a matter best handled within the school system at the national level, through legislation, and at the local level, through decision-making at the municipal level.[15]

The OECD is not alone in pointing out the necessity for academic improvement in Swedish schools. Other Swedish authorities have also noted problems in the school environment that have impaired the schools' ability to reach national goals promoting learning, development, and wellness.[16] In addition, reports show that psychiatric health problems among students have increased.[17] In 2017 the Swedish School Commission noted that while many problems in schools were caused by issues outside of school, schools must work to prevent risk factors within the school environment. It pointed to risk factors within the school environment and aimed its proposals for improvement in increasing access to a good learning environment for students living in lower socioeconomic neighborhoods.[18]

Identification of Special Needs

Practices of inclusion, developed in reaction to earlier practices that segregated and sorted individuals based on cognitive and/or other functional handicaps into state mental institutions or other state facilities for care and treatment, are based on the principle that all individuals have an equal value within a collective educational system.[19]

The National Agency for Education has pointed out that Swedish schools have difficulty with early identification of children with special needs.[20] There is no national program or method for identifying pupils in need of support. However, even if there is difficulty in identifying children with special needs, the process of defining who has a special educational need is thought to be done best at the local level.[21] Government guidelines are therefore weakly formulated, and different needs and student categories are not named.[22] This is deliberate. The decentralization of Swedish compulsory school endorsed a local government model based on discretion delegated to local governments by the state.

Improvement Efforts

A key 2011 report by the National Agency for Education evaluating antibullying methods included a simultaneous evaluation of eight antibullying programs, followed vulnerable pupils over a longer time period, and gathered both qualitative and quantitative material. The evaluation pointed out a number of problems when schools purchase a packaged program and adapted school routines and school organization to it. The evaluation pointed out that given the wide variation and shifts in the everyday life of schools, commercial antibullying programs were poorly formulated and lacked flexibility by using a one-size-fits-all approach. The report concluded that it could not recommend that schools use any of the evaluated programs (in their present form) as a preventive program against bullying.[23] Instead, it recommended that schools use the guidelines they themselves produced, which would allow schools to build a systematic strategy against abusive behavior based on the unique situation of the individual school.

In terms of preventing discrimination and other abusive behavior, the Swedish School Commission cited problems with the learning environment as one systemic weakness.[24] Although the school system has a central goal of inclusion and of protecting the rights of all students to an education, it is uncertain whether those in need of help are detected at an early stage. More knowledge of a student's support requirement is a prerequisite for enabling correct action.

Instructional Efforts or More Comprehensive Improvement Strategies?

According to the School Commission, there are no general national guidelines or support programs available to improve school strategies for increased safety. The National Agency for Education has, however, produced a legal guide on school security and school climate, where the work done in advance of the Education Act of 2010 is presented and guidelines and supporting material concerning the work of schools against violence in school, harassment, and abusive behavior are given.[25] The guide also includes a section on security and school climate and makes a connection between the basic values of school and a peaceful school environment.[26] Although the Swedish School Commission does point out that the work done by the National Agency for Education is available, it does not view it as support material because it does not instruct schools on what methods will effectively promote security and a peaceful school climate and does not inform the schools about how to deal with problems concerning their specific school climate and the individual behavior of students.[27]

In 2014 the National Agency for Education published a report on how schools can work to prevent discrimination, harassment, and other abusive behavior.[28] It pointed out in the preface that "it is not possible to produce a model for how to treat the complex social interaction that lies behind abusive behavior and harassment. However, it is possible that the use of theoretical knowledge strengthened by a stable system of values together with their own and others' experience can give a basis for different types of alternative action that can function for different groups of students."[29] This view is also supported by the DO. In January 2018 the DO wrote about programs to prevent discrimination, noting that "it is not possible to state what measure a school should apply. This must be judged from the results of analysis and with consideration taken to needs, resources, and other circumstances. But the main rule is that the person legally responsible for locally coordinating the educational system shall take measures necessary to eliminate risks and other barriers that have been discovered."[30]

MEASUREMENT TRENDS

Sweden has a high level of formal accountability mechanisms. The OECD pointed out in 2015 that in Sweden, almost all (96 percent) students were in schools that used assessment data that monitored school progress; this was well above the average of 81 percent across OECD countries.[31]

The National Agency for Education produces two publicly available databases, both with a comprehensive set of educational statistics: SIRIS (Skolverkets Internetbaserad Resultat och Kvalitets Information System) provides information on individual schools, such as pupil-teacher ratios and student achievement in national tests; and SALSA (Skolverkets Arbetsverktyg för Lokala Sambands Analyser) presents the results of final grades of students leaving compulsory school in relationship to a number of background factors. SIRIS has been in operation since September 2001 as a tool for schools to use in their improvement efforts. An example of SIRIS data are results from nationwide tests in grades 3, 6, and 9, as well as reported final grades for students in grade 9, as the final grades might be higher or lower than student grades on the nationwide tests. With this data, schools are able to evaluate their grading systems as compared with other schools with a similar number of students and a similar student-teacher ratio. They can also evaluate student results in relationship to quality survey investigations done by SSI and made available through SIRIS. SALSA gives a more nuanced picture of student grades. It is based on a statistical regression model and is intended primarily for school administrators, principals, teachers, and elected municipal council members in their function as school board members. SALSA presents parents' educational level, composition of boys and girls, and proportions of students with a non-Swedish background and newly arrived immigrant students as important background factors in influencing grade achievements.

Since 1993, the National Agency for Education has administered an attitude survey to compulsory school students and teachers every three years. In 2015, 5,300 students and 1,600 teachers completed the survey.[32] The survey features a variety of questions, including questions about security, relationships between students and teachers, teachers' competence, stress and demand in school, and abusive behavior. An important purpose of the survey is to contribute to discussions about school environment and to signal future analysis. The number of pupils who said that they had experienced their school climate as "always" or "generally" peaceful has remained stable since 2006. There was, however, between 2012 and 2015 an increase of almost 50 percent among younger pupils reporting "always being disrupted" in their classwork by another student. There is no difference in reported abusive behavior between 2012 and 2015. A question in all of the surveys since 1993 asks students if their school actively works to prevent abusive behavior at school. The number of students who described their school as doing this "always" or "generally" increased each year, reaching a high in 2008 for högstadiet students at 85 percent; in 2015 it was at 78 percent, and in 2019 it had decreased to 60.3 percent.[33]

The National Agency for Education also offers a program of self-assessment for teams of teachers or other units at a school striving to improve quality in accordance with the national goals set forth in the Education Act of 2010.

BRUK is a self-assessment tool commissioned through a government initiative in 1998 and totally revised in 2011–14 to improve its format and make it more user friendly around both national school goals and relevant research.[34] School administrators or personnel use indicators to assess their individual school, plan for goals, and evaluate themselves along certain criteria. This is designed to lead to discussion around possible actions with a process of continual self-assessment to evaluate the progress made toward meeting goals. BRUK is a part of a school's systematic evaluation and improvement/development of quality in the work environment. It is designed to give a picture of how a particular part of a school's organization meets the national educational goals within different areas.

In 2018 the National Agency for Education established the Quality Workshop as an internet-based process support instrument to be used by municipal authorities with responsibility for schools.[35] This computer program is interactive and poses questions to a group of teachers to help them formulate a description of the quality of the learning environment at their particular school and then guides them through stages of improving or maintaining the quality.

The SSI also conducts a survey. Every two years, it surveys students, school personnel, and parents in all the schools twice a year, in the fall and in the spring. The survey is based on a number of questions that form fifteen indexes. Some of the indexes important for an analysis of abusive behavior and success of preventive programs are Feelings of Safety at School, Prevention of Abusive Behavior at School, Student Health Unit, Satisfaction at School, School Climate, School Regulations, Basic Values at School, and Participation and Influence. Many of the questions in the survey are available on the SSI webpage, which allows the public to look up a particular school and see its results. The school survey is given to students in grades 5 and 9 in the compulsory school system and the second year of upper-secondary school (*gymnasiet*) and to all pedagogical personal within the compulsory and the upper-secondary schools. In the spring of 2019, 1,642 schools participated in the survey, with 46,723 students (86.5 percent), 16,755 educators (71.7 percent), and 89,098 parents (35.3 percent) responding.[36]

The Swedish Association of Local Authorities and Regions (SALAR) is a consultative body that represents, advocates for, and advises local governments and its employees. Roughly half of all municipalities participate in improvement programs offered by SALAR around school issues. Most notably,

SALAR publishes its own analysis of the National Agency for Education data and has developed indicators and rankings of individual schools for the Open Comparison database, which looks at national test results, school costs, and staffing, to name a few indicators. It also provides a handbook on how to use these comparisons to analyze and improve a municipality. The OECD found that schools rely heavily on SALAR's Open Comparison databases for assessment of their performance and rarely use the many other diagnostic tools available.[37] The Open Comparison program is easy to use and provides an overview of one municipality's situation in relationship to other municipalities.[38]

In their work on school evaluation in Sweden at the municipal level, Hanberger and colleagues found that a multiple accountability problem emerges because there are so many overlapping evaluation systems within a crowded policy space.[39] They noted that local municipalities adapted an "evaluation marketplace," whereby municipalities adapt evaluations that favor their own school governance needs and that can be used to depict the municipality in a positive spirit. Similarly, Hult and Edström found that principals and teachers mainly used informal, word-of-mouth evaluations to improve teaching and school practice.[40]

RECOMMENDATIONS

Sweden has built a pyramid of efforts to make school climate a safe place for all students. Countries grappling with trying to decide which methods to use in compulsory schools to achieve and maintain a safe, positive, challenging learning environment could learn from the Swedish experience of opening schools to a variety of patterns of reorganization of the classroom, of understanding behavior outside of the classroom, and of encouraging participation of both students and parents in the everyday life at school by including them in active decision-making processes.

Yet, all of the changes over time have not eradicated abusive behavior from Swedish schools. New problems arise, and new situations have to be taken into account. Sweden is, however, at the international forefront of recognizing and taking action to combat abusive behavior at schools. The concept of "abusive behavior" in school goes far beyond traditional concepts of bullying. It considers the student who subjectively experiences—even if only one time—exclusion by others at school.

Given national and local ambition to advance compulsory school as a place absent all types of behavior that are experienced as abusive, I offer two recommendations to Swedish schools in their work to achieve that goal. These are based primarily on my own empirical research but also on the numerous reports presented by national and international commissions, the work done by Swedish researchers, and the SSI and the National Agency for Education publications on quality work within compulsory schooling, as presented in this chapter. They should be considered as guides to further the development of Sweden's schools and to guarantee and preserve school as a safe place. They focus on possible "soft points" in need of attention by both national and local authorities, as well as individual schools and regulating authorities.

Strengthening Local Decision-Making

The decentralization of schools remains a political issue in Sweden. The disparity between power and local knowledge exists in lines of communication within the municipalities and between the municipalities and the central government. Declining school results in international surveys confirm that student performance has been deteriorating in Sweden since 2003, with a slight improvement in 2015 and a stabilization in 2018. However, a gap has emerged between top- and bottom-performing schools. Stabilization of school results internationally seems to be the result of slightly better results for schools in Sweden with a student population at the lower end of the socioeonomic scale. Even if there is strong variation around school culture throughout Sweden, a number of studies I've mentioned here conclude that the schools have become more performance oriented in recent years. That is, student performance has become the focus of national discussions around school development. Personal development and respect for human dignity seem to be out of the spotlight. If student academic performance can be stabilized and even improved despite municipalization, it is reasonable to recommend that a focus on the micro processes of student behavior differences within the local community can result in improvement.

- Broaden goal setting and local responsibility through better use of existing data.
- Involve parents and other members of the school community, such as leaders of sports group and other afterschool activities, in discussions

about school climate, responsibility, and comparisons of local results with government guidelines.

- Encourage students to become involved in creating an "ecological map" of their school that shows which, and explains why, places are secure and which are not.

Build Local Capacity and Strengthen Lines of Communication

According to the 2015 OECD report, there is a mismatch in Sweden between knowledge and power within the municipality: top municipal authorities have the power to allocate funding to schools, but it is usually done on the basis of oversimplified evidence and with little input from principals or those who have more knowledge of education in general and local schools in particular. There also appears to be a mismatch between the introduction of new programs, school reforms, and increased national school regulation and knowledge of municipal issues. This is not surprising considering that in the last twenty years Sweden has seen fifty-five large school reforms.

- Provide guidance on priority setting in such a way that risk assessments and consequences of a hierarchy of priorities are apparent in a feedback loop between knowledge of local or municipal needs and authorities with the power to allocate funding, distribute grants, and/or increase regulation.
- Make available collaboration forums for local schools, school boards, and municipal councils to facilitate a fluid integration of new school reforms within the everyday life of schools.
- Build capacity to use the assessment data available to incorporate relevant expert knowledge to create a culture of evaluation from a holistic perspective that includes not only performance measures but qualitative indicators that promote information exchange networks.

CLOSING COMMENTS

Sweden has been shocked by lower results in international evaluations since 2013 and by the realization that the central government does not know or have control over what is happening in local schools. Yet, even if the international and national emphasis is largely on investing in education and training to avoid a decline in basic knowledge proficiency, this chapter makes it clear that it is equally important to prepare students to function well in a group, community, or nation-state and to have a strong allegiance to the democratic principle of respecting the human dignity of every person. This includes zero tolerance of all abusive behavior. Current data shows that Sweden is advancing in that endeavor. It should be self-evident that student performance does not take place in a vacuum. School climate, student performance, and respect for the dignity of others are part of a chain of behaviors that, by necessity, function together to educate the whole person. The aim of this chapter and my own research is to show how Sweden continually works with new challenges and different local community conditions to contain extreme violent behavior at school and, at the same time, to promote well-being for all students.

CHAPTER 12

CREATING SAFE, SUPPORTIVE, AND ENGAGING K–12 SCHOOLS IN THE UNITED STATES

JONATHAN COHEN AND DOROTHY L. ESPELAGE

AMERICAN PUBLIC EDUCATION was founded on an extraordinary vision: to support the development of an engaged democratic citizenry. In fact, founding fathers Jefferson, Adams, and Franklin suggested that education was the foundation for democracy. Although they did not delineate what specific skills, knowledge, and dispositions provide the foundation for an engaged citizenry, they were clearly referring to socially, emotionally, and civically informed competencies as well as linguistic, mathematical, and scientifically informed abilities. Tellingly, feeling safe—and happy—was recognized as a foundational goal in the second paragraph of the *Declaration of Independence*: "Whenever any Form of Government becomes destructive of these ends, it is the Right of the People to alter or to abolish it, and to institute new Government, laying its foundation on such principles and organizing its powers in such form, as to them shall seem most likely to effect their Safety and Happiness."

For almost two hundred years, American educators recognized and focused only on physical aspects of safety and feeling safe from physical violence in schools.[1] In 1979, a report from the US Surgeon General's office, *Healthy People: The Surgeon General's Report on Health Promotion and Disease Prevention*, recognized and identified violence as one of priority areas for the nation. There were several factors that contributed to this landmark report.

As the US became more successful in preventing and treating many infectious diseases, homicide and suicide rose in the rankings of causes of death. In addition, the risk of homicide and suicide were reaching epidemic proportions during the late 1970s and 1980s among specific segments of the population, including youth and members of minority groups.[2]

The emergence of violence as a recognized national issue spurred a growing set of responses from the public health sector in the 1980s. In 1983, the Centers for Disease Control and Prevention (CDC) established the Violence Epidemiological Branch. Public health professionals utilized epidemiological methods to characterize the problem and began to identify empirically based risk and protective factors. Beginning in the early 1990s, the public health approach began to shift from describing the problem to understanding what worked in preventing violence. These early efforts were focused on the high rates of homicide among youth. In 1992, the CDC issued *The Prevention of Youth Violence: A Framework for Community Action*, which set in motion the development of more empirically grounded violence prevention efforts in the US.[3]

In 1994, the US Congress mandated that the Department of Education begin to collect information on efforts to prevent violence in schools. This led to a series of Department of Education and Justice Department studies that revealed three major sets of findings.[4] First, the vast majority of schools have relatively low levels of serious crime. In fact, since the 1990s, schools have become one of, if not *the*, safest places for many K–12 students to be, physically. Second, disciplinary data and findings were recorded in a range of ways, and few schools were adhering to recommended data collection principles. Third, there were four major prevention efforts that schools were focused on: prevention activities, which were typically not being monitored and/or evaluated; school security measures (e.g., hiring special security personnel, use of metal detectors, random searches), which were often inconsistently implemented; school discipline practices and policies that focused on punitive rather than health promotion practices; and school climate–informed improvement practices, which tended to focus on staff-student relations, explicit improvement goals, rules and expectations (too often focused on disciplinary practice as well as positive expectations), and the environment (e.g., ensuring that schools were clean).

The 1999 school shooting at Columbine High School in Colorado prompted a sense of urgency to better understand school violence and to ensure that students feel safe in school. While there had been certainly school shootings prior to Columbine, virtually all of them had involved very small numbers of students being hurt, and they typically occurred in economically disadvantaged communities. And the growing number of school shootings since Columbine has, understandably, increased public alarm. Since the school shooting at Sandy Hook Elementary School in Connecticut in 2012, for example, there have been more than 300 school shootings. However, the CDC reported that there have been more than 100,000 shootings outside of schools each year between 2012 and 2017—about 275 shootings every day resulting in approximately 92 deaths and 183 injuries.[5]

Violence in US schools is just a small part of the larger problem of gun violence in US society. Children are exposed to violence in many other settings in their communities. Over the past 20 years, the US has experienced an average of 22 students murdered at school each year. In other words, students are 67 times more likely to be murdered outside of school than in school.[6] As Dewey Cornell and others have underscored, the US does not have a school violence problem; it has a gun violence problem.[7] Yet, a March 2019 survey of more than 1,000 adults revealed that 74 percent of parents of school-age children and 64 percent of nonparents believed schools were more unsafe today than they were in 1999.[8] These fears have fueled a new K–12 school security industry that focuses on metal detectors, armed guards, and physical dangers, though there is no evidence that these efforts to "harden schools" are effective.[9]

Since 2000 there have been two important understandings around safety. First, as relatively physically safe as students are in schools, they are not safe socially, emotionally, or intellectually. Bullying and bully-victim-bystander dynamics are a major worry for many students. In fact, the CDC has recognized that bullying is a public health concern.[10] Second, research underscores the idea that measures supporting students feeling safe and preventing school violence need to be based on an ecologically informed public health model that interactively supports prevention and health/mental health promotion efforts with academic learning. This public health model needs to recognize and further universal programs that promote prosocial learning (e.g., social-emotional learning, character education, mental health promotion efforts) and healthy development for everyone, secondary-level programs designed to reduce risk factors, and tertiary-level interventions for individuals who are struggling in significant ways and/or where illness is imminent.[11]

According to the National Center for Educational Statistics, in the US there are roughly 56.6 million students (2018) in 98,200 public schools (2015), which includes roughly 6,700 charter schools.[12] (There are also more than 33,000 independent schools and home schooling networks, which we do not focus on here.) Public education in the US is largely shaped by state-level policy and practice guidelines. In this chapter we summarize how the US currently understands what it means to "feel safe," as well as how states address mean, bullying, and/or disrespectful behaviors in K–12 schools. We consider how this understanding shapes school improvement goals and strategies as well as how improvement is measured. Finally, we make a series of recommendations based on these trends and our understanding of relevant research.

Documenting national trends is inherently challenging. In the US, state education departments largely shape educational policy and practice guidelines, and there is variability between states and within a given state. In addition, a state's policy does not necessarily shape what each district and school is actually doing. The major source of data we used to make statements about US trends is a 2011–17 educational policy scan that looked at how states were focused on bully prevention, social-emotional learning (SEL), and school climate.[13] In addition, we used research findings as well as our own consultative and research experiences with schools, districts, and state education departments. Over the last three decades, we have learned and worked with scores of districts and many states on multiyear improvement projects. In addition, we have worked with an additional dozen states and hundreds of districts and building leaders on a more intermittent consultative basis.

UNDERSTANDINGS

Historically, US educators have only focused on being and feeling safe physically in schools. It is only over the last two decades that federal, state, and district leaders have begun to increasingly focus on the social, emotional, and intellectual aspects of feeling safe in schools. Empirical research that has studied high school dropout rates, the short- and long-term toxic effects of bully-victim-bystander behavior, and the school climate improvement process, as well as SEL-informed studies, have fostered a growing appreciation for and focus on the foundational importance of students feeling safe in school—socially, emotionally, intellectually, and physically.[14]

The 2011–17 policy scan revealed confusion about what school climate, SEL, and school violence are and how to best define these somewhat overlapping ideas. There is confusion about understandings and definitions in two ways: conceptually and with regard to a helpful and sustainable improvement process. There is a lack of consensus about how to define the concepts of school climate, SEL, and bullying.[15] This is a meaningful challenge to research efforts, as investigators focus on and measure these domains in very different ways. This complicates researchers' and policy makers' ability to compare and contrast findings. There is also confusion about what an effective and sustainable school climate, SEL, and bullying prevention improvement efforts mean. These three labels are different conceptually, and they grow out of different educational traditions.[16]

School climate is often not defined in state policy: only ten of the thirty-four states provided a definition. Although two-thirds of these states explicitly supported school climate improvement as a schoolwide improvement process, this was typically not well-defined or in any way yoked to implementation science findings.

Definitions of *social-emotional learning* vary, and there is not a consensus about how to define it. Most states focus on the process of learning that supports the development of social-emotional competencies aligned with the Collaborative for Social Emotional and Academic Learning (CASEL) definition that recognizes and focuses on the following five organizing competences: self-awareness, self-management, social awareness, responsible decision-making, and relationship skills. One state explicitly recognized character development and SEL; another state did not have any definition.

The term *bullying* is complicated, and the policy scan revealed some good as well as some problematic news.[17] The good news is that there is a growing understanding that bullying is not a single behavior but that it reflects a spectrum of behaviors that are hurtful and undermine feeling safe. More than half of the states recognized that cyberbullying is a form of bullying and that sexual harassment represents a form of bullying. Six states even recognized that "teasing" is on the spectrum of behaviors that can undermine feeling safe in schools.

School leaders do not always appreciate that there is complicated spectrum of behaviors that undermine students—and adults—feeling safe in school. On the one hand, individual psychopathology (e.g., major depressive disorders, trauma) represents one important and relatively common set of experiences that undermine students feeling safe. On the other hand, there is a spectrum of additional behaviors undermining people feeling safe in schools that ranges from normative moments of misunderstanding and microaggressions, to intentional communications (verbal or cyber) designed to be hurtful, to more extreme forms of harassment, disrespect, and physical assault, importantly including date rape and rape. There is growing evidence that sexual violence (e.g., unwanted sexual commentary, rape) is as prevalent in middle and high schools as it is on college campuses.[18] Yet, in dramatic contrast to growing conversation about sexual harassment in adult life, there has been a deafening silence about sexual violence, sexual harassment, and rape and related forms of severe disrespect and harassment in K–12 schools.

Sexual harassment is a form of sexual discrimination that involves unwanted sexual conduct, including verbal, nonverbal, and physical behaviors that interfere with an individual's right to receive an equal education by limiting a student's ability to participate in or benefit from educational programs or by creating a hostile or abusive educational environment based on its severity, persistence, or pervasiveness.[19] During adolescence, sexual harassment tends to involve sexual commentary, spreading sexual rumors, and inappropriate touching.[20] Such behavior is common among teens, with one national study reporting sexual harassment rates as high as 56 percent for females and 40 percent for males, including being called "gay."[21] In a 2016 study of sixth-grade students from thirty-six Midwest middle schools, 8 percent admitted to perpetrating at least one incident of sexual harassment, and 15 percent reported being victims of at least one form of sexual harassment in the last year.[22] Additionally, 34 percent of the students reported being targets of homophobic epithets, with 31 percent identifying as victims of homophobic name-calling.

Most states define *bullying* as being related to acts of "discrimination and/ or harassment" based on a student's race, color, weight, national origin, ethnic group, religion, religious practices, disability, sexual orientation, gender identity, and sex. However, the majority of bully prevention policies focus on reporting criteria and methods. Our impression is that this is unhelpful and fosters anxiety about the implications of reporting. In New York City, for example, half of the schools reported zero incidents of bullying.[23] Given epidemiologically informed understandings of bullying, it is extraordinarily unlikely that this number is valid.

Another conceptual shortcoming in definitions of bullying is that current policy is only focused on the individual, or group, who is acting in mean, bullying, and/or disrespectful ways. It is certainly true that bullying is an individual act; however, it is also a social process. There are virtually always witnesses who see or hear bullying behaviors, and how they respond (bystanders or "Upstanders") shapes bullying behaviors.[24] Only one state recognizes that being a witness—bystander or Upstander—matters in helpfully preventing and addressing bullying and disrespectful behaviors.

As with the lack of consensus around definitions, there is not one model that shapes bully prevention, SEL, school climate, and/or health/mental health promotion improvement efforts in the states. Positive Behavioral Interventions and Supports (PBIS) has been funded by the US Department of Education and is certainly one of the major models that many school districts use to further safer and more supportive schools.[25] PBIS began as a targeted intervention and response to behaviorally "out-of-control" special education students. Over the last two decades, it has grown to become a universal intervention designed to support all students. Some consider it to be a school climate improvement model. We suggest that there are commonalities: both PBIS and our understanding of school climate improvement (1) are schoolwide efforts; (2) are focused on supporting positive change; (3) support student learning; (4) support student, family, school personnel, and community partnerships; (5) are data driven; (6) appreciate that adult behavior and "adult modeling" matter; and (7) are focused on advancing policies and procedures that support effective practice. However, they are actually more different than similar in a number of fundamentally important ways.[26] They have very different goals. They use very different data sets. PBIS is based on a behaviorally informed model that narrowly focuses on providing supports to prevent, teach, and reinforce desirable behavior, while school climate reform supports the development of SEL and intrinsic motivation through engaging community members who support the school improvement process together. And rather than being an adult driven, top-down effort, school climate reform is a much broader, more systemic effort grounded in a democratically informed process of engaging students, parents/guardians, school personnel, and even community members in being co-learners and co-leaders (under the leadership of the principal). Also, PBIS's policy efforts focus on supporting the design and implementation of effective interventions to change student behavior through behavioral contingencies, while school climate reform focuses on supporting policies that support school communities, thereby furthering an iterative process of learning and improvement and promoting positive relationships.

Our consultative experiences underscore the statistical and research findings: there is confusion about how school climate, SEL, and violence prevention efforts are similar and different and about what an effective and sustainable school improvement process is. Yet, over the last decade that there has been a growing appreciation for the idea that effective improvement efforts in SEL, school climate, and violence prevention are part of an ongoing and, ideally, iterative process.

Until very recently, the majority of school leaders needed and wanted to understand what were relevant and appropriate evidence-based instructional improvement efforts. There was less appreciation for the importance of thinking systemically as well as instructionally. And rather than developing plans to integrate social, emotional, and civic teaching and learning, as well as efforts to support all students feeling safe, supported, and engaged throughout the school day, the focus was on "programs" that would support language, math, and science learning "this year." This was very understandable, as the 2002–15 No Child Left Behind (NCLB) Act insisted that districts use "evidence-based" programs and promoted annual reading, math, and science scores—"what is measured is treasured."

There is an important shift occurring in the US today that is supporting school leaders who are beginning to measure and focus on the "nonacademic" aspects of student learning and school life. In part, this is being spurred by the new federal Every Student Succeeds Act, which, for the first time, mandates that states and districts measure a "nonacademic" aspect of student learning and/or school life. In addition, there is a growing understanding that school leaders need to consider findings from implementation science.[27] Implementation science, which focuses on supporting effective and sustainable school improvement, underscores the following understandings. First, schools will never be perfect, and what is important is being clear about improvement goals, the strategies to actualize these goals, and measurement that supports learning and improvement in an iterative manner.[28] Second, the development of transparent learning communities (e.g., professional learning communities within schools and/or network improvement communities between schools) supports educators learning from one another in ways that further sustainable improvement efforts.[29] Third, effective instruction plus effective implementation plus enabling supportive systems can support educationally significant outcomes.[30] Fourth, it really does take a "village"—students, parents, school personnel, and even community members/leaders—to be co-learners and co-leaders in a helpful and sustainable improvement process.[31] And the whole village needs to intentionally promote both individual (student and educator) and organizational well-being, the foundation for effective and sustainable violence prevention efforts.[32] These implementation science findings are still more an idea and an emerging goal for school leaders and not yet common practice.

Finally, US educators have only recently begun to focus on the importance of educators feeling safe in schools. In fact, violence directed against K–12 teachers is a serious problem.[33] There is a significant, meaningful, and growing appreciation that we can and need to focus not only on the safety of teachers but on their ongoing SEL as well.[34]

GOALS

Today, the goal for both federal and state educational leaders is to ensure that all students are able to learn and develop in healthy ways. But there are profound gaps between this ideal and current policy and practice guidelines.

The 2011–17 policy scan revealed that state Departments of Education are providing very little guidance on how to consider delineating helpful school climate, SEL, and/or bully/violence prevention improvement goals. Although every state now has a bully prevention policy or law, 90 percent of the states are focused on the following two terribly unhelpful goals: identifying the "bully" and disciplining or punishing the "bully." We know that only focusing on identifying, reporting, and criminalizing is not helpful. In fact, it inadvertently furthers the socially unjust "high school to prison pipeline."[35]

There is dramatic and growing interest in school climate and SEL-informed policy at the state and district levels. In 2011 there were 24 state school climate policies, and in 2017 there were 34. School climate policy in the US focuses on the school environment and how it is supporting schoolwide patterns that foster students feeling safe, supported, and engaged. In 2011 there were 48 pre-K SEL policies and one K–12 SEL policy that focused on learning standards.[36] In 2017, all 50 states had pre-K SEL policies, and eight had K–12 policies, and there are more than a dozen states that are now developing SEL-informed policy. SEL policies are focused on learning standards or information and grade-by-grade guidelines for what students should know and be able to do, socially and emotionally, as a result of educational instruction.

At the building, district, and state levels, there is very significant and growing interest in school climate, SEL, and bully/violence prevention efforts. The fact that two major bully prevention reports have underscored and supported the comprehensive school climate and SEL universal improvement efforts in conjunction with "at-risk" and targeted interventions is fueling interest in this iterative, data-driven, and fundamentally collaborative improvement effort.[37] Also, the Aspen Institute's National Commission on Social Emotional and Academic Development educational reports are also helping to raise national awareness about effective and sustainable SEL/character education and K–12 school climate improvement efforts.[38]

Our consultative experiences do not easily fit within or support these findings, however. We learn from and work with a growing number of educational leaders who are invested in understanding and furthering an intentional, strategic, and fundamentally collaborative process that promotes prosocial instruction and schoolwide efforts to foster safer, more supportive, and engaging climates for learning, as well as preventing the spectrum of experiences that undermine students feeling safe. Naturally, school leaders who invite us to learn and work with them are more or less knowledgeable about, and very motivated to further, *sustainable* school climate, SEL/character education improvement, and/or effective violence prevention efforts. There are several important challenges we have consistently seen in our consultative work. First, building and district leadership are essential. Yet, there is less, not more, effective and sustained education/professional development for future and current school leaders around school climate, SEL, and violence prevention. Second, we know from the work of James Comer, Tony Bryk, and others that creating a climate of trust among and between educators is an essential foundation for school improvement of any and all sorts.[39] Again, there is less rather than more pre- and in-service education that is focused on team building and the science of teamwork.[40] Although whole-school improvement efforts are, by definition, based on students, parents/guardians, school personnel, and even community members/leaders learning and working together, there is virtually no focus on what it means to develop effective intergenerational teams that are focused on school improvement. Finally, the NCLB-informed focus on annual assessments has inadvertently contributed to school leaders not adopting a multiyear school improvement framework that meaningfully supports iterative learning and to school leaders embracing the notion that "failure is the foundation for learning."[41]

STRATEGIES

Since the late 1990s, there has been a pronounced focus on evidence-based educational, as well as risk-prevention and health promotion/improvement, programs and strategies. In a number of ways this has been important. In the US there are "approved lists" of evidence-based improvement strategies (e.g., Blueprints, the Departments of Education and Justice, What Works Clearinghouse). These approved improvement strategies have been problematic in two important ways. First, until very recently, the primary focus of improvement efforts has been curricular based. As a result, there was less focus on the essential schoolwide improvement goals (e.g., district-level policy; codes of conduct/school rules; an understanding of "shared values" and/or a "vision" about the desired kind of school; leadership development; measurement practices that recognize and support social, emotional, and civic as well as academic aspects of student learning and school life) that complement and support instructional improvement efforts. Second, until very recently, certain curricular and other improvement strategies were "approved" only if they had undergone randomized controlled experimental study. As valuable as these rigorous methods are, there is a growing body of research findings that underscore how school improvement efforts are inherently complicated, multifaceted, and continually evolving. What may be helpful in a controlled study does not necessarily work effectively in the complicated and "messy" life of schools dealing with anywhere between four and fifteen new improvement initiatives. Interestingly, other countries (e.g., Japan, Sweden) have moved away from insisting on evidence-based programs and toward adopting teacher- and/or administration-driven initiatives designed to support change throughout the school as a system.

Today, there is a growing understanding that school climate and SEL improvement efforts have significant and positive implications for violence prevention efforts. School climate–informed research has shown that positive school climate improvement efforts are associated with effective prevention of bully/victim/bystander behavior and high school dropout prevention, as well as enhanced school violence prevention, healthy and connected relationships, student learning and achievement, and higher teacher retention rates.[42]

As a result of these findings, the Department of Education, the CDC, and the Institute for Educational Sciences have endorsed or supported school climate reform as the single-most-effective prevention strategy for bully/victim/bystander behavior and high school dropouts.[43] Research has shown that universal school-based SEL informed improvement efforts promote helpful attitudes about self, others, and school; positive classroom behavior and student achievement; and fewer conduct problems.[44]

Our consultative experiences underscore several overlapping trends. There is very significant and growing interest in school climate improvement, SEL, and effective bully prevention efforts.[45] This means that there is growing interest in understanding the range of instructional and schoolwide improvement strategies. There is also a growing interest in practical and/or district improvement models or road maps.

Although there is growing interest in schoolwide improvement strategies, there is still a primary focus on instruction. And there is also a continuing and terribly problematic focus on punishment; too often building and district leaders rely on disciplinary/punitive methods of managing disruptive and bullying behaviors. In addition, too often school leaders continue to believe that they can and should only focus on academic achievement "this year," undermining a longer-term iterative framework.

MEASUREMENTS

The Every Student Succeeds Act is positive in several important ways. First, it mandates that all states measure a "nonacademic" aspect of student learning and/or school life. Most states will use rates of chronic absenteeism (absent for fifteen or more days in a school year) as their metric, while others will use school climate surveys that recognize student, parent, and school personnel voices on a range of safety, relationship, teaching and learning, and environmental issues.

The 2011–17 policy scan revealed that there are several major challenges with regard to measurement. First, there are a range of school climate–informed measurement practices due to the lack of consensus about how to define both school climate and an effective school climate improvement process. Bullying-related measurement is largely and problematically focused on reporting, which is linked to "consequences" and punishment for the "bully." This is profoundly unhelpful and socially unjust.

Educators and researchers are in the midst of considering how to best evaluate students' social and emotional learning. There is a range of ways the twelve states that have K–12 standards recommend SEL-informed measurement practices. Most are grounded in delineating indicators that support teacher observations (with or without checklists) and understandings about social emotional learning at the classroom level. Several states underscore the importance of using multiple sources of data without detailing what this means practically. There is a consensus that SEL-informed student measures are helpful formatively but are not ready to be used as measures of accountability.

Our impression is that school and district leaders are generally not thinking about fidelity informed concerns. And, much more often than not, academic, behavioral, school climate and other sources of data are only seen and reviewed by school leaders. Measurement findings are not being used to engage youth, parents and colleagues to collaboratively learn together, to compare current findings with our "shared vision" of what kind of school we want ours to be and/or to support inter-generational school improvement efforts.

Our consultative experiences underscore the important and widespread interest in school climate and SEL-informed measures. More and more school leaders appreciate that they can and need to integratively consider academic, behavioral, and school climate–informed measures.[46]

IMPROVEMENT TRENDS

It is difficult to understand the nature of school safety improvement trends in the US for several reasons. First, reports from educators about the prevalence of bullying are not reliable. Education leaders fear that if they report too many instances of bullying they, or their schools, will be penalized. Second, a number of experiences that undermine students feeling safe are not measured at all.[47]

There are indications that homicides and serious crime have been decreasing over time.[48] Yet, rates of youth suicide are on the rise, with the largest increase, a rate that has doubled, between 2008 and 2017among young girls aged ten to twenty-four. Moderate to high rates of sexual violence against youth are also prevalent. The 2011 Youth Risk Behavior Survey, a national survey of students in grades 9–12, found a lifetime reported prevalence of unwanted physically forced sexual intercourse of 11.8 percent for female students and 4.5 percent for male students.[49] Four years later, the rates were quite similar, with 11.3 percent of females and 3.5 percent of males in US schools (grades 9–12) reporting physically forced sexual intercourse at some point during their childhood or adolescence, and 15.2 percent of female and 4.3 percent of males reporting that they had been forced to do "sexual things" (e.g., kissing, touching, or physically forced to have sexual intercourse) in the twelve months before the survey.[50]

Despite high rates of sexual harassment and prevalence of homophobic language in our schools, teachers and other school personnel often feel ill-equipped to address the problem, reporting a lack of professional development and support in this area.[51] Educators need to understand that sexual harassment comes in various forms, from physical (e.g., being "pantsed" or forced to do something sexual) to nonphysical (e.g., homophobic verbal harassment, sexual commentary). They also need to monitor areas where sexual harassment is most likely to take place, such as in hallways and classrooms. The US Department of Education's Office of Civil Rights notes the legal obligations of schools to protect their students from gendered harassment under Title IX.[52] In accordance, school districts must consistently enforce policies around sexual harassment and provide training and guidelines for how to deal with incidents and what to do when a student reports being sexually harassed.

There are indications that the prevalence of bullying and related behaviors have decreased from 2005 to 2015 showing the greatest improvements in school climate and reductions in bullying.[53] However, this study did not include surveys of youth with disabilities or in alternative school settings, which are highly vulnerable populations for victimization.[54] Thus, results should be viewed with caution.

RECOMMENDATIONS

The following school improvement recommendations for teachers and school and district leaders grow out of our trend analysis.

Understandings

Five questions have the potential to further helpful understandings about school safety for classroom, school, and district leaders:

- What is the spectrum of experience that undermines students feeling safe?
- What are effective and sustainable violence prevention efforts?
- When students' misbehave, what are they communicating?
- What can we do to foster a community of Upstanders, people who not only notice others who are hurting or being hurt but who also struggle to "do the right thing"?
- How can we embrace the notion that learning and school improvement is an ongoing, iterative process?

It is most helpful to support authentic conversations around these questions with peers and, potentially, students and their parents/guardians. When students, parents, and school personnel are all thinking about these and related foundational questions about safety, they have the potential to become a team, a school community that is learning and working together. Teamwork is the essential foundation for transformative school improvement efforts.

Measurement

There are three essential questions which shape measurement practices that will potentially enhance students feeling and being safe:

- What are nonacademic measures we can use to complement and extend our current academic and behavioral measurement practices?
- How can and will we use measurement findings to support engagement, meaningful learning, and revised school improvement plans?
- How can we make measurement a part of a meaningful and iterative process of continuous learning and school improvement?

Measurement is just one step in the school improvement process. Administering nonacademic surveys is an opportunity to engage students, parents, and school personnel in a process of learning and developing and enacting intergenerational school improvement efforts. School leaders also need to actively consider how to develop multiyear improvement cycles. The National Center on Safe and Supportive Learning Environments has curated a helpful compendium of scientifically sound school climate surveys.[55] Also, in another study we summarize other school climate informed measures (e.g. readiness, process and community scales) that complement student/parent/school personnel school climate surveys.[56] And CASEL issued a compendium of individual, student SEL-informed measures in 2019.[57]

Disciplinary Practice

Policy leaders need to provide detailed disciplinary and classroom management guidelines that support learning and school engagement rather than reporting, punishment, and disengagement. Policy leaders need to understand and use the empirical findings that have grown out of twenty-plus years of empirical research on helpful disciplinary and classroom management practices. These research findings show that punitive practices and the criminalization of students support the socially unjust "high school to prison pipeline."

There is now a robust set of policy and practice guidelines that support helpful disciplinary practice in schools and school-justice partnerships that promote learning and higher graduation rates.[58] There are toolkits and case studies that will potentially support classroom, school, and district leaders in aligning disciplinary practice with research findings.[59]

Implementation

We offer three sets of school improvement recommendations.

First, all policy and practice leaders need to learn about the growing body of implementation science findings.[60] The important learning, policy, and practice recommendations from the UCLA Center for Mental Health in Schools complements and supports implementation science as well as virtually all prosocial educational, risk prevention, and health/mental health promotion efforts.[61] Educational policy needs to recognize and support this fundamentally important body of research that sheds light on what works with regard to sustainable school improvement efforts. Importantly, this includes supporting school and district leaders in being clear about their short-term and multiyear improvement goals in three ways: (1) systemically, such as through district-level policy review and reform, by utilizing school climate–/SEL-informed metrics, by understanding the school communities' "shared vision" and/or shared values, by ensuring that SEL-/character education–informed teaching and learning is a schoolwide practice; (2) instructionally, such as by being a helpful role model, using disciplinary practices that support learning rather than punishment, developing a pedagogy that is designed to promote social, emotional, and academic learning as well as curriculum; and/or (3) relationally, such as by fostering more connected teacher-student, adult-adult and student-

student relationships.[62] Understanding how to be an effective member of a team encourages learning and improvement in virtually all of these areas. Surprisingly, there has been very little conversation about the science and practice of effective teamwork in K–12 education.[63]

Second, implementation-informed policy must explicitly support youth voice and engagement, as well as intergenerational school improvement efforts. A growing body of research suggests that intergenerational efforts are one of the most important steps school leaders can take in setting in motion improvement processes that are actually transformational.[64] There are numerous examples that illustrate the transformational power of supporting youth *at the center* of policy and practice improvement efforts.[65]

Third, three overlapping sets of research findings should shape future school climate, SEL, and bully prevention policy and practice improvement efforts:

- *The most effective ways to support SEL- and school climate–informed improvement efforts as well as deal with bullying are built on a whole-school approach.*[66] All educators and other school personnel, students, and parents need to develop a shared vision of what kind of school they want theirs to be, as well as action plans, procedures, and ways of communicating that support the positive shared goals and address barriers to learning in an iterative, data-driven, and fundamentally collaborative manner.
- *Creating a welcoming, supportive, engaging, and positive school climate; intentionally integrating SEL into instructional improvement efforts; and understanding and addressing the challenges (e.g., bully/victim/bystander behavior) that undermine these efforts promotes effective risk prevention and health/mental health promotion efforts.*[67]
- *A positive school climate, SEL, academic achievement, and violence prevention are interconnected.*[68] Longitudinal studies and comprehensive research reviews show that a positive school climate as well as SEL can contribute to better mathematics, reading, and literacy outcomes. This research suggests that schools which emphasize academics *and* include efforts to improve school climate and prevent violence have increases in academic achievement as well as significant reductions in bullying. Schools that only focus on improving the climate or reducing violence do not seem to significantly raise academic achievement.

PART II

COMMENTARIES ON INTERNATIONAL TRENDS

CHAPTER 13

REFLECTIONS ON SCHOOL SAFETY INTERVENTIONS ACROSS CULTURES

PETER K. SMITH

THIS COLLECTION OF eleven country case studies on school safety provides a very valuable overview of actions being taken across the globe on five continents—North America, South America, Europe, Asia, and Australasia. Contributions from Africa are missing; there is a lower volume of research coming from African countries, although some relevant work is being done, for example in South Africa.[1] Internationally, the topic has had a relatively low profile until the 1980s or 1990s. This historical trend has been explicitly documented for the topic of school bullying.[2] However, the last thirty to forty years of research and action on school safety issues have greatly raised awareness, produced a lot of research and many publications, and also resulted in legislative actions, resources for schools, and a range of relevant interventions. These have had some impact.

The evidence for such impact may again be clearest in the case of school bullying, where, for example, the Health Behaviour of School-Aged Children (HBSC) surveys have shown some declines in school victimization rates in many (not all) countries over a twenty-year period, a trend supported by other evidence.[3] This is encouraging; but the reductions are often relatively modest, and as the evidence from the chapters in this book shows, levels of school safety are often not as good as they should be and as students, parents and teachers would wish and expect them to be.

In this commentary I discuss some thoughts around when and why the topic becomes an important issue, the scope of the problem, the types and range of initiatives taken to improve school safety, and some issues around cultural differences and the extent to which knowledge in this area can be transferred from one country to another.

WHEN AND WHY DOES SCHOOL SAFETY BECOME AN IMPORTANT ISSUE?

What drives concern and action about school safety and topics such as school bullying? What is often needed is a combination of incidents which raise public awareness, media take-up that ensures wide publicity, and research findings that can back up the generality of concern. This needs to be coupled with some political willingness to further relevant actions through legislation and/or financial support.

Unfortunately, the incidents that may trigger concerted actions are often tragic ones. This was the case in Norway, where three suicides in 1982 were the initial stimulus for the first nationwide campaign against school bullying in 1983.[4] In Japan, too, suicides due to *ijime* had a dramatic effect.[5] This was also the case in the US, where the Columbine school shootings had a huge impact. However, the trigger might also be a student demonstration, as in France, or findings on the prevalence of school bullying, as in the UK.[6] In all these cases, the incidents or events were highlighted in the media. For example, in the UK, the research findings on the prevalence of school bullying led to headlines like "Is Britain the Bullying Capital of Europe?" which led to questions in Parliament and resources being allocated to antibullying work.[7] Even if not initially noticed, research findings can reinforce the public awareness message coming from other events. In Norway, the research findings already produced by Olweus on school bullying, demonstrated that the suicides were not isolated events but evidence of many victims suffering in school.[8]

Another impetus for action can come from charities and public organizations, which can act as a focus for parent and teacher concerns, as well as support websites, phone helplines, and resources to help children, young people, and adults. In the UK, organizations like the Antibullying Alliance, Kidscape, YouthWorks Consulting, and Ditch the Label have carried out these functions.[9]

THE SCOPE OF THE PROBLEM

School safety is, in essence, a positive concept, or at least it is an absence of negatives. In a safe school environment, students can follow the school curriculum, socialize with peers, and enjoy the various extracurricular opportunities that schools offer. A related, slightly broader, concept is school climate. According to Gregory and Cornell, two aspects of school climate are important for a school that is both safe and effective.[10] The first is high disciplinary and academic expectations for students, which they refer to as the "demandingness" or structure of the school climate. The second is the responsiveness to or supportiveness of teacher-student relationships, such that teachers and other school staff members interact with students in a respectful, caring, and helpful manner. The combination of these two aspects makes for an "authoritative school climate." There is evidence, at least from the US, that victimization rates are less in such schools.[11] A similar perspective on the importance of school climate comes from Israel. Also, the term *convivencia* in Spain and Spanish-speaking countries, as in Chile and Colombia,) emphasizes the positive aspects of getting on with each other at school.

However, concern about school safety almost inevitably often focuses on what can disrupt it. These can be various ways in which relationships, and also school property or rules, are disrespected, such as through abuse, harassment, bullying, violence. In Sweden, the term abusive behavior is used. School bullying has come to be a very substantial focus of research and action in many countries over the last two decades (e.g., Italy). If bullying is understood to be a "systematic abuse of power," then it could cover many forms of abuse and harassment, including sexual harassment, racial harassment, other kinds of bias bullying, repeated aggression involving teachers and students, and even abuse in the home, which may carry over into school.[12] However the definition recently adopted by the US Centers for Disease Control and Prevention is narrower: "Bullying is any unwanted aggressive behavior(s) by another youth or group of youths who are not siblings or current dating partners that involves an observed or perceived power imbalance and is repeated multiple times or is highly likely to be repeated."[13] This would make "teacher-student bullying" a misnomer, although it is an important, if under-researched, topic of investigation.[14]

Bullying is an Anglo-Saxon term, and there are issues of translation that affect definitions of this and related terms, such as *school climate*. This is thoroughly discussed in relation to terms such as *ijime* and *bouryoku* in the Japan chapter. Ijime is similar in meaning to *bullying*, but not identical. The chapter on China includes a discussion of bullying and laws addressing it, but it would be relevant to know what Chinese term for *bullying* is used in these laws. Zhang, Chen, and Chen state that *qifu* is the closest Chinese term, although they mention several others. Qifu is defined as "a kind of behaviour to intimidate, oppress, or embarrass others with an arrogant attitude and in unreasonable ways."[15] Again, it is similar to *bullying* but not identical, and Zhang and colleagues comment that qifu may underrepresent social exclusion types of bullying.

THE TYPES AND RANGE OF INITIATIVES TAKEN TO IMPROVE SCHOOL SAFETY

If awareness and concern have been raised, and at least some political support is forthcoming, what can be done to improve school safety and reduce bullying and violence? The case study chapters in this book give a considerable range and variety of actions. Drawing from ecological systems theory, we can think of these at various levels—notably, at the society, school, class, family, and individual levels.[16]

At the societal level, there may be national laws enacted about bullying, harassment, and/or cyberbullying (sometimes at the state level within a national federation, as in Australia and the US). These obviously signify importance given to the issue and can be a recourse for victims, parents, and schools. There is some evidence from the US of how such laws may impact rates of bullying. Hatzenbuehler and colleagues found that, in twenty-five states, having some legislative component to antibullying laws was correlated with reduced rates of being both bullied and cyberbullied.[17] Using a longitudinal design, Ramirez and colleagues examined victim rates in Iowa in 2005, just before an antibullying law was introduced, and again in 2008 and 2010 and found an increase in victim rates in 2008, possibly due to increased reporting, but then a decrease by 2010.[18]

Laws generally target certain abusive behaviors but can be used in other ways. For example, in the UK it has been a legal requirement since 1998 for schools to have some form of antibullying policy. Such a policy is typically a written document (also available on the school website) setting out what bullying is, that it is not acceptable, what anyone who experiences or sees bullying should do, what actions the school will take if it happens, and what records will be kept. Studies in the UK have found that policies do vary greatly in content and quality, and there is only slight evidence that this correlates with school victim rates.[19] Nevertheless, a school antibullying policy can be seen as an important first step in setting out the school's aims and in providing a recourse for victims and their parents. A policy may, of course, be broader than just bullying and cover behavior and school climate issues more generally.

Resources for schools can be provided at national or local levels. In England, the Department of Education issued the course packs *Don't Suffer in Silence* and, later, *Safe to Learn*, which gave advice and practical steps mainly for teachers but also for parents and students. Currently, organizations like the Anti-Bullying Alliance, among others, provide a range of useful resources around bullying and school safety on their websites.

In the UK, these resources are available for schools, and each school chooses which curriculum program or interventions it wishes to use. There is an expectation of a whole-school approach (and a behavior or antibullying policy), but within that there can be great variation in actions taken, kinds of sanctions used, etc. This could be called an à la carte *approach*, in contrast to a *set menu approach*. The set menu approach is exemplified by some well-established antibullying programs, such as the Olweus Bullying Prevention Program (OBPP) started in Norway, KiVa in Finland, ViSC in Austria, Steps to Respect in the US, and Friendly Schools in Australia. These programs have a well-defined set of components and operate at whole-school, class, and individual levels.

There can be pros and cons to either approach. In an à la carte approach, schools can choose those components most suitable for their needs and philosophy, and they may feel more ownership of their antibullying actions, rather than having to fit into a preexisting framework. Yet, programs such as OBPP and KiVa are ready to use, teachers can be trained in them, and they have had replicated success in reducing rates of victimization. The divergence between these two approaches can, however, be overemphasized, as schools and teachers tend to adapt any programs that are presented to them. Flygare and colleagues compared eight antibullying programs in Sweden and found that all thirty-nine schools studied that were supposedly using one particular program were actually using components from more than one program.[20]

The kinds of actions or components available, whether in a program or available to choose from a range of resources, are greatly varied. Some are preventative, or proactive, laying a foundation of respect in interpersonal relationships. Some are more reactive, are ways to respond when bullying or violence happens. Both proactive and reactive strategies are needed in any comprehensive approach.

Proactive strategies could include a wide range of curriculum approaches, such as education for citizenship, social and emotional learning, social skills training, assertiveness training, e-safety curricula, and so on. These can have some impact(see especially the Israel and US chapters).[21] Outside the classroom, an interesting and well-supervised playground area can be helpful.[22] Peer support schemes can be useful, given certain provisos.[23] Peer supporters can act proactively (e.g., facilitating prosocial and inclusive playground activities) or reactively (e.g., in peer counseling when approached by students with difficulties). Similarly, the existence of peer support schemes may encourage a wider peer climate of supporting victims or the changing of bystanders to "Upstanders."[24]

Reactive strategies also have a wide range, from more punitive sanctions, to serious talks, to restorative approaches, to support group methods that avoid directly sanctioning the perpetrator. This spectrum of responses is clear from the chapters in this book—for example, from an emphasis on "punishment" (China), to both "punitive" and "formative" approaches (Chile), to "mediation" and "reconciliation" (Colombia) and "rehabilitation" (Canada). There is continuing debate about the relative effectiveness of these approaches, but there is some consensus that a consistent approach of whatever kind is important, as compared with ignoring incidents or providing ad hoc responses.[25]

While most actions and interventions center around actions by school staff, clearly the role of parents is important. Parents can support school safety and antibullying initiatives and liaise with schools if they have concerns about a child's behavior. In turn, schools can involve parents through information in newsletters or websites and/or parent-teacher meetings. Axford and colleagues provide a review of issues around the involving parents in antibullying work.[26] Parents have a particular role in internet safety and cyberbullying in terms of knowing about and advising on their child's internet use, which is probably best done by concerned involvement but without being overly restrictive.[27]

Another aspect to bear in mind is what has been called student "voice." Australian colleagues in particular have called for initiatives to involve students themselves more in decisions that concern them, as well as in research about them.[28] This is particularly relevant for work on e-safety and cyberbullying, where students may well know more about various aspects, including the latest forms of cyberbullying, then teachers and parents do. With colleagues from other European countries, I have been involved in the project Blurred Lives, where we have engaged fourteen- to sixteen-year-old students through focus groups and quality circles to get their opinions and ideas about resources and advice on internet safety.[29] While internet safety is not strictly a matter of school safety, there is considerable overlap. For example, cyberbullying and schoolyard bullying are often related.[30]

Other aspects important for effective and sustainable interventions include early involvement of stakeholders in the society and community, adequate preparation for teachers and other staff, follow-up after the initial launch of any new approach, and proper evaluation of the extent of success of any intervention. Student-reported data on a national basis is invaluable, but it is only available in some countries—Australia (for mental health and well-being but not bullying), Israel, Italy (until recently), and Norway—but not in the UK, for example. Also, increasingly necessary to persuade policy makers will be evidence of the cost benefits of intervention work.[31] Issues around maximizing the practical impact of antibullying interventions in a number of countries are discussed in a recent edited book.[32]

SOME ISSUES AROUND CULTURAL DIFFERENCES AND KNOWLEDGE TRANSFER

In a number of cases, programs have been shared across countries. For example, the OBPP, KiVa, and the Viennese Social Competence programs have been used in several other countries beyond the initiating countries. While these have generally been in Western countries, there has also been influence from Western countries on, for example, Japan.[33] It is important that we learn and profit from the experiences of others cross-nationally as well as within any particular country. There are obvious benefits of learning from the successes and failures of others. Indeed, this book aims to facilitate this kind of sharing of cross-national expertise.

However, there are also obstacles to taking programs and expertise from one country to another, namely translation of terms and cultural values. Unless sharing the same language, a program being used in a country different from the initiating country will need translating. Much of this may be straight-forward, but terms for concepts, such as *bullying*, will not be identical in dif-ferent languages. Thus, what is considered as being or not being *bullying*, or the cognate term used in translation, may vary too. This has been demon-strated in studies using the stick figure cartoon test.[34] As one example, a car-toon with the caption "The rest of the team won't let Millie take part in a competition, even though she is one of the best players, because she is from a lower year group" was described as "bullying" by a majority (around 75 per-cent) of fourteen-year-old students in England and Canada. However, this fell to 46 percent of students in China who described it as "qifu" and as low as 29 percent of students in Japan who described it as "ijime." There were also substantial differences for situations around severe social exclusion (very often see as ijime) and for cartoons around gender discrimination in games (often see as bullying in England, but much less frequently in many other countries, at least in 2005–06).

Thus, objectively, the same situation in terms of behaviors may be inter-preted differently by students in different countries. In the case of being ex-cluded from the team because of age, we may think of the extent to which hierarchy (by age or in other ways) may be accepted in some societies more than in others—in Japan and China more than in England and Canada, for example. Yet, sensitivity to social exclusion might be related more to the individualism-collectivism dimension. These findings clearly have implica-tions for how such situations are dealt with in different countries.

The EU Kids Online team produced a model for looking at country vari-ations in internet risks, which also is suitable for looking at school safety is-sues and bullying.[35] Adopting an ecological perspective, the model includes factors about the individual, their social network (parents, peers, school), and also broader country factors. Their country level factors include five aspects:

- cultural values, such as power distance, tradition, benevolence, individualism vs. collectivism;
- education system, such as levels by age, grade retention, class groupings, school and class size, structure of school day, break times and supervision;
- technological infrastructure, such as penetration of mobile phones, smart phones, and internet;

- regulatory framework, such as school policies, legal aspects, antibullying initiatives); and
- socioeconomic stratification, such as income, internet access, health, crime).

All five aspects are important to consider in the context of transferability, or adaptation, of programs from one country to another. Cultural values are clearly important in how different kinds of "possibly bullying" situations are perceived. They may also impact the prevalence of bullying, as well as the types of behavior recognized as such. Hofstede, Hofstede, and Minkov proposed six main dimensions of cultural values: power distance, individualism-collectivism, masculinity-femininity, uncertainty avoidance, long-term orientation, indulgence vs. restraint.[36] Predictions can be made about the influence of these on victimization.[37]

Theoretically, collectivist societies might be expected to have lower rates of victimization, because in these societies group harmony is emphasized and conflict should be avoided.[38] However, using data from the HBSC surveys, Smith and Robinson found that overall there is *less* victimization in individualist societies, but only in more recent years.[39] They advanced the hypothesis that regulatory frameworks and resources have reduced victimization primarily in more individualist societies during this century. If this is so, as well as other evidence on the success of interventions, it points to the importance of continuing efforts to improve school safety and student well-being.[40]

The chapters in this book typically end with recommendations for policy makers, educators, and school communities. Increasingly, such recommendations can be based on practical experience and research findings. Students and teachers deserve a safe environment at school, without exception. There will be successes and failures in this endeavor, but the cause is worthwhile, and the efforts described in this book can help move it forward.

CHAPTER 14

IMPLEMENTING SOCIAL AND EMOTIONAL INNOVATIONS TO ELIMINATE BULLYING

DEAN L. FIXSEN, KAREN A. BLASE, AND MONISA AIJAZ

IT IS RECOGNIZED that experiences of school violence like bullying and mean and disrespectful behavior produce feelings of being unsafe physically, socially, emotionally, and intellectually. These experiences are interactive processes involving individuals and groups. The social-emotional development that is the solution to address them is an equally interactive process. In interactions, the behavior of each person influences the behavior of the other person. Thus, teacher and student attempts to intervene in helpful ways to influence those involved are influenced themselves by the responses and the social environment.

Given the interactive and mutual influence, the challenges of changing the behavior of teachers and those involved at the receiving and the giving end of these experiences must be met with thoughtful and effective support from schools and education systems. This is the domain of implementation practice and science. Experts who wrote the chapters in this book have provided ample evidence regarding what to do and why those things need to be done. For example, table 14.1 lists many of the recommendations offered by these international author-experts for what teachers and students should do to prevent or constructively respond to various forms of school violence. If a country has ten thousand or ten million teachers, how will each teacher know what to do and how to do it effectively to end bullying and other forms of school violence and establish a healthy social-emotional environment for

TABLE 14.1 International recommendations for teacher responses to various forms of school violence

Recommendations to improve social-emotional learning across countries
• For teachers, it is helpful to have conversations with students and guardians about the following questions: (1) What undermines student safety? (2) What are effective violence prevention efforts? (3) What is the meaning behind misbehaving? (4) How can you create a community of upstanders?
• School improvement practices should take place systemically, instructionally, and relationally. Integrating school climate, SEL, and restorative practices requires careful implementation. Implementation should also be informed by students and all other members of the school community and take an approach that integrates SEL, positive school climate, academic achievement, and violence prevention efforts, as this integrative approach is best for risk prevention and health/mental health promotion.
• Teachers need be more aware of school and school district's *ijime* policies. Also, teachers need to collaborate more with other teachers to discuss survey results and improvement efforts.
• School policies need to involve all members in a school community and need to be implemented on a local level. It is suggested that teachers pay close attention to students and not neglect even petty aggressions in the classroom. It is recommended that discipline should be neither repressive nor too relaxed.
• Teacher development should be focused on (1) creating classrooms that promote equality of respect and recognition and more horizontal student-teacher relations; (2) developing practices that promote student voice and decision-making; (3) restorative discipline; and (4) integrating creative mediums for students to express their thoughts and feelings.
• Teachers should pay more attention to each student's needs and to student dynamics to prevent various forms of school violence. They also can provide more targeted education that includes making students aware of how they can cope with bullying.
• Use fewer punitive practices and encourage school staff to be involved in peer-to-peer methods.

students and staff? What is missing are recommendations concerning *how* to do what needs to be done.

If millions of teachers are to change their approaches to social and emotional development, then schools must support teachers in multiple ways. Table 14.2 lists many of the recommendations for changes in schools made by the authors of the country case studies. There is a laudable emphasis on leadership, parent and community involvement, and data collection and the use of data to guide improvement. What is missing is *how* to support teachers so they can realize the ambitions of each school.

Of course, schools operate in the context of education systems and social norms. Many of the authors recommend changes in national policy. Some of these recommendations are listed in table 14.3. While the recommendations

TABLE 14.2 Recommended changes in schools to support healthy student development

• Administer nonacademic surveys to monitor school improvement and use the results to involve other school members in the improvement process. Principals also should implement multiyear improvement cycles to create and sustain intergenerational change.
• School leaders must go against the ideology that schools should only focus on academics and promote learning about life skills in their classes. It is important that principals foster a positive school climate based on democratic values and a "shared responsibility for a positive daily atmosphere."
• Principals need to strengthen school safety programs and work on communicating ideas behind bullying prevention to every child.
• Recommendations include increasing parental and community involvement
• A whole-school approach is necessary for changes in school climate. For principals and superintendents, it is important to note that the effectiveness of prevention programs often is determined by the quality of leadership, since leasers help actualize the quality of implementation.

TABLE 14.3 Recommendations for changes in national policies

State/Nation	• Policy leaders should shift to disciplinary guidelines that are more restorative than punitive.
	• On the policy level, some recommendations are to promote transparency and ensure accountability in regard to school safety; involve other stakeholders (state, public-private sector, etc.) in collaborating on strategies, interventions, and data sharing; and evaluate a three-tiered approach to prevention and intervention.
	• Increase the government's role by passing bullying laws to promote prevention and to ensure appropriate consequences for bullying and other forms of school violence. Also, schools, families, and society should come together to create a three-in-one system of prevention and control.
	• Create a national database for informing policy and practice
	• Identify and test evidence-based programs that reduce bullying and increase mental health and well-being.
	• Include the Bill of Rights principle (the duty to educate and protect minors, whether they are victims, perpetrators, or witnesses) into educational legislation to make this commitment a reality.
Profession	• Bullying prevention models should be incorporated into teacher training. Teacher training can be used to spread awareness, recognize different types of bullying, increase collaboration, enhance classroom climate, foster socio-affective competence, and mobilize bystanders.
	• Strengthen preservice and in-service teacher training.

provide some guidance for policy makers, they do not provide a pathway for policy to support changes in schools so they can support changes in teacher behavior, although the suggestions for changes in teacher professional preparation is a nod in that direction.

IMPLEMENTATION-INFORMED RECOMMENDATIONS

Missing from the recommendations made by the authors of the country case studies is any reference to the importance of implementation supports for innovations so that goals can be realized for students. Innovations include interventions by teachers and schools to encourage healthy social-emotional development and an end to bullying. Innovations are, by definition, new ways of work in education and elsewhere. To use an innovation, teachers and school staff must be able to learn how to engage in the new ways of work in practice in classrooms and schools. New ways of work are disruptive to teachers and school staff, and organizations must change in subtle or radical ways to accommodate and support the quality use of an innovation by teachers and school staff. Without attention to implementation factors, the science-to-service gap continues to grow, and potentially effective innovations languish while problems persist.[1]

Initiating and managing disruptive change in practices and organizations is the work of implementation. Implementation practice and science has been summarized and organized in the Active Implementation Frameworks and is generalizable across all human services, including education.[2] The foundation of implementation of any innovation is support for changes in practice. For social and emotional learning to occur as recommended, teachers must change how they interact with students and others. The Active Implementation Drivers are specific to supporting behavior change at the teacher level: Competency Drivers, Organization Drivers, and Leadership Drivers.

Active Implementation Drivers

The Implementation Drivers are required to produce, sustain, and improve the effective and efficient use of innovations. A review and synthesis of the implementation evaluation literature provides strong evidence for the benefits of Active Implementation.[3] Experience and research continue to build on and expand the knowledge base.

The definition of *implementation* discriminates between *innovations* and *implementations*—an innovation is one thing, and an implementation is another thing altogether.[4] Like computer software and hardware, or serum and a syringe, while they are very different, they need to work together to produce reliable outcomes. The idea of evidence-based implementation methods is new. Practical assessments of the Implementation Drivers have been developed and tested.[5] The strong links between the Implementation Drivers assessment (fidelity of the use of the Drivers) and intervention assessment (fidelity of the use of an innovation) are being established in practice.[6]

The Active Implementation Drivers are shown in figure 14.1. An innovation is a new way of work that must be learned by those who will do the work (teachers and school staff). The Implementation Drivers triangle places fidelity at the top as the essential link between the Implementation Drivers and the innovation—that is, between implementation outcomes and using social-emotional and bullying intervention innovations to achieve desired outcomes. Innovation outcomes cannot be interpreted without knowing the fidelity with which an innovation is being delivered. Poor outcomes may be the result of an ineffective innovation or may be the result of an effective

FIGURE 14.1   The Implementation Drivers for developing practitioner competency, establishing hospitable organizations, and providing leadership for using innovations with fidelity and good outcomes

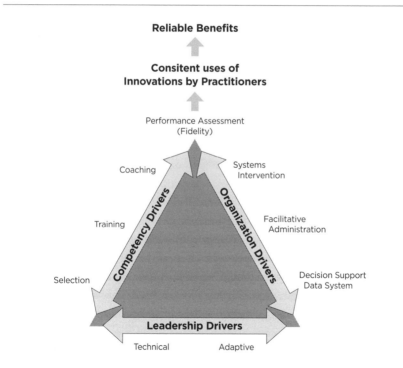

Source: Used with permission from Dean Fixsen and Karen Blase.

innovation used poorly in practice (with low fidelity).[7] Without a measure of fidelity, there is no way to attribute poor (or good) outcomes to an innovation.[8] High fidelity is the outcome of using the Implementation Drivers well, and it results in consistent uses of the innovation and reliable benefits to recipients. A description in a methods section of an article is no substitute for a measure of the innovation (independent variable) as it is used in practice (fidelity).

The Competency Drivers illustrate how teachers and school staff are introduced to an innovation and are supported in their efforts to use it as intended (with fidelity). To be repeatable and sustainable, the uses of an innovation by teachers and school staff and the uses of the Competency Drivers almost always require changes in organization (school) roles, functions, and structures. The Organization Drivers describe how school leaders and staff sense and measure the need for change (Decision Support Data System) and make changes (Facilitative Administration, System Intervention) to fully support teacher and school staff uses of innovations (with fidelity). The third side of the triangle is the Leadership Drivers to initiate the uses of innovations, support the constant changes required to align organization components with intended outcomes, and constructively cope with unintended outcomes, adaptive challenges, and wicked problems that arise.

All three sets of Drivers need to be in place and fully functioning to produce and sustain consistent uses of innovations by teachers and school staff and, therefore, to produce reliable outcomes for students, the intended recipients of an innovation. After a few years, the Implementation Drivers and the innovation practices become the new ways of work in an education system and, eventually, become the standard ways of work.

Integrated and Compensatory Nature of Active Implementation Drivers

Organizations using the Active Implementation Frameworks are learning organizations. They use innovations on purpose, they support the use of innovations on purpose, they teach new teachers and staff members innovation and implementation best practices, they collect data on effectiveness and efficiency, and they use data to make better decisions, improve practices, and improve benefits. Teaching, learning, learning to learn, and improvement are hallmarks of a learning organization.[9]

Given the changing sociopolitical, economic, and cultural conditions in which education organizations operate, nothing is expected to stay the same.

Complexity theory points to the need to be aware of uncertainty and unexpected conditions in society, systems, and organizations.[10] To cope with "environments where change is imminent and frequent," Dooley suggests some general guidelines for organizations: "(a) create a shared purpose, (b) cultivate inquiry, learning, experimentation, and divergent thinking, (c) enhance external and internal interconnections via communication and technology, (d) instill rapid feedback loops for self-reference and self-control, (e) cultivate diversity, specialization, differentiation, and integration, (f) create shared values and principles of action, and (g) make explicit a few but essential structural and behavioral boundaries."[11]

The Implementation Drivers provide ways to respond purposefully and constructively to changes that are inevitable and to follow the guidelines listed by Dooley. Leadership Drivers, Competency Drivers, and Organization Drivers enhance one another in multiple ways in response to internal and external change and uncertainty. Implementation Teams "cultivate diversity, specialization, differentiation, and integration," as managers and leaders also conduct selection interviews and teach sections of training workshops and coaches and trainers also do fidelity assessments and data management, and so on. Decision Support Data Systems detect trends and "instill rapid feedback loops for self-reference and self-control." Systems Interventions "enhance external and internal interconnections via communication and technology." Leaders, managers, trainers, coaches, and fidelity assessors work together to "create a shared purpose" and "create shared values and principles of action." The use of data in action planning and Improvement Cycles helps to "cultivate inquiry, learning, experimentation, and divergent thinking." And the Active Implementation Frameworks "make explicit a few but essential structural and behavioral boundaries."[12]

The Implementation Drivers are integrated so that each supports the others. And they are compensatory in that a weakness in one (e.g., training) can be accommodated by strengthening others (e.g., coaching and fidelity assessment). Given the complexity of providing interaction-based services in capricious operating environments, the Active Implementation Frameworks provide a way to sense changes and a way to rapidly compensate for those changes without losing sight of the mission and goals. Using innovations as intended is the work of teachers and school staff. Using Implementation Drivers as intended is the work of the Implementation Team.

INTERACTION OF INNOVATIONS, CONTEXT, AND DRIVERS

In interaction-based education, thought needs to be put into how to use innovations in practice, and it is best to do this thinking before attempting to begin using an innovation. For example, table 14.4 shows the interaction between the context in which an innovation is used and the skills required to use an innovation. Innovations that significantly depart from standard practice and are used outside typical contexts likely will require more careful consideration and more precise use of the Competency, Organization, and Leadership Drivers. But innovations that are close to standard practice and within existing skill sets of typical teachers and school staff and conducted within a familiar context (e.g., typical classroom settings) may require less attention to the Implementation Drivers. In each quadrant, the goal is to support high-fidelity use of an innovation with good outcomes; the intensity and precision of implementation supports are adjusted to achieve the goal.

The relevance of implementation supports for social-emotional learning programs is described in detail by Oberle and colleagues.[13] The development of a shared vision and adequate resources (Leadership Drivers), providing support for social-emotional learning programs in the midst of other initiatives (Facilitative Administration), embedding ongoing professional development (Competency Drivers) to ensure quality instruction (Fidelity), aligning school and state policies to support social-emotional learning programs in every school (Systems Intervention), and continuously examining data to guide improvements in instruction and outcomes (Decision Support Data System) are recommendations made by these experts that point to using the Implementation Drivers to ensure full and effective uses of social-emotional learning programs.

TABLE 14.4 Support required for innovations of varying complexity

	Close to current skills	Requires new skills
Familiar context	Little departure from standard practice; less intensive support required	Significant departure from standard practice; more intensive support required
Unfamiliar context	Changes required in standard organization operating procedures; more intensive support required	Significant changes required in practitioner and organization behavior and operating procedures; very intensive support required

SUMMARY

Interventions to prevent or reduce the incidence of bullying and to promote healthy social-emotional development are badly needed in education settings around the world. The chapters in this volume provide excellent accounts of the extent of the problems and the initiatives under way or being considered to eliminate problems associated with various forms of school violence and its unwanted outcomes for students, families, and societies. This commentary brings attention to a missing and essential component when considering current and future initiatives: evidence-based implementation supports for evidence-based interventions in schools and education systems.

Students cannot benefit from interventions they do not experience. Supporting teachers as they learn and use evidence-based promotion and intervention practices is the work of the Implementation Drivers and the other components of the Active Implementation Frameworks.

CHAPTER 15

THE INTEGRATION OF LEARNING AND WELL-BEING AS THE NEXT FRONTIER IN WHOLE-SYSTEM CHANGE

MICHAEL FULLAN AND SANTIAGO RINCÓN-GALLARDO

THE CASES IN THIS BOOK broaden and deepen our knowledge about how student safety and well-being have been understood and pursued in a widely diverse set of countries in North America, South America, Europe, Asia, and Oceania. There are many important things that the cases, taken as a whole, reveal. The first is that student well-being has recently become an important concern for education leaders around the globe, with a few of the countries showcased, such as Sweden, having longer histories of advancing student well-being through education policy and practice. While there is wide variation in the historical and contextual factors that might have prompted a particular country to embrace student well-being as a core priority (e.g., a five-decade-long armed conflict in Colombia; student demonstrations in France in the 1990s; the complexity and diversity of cultural, religious, and ethnic affiliation in Israel), shifts toward broader understandings of and greater attention to student well-being are reported in each of the eleven cases featured in this book.

The second thing that the cases demonstrate is that there have been important shifts, across nations, in how student safety and well-being are understood and promoted—from a narrow focus on physical safety toward broader understandings that include the social and emotional dimensions of well-being. Some of the countries featured have shifted from punitive approaches focused on victim and perpetrator toward more holistic, restorative practices that involve the larger school community. In countries with some of the most sophisticated understandings of student well-being, such as Israel, an "ecological" perspective has been adopted, which looks at and deals with things such as bullying and connectedness as social-environmental, rather than merely individual, phenomena.

A third thing that the cases teach us is that there is wide variation in the extent and depth with which different education systems across the world have prioritized and intentionally pursued the promotion of student well-being in schools. At the most basic level there is, across all countries, growing awareness of the need to attend to the socioemotional dimensions of student safety and well-being, not merely the physical dimension. In the countries with the most advanced systemwide strategies to tackle violence in schools and promote student well-being, this awareness has translated into the development of comprehensive frameworks, detailed guidelines for policy and practice, and specific policies or programs to promote student safety and well-being in schools. For example, in countries such as Israel, Sweden, and France, student well-being has been incorporated as a central area of focus that schools are expected to include in their strategic plans.

All these developments are important and encouraging. At the same time, current times require a substantive revamp of the purpose and strategies of education systems, particularly around the well-being agenda. Of course, keeping students safe in schools is fundamental—and in countries like the United States it is urgent—but we will fail our children and youth if that is how high we set the bar. Effectively preparing younger generations to survive, thrive in, and change the world for the better requires a fundamental redefinition of the purpose and role of schools, particularly their role in fostering student well-being.

This book is a very important accomplishment in that it outlines the current international landscape on policy and practice to promote student safety and well-being in schools. With this landscape laid out, we feel compelled to push our collective thinking toward what we believe is the next frontier in systemwide student well-being. Here we stretch the thinking about and the policy and practice approaches to student safety and well-being offered in this important book. We use existing and emerging knowledge on educational change as a lens to identify five key conceptual or strategic gaps in the systemwide approaches to student well-being that have been designed and carried out so far.

FIVE GAPS

The Absence of Ill-Being versus Well-Being

The idea that well-being is the absence of ill-being—similar to the idea that peace is the absence of war—seems to be pervasive in many education policy circles around the world. To be sure, there are countries, including some featured in this book (e.g., Colombia, Sweden, Israel), that have adopted more holistic views on student well-being. In these countries, policies and guidelines have been created with the intention of simultaneously addressing the prevention of harm and proactively fostering well-being. In most cases, however, preventing and reacting to harm takes precedence over the positive development of well-being. To be fair, in a country like the United States, where school shootings have become painfully common and widespread, and where some of the most blatant forms of discrimination and violence are on the rise, simply keeping young people safe from harm in schools would be a tremendous accomplishment. Yet, keeping the bar this low would be a tremendous disservice to young people.

Looking across the cases in the book, it seems that *ill-being* has been more precisely defined and intentionally dealt with than *well-being*. Take, for example, the spectrum of biopsychosocially informed experiences that shape feeling safe presented in chapter 1, which organizes experiences on a spectrum that ranges from experiencing psychological harm due to a misunderstanding to the most extreme forms of physical harm (e.g., homicide, suicide, war). This spectrum offers precise and clearly defined levels of experiences that undermine students feeling safe. We could not help but notice the absence of a similarly detailed spectrum of student experiences *in the opposite direction*—that is, a spectrum of positive experiences that create a sense of safety and well-being among students. In broad strokes, this spectrum could range from absence of feeling unsafe (which would count as point zero on the spectrum of negative experiences) to experiences of *flow*, a mental state of total absorption into an activity of interest when the sense of time disappears.

To be sure, some countries featured, such as Sweden, Australia, Canada, and Israel, are grounding their policies and strategies for student well-being on the dual purpose of reducing and responding to experiences of harm while proactively cultivating positive experiences of student well-being. But our point is that these positive examples are treated throughout the book more as an add-on than as conceptually integrated with and complementary to the efforts aimed at reducing student ill-being. We see the development of a full spectrum of student experience, with increasing levels of both positive and negative experiences, as well as its use to shape and inform policies on student well-being, as an important conceptual next step.

The Learning/Well-Being Divide

In this book and the case studies that comprise it, student safety and well-being are conceptualized most prominently as a precondition for student learning, as something that needs to be guaranteed so that students can focus and concentrate on their schoolwork. Well-being and learning are seen, for the most part, as separate issues connected mostly on the grounds that you need the former in order to get the latter.

There is tremendous potential in the idea of integrating learning and well-being as a unified construct. This involves three major ideas. The first idea is that deep learning—understood as experiences of engaging the world and changing the world that foster key global competencies such as critical thinking, creativity, collaboration, communication, citizenship, and character—produces well-being. Full immersion in self-driven learning nurtures intrinsic motivation and thus contributes to the development of a sense of efficacy and fulfillment. Furthermore, in our work cultivating deep learning in over a thousand schools in eight countries, we're finding that deep learning is good for all students but especially beneficial for students traditionally disengaged from conventional school. When you create conditions for deeper learning in schools and across school systems, learning and well-being feed each other.

The second idea represents one of the most important blind spots in education systems across the world. Conventional schooling might be a key contributing factor, albeit unintentionally, to the undermining of student well-being. Stress is on the rise among school-age students. Engagement and enthusiasm with school declines sharply over time in school. Creativity, imagination, and the joy of learning practically disappear among the vast majority of young people as they progress through school. And things are not significantly better for students who are "doing well" in school. Schools are producing cadres of students who are good at school but not necessarily good in life. We said that deep learning produces well-being. But schooling, as we know it, has proven to be a very ineffective vehicle to foster deep learning.

Massive compulsory school systems were not designed to produce deep student learning. Their historical role has been around control, custody, and sorting. Even in the best cases, students learn to be taught—to sit in silence, to listen attentively to what the teacher is saying, to understand and fulfill the expectations of the adults in the school. But this is not the same as, and indeed is a deterrent to, deep learning. Boredom is common currency in school classrooms around the world. And as neuroscience is demonstrating, boredom activates the same neuronal pathways and releases the same biochemical substances as stress.

The most powerful systemwide strategies and policies to enhance student well-being will unify learning and well-being into a single purpose. And this will require profound changes in how we think and go about educating young people in schools.

Where Are the Students?

Just as with the learning agenda, in the well-being agenda students are overwhelmingly seen and treated as recipients or beneficiaries of the policies and programs designed in ministries of education. A few exceptions can be found in Japan's concept of *kizuna-zukuri*, which refers to the role that students play in creating environments of caring and belonging in schools, as well as in Sweden's intentional work to promote meaningful student participation in school improvement efforts. But even in these cases, the role of students in promoting well-being is confined to the management of individual classrooms or their schools.

There are very encouraging signs that young people are eager and ready to change the world. Some of the most prominent examples include the gun violence prevention movement galvanized around March for Our Lives in the United States, the climate change strikes that have spread across the globe, and the recent student protests in Ontario against proposed funding cuts in education. Seeing and treating students as equals and creating conditions and environments for their active involvement in designing, carrying out, assessing, and continuously developing initiatives to deepen their learning and their well-being represents one of the most exciting and promising opportunities for educational change moving forward.

. . . and the Larger Community?

Schools and school systems alone cannot control the multiple variables and circumstances that might compromise their students' feelings of safety. While there are a couple cases, namely Australia and Israel, that mention the intentional development of school-community partnerships to prevent harm and promote well-being, in most cases the focus is confined to the work carried out within school systems. This does not necessarily mean that school-community partnerships don't exist in the other countries; it may be that these are simply not included in the chapter discussion. Yet, we believe that partnerships of this kind will have to be intentionally looked at and developed moving forward.

Fully realizing the dual purpose of student learning and well-being requires simultaneously changing what happens inside schools and what happens outside schools. These two goals are often treated as dichotomous options in a zero-sum game, where investment in one means divestment in the other. But there is no reason why the problem of changing schools and changing the context in which they operate has to stay framed in this way. School-community partnerships can take several forms. At the most basic level, networks can be created to link schools, communities, and social agencies and organized in such way that each part assumes direct responsibility for the portion of the problem most under its control. Another possible type of partnership might involve the creation of "education cities," where the infrastructure and institutions of cities (e.g., libraries, public parks, government offices, laboratories) open their doors to students and thus create a much wider learning environment. Yet another type of partnership rests on creating opportunities for students to identify challenges that affect their lives and their communities, to examine their key causes, and to design, launch, test, and refine solutions.

The Gap Between Good Intentions and Everyday Practice

A fifth gap in the case studies presented in this book relates to the large divide between good intentions and everyday practice. Only a few systems in the cases presented have created specific frameworks, tools, and/or processes to bridge this divide. In Sweden and France, for example, schools are expected to include well-being as a key priority in their school improvement plans and to develop and report progress on schoolwide strategies to address it. In Israel, standards for "optimal and positive climate" are included as part of the national education accountability standards, alongside academic achievement. These examples can offer important guidance to other countries interested in ensuring that the good intentions of policies designed to address student well-being effectively make their way into the everyday lives of students in schools.

At the same time, a full-on embrace of learning and well-being as a tightly intertwined and unified purpose will require more than incorporating these as key priorities in school improvement plans. It will also require fundamental changes in the logic of operation of the systems where schools are embedded. There's growing evidence on the key features of successful systemwide reform, which include:

- awareness that achieving clarity "on paper" is 20 percent of the work, while the remaining 80 percent is developing clarity in the minds and hearts of frontline staff (what we call *coherence making*);
- intentional effort to shape the culture of the organization (focus on shared goals; processes of collaborative inquiry to continuously examine evidence of impact and refine/enhance the strategy over time) across all levels of the education system;
- development of theories of action that explain simply and clearly how and why the key actions of the strategy will produce the intended results;
- creation of multiple opportunities for actors across the system to learn to do their work differently, grounded in a clear understanding of how and under what conditions adults learn to change their practice (e.g., site-based coaching, direct links between professional learning and practice in the classrooms and schools where trainees work, observation of or mentorship from more experienced practitioners, collaborative inquiry with peers); and
- intentional development of ongoing, purposeful interaction among actors, both laterally among peers and vertically across all levels of the system.

THE NEXT FRONTIER IN WHOLE-SYSTEM CHANGE

In schools as we know them, doing well in school and doing well in life are not necessarily the same thing. In the school systems of the future, if the future is to be bright, doing well in school and doing well in life will have to go hand in hand. An overemphasis on student achievement to the neglect of everything else will give way to an integral emphasis on the development of children as whole human beings. Learning and well-being will no longer be seen and treated as separate but instead will be seen and treated as one and the same phenomenon, making for a more complete human being. (Michael Fullan has suggested elsewhere that the unification of the two elements is the new moral imperative for educational change.[1])

In the education systems of the future, an overemphasis on reducing negative, harmful experiences in schools will give way to a wider spectrum that also includes and prioritizes the development of environments and practices that allow students to experience well-being in its full expression.

With this in mind, students and communities should play an active role in advancing the waves of cultural change that will be required to create the education systems of the future. This will make important contributions to the profound changes that are required to turn obsolete schooling systems into vibrant learning organizations and, at the same time, nurture a sense of efficacy, worthiness, fulfillment, and self-respect among our younger generations and within the communities where they belong. The next decade will be crucial in determining whether schools and the systems where they operate will turn themselves into effective vehicles to prepare our children and youth to survive, thrive in, and change the world for the better.

CHAPTER 16

A WORLD FOCUS ON KEEPING CHILDREN SAFE

GRACE SKRZYPIEC

MUCH HAS CHANGED in the world for children since the Industrial Revolution of the 1700s, when child labor was commonplace.[1] Within two centuries, since the early 1900s, the world has seen laws against child labor prevail, and the focus for children has become their education. Most countries in the world, as the eleven case chapters in this volume note, have taken steps to ensure that education is available to all children well into their teens. The world's acceptance of childhood as an important stage of human development and the understanding that children must be protected and permitted to flourish formed the backdrop for the creation of the United Nations' Convention on the Rights of the Child (CRC), which was signed in November 20, 1989.[2] The CRC stresses that every child has the right to be sheltered from all kinds of violence:

1. States Parties shall take all appropriate legislative, administrative, social and educational measures to protect the child from all forms of physical or mental violence, injury or abuse, neglect or negligent treatment, maltreatment or exploitation, including sexual abuse, while in the care of parent(s), legal guardian(s) or any other person who has the care of the child.

2. Such protective measures should, as appropriate, include effective procedures for the establishment of social programmes to provide necessary support for the child and for those who have the care of the child, as well as for other forms of prevention and for identification, reporting, referral, investigation, treatment and follow-up of instances of child maltreatment described heretofore, and, as appropriate, for judicial involvement.

The country case studies are historical testimonials of the world's progress in recognizing the rights of children to live in safe and nurturing environments and of the actions taken in these countries to ensure that child-promoting entreaties are realized.

In providing all children with access to education, governments and educational jurisdictions have accepted that they are primarily responsible for the safety of young people during their schooling and while they are in the care of the educators entrusted to instruct them. This responsibility has been exercised by making certain that schools are safe environments for young people and that school campuses are protected from external threats arising from outside the school. This has included keeping children safe from perils associated with weapons, drugs, and undesirable personnel. In some countries (e.g., Australia) schools control who has access to children during school hours and on school premises, including who may pick children up at the end of the day (e.g., in cases involving child custody orders). However, governments and educational jurisdictions have progressed in their views about the complexities of school safety and what children's safety entails.

The case study authors note that the safety of young people at school extends beyond keeping them physically safe. As Antoinette Hetzler explains in her case study of Sweden, curbing school violence "is not dependent on the use of metal detectors or armed guards." The case studies describe the importance of school climate and social-emotional learning (SEL) as important facets of school safety. A positive school climate involves five dimensions—safety, relationships, teaching and learning, institutional environment, and institutional improvement processes—and is of prime importance in all of the countries studied.[3] By addressing these five elements, school climate is enhanced and improvements occur in all areas of young people's lives. The resultant outcome is an enriched school environment where students flourish and school violence is minimized.

In Israel, the importance of SEL is part of the holistic effort to create a positive school climate where "the acquisition of [social and emotional skills] is expected, among other outcomes, to help students empathize with others, understand their point of view, and deal peacefully with conflict." In some ways this is akin to an approach that requires an understanding of others through the concept of *convivencia escolar*, or school coexistence, in Chile and Colombia. Such approaches seek to develop an understanding among individual students that extends to the creation of a democratic school climate "where children construct academic and socioemotional learning and learn to live together in a democratic way, becoming the protagonists of more just and participatory societies," in accordance with UNESCO declarations.[4]

In several countries, documents that reflect this understanding have contributed to the advancement of policies and strategies to keep children safe at school. In France, "since 2011 . . . there has been a growing appreciation for a wider spectrum of behaviors—social, emotional, and intellectual factors— that undermine students feeling safe," particularly around the recognition that bullying and harmful peer aggression is objectionable behavior. Where once bullying was accepted behavior believed to be part of growing up, it is now considered unacceptable and the most harmful form of peer aggression.[5] Indeed, the World Health Organization declared bullying to be "a worldwide health problem among children and adolescents; a subject which has demanded much attention due to its detrimental and enduring consequences."[6] While all case study authors note that there are problems with the definition of *bullying*, it is nonetheless being acknowledged as a feature of school life that demands the attention of educational authorities. This is another facet of school life that requires consideration for policies and laws enacted with the goal of keeping students safe at school.

All countries, too, collect data and seek an evidence base through surveys and other means to monitor progress and inform policy direction. Since the nature of bullying varies by locality (e.g., *ijime* in Japan), it is understandable that each jurisdiction has provided its own definition of bullying, harassment, or degrading behavior. Other than limiting comparisons between countries, it matters little how deliberate, harmful, and repeated aggressive behavior is defined by each country's government, provided it remains stable, unchanged, and well understood by the authorities seeking to promote student safety and well-being. What is problematic is when the bullying phenomenon is not well understood by individuals within a particular jurisdiction. This is something that should not be dismissed as insignificant, as it will hamper intervention efforts to reduce bullying. Without proper definitions, it is difficult to make comparisons year to year, yet alone determine the effectiveness of any interventions.[7] For example, the use of questions like "How often were you bullied?" in pre- and post-tests to investigate the effectiveness of an intervention could be misleading if respondents' understanding of what constitutes bullying changes during the intervention. A program may appear to be effective if respondents decide that what they thought was bullying in the pretest was not in fact bullying, so they report that they were not a victim of bullying in the post-test, falsely suggesting that the incidence of bullying victimization has reduced. It is important that everyone—researchers, educators, parents and students—all have the same understanding of the behavior that they are aiming to eradicate.

As has been the case with matters involving children in the past, laws have been passed in some countries that seek to ensure not only children's right to an education but also their safety. These have been enacted to protect children from threats from peers, such as bullying and harassment. In some countries where laws have not been enacted, the issue of school bullying is nonetheless a prominent issue within the public, sociopolitical domain. For example, in China the term *school bullying* appears in legal documents and school governance orders issued by the Ministry of Education in 2016, such as "Guidelines on Prevention and Management of Bullying and Violence in Primary and Secondary Schools."

In some countries, such as Australia, Canada, and China, there are no laws against bullying. In these countries existing laws may be used to deal with peer physical violence (assault), sexting (child pornography), and spreading rumors (defamation and libel) if legal action is required. With the advent of new digital technologies that can be used to deliberately harm others, however, some countries have found it necessary to legislate against cyberbullying. For example, in 2017 the Italian government approved legislation against cyberbullying.

Whether or not each of the countries studied has followed a legislative pathway against bullying and cyberbullying, all case study authors describe policies and guidelines developed primarily by educational ministries and departments to assist schools in countering school violence. Various national programs and strategies have been developed that are available for school staff to select and use in their school. For example, in Canada the Department of Public Safety instigated a National Crime Prevention Strategy and "has spent the last twenty years providing support for the development and assessment of several antibullying school programs." Other examples are the P.E.A.C.E. Pack program developed for Australian schools and the cyclical intervention process developed in Japan to reduce ijime.

Yet, while legislative measures send a message of what is unacceptable behavior, laws and the policing of them do not necessarily have a preventative or deterring effect.[8] It is fortunate that many governing bodies have recognized that more is needed in schools to prevent school violence and keep children safe. As children grow and learn, they require guidance for healthy social and psychological development.[9] Many countries are moving forward with policies and recommendations with child development in mind.

Policies and guidelines against bullying and school violence exist in many countries, but schools, for the most part, appear to have been left to find their own way in their quest to reduce school violence. It is evident that political parties and governing bodies have met their obligations and responded to the demands of their constituents by providing financial support and enacting laws and policies against school violence, and bullying. However, while government and ministerial policies exist, their uptake by schools in uncertain. For example, in Australia the National Safe Schools Framework created in 2003 and endorsed by all state ministers of education was not widely implemented in schools as a strategy to deal with bullying. While this framework has since been updated and made available online, schools are not mandated to use it, although because of the materials and resources available it is hoped that they will. Similarly, in Italy "schools have autonomy in applying all these suggestions, and there is no formal control mechanism for control over their implementation," so there is considerable variation among Italian regions and among schools in the same local territory in their uptake of policies and antibullying strategies. And in France, where laws against bullying exist, "each school must, on the one hand, design and implement policies to prevent and handle bullying situations positively, and on the other hand design a whole school policy to ensure safety against major risks such as terrorism."

Although policies, laws, and interventions constitute a positive development in a nation's quest to keep children safe at school, the need for a more integrated and holistic approach is a common point raised by most case study authors. Since children exist in a multilevel environment where they are influenced by the beliefs and values of the people around them, it makes sense to involve people at all levels if an effort to reduce school violence is to be successful.

One country that stands out in this respect is Israel, which follows an ecological systems model involving students, teachers, parents, and other relevant bodies.[10] A consideration of child development is demonstrated by having specially trained counselors from the national psychological and counseling service who play an important role in assisting schools with school climate and violence prevention, although they do not deal directly with students.

This approach is well thought out: specialist counselors work with leadership and help provide guidance that incorporates a specialist's understanding of children and their needs and consideration of solutions that fit within the educational realm. Furthermore, the school as a whole, which includes students, parents, and education staff, works together in implementing prevention and intervention activities that are adapted and tailored for their particular school context.

It is important that there be a shared vision among stakeholders of the collaborative goal of shaping a school to have a positive school climate and culture. This appears to be an important and uniting factor that may be missing in many of the approaches in the country case studies. It is not clear whether there is a common understanding of what "keeping students safe at school" actually entails and whether this is incorporated into a common vision that unites governments and policy makers (who provide directives), school leaders (who must manage staff and students), parents (who seek the best for their children), and students (who attend school for an education) or whether each stakeholder has their own view of the matter. Without a common vision, these stakeholders will have different goals and agendas, and any intervention process will be disjointed and limited in its effectiveness. One country that appears to be close to developing a cohesive approach is Israel, where a "unifying conceptual framework" provides "directives and guidelines while providing a comprehensive infrastructure designed to support and promote school-level innovation and localized solutions," which "helps direct schools to improve their social climate, reduce school violence and bullying, and promote well-being of students and educational staff as part of their core educational mission." However, it was not clear from the chapter whether a unifying vision was present within each localized school community.

To ensure effectiveness, it is important to determine exactly and explicitly what stakeholders should be involved in actualizing the shared vision and the role they should play. It is not satisfactory to use rhetoric that states that bullying is being addressed without having a basis and terms of reference for action. It is not sufficient to state that a whole-school approach will be taken to prevent school violence without stipulating how this is to be done and what role each group of players (students, teachers, administrators, parents) will take. As Claire Beaumont states in her case study of Canada, "Creating a positive school climate and responding appropriately to violence as it occurs should not be subject to improvisation; it requires a range of planned and calibrated interventions." Despite national efforts described by these authors, it does not appear that we are there yet, as evidenced by continued incidents of peer aggression, bullying, cyberbullying, and "bullycide."

The recommendations the case study authors make outline the blueprint for ensuring students are safe at school. This includes ensuring that data is collected and shared; that antiviolence and antibullying programs are evidence-based; that there is training for preservice as well as in-service teachers; that the entire community is mobilized; that there is a positive approach toward discipline, where restorative principles prevail and punishment is avoided; and that a broader and concerted vision is developed among stakeholders. However, it is paramount that interventions, programs, and processes are thoroughly investigated, tested, and evaluated. As Fishbein notes, "Just as one cannot 'throw together' a vaccine, one cannot 'throw together' an intervention."[11] There are interventions and programs that make sense at an intuitive level, but can they have an antipodal effect? Do feelings of alienation and disenfranchisement arise when students are suspended or punished for their involvement in bullying? For example, Beaumont raises questions about the progress being made and the effectiveness of current punitive methods in Canada, asking about the programs and interventions: "Do they truly provide better social skills to those who assault their peers? Do they provide young victims with the support they need to heal their emotional wounds? Do they help victims develop resilience through coping strategies that can help them better manage peer aggression in the future?" Answers to such questions can be achieved through careful and rigorous mixed-methods research.

While the case studies demonstrate the great progress made in countries seeking to develop safe environments for children, there remains so much more to be done. As Eric Debarbieux points out in his study of France, "Since violence in schools is not the consequence of the intrusion from outsiders on the school premises, and because it is influenced by the quality of the relationships among all the members of the school community, it will not be possible to eradicate it through the intervention of external agencies." Schools must work on the problem of school violence as it is present in their school. What outside agencies, researchers, and specialists in child development can do is collaborate with them to provide knowledge and information, as well as make tools available to assist school leaders in their quest to curb school violence at the local level. As Jonathan Cohen and Dorothy Espelage point out about the United States, to curb school violence, "all educators and other school personnel, students, and parents need to develop a shared vision of what kind of school they want theirs to be." And without "an iterative, data driven, and fundamentally collaborative manner," attempts to address school violence with a whole-school approach will prove challenging.

The case studies outline laws and policies and guidelines about what is needed to prevent school violence and keep children safe. It is accepted that a holistic approach which involves the development of a positive school climate, the teaching of SEL skills, the incorporation of a three-tiered (primary, secondary, and tertiary) strategy, and the involvement of people at all levels of the school milieu are needed. However, while we have a road map, and nations have made great progress since the 1989 CRC, we are only in the early stages of actualizing what is needed to keep all children safe at school.

CHAPTER 17

TRENDS IN UNDERSTANDINGS, POLICY, AND PRACTICE IN ELEVEN COUNTRIES

AMERICA J. EL SHEIKH, JONATHAN COHEN,
AND DOROTHY L. ESPELAGE

THIS CHAPTER PROVIDES a systemic examination of the themes, similarities, and differences among understandings, policy, and practice around school safety in the eleven country case studies presented in this volume. In developing the volume, the editors gave each case study author a set of questions regarding their country's understandings, goals, strategies, measures and measurement systems, improvement trends (if any), and recommendations in regard to bullying, school climate, safety, and violence. Here we reflect on how each author answered these questions, breaking down the responses and noting common themes and key terms for conceptualizing bullying, school climate, safety, and violence to provide a comprehensive, digestible comparison for readers.

A GROWING WORLDWIDE APPRECIATION FOR A SPECTRUM OF HARM

The chapters and the commentaries in *Feeling Safe in School: Bullying and Violence Prevention Around the World* illustrate that, despite the variety of definitions and approaches taken by the eleven featured countries, there has been a worldwide shift from focusing only on the physical aspects of feeling and/or being safe in school to a wider recognition and appreciation that there are social, emotional, and intellectual aspects to feeling safe in K–12 schools.

Some countries (e.g., Sweden and the US) have, for over forty years, appreciated this wider spectrum of experiences that undermine students feeling safe. Others have only begun to focus on these issues in the last few years. For example, France first started studying school climate in 1991, but it wasn't until after the 2011 National Assembly Against School Bullying that it showed an expanded understanding of school safety and climate by acknowledging multiple factors (social, emotional, and intellectual) that undermine student safety, compared to its previous sole emphasis on physical violence. In Italy, the Ministry of Education did not address bullying until 2007, and "safety" wasn't addressed in either the behavioral or psychological senses until 2015. And school bullying research was almost nonexistent in China until 2015, and to date China still does not have legislation against bullying, only laws pertaining to crime, juvenile protection, and juvenile delinquency, though the Ministry of Education's definition of bullying does acknowledge the impact of bullying on mental health.

Most countries have focused on bullying as the source of students feeling and/or being unsafe socially, emotionally, and intellectually, as well as physically. Many, but not all, of the case study authors mentioned the importance of measuring cyberbullying and sexual violence and harassment in their countries. There is a lot of overlap among the definitions of *bullying* in these eleven countries, including having physical and psychological or emotional consequences, being repetitive, and involving a difference in power. Bullying is both an individual act (a person or group is intentionally mean and/or disrespectful toward another person or group) and a social process, as there are virtually always witnesses who hear and/or see bullying behaviors. This trend aligns with a growing body of research underscoring the importance of social norms that implicitly support bystander behavior on the one hand and communities that foster communities of "Upstanders" or social responsibility on the other. Many countries take into account the effects that school violence have on witnesses and bystanders, but few are actively supporting efforts to create communities of Upstanders. The only country that appears to create large-scale, country-wide efforts is Israel, where the social-emotional curriculum uses an Upstander promotion module. Japan appears to have the most unique definition of *bullying*: no single term encompasses both the physical and psychological aspects of bullying but, instead, two different terms. Since most students in Japan are perpetrators of *ijime* (the relational, psychological form), Japan has taken an ecological approach to its prevention. More countries had better defined ideas around bullying than around school climate. In terms of school climate, countries such as Chile, Colombia, France, Italy, Sweden, and the US include the concept of democratic participation and/or citizenship as part of a broader vision of school climate. This is especially true for Chile and Colombia, where *convivencia escolar*, or school coexistence, defines their goals.

Importantly, over the last decade, there has been a growing research-based understanding that effective school violence prevention efforts need to rest on universal efforts to promote health/mental health/social-emotional-civic competencies, both individually and systemically. According to the country case studies, this understanding has shaped goals but not explicitly shaped policy guidelines, except in Sweden and Israel. Sweden's Education Act of 2010 provides a guideline for promoting social-emotional-civic competencies on both national and individual levels. It has also helped coordinate school-student welfare teams, which give students access to medical, psychological, social-psychological, and special pedagogical competencies. Israel also promotes social and emotional skills on a large scale with its K–12 Life Skills curriculum. Although not on a policy or even a national scale, two countries (Italy and Israel) promote life skills, and six other countries (Canada, Colombia, Chile, Italy, Japan, US) promote social-emotional competencies. These competencies/skills are described in different ways, from being socioaffective and sociocognitive (Colombia) to socioemotional (Canada). Some countries do recognize the value and need to integrate the community into school bullying prevention efforts or at least consider what's going on in communities, since violence or systemic problems in the community make their way into schools. For example, immigration is a salient topic in Italy, where immigrants are bullied more and do worse in school when compared to their nonimmigrant counterparts.

A NEED FOR ACCOUNTABILITY AND GUIDELINES

Many countries have policies and laws in place to prevent school violence and bullying, but there appears to be an absence of measures to hold schools accountable to these laws. Policies focused on individual and/or organizational learning and health promotion as well as violence prevention do not provide guidelines that support effective and sustainable school improvement efforts. In an overlapping manner, many countries seem to value the importance of adapting an ecologically informed perspective but do not provide information or guidelines that support effective and sustainable ecologically informed school improvement efforts. Some authors mentioned that their countries' (e.g., Chile and China) ambiguous policies were a barrier to prevention efforts. And some countries (e.g., France and US) have disciplinary policies that problematically "punish" schools/districts that report high levels of bullying, which has resulted in underreporting. So while there is a growing conversation around the world about social, emotional, and academic teaching/learning, safe and supportive school environments, and coordinating universal prosocial (individual and schoolwide) improvement around violence prevention, this is not evident in most educational policies internationally today. And when school climate and/or social emotional learning is mentioned, it is only rarely linked to standards and/or detailed implementation guidelines.

Many countries give a nod to the importance of positive school climate, social-emotional learning, and/or restorative practices, but few support these practices with detailed standards, implementation guidelines, and/or monitoring systems that address iterative and continuous learning and school improvement. In addition, most countries have not evaluated the effects these practices have on school climate and bullying. Few country case studies mentioned the importance of peer support or prevention focused on peer-to-peer interaction, suggesting that this is not a priority yet internationally. Some countries' prevention efforts come from the ground up or from the individual school level. Some countries recognize that a whole-school approach would be beneficial, but there are often barriers to this (e.g., France believes that academic knowledge really matters). In many countries, measurement and related learning systems are too often not mandated or recommended, or in place at all, at the national, regional, and school levels. Instead, it is up to individual researchers to study the phenomenon of school climate and bullying.

Almost no case studies focus on strengthening norms and values that support nonviolent, respectful, nurturing, positive, and gender-equitable relationships for all children and adolescents. One branch of Sweden's National Agency for Education is dedicated to issuing legislation relating to rules, norms, and values, setting goals around these for each student. For example, "respecting the intrinsic value of other people" and "rejecting the subjection of people to oppression and degrading treatment" are goals set by the Education Act of 2010. One important aspect of social norms relates to what we learn to do when we see someone else causing harm or being harmed, yet we are not aware of any countries that recognize and support school leaders in transforming norms that typically implicitly support bystander behavior into norms that support communities of Upstanders.

Yet, it is encouraging that there is a growing appreciation around the world for how disciplinary practices (at home and in school) that foster learning rather than punishment and healthy connected relationships between students and their teachers, as well as their parents, are an essential foundation for feeling and being safe in school. But while there is growing interest in these practices, there is less actual support and guidance for them. The countries that mentioned restorative, rehabilitative, and/or formative practices recognized that these approaches would benefit school climate, but almost none had programs or policies in place. Colombia has legislation that recommends restorative approaches, but more teacher development with these approaches is needed.

· · ·

THE NEXT STEPS NECESSARY for preventing mean, cruel, and/or bullying behaviors and improving well-being and school climate vary considerably, depending on the country. In countries where bullying and school climate research is fairly new, such as China, developing legislation against mean, cruel, and/or bullying behaviors and furthering an understanding of how bullying manifests is crucial. For countries with legislation and measurement systems already in place, it is necessary to develop, evaluate, and adjust prevention programs.

Most countries are still primarily focused on promoting linguistic, mathematical, and scientific literacy in K–12 schools—on teaching and learning in the classroom. In many ways, this is understandable. However, teaching and learning are always social, emotional, and civic endeavors. And communities of students, school personnel, and parents are always creating climates for learning that support, or undermine, students feeling safe, supported, and engaged. There are problematic gaps between what school climate, school safety, and prosocial (e.g., social-emotional learning, character education, mental health promotion) learning research suggests and current educational policy and practice in most countries around the world. The very good news is that there is dramatic and growing interest in social-emotional learning, school climate, and social-emotional safety improvement efforts.

The bad news is that too many countries continue to prioritize academic learning, practice punitive methods of school discipline, and fail to provide research-based measurement and school improvement guidelines. School systems, like people, will always have problems as well as strengths. As such, creating school improvement systems that are iterative and truly embrace "failure as the foundation for learning" is foundationally important.

In many countries, increased attention is being paid to restorative practices rather than an overreliance on traditional disciplinary approaches of suspension and expulsion. Restorative practices have emerged as one potential approach to address inequities that have risen out of zero-tolerance approaches to school violence and discipline infractions. However, restorative approaches are difficult to implement and sustain because they require intensive and ongoing training for all school members. This has led to restorative approaches being viewed by school staff and parents as "letting kids off the hook" or creating schools where "there are no consequences for violating rules"—phrases we hear from parents and teachers on a daily basis. In fact, and unfortunately, in our qualitative work on violence directed at educators, we note that many teachers are calling for more punitive approaches rather than embracing reparation.[1] In reality, the impact of restorative approaches depends largely on consistent implementation, which is often largely undermined by teachers and staff who do not agree with the approach.

Our hope is that the spectrum of experiences that address children feeling safe at school presented in the country case studies and the commentaries in this volume will spur conversations among research, policy, practice, and youth leaders.

NOTES

PREFACE

1. Pamela Cantor, David Osher, Juliette Berg, Lily Steyer, and Todd Rose, "Malleability, Plasticity, and Individuality: How Children Learn and Develop in Context," *Applied Developmental Science* 23, no. 4 (2019): 307–37; David Osher, Pamela Cantor, Juliette Berg, Lily Steyer, and Todd Rose, "Drivers of Human Development: How Relationships and Context Shape Learning and Development," *Applied Developmental Science* (2018), doi:10.1080/10888691.2017.1398650.

2. Aspen Institute, *From a Nation at Risk to a Nation at Hope: Recommendations from the National Commission on Social Emotional and Academic Development* (2019), http://nationathope.org/; Stephanie M. Jones and Jennifer Kahn, *The Evidence Base for How We Learn: Supporting Students' Social, Emotional and Academic Development: Consensus Statement of Evidence from the Council of Distinguished Scientists* (Washington, DC: Aspen Institute's National Commission on Social, Emotional and Academic Development, 2017).

3. Future of Education and Skills 2030, https://www.oecd.org/education/2030-project.

4. International Observatory for School Climate and Violence Prevention, https://intobservatory.org.

5. See http://www.ijvs.org/.

CHAPTER 1

1. J. Cohen, E. Gordon, and K. Kendziora, "School Safety, Wellness, and Learning: Conditions for Learning, Barriers to Learning, and School Improvement," in *Keeping Students Safe and Helping Them Thrive: A Collaborative Handbook on School Safety, Mental Health, and Wellness*, ed. M. J. Mayer, D. Osher, K. Kendziora, and L. Wood (New York: Praeger, 2019); A. H. Maslow, "A Theory of Human Motivation," *Psychological Review* 50, no. 4 (1943): 370–96, doi:10.1037/h0054346; Douglas T. Kenrick, Vladas Griskevicius, Steven L. Neuberg, and Mark Schaller, "Renovating the Pyramid of Needs: Contemporary Extensions Built upon Ancient Foundations," *Perspectives on Psychological Science* 5, no. 3 (2010): 292–314, doi:10.1177/1745691610369469.

2. M. J, Mayer and D. G. Cornell, "Why Do School Order and Safety Matter?" *Educational Researcher* 39, no. 1 (2010): 7–15; Carolyn Côté-Lussier and Caroline Fitzpatrick, "Feelings of Safety at School, Socioemotional Functioning, and Classroom Engagement," *Journal of Adolescent Health* 58, no. 5 (2016): 543–50, doi:10.1016/j.jadohealth.2016.01.003; Johanna Lacoe, "Too Scared to Learn? The Academic Consequences of Feeling Unsafe in the Classroom," *Urban Education* (2016), doi:10.1177/0042085916674059;

D. Osher Moroney, and S. Williamson, eds., *Creating Safe, Equitable, Engaging Schools: A Comprehensive, Evidence-Based Approach to Supporting Student* (Cambridge, MA: Harvard Education Press, 2018).\

3. N. K. Bowe and G. L. Bowen, "Effects of Crime and Violence in Neighborhoods and Schools on the School Behavior and Performance of Adolescent," *Journal of Adolescent Research* 14, no. 3 (1999): 319–42; Ross Macmillan and John Hagan, "Violence in the Transition to Adulthood: Adolescent Victimization, Education, and Socioeconomic Attainment in Later Life," *Journal of Research on Adolescence* 14, no. 2 (2004): 127–58, doi:10.1111/j.1532-7795.2004.01402001.x; Christopher J. Schreck and J. Mitchell Miller, "Sources of Fear of Crime at School: What Is the Relative Contribution of Disorder, Individual Characteristics, and School Security?" *Journal of School Violence* 2, no. 4 (2003): 57–79, doi:10.1300/J202v02n04_04.

4. H. Koo, "A Time Line of the Evolution of School Bullying in Differing Social Context," *Asia Pacific Education Review* 8, no. 1 (2007): 107–16.

5. J. Archer, "The Nature of Human Aggression," *International Journal of Law and Psychiatry* 32 (2009): 202–08; D. M. Buss and T. K. Shackelford, "Human Aggression in Evolutionary Psychological Perspective," *Clinical Psychology Review* 17, no. 6 (1997): 605–19; D. Hart, *Man the Hunted: Primate, Predators, and Human Evolution* (New York: Routledge, 2008); L. S. Leakey, "Development of Aggression as a Factor in Early Human and Pre-Human Evolution," *UCLA Forum in Medical Sciences* 7 (1967): 1–33; T. Pickering, *Rough and Tumble: Aggression, Hunting and, Human Evolution* (Berkeley: University of California Press, 2013).

6. A. Gat, *War in Human Civilization* (Oxford, UK: Oxford University Press, 2006).

7. C. Hedges, *What Every Person Should Know About War* (New York: Free Press, 2003).

8. S. Pinker, *The Better Angels of Our Nature: Why Violence Has Declined* (New York: Penguin Books, 2012); United Nations, "World Report on Violence Against Children," 2006, https://www.unicef.org/violencestudy/reports.html; Centers for Disease Control and Prevention, "Suicide Rates in the United States Continue to Increase," 2018, https://www.cdc.gov/nchs/products/databriefs/db309.htm.

9. D. Olweus, "Bully/Victim Problems Among Schoolchildren: Long-Term Consequences and an Effective Intervention Program," in *Mental Disorder and Crime*, ed. S. Hodgins (Thousand Oaks, CA.: Sage, 1993), 317–49; Philip C. Rodkin, Dorothy L. Espelage, and Laura D. Hanish, "A Relational Framework for Understanding Bullying: Developmental Antecedents and Outcomes," *American Psychologist* 70, no. 4 (2015): 311–21, doi:10.1037/a0038658.CA.","page":"317-349

10. Engineering National Academies of Sciences and Medicine, Preventing Bullying Through Science, Policy, and Practice (Washington, DC: National Academies Press, 2016); Dorothy L. Espelage, "Leveraging School-Based Research to Inform Bullying Prevention and Policy," *American Psychologist* 71, no. 8 (2016): 768–75, doi:10.1037/amp0000095; S. Jimerson Swearer and Dorothy Espelage, eds., *International Handbook of Bullying* (New York: Routledge, 2009); Committee on the Biological and Psychosocial Effects of Peer Victimization: Lessons for Bullying Prevention et al., *Preventing Bullying Through Science, Policy, and Practice*, ed. Frederick Rivara and Suzanne Le Menestrel (Washington, DC: National Academies Press, 2016); P. K. Smith, S. Kwak and Y. Toda, eds., *School Bullying in Different Cultures: Eastern and Western Perspectives* (Cambridge, UK: Cambridge University Press, 2016); P. K. Smith, S. Sundaram, B. Spears, C. Blaya, M. Schäfer, and D. Sandhu, eds., *Bullying, Cyberbullying and Student Well-Being in*

Schools: Comparing European, Australian and Indian Perspectives (Cambridge, UK: Cambridge University Press, 2018).

11. Grace Skrzypiec, Earvin Alinsug, Ulil Amri Nasirdddin, Eleni Andreou, Antonella Brighi, Eleni Didaskalou, Annalisa Guarini, Soon-Won Kang, Kirandeep Kaur, Soon-jung Kwon, Rosario Ortega-Ruiz, Eva M. Romera, Christina Roussi-Vergou, Damanjit Sandhu, Iwona Sikorska, Mirella Wyra, and Chih-Chien Yang, "Self-Reported Harm of Adolescent Peer Aggression in Three World Regions," *Child Abuse & Neglect* 85 (2018): 101–17, doi:10.1016/j.chiabu.2018.07.030.

12. U. Bronfenbrenner, ed., *Making Human Beings Human: Bioecological Perspectives on Human Development* (Thousand Oaks, CA.: Sage, 2005).

13. E. J. Langer, *Mindfulness* (Boston: Addison-Wesley, 1989); Jennifer L. Frank, Patricia A. Jennings, and Mark T. Greenberg, "Validation of the Mindfulness in Teaching Scale," *Mindfulness* 7, no. 1 (2016): 155–63, doi:10.1007/s12671-015-0461-0; Patricia A. Jennings, Joshua L. Brown, Jennifer L. Frank, Sebrina Doyle, Yoonkyung Oh, Regin Davis, Damira Rasheed, Anna DeWeese, Anthony DeMauro, Heining Cham, and Mark T. Greenberg, "Impacts of the CARE for Teachers Program on Teachers' Social and Emotional Competence and Classroom Interactions," *Journal of Educational Psychology* 109, no. 7 (2017): 1010–28, doi:10.1037/edu0000187.

14. Less Jussim, *Social Perception and Social Reality* (New York: Oxford University Press, 2012).

15. Diana E. Hess, *Controversy in the Classroom: The Democratic Power of Discussion* (New York: Routledge, 2009).

16. Diana E. Hess and Paula McEvoy, *The Political Classroom: Evidence and Ethics in Democratic Education* (New York: Routledge, 2015).

17. Jennifer L. DePaoli, Matthew N. Atwell, John M. Bridgeland, and Timothy P. Shriver, "Respected: Perspectives of Youth on High School and Social Emotional Learning" (report, Collaborative for Academic, Social and Emotional Learning [CASEL], 2018); see https://allstatefoundation.org/new-research-shows-u-s-students-feel-unprepared-without -social-and-emotional-skills/.

18. E. J. Costello, W. Copeland, and A. Angold, "Trends in Psychopathology Across the Adolescent Years: What Changes When Children Become Adolescents, and When Adolescents Become Adults?" *Journal of Child Psychology and Psychiatry* 52, no. 10 (2011): 1015–25, doi:10.1111/j.1469-7610.2011.02446.x; UNICEF, "Measurement of Mental Health Among Adolescents (MMHA): Road Map 2018–2019," 2018, https://data .unicef.org/wp-content/uploads/2018/05/MMHA-Roadmap.pdf; W. E. Copeland, A. Angold, L. Shanahan, and J. E. Costello, "Longitudinal Patterns of Anxiety from Childhood to Adulthood: The Great Smoky Mountains Study," *Journal of the American Academy of Child and Adolescent Psychiatry* 53, no. 1 (2014): 21–33.

19. R. F Anda, A. Butchart, V. J. Felitti, and D. W. Brown, "Building a Framework for Global Surveillance of the Public Health Implications of Adverse Childhood Experience," *American Journal of Preventative Medicine* 39, no. 1 (2010): 93–98.

20. E. Clous, K. Beerthuizen, K. J. Ponsen, J. Luitse, M. Olff, and C. Goslings, "Trauma and Psychiatric Disorders: A Systematic Review," *Journal of Trauma and Acute Care Surgery* 82, no. 4 (2017): 794–801, doi:10.1097/TA.0000000000001371.

21. W. E. Copeland, G. Keeler, A. Angold, and E. J. Costello, "Traumatic Events and Posttraumatic Stress in Childhood," *Archives of General Psychiatry* 64 (2007): 577–84.

22. "Trauma Informed Schools for Children in K–12: A Systems Framework" (policy brief, National Child Traumatic Sites Network, Rockville, MD, 2017), https://www.nctsn .org/resources/creating-supporting-and-sustaining-trauma-informed-schools-system -framework.

23. Ron Avi Astor and Rami Benbenishty, *Bullying, School Violence, and Climates in Evolving Contexts: Culture, Organization and Time* (New York: Oxford University Press, 2019); Phillip M. Brown, Michael W. Corrigan, and Ann Higgins-D'Alessandro, eds., *Handbook of Prosocial Education* (New York: Rowman & Littlefield, 2012).

24. Phillip T. Slee, Grace Skrzypiec, and Carmel Cefai, eds., *Child and Adolescent Well-Being and Violence Prevention in Schools* (New York, Routledge, 2018); Michael J. Furlong, Richard Gilman, and E. Scott Huebner, eds., *Handbook of Positive Psychology in Schools,* 2nd ed. (New York: Routledge, 2014); Stephanie A. Moore, Erin Dowdy, Karen Nylund-Gibson, and Michael Furlong, "A Latent Transition Analysis of the Longitudinal Stability of Dual Factor Mental Health in Adolescence," *Journal of School Psychology,* 73 (2019): 56–73, doi:10.1016/j.jsp.2019.03.003.

25. William Ming Liu, Rossina Z. Liu, Yunkyoung L. Garrison, Cindy J. Y. Kim, Laurence Chan, Yu C. S. Ho, and Chi W. Yeung, "Racial Trauma, Microaggressions, and Becoming Racially Innocuous: The Role of Acculturation and White Supremacist Ideology," *American Psychologist* 74, no. 1 (2019): 143–55, doi:10.1037/amp0000368; Derald Wing Sue, Christina M. Capodilupo, Gina C. Torino, Aisha M. Holder, Kevin L. Nadal, and Marta Esquilin, "Racial Microaggressions in Everyday Life: Implications for Clinical Practice," *American Psychologist* 62, no. 4 (2007): 271–86, doi:10.1037/0003-066X.62.4.271.

26. Scott O. Lilienfeld, "Microaggressions: Strong Claims, Inadequate Evidence," *Perspectives on Psychological Science* 12, no. 1 (2017): 138–69, doi:10.1177/1745691616659391.

27. Peter K. Smith, Keumjoo Kwak, and Yuici Toda, *School Bullying in Different Cultures: Eastern and Western Perspectives* (Cambridge, UK: Cambridge University Press, 2017).

28. Astor and Benbenishty, *Bullying, School Violence, and Climates.*

29. K. C. Basile, S. G. Smith, M. J. Breiding, M. C. Black, R. R. Mahendra, "Sexual Violence Surveillance: Uniform Definitions and Recommended Data Elements, Version 2.0." (2014).

30. S. G. Smith, J. Chen, K. C. Basile, L. K. Gilbert, N. Patel, M. T. Merrick, A. Jain, and M. L. Walling, "The National Intimate Partner and Sexual Violence Survey (NISVS): 2010–2012 State Report" (report, Centers for Disease Control and Prevention, Atlanta, 2017), https://stacks.cdc.gov/view/cdc/46305.

31. Ibid.

32. Catherine Hill and Holly Kearl, "Crossing the Line: Sexual Harassment at School" (white paper, American Association of University Women, Washington, DC, 2011), https://files.eric.ed.gov/fulltext/ED525785.pdf.

33. Michele L. Ybarra and Richard E. Thompson, "Predicting the Emergence of Sexual Violence in Adolescence," *Prevention Science* 19, no. 4 (2018): 403–15, doi:10.1007/s11121 -017-0810-4.

34. D. L. Espelage, K. C. Basile, and M. E. Hamburger, "Bullying Perpetration and Subsequent Sexual Violence Perpetration Among Middle School Students," *Journal of Adolescent Health* 50 (2012): 60–65; D. L. Espelage, K. C. Basile, L. De La Rue, and M. E. Hamburger, "Longitudinal Associations Among Bullying, Homophobic Teasing, and Sexual Violence Perpetration Among Middle School Students," *Journal of Interpersonal*

Violence 30, no. 14 (2015): 2541–61; Michele L. Ybarra, Dorothy L. Espelage, Jennifer Langhinrichsen-Rohling, Josephine K. Korchmaros, and Danah Boyd, "Lifetime Prevalence Rates and Overlap of Physical, Psychological, and Sexual Dating Abuse Perpetration and Victimization in a National Sample of Youth," *Archives of Sexual Behavior* 45, no. 5 (2016): 1083–99, doi:10.1007/s10508-016-0748-9.

35. J. Bennett, "The #MeToo Moment: Navigating Sex in the 'Grey Zone,'" *New York Times*, February 23, 2018; Katie Roiphe, *The Morning After: Sex, Fear, and Feminism* (Boston: Little, Brown, 1994), 1; Kristen Roupenian, "Cat Person," *New Yorker*, December 4, 2017, https://www.newyorker.com/magazine/2017/12/11/cat-person.

36. Anlan Zhang, Ke Wang, Jizhi Zhang, Jana Kemp, Melissa Dilberti, and Barbara A. Oudekerk, "Indicators of School Crime and Safety: 2017 (NCES 2018-036/NCJ 251413)," National Center for Educational Statistics, March 2018, https://eric.ed.gov/?id=ED581798.

37. Centers for Disease Control and Prevention, "Suicide Rates in the United States Continue to Increase," June 2018, https://www.cdc.gov/nchs/products/databriefs/db309.html.

38. World Health Organization, "Suicide," 2018, https://www.who.int/en/news-room/fact-sheets/detail/suicide.

39. US Government Accountability Office, "K–12 Education: Discipline Disparities for Black Students, Boys, and Students with Disabilities: Report to Congressional Requesters," 2018, https://www.gao.gov/assets/700/690828.pdf; Richard O. Welsh and Shfiqua Little, "The School Discipline Dilemma: A Comprehensive Review of Disparities and Alternative Approaches," *Review of Educational Research* 88, no. 5 (2018): 752–94.

40. R. M. Diaz, G. Ayala, E. Bein, J. Henne, and B. V. Marin, "The Impact of Homophobia, Poverty, and Racism on the Mental Health of Gay and Bisexual Latino Men: Findings from Three US Cities," *American Journal of Public Health* 91, no. 6 (2001): 927–32; M. E. Newcomb and B. Mustanski, "Internalized Homophobia and Internalizing Mental Health Problems: A Meta-Analytic Review," *Clinical Psychology Review* 30, no. 8 (2010): 1019–29.

41. I am grateful to Dewey Cornell for the conversations we have had about feeling safe and being safe.

42. Matthew J. Mayer and Michael J. Furlong, "How Safe Are Our Schools?" *Educational Researcher* 39, no. 1 (2010): 16–26, doi:10.3102/0013189X09357617.

43. Lauren O'Neill and Jean Marie McGloin, "Considering the Efficacy of Situational Crime Prevention in Schools," *Journal of Criminal Justice* 35, no. 5 (2007): 511–23, doi:10.1016/j.jcrimjus.2007.07.004.

44. Schreck and Miller, "Sources of Fear of Crime at School."

CHAPTER 2

1. Ken Rigby and Phillip T. Slee, "Dimensions of Interpersonal Relations Among Australian School Children and Implications for Psychological Well-Being," *Journal of Social Psychology* 133, no. 1 (1993): 33–42.

2. House of Representatives Standing Committee, *"Sticks and Stones": Report on Violence in Australian Schools* (Canberra: Australian Government Publishing Service, 1994).

3. Ministerial Council on Education, Employment, Training and Youth Affairs (MCEETYA), *National Safe Schools Framework*, 2003, https://www.mdc.wa.edu.au/assets/About-Us/Policies/SafeSchools-Framework.pdf.

4. Ministerial Council for Education, Early Childhood Development and Youth Affairs (MCEECDYA), *National Safe Schools Framework: All Australian Schools Are Safe, Supportive and Respectful Teaching and Learning Communities that Promote Student Wellbeing*, 2011, https://docs.education.gov.au/system/files/doc/other/national_safe_schools_framework.pdf;

5. "Be You Mental Health Initiative," 2018, https://beyou.edu.au/about-be-you and https://beyou.edu.au/history.

6. Council of Australian Governments (COAG) Council of Education, 1992, https://www.coag.gov.au/about-coag.

7. Kathryn Anderson-Levitt, "A World Culture of Schooling?" in *Local Meanings, Global Schooling: Anthropology and World Culture Theory*, ed. Kathryn Anderson-Levitt (New York: Palgrave Macmillan, 2003), 1–26.

8. Barbara A. Spears, Carmel Taddeo, Lesley Ey, Toby Carslake, Alexander Stretton, Colette Langos, Damanjit Sandhu, and Suresh Sundaram, "Pre-Service Teachers' Understanding of Bullying in Australia and India," in *Bullying, Cyberbullying and Student Well-Being in Schools: Comparing European, Australian and Indian Perspectives*, ed. Peter K. Smith, Suresh Sundaram, Barbara A. Spears, Catherine Blaya, Mechthild Schäfer, and Damanjit Sandhu (Cambridge, UK: Cambridge University Press, 2018), 208–35.

9. Marilyn Campbell, Barbara A. Spears, Donna Cross, and Phillip T. Slee, "Cyberbullying in Australia," in *Cyberbullying: A Cross-National Comparison*, ed. Joaquín A. Mora Merchán and Thomas Jager (Landau, Germany: Verlag Empirische Pädagogik, 2010), 232–44.

10. Australian Bureau of Statistics, "Schools, Australia 2017," http://www.abs.gov.au/ausstats/abs@.nsf/mf/4221.0.

11. Australian Government Department of Education and Training, https://www.australia.gov.au/directories/australia/education.

12. COAG Council of Education.

13. "Australian Education Act," 2013, https://www.education.gov.au/australian-education-act-2013.

14. Rigby and Slee, "Dimensions of Interpersonal Relations," 33–42.

15. House of Representatives Standing Committee, *"Sticks and Stones."*

16. Australian Education Authorities, "Bullying. No Way!" https://bullyingnoway.gov.au/.

17. Education Services Australia Student Wellbeing Hub, https://www.studentwellbeinghub.edu.au/glossary#/.

18. Australian Government Office of the eSafety Commissioner, "Glossary," https://www.esafety.gov.au/education-resources/iparent/glossary.

19. Australian Education Authorities, "Bullying. No Way!"

20. Sheryl A. Hemphill, Jessica A Heerde, and R. Gomo, *A Conceptual Definition of School-Based Bullying for the Australian Research and Academic Community* (Canberra: Australian Research Alliance for Children and Youth, 2014).

21. Colette Langos, "Cyberbullying: The Challenge to Define," *Cyberpsychology, Behavior, and Social Networking* 15, no. 6 (2012): 285–89.

22. Urie Bronfenbrenner, "Toward an Experimental Ecology of Human Development," *American Psychologist 32*, no.7 (1977): 513; Urie Bronfenbrenner, "Developmental Ecology Through Space and Time: A Future Perspective," in *Examining Lives in Context: Perspectives on the Ecology of Human Development*, ed. P. Moen, G. H. Elder Jr., and K. Lüscher (Washington, DC: American Psychological Association, 1995).

23. Phillip T. Slee, *School Bullying: Teachers Helping Students Cope* (New York: Routledge, 2017).
24. Rosalyn H. Shute and Phillip T. Slee, *Child Development: Theories and Critical Perspectives* (New York: Routledge, 2015).
25. Ibid.; Slee, *School Bullying.*
26. Phillip T. Slee and Grace Skrzypiec, *Well-Being, Positive Peer Relations and Bullying in School Settings* (Dordrecht, The Netherlands: Springer, 2016).
27. Corey L. M. Keyes, "Mental Health in the Adolescence: Is America's Youth Flourishing?" *American Journal of Orthopsychiatry* 76, no.3 (2006): 4, 5.
28. House of Representatives Standing Committee, *"Sticks and Stones."*
29. Council of Australian Governments, *The Roadmap for National Mental Health Reform, 2012–2022* (Canberra: Council of Australian Governments, 2012), https://www.coag .gov.au/sites/default/files/communique/The%20Roadmap%20for%20National%20 Mental%20Health%20Reform%202012-2022.pdf.
30. MCEETYA, *Melbourne Declaration on Educational Goals for Young Australians*, 2008, http://www.curriculum.edu.au/verve/_resources/National_Declaration_on_the _Educational_Goals_for_Young_Australians.pdf.
31. Ibid.
32. Ibid.
33. Australian Curriculum Assessment and Reporting Authority (ACARA), "General Capabilities," https://australiancurriculum.edu.au/f-10-curriculum/general-capabilities /personal-and-social-capability/.
34. ACARA, "Health and PE," https://australiancurriculum.edu.au/resources/curriculum -connections/dimensions/?Id=46754&YearLevels=42683&searchTerm=bullying# dimension-content.
35. Australian Institute for Teaching and School Leadership (AITSL), https://www.aitsl .edu.au/.
36. Australian Department of Education, Employment and Workplace Relations (ADEEWR), Office for Youth, *National Strategy for Young Australians*, 2009, http:// www.voced.edu.au/content/ngv:43206.
37. Australian Government Department of Education and Training (AGDoET), *Review to Achieve Excellence in Australian Schools*, 2018, https://www.education.gov.au/review -achieve-educational-excellence-australian-schools.
38. Barbara A. Spears, Neil Tippett, Carmel Taddeo, and Alan Barnes, *Final Report: Review and Update of the National Safe Schools Framework* (Adelaide: University of South Australia, 2017); Education Services Australia, *A Summary of the Review Process and Key Findings to Inform the Update of the National Safe Schools Framework*, 2018, https:// www.studentwellbeinghub.edu.au/docs/default-source/nssf-summary-report-pdf.pdf ?sfvrsn=0.
39. "Be You Mental Health Initiative."
40. Australian Institute of Family Studies, "National Support for Child and Youth Mental Health Program," 2018, https://aifs.gov.au/cfca/2018/04/04/introducing-national -workforce-centre-child-mental-health-focus-all-health-and-welfare.
41. "UNICEF: The United Nations Convention on the Rights of the Child," 1989, http:// www.unicef.org.uk/wp-content/uploads/2010/05/UNCRC_united_nations_convention _on_the_rights_of_the_child.pdf; "United Nations Sustainable Development Goals," 2018, www.un.org/sustainabledevelopment.

42. House of Representatives Standing Committee, *"Sticks and Stones,"* v.

43. MCEETYA, *National Safe Schools Framework*, 2003, https://www.mdc.wa.edu.au/assets /About-Us/Policies/Safe- Schools-Framework.pdf, 3–6.

44. Helen McGrath, *Making Australian Schools Safer: A Summary Report of the Outcomes from the National Safe Schools Framework Best Practice Grants Programme (2004–2005)* (Canberra: Department of Education, Science and Training, 2005).

45. Donna Cross, Thérèse Shaw, Lydia Hearn, Melanie Epstein, Helen Monks, Leanne Lester, and Laura Thomas, "Australian Covert Bullying Prevalence Study (ACBPS)" (report, Child Health Promotion Research Centre, Edith Cowan University, Perth, 2009).

46. Donna Cross, Melanie Epstein, Lydia Hearn, Phillip Slee, Thérèse Shaw, and Helen Monks, "National Safe Schools Framework: Policy and Practice to Reduce Bullying in Australian Schools," *International Journal of Behavioral Development* 35, no. 5 (2011): 398–404.

47. MCEECDYA, *National Safe Schools Framework*, 2.

48. Standing Council, *National Safe Schools Framework (Updated)*.

49. Carmel Taddeo, Barbara A Spears, Lesley-Anne Ey, Deborah Green, Deborah Price, Toby Carslake, and Greg Cox, *A Report on the Evaluation of the Safe Schools Hub* (Adelaide: University of South Australia, 2015).

50. Education Services Australia, "Summary Report: Review and Update of the National Safe Schools Framework," 2017, https://www.studentwellbeinghub.edu.au/docs/default -source/nssf-summary-report-pdf.pdf?sfvrsn=0.

51. Ibid.

52. House of Representatives Standing Committee, *"Sticks and Stones."*

53. MYCEETA, *National Safe Schools Framework*.

54. Ibid.

55. SCSEEC, *National Safe Schools Framework*.

56. Education Services Australia, "Australian Student Wellbeing Framework."

57. House of Representatives Standing Committee, *"Sticks and Stones."*

58. Shute and Slee, *Child Development*.

59. Barbara Spears and Jette Kofoed, "Transgressing Research Binaries: Youth as Knowledge Brokers in Cyberbullying Research," in *Cyberbullying Through the New Media: Findings from an International Network*, ed. Peter K. Smith and Georges Steffgen (London: Psychology Press, 2013), 201–21.

60. Phillip T. Slee, Marilyn Campbell, and Barbara A. Spears, *Child, Adolescent and Family Development*, 2nd ed. (Melbourne, Australia: Cambridge University Press, 2012).

61. Spears and Kofoed, "Transgressing Research Binaries."

62. Barbara A. Spears and Mike Zeederberg, "Emerging Methodological Strategies to Address Cyberbullying: Online Social Marketing and Young People as Co-Researchers," in *Principles of Cyberbullying Research: Definitions, Measures and Method*, ed. Sheri Bauman, Donna Cross, and Jenny L Walker (New York: Routledge, 2013), 273–85; Rosalyn Shute and Phillip T. Slee, *Mental Health and Wellbeing Through Schools: The Way Forward.* (Routledge: London, 2016); Phillip T. Slee. Grace Skrzypiec, Damanjit Sanhdu, Kirandeep Kaur, and Marilyn Campbell, "Photostory: A Legitimate Research Tool in Cross-Cultural Research," in *Bullying, Cyberbullying and Student Well-Being in Schools*, ed. Peter K. Smith et al. (London: Cambridge University Press, 2018).

63. Education Services Australia, "Australian Student Wellbeing Framework."

64. ACARA, "Personal and Social Capability," 2008, https://australiancurriculum.edu.au
/resources/curriculum-connections/dimensions/?Id=46754&YearLevels=42683&search
Term=bullying#dimension-content; https://australiancurriculum.edu.au/f-10-curriculum
/general-capabilities/personal-and-social-capability/; https://australiancurriculum.edu
.au/resources/curriculum-connections/portfolios/food-and-wellbeing/general-capabilities/.

65. World Health Organization, "The Health Behaviour in School-Aged Children Survey,"
2018, http://www.hbsc.org/.

66. Programme for International Student Assessment, "Wellbeing," http://www.oecd.org
/pisa/searchresults/?q=wellbeing.

67. Australian Government Department of Social Services, "Building a New Life in Australia: The Longitudinal Study of Humanitarian Migrants (BNLA)," https://www.dss
.gov.au/our-responsibilities/families-and-children/programmes-services/building-a-new
-life-in-australia-bnla-the-longitudinal-study-of-humanitarian-migrants; Australian
Government Department of Social Services, "Footprints in Time: The Longitudinal
Study of Indigenous Children (LSIC)," https://www.dss.gov.au/about-the-department
/publications-articles/research-publications/longitudinal-data-initiatives/footprints-in
-time-the-longitudinal-study-of-indigenous-children-lsic; Australian Government Department of Social Services, "Growing Up in Australia: The Longitudinal Study of
Australian Children (LSAC)," https://growingupinaustralia.gov.au/; Australian Government Department of Education and Training, "Longitudinal Surveys of Australian Youth," https://www.lsay.edu.au/; Australian Government Department of Social
Services, "Household, Income and Labour Dynamics in Australia (HILDA)," https://
www.dss.gov.au/our-responsibilities/families-and-children/programmes-services/the
-household-income-and-labour-dynamics-in-australia-hilda-survey.

68. Slee, *School Bullying*.

69. Cross, *Covert Bullying Prevalence Study*.

70. David Lawrence, Sarah Johnson, Jennifer Hafekost, Kartina Boterhoven de Haan,
Michael Sawyer, John Ainley, and Stephen R Zubrick, *The Mental Health of Children
and Adolescents: Report on the Second Australian Child and Adolescent Survey of Mental
Health and Wellbeing* (Canberra: Department of Health, 2015).

71. Cross, *Covert Bullying Prevalence Study*.

72. Barbara A. Spears, Matthew Keeley, Shona Bates, and Ilan Katz, "Research on Youth
Exposure to, and Management of, Cyberbullying Incidents in Australia: Part A—Literature Review on the Estimated Prevalence of Cyberbullying Involving Australian
Minors" (report, Social Policy Research Centre [SPRC], University of Southwest Australia, Sydney, September 2014), https://www.arts.unsw.edu.au/sites/default/files
/documents/Youth_exposure_to_and_management_of_cyberbullying_in_Australia
_Part_A.pdf.

73. Australian Government Office of the eSafety Commissioner, https://www.esafety.gov.au.

74. Australian Government Office of the eSafety Commissioner, https://www.esafety.gov.
au/about-the-office/research-library; Commonwealth of Australia, *Australian Communications and Media Authority Annual Report 2017–18* (Canberra: Commonwealth of
Australia, 2018).

75. Caitlin Chalmers, Marilyn A Campbell, Barbara A Spears, Des Butler, Donna Cross,
Phillip Slee, and Sally Kift, "School Policies on Bullying and Cyberbullying: Perspectives Across Three Australian States," *Educational Research* 58, no. 1 (2016): 91–109.

76. Barbara A. Spears, "A Review of Initiatives Using Technology to Promote Cyber-Safety and Digital Citizenship," in *The Impact of Technology on Relationships in Educational Settings*, ed. Angela Costabile and Barbara A. Spears (London: Routledge, 2012), 188–203.

77. "Senate Enquiry: The Adequacy of Existing Cyberbullying Laws," 2019, https://www.aph.gov.au/Parliamentary_Business/Committees/Senate/Legal_and_Constitutional_Affairs/Cyberbullying.

78. Queensland Anti-Cyberbullying Task Force, "Adjust Our Settings: A Community Approach to Address Cyberbullying Among Children and Young People in Queensland," 2018, https://campaigns.premiers.qld.gov.au/antibullying/taskforce/assets/anti-cyberbullying-taskforce-final-report.pdf.

79. New South Wales Department of Education, "Anti-Bullying," https://antibullying.nsw.gov.au/.

80. Bill Cossey, "Review of Procedures and Processes Related to Bullying and Violence in Schools" (report, Department of Education and Children's Services, Adelaide, 2011, http://www.saasso.asn.au/wp-content/uploads/2012/11/Cossey-Review-Implementation-of-Requirements.pdf.

81. "Anti-Bullying Policies Inadequate in Many SA Public Schools," *Adelaide Advertiser*, May 23, 2018.

82. Department for Education, "Wellbeing and Engagement Collection," 2017, https://www.education.sa.gov.au/sites/g/files/net691/f/2017-wellbeing-engagement-survey-report.pdf.

83. COAG, "Enhancing Community Responses to Student Bullying, Including Cyberbullying: Report and Work Program," 2018, https://www.coag.gov.au/sites/default/files/communique/bcsowg-report-work-program.pdf.

84. Price Waterhouse Coopers, *The Economic Cost of Bullying in Australian Schools* (Melbourne: The Alannah and Madeline Foundation, 2018), https://www.ncab.org.au/media/2505/amf-report-280218-final.pdf.

CHAPTER 3

1. Council of Ministers of Education, "Some Facts About Canada's Population," 2016, https://www.cmec.ca/299/Education_in_Canada__An_Overview.html.

2. David M. Day, Carol A. Golench, Jyl Macdougall, and Cheryl A. Beals-Gonzaléz, *School-Based Violence Prevention in Canada: Results of a National Survey of Policies and Programs* (Ottawa: Ministry of the Solicitor General of Canada, 1995), https://www.ncjrs.gov/App/Publications/abstract.aspx?ID=156716.

3. Ken Rigby, *Bullying Interventions in Schools: Six Basic Methods* (Camberwell, Australia: ACER, 2010), 37.

4. Organisation for Economic Co-operation and Development (OECD), *PISA 2015 Results (Volume III): Students' Well-Being* (Paris: OCDE, 2017), 60, doi:10.1787/9789264273856-en.

5. Mental Health Commission of Canada, *Changing Directions, Changing Lives: The Mental Health Strategy for Canada* (Calgary: Mental Health Commission of Canada, 2012), 11, www.mentalhealthcommission.ca/sites/default/files/MHStrategy_Strategy_ENG.pdf.

6. Katherine Weare, "Mental Health and Social and Emotional Learning: Evidence, Principles, Tensions and Balances," *Advances in School Mental Health Promotion* 3, no. 2 (2010): 5–17, https://www.tandfonline.com/doi/abs/10.1080/1754730X.2010.9715670.

7. Jean-Pierre Bellon and Bertrand Gardette, *Harcèlement scolaire: Le vaincre c'est possible: la méthode Pikas, une technique éprouvée* (Paris: ESF, 2016), 15.

8. Dan Olweus, *Violences entre élèves, harcèlements et brutalités: Les faits, les solutions* (Paris: ESF, 1999), 20.

9. Ercilia Menesini and Christina Salmivalli, "Bullying in Schools: The State of Knowledge and Effective Interventions," *Psychology, Health & Medicine* 22, no. 1 (2017): 240–53, https://www.researchgate.net/publication/312869444_Bullying_in_schools_the_state_of_knowledge_and_effective_interventions.

10. Alana Vivolo-Kantor, Melissa K. Holt, and Gretta M. Massetti, "Individual and Contextual Factors for Bullying and Peer Victimization: Implications for Prevention," *Journal of School Violence* 10, no. 2 (2011): 210–12, https://www.tandfonline.com/doi/abs/10.1080/15388220.2010.539169.

11. John G. Freeman, Mathieu King, and William Pickett, "Health Behaviour in School-Aged Children (HBSC) in Canada: Focus on Relationships" (report, Public Health Agency of Canada, Ottawa, 2016), http://healthycanadians.gc.ca/publications/science-research-sciences-recherches/health-behaviour-children-canada-2015-comportements-sante-jeunes/alt/health-behaviour-children-canada-2015-comportements-santé-jeunes-eng.pdf; OECD, *PISA 2015 Results (Volume III)*.

12. OECD, *PISA 2015 Results (Volume III)*; Freeman et al., "Health Behaviour in School-Aged Children."

13. Reynol Junco, "Resharing of Images or Videos Without Consent: A Form of Relationship Violence and Harassment," in *Perspectives on Harmful Speech Online* (Cambridge, UK: Berkman Klein Center for Internet and Society, 2016), 16–17, https://cyber.harvard.edu/sites/cyber.harvard.edu/files/2017-08_harmfulspeech.pdf.

14. Matthew Johnson, Faye Mishna, Moses Okumu, and Joanne Daciuk, *Non-Consensual Sharing of Sexts: Behaviours and Attitudes of Canadian Youth* (Ottawa: MediaSmarts, 2018), http://mediasmarts.ca/sites/mediasmarts/files/publication-report/full/sharing-of-sexts.pdf.

15. Sylvie Parent and Kristine Fortier, "La violence envers les athlètes dans un contexte sportif," in *Rapport québécois sur la violence et la santé*, ed. Julie Laforest, Pierre Maurice, and Louise Marie Bouchard (Québec: Institut national de santé publique du Québec, 2018), 229–53, https://www.inspq.qc.ca/sites/default/files/publications/2380_rapport_quebecois_violence_sante.pdf.

16. Debra Pepler and Wendy Craig, "Peer Dynamics in Bullying: Considerations for Social Architecture in Schools," in *Building Capacity for Diversity in Canadian Schools*, ed. Judy Lupart and Anne McKeogh (Markham, Ontario: Fitzhenry & Whiteside, 2009), 285–303; Kimberly A. Schonert-Reichl, Jennifer L. Hanson-Peterson, and Shelley Hymel, "Social and Emotional Learning and Pre-Service Teacher Education," in *Handbook of Social and Emotional Learning*, ed. Joseph A. Durlak, Celene E. Domitrivich, Roger P. Weissberg, and Thomas Gullotta (New York: Guilford Press, 2015), 406–21.

17. Mona Paré and Tara Collins, "Government Efforts to Address Bullying in Canada: Any Place for Children's Rights?" *Journal of Law and Social Policy* 25, no. 3 (2016): 54–77, https://digitalcommons.osgoode.yorku.ca/cgi/viewcontent.cgi?article=1224&context=jlsp; Brenda E. Morrison and Dorothy Vaandering, "Restorative Justice: Pedagogy, Praxis, and Discipline," *Journal of School Violence* 11, no. 2 (2012): 138–55, https://www.tandfonline.com/doi/full/10.1080/15388220.2011.653322. The 1989 UN

Convention on the Rights of the Child is an international treaty recognizing specific rights for children (https://www.ohchr.org/en/professionalinterest/pages/crc.aspx).

18. Frédéric N. Brière, Sophie Pascal, Véronique Dupéré, and Michel Janosz, "School Environment and Adolescent Depressive Symptoms: A Multilevel Longitudinal Study," *Pediatrics* 131, no. 3 (2013): 702–8, doi:10.1542/peds; Claire Beaumont, Eric Frenette, and Danielle Leclerc, "Les mauvais traitements du personnel scolaire envers les élèves: Distinction selon le sexe et l'ordre d'enseignement," *International Journal on School Climate and Violence Prevention* 1 (July 2016): 65–95, https://www.violence-ecole.ulaval.ca/fichiers/site_chaire_cbeaumont/documents/Beaumont_al._2016.pdf.

19. Gouvernement du Québec, *Loi sur l'instruction publique* (Québec: Gouvernement du Québec, 2012), http://www.legisquebec.gouv.qc.ca/en/pdf/cs/I-13.3.pdf.

20. Gouvernement du Québec, *Rapport du comité d'experts sur la cyberintimidation* (Québec: Gouvernement du Québec, 2015), https://www.mfa.gouv.qc.ca/fr/publication/documents/rapport-com-experts-cyberintimidation.pdf.

21. Patricia I. Coburn, Deborah Connolly, and Ronald Rosech, "Cyberbullying: Is Federal Criminal Legislation the Solution?" *Canadian Journal of Criminology and Criminal Justice* 57, no. 4 (2015): 566–79, doi: 10.3138/cjccj.2014.E43.

22. Gouvernement du Québec, *Rapport du comité d'experts sur la cyberintimidation*.

23. UN Human Rights Council, "Convention on the Rights of the Child," http://www.unhcr.org/uk/4d9474b49.pdf.

24. Public Safety Canada, *Building a Safe and Resilient Canada: Overview of Approaches to Address Bullying and Cyberbullying* (Ottawa: Government of Canada, 2018), https://www.securitepublique.gc.ca/cnt/rsrcs/pblctns/2018-ddrss-bllyng-cybrbllyng/2018-ddrss-bllyng-cybrbllyng-en.pdf.

25. Gouvernement du Québec, *Rapport annuel de gestion 2012–2013* (Québec: Gouvernement du Québec, 2013), http://www.education.gouv.qc.ca/fileadmin/site_web/documents/PSG/politiques_orientations/RAG_2012-2013p.pdf; Gouvernement du Québec, *Le Québec chiffres en main* (Québec: Institut de la Statistique du Québec, Gouvernement du Québec, 2018), http://www.bdso.gouv.qc.ca/docs-ken/multimedia/PB01600FR_qcem2018H00F00.pdf.

26. Rami Benbenishty and Ron Avi Astor, *School Violence in Context: Culture, Neighborhood, Family, School, and Gender* (New York: Oxford University Press, 2015), 5.

27. Steve Bissonnette, Carl Bouchard, and Normand St-Georges, "Soutien au comportement positif (SCP): Un système efficace pour la prévention des difficultés comportementales," *Formation et profession* 4 (December 2011): 16–19, http://r-libre.teluq.ca/361/1/Dossier_4%20%282%29.pdf.

28. Claire Beaumont and Natalia Garcia, "La formation initiale des futurs enseignants du primaire les prépare-t-elle à soutenir le développement socioémotionnel de leurs élèves?" (keynote address, Colloque Innovation 2018, Lausanne, Switzerland, February 2018).

29. Sylvie Parent and Kristine Fortier, "La violence envers les athlètes dans un contexte sportif," in *Rapport québécois sur la violence et la santé*, ed. Julie Laforest, Pierre Maurice, and Louise Marie Bouchard (Québec: Institut national de santé publique du Québec, 2018), https://www.inspq.qc.ca/sites/default/files/publications/2380_rapport_quebecois_violence_sante.pdf.

30. Government of Québec, *Loi sur l'instruction publique*, art. 1–13.3, p. 9.

31. Jacques Pain, "Foreword," in *Violences entre élèves, harcèlements et brutalités. Les faits, les solutions*, by Dan Olweus (Paris: ESF, 1999), 15.

32. Ibid.; Gouvernement du Québec, *Rapport du comité d'experts sur la cyberintimidation.*
33. Claire Beaumont, Danielle Leclerc, and Eric Frenette, *Évolution de divers aspects associés à la violence dans les écoles québécoises 2013–2015–2017* (Québec: Collection de la Chaire, 2018), https://www.violence-ecole.ulaval.ca.
34. The empirically tested model lists the results according to the following forms of aggression: (1) direct/insults, threats; (2) direct/physical; (3) indirect/social; (4) indirect/electronic; and (5) indirect/material. See Claire Beaumont, Danielle Leclerc, Eric Frenette, and Marie-Ève Proulx, Gouvernement du Québec, *Rapport du comité d'experts sur la cyberintimidation* (Québec: Gouvernement du Québec, 2015), https://www.mfa.gouv.qc.ca/fr/publication/Documents/rapport-com-experts-cyberintimidation.pdf. (Québec: Collection de la Chaire, 2014), https://www.violence-ecole.ulaval.ca.
35. Auditor General of Quebec, "Report to the National Assembly for 2004–2005: Interventions Related to Violence in Public Secondary Institutions," 2005, https://www.vgq.qc.ca/en/en_publications/en_rapport-annuel/en_fichiers/en_Rapport2004-2005-T1.pdf.
36. Gouvernement du Québec, *Plan d'action pour prévenir et traiter la violence à l'école 2008-2011* (Québec: Gouvernement du Québec, 2008), http://www.education.gouv.qc.ca/fileadmin/site_web/documents/dpse/adaptation_serv_compl/FeuilletViolence_Intimidation.pdf.
37. Government of Québec, *Education Act* (Québec: Government of Québec, 2012), http://www.legisquebec.gouv.qc.ca/en/pdf/cs/I-13.3.pdf.
38. François Bowen, Caroline Levasseur, Claire Beaumont, Éric Morissette, and Paula St-Arnaud, "La violence en milieu scolaire et les défis de l'éducation à la socialisation," in *Rapport québécois sur la violence et la santé*, ed. Julie Laforest, Pierre Maurice, and Louise Marie Bouchard (Québec: Institut national de santé publique du Québec, 2018), 219, https://www.inspq.qc.ca/rapport-quebecois-sur-la-violence-et-la-sante.
39. Ibid., 221.
40. Ibid., 220–24.
41. Johan Deklerck, "Problem Behaviour and Prevention," *International Journal of Violence and School* 10 (December 2009): 3–34, http://www.cndp.fr/tenue-de-classe/fileadmin/user_upload/PDF/international/ijvs/ijvs10_en.pdf; Claire Beaumont, "Peut-on former le personnel scolaire contre la violence à l'école?" in *L'école face à la violence: Décrire, expliquer, agir*, ed. Éric Debarbieux (Paris: Armand Colin, 2016), 208–20.
42. Claire Beaumont, Danielle Leclerc, and Eric Frenette, *Évolution de divers aspects associés à la violence dans les écoles québécoises 2013–2015–2017* (Québec: Collection de la Chaire, 2018), https://www.violence-ecole.ulaval.ca.
43. Beaumont and Garcia, *La formation initiale des futurs enseignants.*
44. Gérald Boutin and Simon Forget, "Programmes québécois de lutte contre la violence scolaire : description, apports et limites," *Sociétés et jeunesses en difficulté* 10 (December 2010): 1–32, https://journals.openedition.org/sejed/6812.
45. Bowen et al., "La violence en milieu scolaire," 224.
46. Ibid., 220.
47. Coburn et al., "Cyberbullying."
48. Anatol Pikas, "A Pure Concept of Mobbing Gives the Best Results for treatment," *School Psychology International* 10, no. 2 (1989): 95–104, https://doi.org/10.1177/0143034389102003.
49. Ibid.; Paré and Collins, "Government Efforts to Address Bullying in Canada."

50. Beaumont et al., *Évolution*; Beaumont et al., "Les mauvais traitements du personnel scolaire."

51. Éric Debarbieux and Catherine Blaya, "Le contexte et la raison: Agir contre la violence à l'école par l'évidence?" *Criminologie* 42, no. 1 (2009): 13–31, https://www.erudit.org /fr/revues/crimino/2009-v42-n1-crimino2907/029806ar/.

52. Beaumont, "Peut-on former le personnel scolaire contre la violence à l'école?"

53. Mona Paré and Tara Collins, "Government Efforts to Address Bullying in Canada: Any Place for Children's Rights?" *Journal of Law and Social Policy* 25, no. 3 (2016): 54–77, https://digitalcommons.osgoode.yorku.ca/cgi/viewcontent.cgi?article=1224 &context=jlsp.

CHAPTER 4

I acknowledge funding from FONDECYT 1140960, FONDECYT 1191267, and PIA CONICYT 160009.

1. Patricia Carbajal Padilla and María C. Fierro, "Convivencia escolar: Una revisión del concepto," *Psicoperspectivas 18*, no. 1 (2019): 1–19.

2. Jonathan Cohen, Catherine Blaya, and Verónica López, *K–12 School-Based Bully Prevention/Mental Health Promotion Trends: Research, Policy and Practice in the European Union, North and South America* (paper, American Society for Adolescent Psychiatry and International Society for Adolescent Psychiatry and Psychology, New York, March 2015).

3. María C. Fierro, "Convivencia inclusiva y democrática: Una perspectiva para gestionar la seguridad escolar," *Revista Electrónica Sinéctica* 40 (2013): 1–18.

4. Jacques Delors, *Learning: The Treasure Within: Report to the UNESCO of the International Commission on Education for the Twenty-First Century* (Paris: UNESCO, 1996), http://goo.gl/e2LDvx; Nicholas Burnett, "The Delors Report: A Guide Towards Education for All," *European Journal of Education* 43, no. 2 (2008): 181–87, doi:10.1111 /j.1465-3435.2008.00347.x; UNESCO, *Education for All: Ten Years After Jomtien* (Paris: UNESCO, 2000); UNICEF, *World Declaration on Education for All and Framework for Action to Meet Basic Learning Needs* (paper, World Conference on Education for All, Jomtien, Thailand, April 1990).

5. Delors, *Learning*, 182.

6. Verónica López, "Convivencia Escolar," *UNESCO, Apuntes Educación y Desarrollo Post-2015* 4 (2014): 1–18.

7. OECD, *Evaluaciones de políticas nacionales de educación: Educación en Chile* (Santiago, Chile: OECD, 2017), https://goo.gl/bbzmKD.

8. UNICEF, *The State of Education in Latin America and the Caribbean: Towards a Quality Education for All* (Santiago, Chile: OREALC/UNESCO, 2013).

9. Juan Casassus, *La escuela y la (des) igualdad* (Santiago, Chile: LOM Ediciones, 2003).

10. Verónica López, Claudia Carrasco, Macarena Morales, Álvaro Ayala, Joedith López, and Michelle Karmy, "Individualizando la violencia escolar: Análisis de prácticas discursivas en una escuela municipal de la Región de Valparaíso," *Psykhe* 20, no. 2 (2011): 75–91, doi:10.4067/S0718-22282011000200022011; Verónica López, Paula Ascorra, Marian Bilbao, Juan Carlos Oyanedel, Iván Moya, and Macarena Morales, "El ambiente escolar incide en los resultados PISA 2009: Resultados de un estudio de diseño mixto," in *Evidencias para las políticas públicas en Educación: ¿Qué aprendemos de los resultados PISA 2009*, ed. Ministerio de Educación (Santiago, Chile: MINEDUC, 2012), 49–94.

11. UNESCO América Latina y el Caribe, *Revisión regional 2015 de la educación para todos* (Santiago, Chile: OREALC/UNESCO, 2014), http://unesdoc.unesco.org/images/0023/002327/232701s.pdf; Jonathan Cohen, "Social, Emotional, Ethical, and Academic Education: Creating a Climate for Learning, Participation in Democracy, and Well-Being," *Harvard Educational Review* 76, no. 2 (2006): 201–37, doi:10.17763/haer.76.2.j44854x1524644vn2006; Jonathan Cohen, Elizabeth McCabe, Nicholas Michelli, and Thomas Pickeral, "School Climate: Research, Policy, Practice, and Teacher Education," *Teachers College Record* 111, no. 1 (2009): 180–213, http://ww.ijvs.org/files/Publications/School-Climate.pdf; OREALC/UNESCO/LLECE, *Segundo estudio regional comparativo y explicativo (SERCE)* (Santiago, Chile: OREALC/UNESCO, 2006), http:// goo.gl/h868NG.

12. López, "Convivencia escolar"; Organización de Estados Iberoamericanos (OEI), *Educational Goals for 2021: Metas educativas* 2021 (Madrid: Secretaría General, 2008), https://goo.gl/H1XxY7.

13. UNESCO, *Informe de Actividades 2001–2002* (Buenos Aires: IIPE-UNESCO Sede Regional Buenos Aires, 2002); UNESCO América Latina y el Caribe, *Revisión regional 2015*; Cohen, "Social, Emotional, Ethical, and Academic Education."

14. APA Zero Tolerance Task Force, "Are Zero Tolerance Policies Effective in the Schools? An Evidentiary Review and Recommendations," *American Psychologist* 63, no. 9 (2008): 852–62, doi:10.1037/0003-066X.63.9.852; Joseph Calvin Gagnon, Sungur Gurel, and Brian R. Barber, "State-Level Analysis of School Punitive Discipline Practices in Florida," *Behavioral Disorder* 42, no. 2 (2017): 65–80, doi:10.1177/0198742916688652; Anthony A. Peguero and Nicole L. Bracy, "School Order, Justice, and Education/Climate, Discipline Practices, and Dropping Out," *Journal of Research on Adolescence* 25, no. 3 (2014): 412–26, doi:10.1111/jora.12138; Russell J. Skiba and Kimberly Knesting, "Zero Tolerance, Zero Evidence: An Analysis of School Disciplinary Practice," *New Directions for Youth Development* 2001, no. 92 (2001): 17–43, doi:10.1002/yd.23320019204; Russell J. Skiba and M. Karega Rausch, "Zero Tolerance, Suspension, and Expulsion: Questions of Equity and Effectiveness," in *Handbook of Classroom Management: Research, Practice, and Contemporary Issues*, ed. Carolyn M. Evertson and Carol S. Weinstein (New York: Taylor & Francis, 2013),1073–100, doi:10.4324/9780203874783.

15. Anna Aizer and Joseph J. Doyle, "Juvenile Incarceration, Human Capital, and Future Crime: Evidence from Randomly Assigned Judges," *Quarterly Journal of Economics* 130, no. 2 (2015): 759–803, https://goo.gl/r7zBBr; Nicole L. Bracy, "Circumventing the Law: Students' Rights in Schools with Police," *Journal of Contemporary Criminal Justice* 26, no. 3 (2010): 294–315, doi:10.1177/1043986210368645; Elora Mukherjee, *Criminalizing the Classroom: The Over-Policing of New York City Schools* (New York: New York Civil Liberties Union, 2007), https://goo.gl/beow1d; Randi Hjalmarsson, "Criminal Justice Involvement and High School Completion," *Journal of Urban Economics* 63, no. 2 (2008): 613–30; Michael F. Lovenheim and Emily G. Owens, "Does Federal Financial Aid Affect College Enrollment? Evidence from Drug Offenders and the Higher Education Act of 1998," *Journal of Urban Economics* 81 (2014): 1–13, doi:10.3386/w18749; Devah Pager, "The Mark of a Criminal Record," *American Journal of Sociology* 108, no. 5 (2003): 937–75, doi:10.1086/3744032003; Joseph P. Ryan, Abigail B. Williams, and Mark E. Courtney, "Adolescent Neglect, Juvenile Delinquency and the Risk of Recidivism," *Journal of Youth and Adolescence* 42, no. 3

(2013): 454–65, doi:10.1007/s10964-013-9906-8; Bruce Western, *Punishment and Inequality in America* (New York: Russell Sage Foundation, 2006).

16. Wolfram Schu, John Ainley, Julian Fraillon, David Kerr, and Bruno Losito, *ICCS 2009 International Report: Civic Knowledge, Attitudes, and Engagement Among Lower Secondary School Students in 38 Countries* (Amsterdam: International Association for the Evaluation of Educational Achievement, 2010).

17. Xavier Crettiez, *Las formas de la violencia* (Buenos Aires: Waldhuter, 2009).

18. Gómez, "Violencia e Institución Educativa," 693; Toledo et al., "Propuesta Tríadica para el Estudio de la Violencia Escolar," 72.

19. Ana María Rodino, *La Educación en Derechos Humanos: Un aporte a la construcción de una convivencia escolar democrática y solidaria* (San José, Costa Rica: OEA, Oficina de Educación y Cultura, 2012).

20. Sonia Eljach, *Violencia escolar en América Latina y el Caribe: Superficie y fondo* (Clayton, Panamá: UNICEF, 2011), https://goo.gl/SWzuMh.

21. Ibid., 70.

22. Macarena Morales and Verónica López, "Políticas de convivencia escolar en América Latina: Cuatro perspectivas de comprensión y acción," *Education Policy Analysis Archives* 27, no. 5 (2019): 1–25.

23. Tomás Moulian, *Chile actual: Anatomía de un mito* (Santiago, Chile: LOM Editores, 1997); Jenny Assaél, Rodrigo Cornejo, Juan González, Jesús Redondo, Rodrigo Sánchez, and Mario Sobarzo, "La empresa educativa chilena," *Educação e Sociedade* 32 (2011): 305–22, doi:10.1590/S0101-73302010002000042011; Nelly P. Stromquist and Anita Sanyal, "Student Resistance to Neoliberalism in Chile," *International Studies in Sociology of Education* 23, no. 2 (2013): 152–78, doi:10.1080/09620214.2013.7906622013.

24. Jaime Portales and Julian Vazquez-Heilig, "Understanding How Universal Vouchers Have Impacted Urban School Districts' Enrollment in Chile," *Education Policy Analysis Archives* 22, no. 72 (2014): 1–35, doi:10.14507/epaa.v22n72.2014; Martin Carnoy, "National Voucher Plans in Chile and Sweden: Did Privatization Reforms Make for Better Education?" *Comparative Education Review* 42, no. 3 (1998): 309–37, doi:10.1086/4475101998.

25. Anwar Shah, *Public Services Delivery* (Washington, DC: World Bank, 2005); World Bank, *The World Bank Annual Report 1996* (Washington, DC: World Bank, 1996), http://goo.gl/MRCX5y.

26. Barbara Bruns, Deon Filmer, and Harry A. Patrinos, *Making Schools Work: New Evidence on Accountability Reforms* (Washington, DC: World Bank, 2011), doi:10.1596/978-0-8213-8679-8.

27. Abdeljalil Akkari and Thibaut Lauwerier, "The Education Policies of International Organizations: Specific Differences and Convergences," *Prospects* 45, no. 1 (2015): 141–57, doi:10.1007/s11125-014-9332-z; Antoni Verger and Mauro Moschetti, *Public-Private Partnerships in Education: Exploring Different Models and Policy Options* (New York: Open Society Foundations, 2016); Eveline Wittmann, "Align, Don't Necessarily Follow," *Educational Management Administration and Leadership* 36, no. 1 (2008): 33–54.

28. Morales and López, "Políticas de convivencia escolar en América Latina," 1–25.

29. Ministerio de Educación de Chile, *Ley no. 20536: Ley de Violencia Escolar* (Santiago, Chile: MINEDUC, 2011), Articulo 16B, http://bcn.cl/1uvxm; ibid., Articulo 16A.

30. María I. Toledo and Abraham Magendzo, "Golpe de estado y dictadura militar: Estudio de un caso único de la enseñanza de un tema controversial en un sexto año básico de un colegio privado de la Región Metropolitana," *Psykhé* 22, no. 2 (2013): 147–60; Claudia Carrasco, Verónica López, and Camilo Estay, "Análisis crítico de la Ley de Violencia Escolar de Chile," *Psicoperspectivas* 11, no. 2 (2012): 31–55, doi:10.5027 /psicoperspectivas-vol11-issue2-fulltext-228.

31. Ministerio de Educación de Chile, *Política nacional de convivencia escolar 2015/2018* (Santiago: MINEDUC, 2015), https://goo.gl/xn9hXR.

32. Carrasco et al., "Análisis crítico de la Ley de Violencia Escolar," 31–55; Abraham Magendzo, María I. Toledo, and Virna Gutiérrez, "Descripción y análisis de la Ley sobre Violencia Escolar (No. 20.536): Dos paradigmas antagónicos," *Estudios Pedagógicos (Valdivia)* 39, no. 1 (2013): 377–91, doi:10.4067/s0718-07052013000100022.

33. David K. Cohen and Susan L. Moffit, *The Ordeal of Equality: Did Federal Regulation Fix the Schools?* (Cambridge, MA: Harvard University Press, 2009), https://goo.gl /RaeMzk.

34. Ministerio de Educación de Chile, *Decreto 381, establece los otros indicadores de calidad educativa a que se refiere el artículo 3º, letra a), de la Ley No. 20.529, que establece el Sistema Nacional de Aseguramiento de la Calidad de la Educación Parvularia, Básica y Media y su fiscalización* (Santiago: MINEDUC, 2013), http://bcn.cl/1wslj.

35. Verónica López, Vicente Sisto, Enrique Baleriola, Antonio García, Claudia Carrasco, Carmen Gloria Núñez, and René Valdés, "A Struggle for Translation: An Actor-Network Analysis of Chilean School Violence and School Climate Policies," *Educational Management Administration & Leadership* (forthcoming).

36. Verónica López, Lorena Ramírez, René Valdés, Paula Ascorra, and Claudia Carrasco-Aguilar, "Tensiones y nudos críticos en la implementación de la(s) política(s) de convivencia escolar en Chile," *Calidad en la Educación* 48 (2018): 96–129.

37. Agencia de Calidad de la Educación de Chile, *Entrega de resultados de aprendizaje 2014* (Santiago: Ministerio de Educación, 2014); Agencia de Calidad de la Educación de Chile, *Resultados educativos 2015* (Santiago: Ministerio de Educación, 2015); Agencia de Calidad de la Educación de Chile, *Resultados educativos 2016* (Santiago: Ministerio de Educación, 2016).

38. Teresa Bardisa Ruiz, "La participación en las organizaciones escolares," in *Consensos y conflictos en los centros docentes no universitarios*, ed. M. García de Cortázar, Javier Gallego, Consuelo del Val, Luis Camarero, Antonio Vallejos, Teresa Bardisa, and Fatima Arranz (Madrid: UNED, 2001); Enrique Chaux, *Educación, convivencia y agresión escolar* (Bogotá: Ed. Taurus, 2012); Eric Debarbieux, "La violencia en la escuela francesa: Análisis de la situación, políticas públicas e investigaciones," *Revista de Educación,* 313 (1997): 79–93.

39. Ron Avi Astor and Rami Benbenishty, "Zero Tolerance for Zero Knowledge: Empowering Schools and Communities with Data and Democracy" (policy brief, Urban Initiative, University of Southern California, Los Angeles, 2006).

40. Catherine L. Dimmit and Amanda L. Robillard, *Evidence-Based Practices: Pro-Social Skill Development and Violence Prevention in K–8 Schools* (Amherst, MA: Fredrickson Center for School Counseling Outcome Research and Evaluation, 2014); A. E. Kazak, K. Hoagwood, J. R. Weisz, K. Hood, T. R. Kratochwill, L. A. Vargas, and G. A., "A Meta-Systems Approach to Evidence-Based Practice for Children and Adolescents," *American Psychologist* no. 65, no. 2 (2010): 85–97, doi:10.1037/a00177842010.

41. Programa de Apoyo a la Convivencia Escolar, Pontificia Universidad Católica de Valparaíso (PACES-PUCV), http://www.paces.cl/.

42. These recommendations for policy makers and educational actors were proposed as a final research objective of a four-year research grant I participated in from the National Commission of Science and Technology of Chile, whose aim was to describe and analyze policies and practices of convivencia escolar in Chile. Research grant FONDECYT 1140960, "Políticas y prácticas de apoyo a la convivencia escolar en ambientes punitivos, segregados y de pruebas estandarizadas con altas consecuencias: el caso de Chile," http://repositorio.conicyt.cl/handle/10533/117951.

43. Morales and López, "Políticas de convivencia escolar en América Latina."

44. "Políticas y prácticas de apoyo a la convivencia escolar en ambientes punitivos."

45. Ministerio de Educación de Chile, "Noticias: Gobierno envía al Congreso Proyecto de Ley 'Aula Segura,'" September 20, 2018, https://www.mineduc.cl/2018/09/20/proyecto-de-ley-aula-segura/.

46. "Piñera firma proyecto para expulsar a estudiantes violentos y los califica de delincuentes," *Radio Biobiochile*, September 21, 2018, https://www.biobiochile.cl/noticias/nacional/chile/2018/09/21/pinera-firma-proyecto-para-expulsar-a-estudiantes-violentos-y-los-califico-de-delincuentes.shtml.

47. The first declaration, dated September 26, 2018, and signed by 27 researchers, can found at https://www.elmostrador.cl/noticias/pais/2018/09/26/investigadores-manifiestan-preocupacion-por-proyecto-aula-segura-y-senala-que-expulsiones-no-resuelven-el-problema/. The second declaration, dated October 23, 2018, and signed by 36 researchers from 15 universities and research centers, can be found at https://www.24horas.cl/nacional/aula-segura-comunidad-cientifica-afirma-que-medidas-como-la-expulsion-acrecientan-la-violencia-2844154.

CHAPTER 5

1. "Statistical Analysis and Summary of the Number of K12 Education Students, Enrollment, Number of Students in School and Number of Graduates in China in 2017–2018," August 1, 2018, http://www.chyxx.com/industry/201808/664173.html.

2. Ibid.

3. "The Ministry of Education Issued the Guidance Manual on Post Safety in Primary and Secondary Schools," *China Youth Daily*, March 26, 2013, http://zqb.cyol.com/html/2013-03/26/nw.D110000zgqnb_20130326_2-07.htm; "Guidelines for Safe Work in Primary and Secondary Schools," *Sohu News*, November 22, 2017, https://www.sohu.com/a/205945498_99957834.

4. Ministry of Education of the People's Republic of China, "Guidelines for Emergency Evacuation Drills for Primary and Secondary Schools and Kindergartens," February 25, 2014, http://www.moe.gov.cn/srcsite/A06/s3325/201402/t20140225_164793.html.

5. Ministry of Education of the People's Republic of China, "The Administrative Standards for Compulsory Education Schools (Trial)," August 4, 2014, http://www.moe.gov.cn/srcsite/A06/s3321/201408/t20140804_172861.html.

6. "Nearly 30 Percent of Primary and Secondary School Students Suffered from School Bullying," *China Daily*, May 29, 2016, http://finance.chinanews.com/sh/2016/05-29/7886776.shtml.

7. "Nearly 20 Percent of Students Have Been Isolated by Their Classmates," *BBC News*, April 20, 2017, http://news.163.com/17/0420/16/.

8. "The Supreme People's Court (SPC) Announced 67 Typical Cases of Criminal Offenses on School Campus," *China Legal Network News*, September 18, 2015, http://www.china.com.cn/legal/2015-09/24/content_36672401.htm.

9. "The Supreme Court Announces Typical Cases of Criminal Crimes on Campus," *Sina News*, September 18, 2015, 9. https://finance.sina.com.cn/sf/news/2015-09-18/16224386.html.

10. Ministry of Education of the People's Republic of China, "School Bullying Special Governance," May 5, 2016, http://www.moe.gov.cn/srcsite/A11/moe_1789/201605/t20160509_242576.html.

11. Ministry of Education of the People's Republic of China, "Guidelines of the Ministry of Education and Nine Other Departments on the Prevention and Management of Bullying and Violence in Primary and Secondary Schools," November 2, 2016, http://www.moe.gov.cn/srcsite/A06/s3325/201611/t20161111_288490.html.

12. Kelei Zhang and Lingwen Zhang, "The Soft and Hard Governance of School Bullying," *Shanghai Education Research* 4 (2017): 16–19.

13. The People's Republic of China, "Student Bullying Management Program," December 27, 2017, http://www.moe.gov.cn/srcsite/A11/moe_1789/201712/t20171226_322701.

14. Haitao Ren, "Definition of 'School Bullying' and Its Legal Liability," *Journal of East China Normal University* (Educational Science Edition) 2 (2017): 43–50.

15. Leijun Ma, "Making Every Student Safe: Problems and Strategies Related to School Bullying," *Management of Primary and Secondary Schools* 8 (2016): 4–8.

16. Linmei Sun and Ling Lin, "Attribution and Countermeasures of Bullying in Children," *School Psychology* 7, no. 3(2009):153–56.

17. Xiang Li et al., "Practical Confusion and Legislative Conception of Anti–School Bullying in China," *Basic Education* 14, no. 1(2007): 28–36.

18. Jianlong Yao, "China's Path to Prevent and Control Student Bullying: An Analysis of the Recent Policy to Manage School Bullying," *China Youth Social Sciences* 36, no. 1(2017): 19–25.

19. Weiyue Yu and Shen Geng, "What Is Student Bullying? What Is School Violence?" *People Education* 8 (2017): 36–41.

20. Jincai Lin, "Types, Formation and Coping Strategies of School Bullying Behavior," *Journal of Educational Science of Hunan Normal University* 2, no. 7 (2017): 1–6.

21. Hanxue Li, "Survey of School Bullying," *Contemporary Education Forum* 5 (2016): 24–30; Ling Wu, "Parenting Style Under Parent-Child Relationship Structure," *Journal of Anhui Normal University* (Humanities and Social Sciences Edition) 6 (2003): 705–09; Zaohuo Cheng et al., "The Influence of Family Environment, Parenting Style and Personality on Juvenile Delinquency and Its Influencing Pathways," *Chinese Journal of Clinical Psychology* 24, no. 2 (2016): 287–92.

22. Yubin Xu and Yanyan Guo, "Causes and Countermeasures of School Bullying," *Journal of Henan Institute of Education* (Philosophy and Social Sciences Edition) 6 (2016): 53–57.

23. Baocun Liu and Jiang Li, "Impact of Cultural Anomie on the Construction of Social Value Culture in the Period of Social Transition," *Journal of Yunnan Institute of Socialism* 4 (2014): 433–34; Jian Liu, "Bullying Behavior and Its Governance in Primary and Secondary Schools in China," *Nanjing Normal University Journal* (Social Sciences Edition) 1 (2017): 75–84; Yanqiu Li, "Overview of Research on School Bullying," *Education Science Forum* 14 (2016): 68–71.

24. Min Xiang, "Comparative Study on Bullying Prevention Between China and America" (paper, Huazhong Normal University, 2016).

25. Xuepeng Dong, "Research on School Bullying and Violence Prevention System," *Legal System and Economy* 5 (2017): 141–42.

26. En'you Zhang and Sheng Chen, "Psychological Thinking on School Bullying in Primary and Secondary Schools," *Chinese Journal of Education* 11 (2016): 13–17.

27. Shuai Zhang, "Study on School Bullying Behavior from the Perspective of Rules Education," *Education Exploration* 9 (2016): 23–26.

28. Li Lu, "Characteristics and Legal Regulations of School Bullying," *Law and Society* 7 (2017): 244–45; Yue Zhou, "An Analysis of the Legalized Approach to School Bullying Management," *Law and Society* 18 (2017): 170–71.

29. Ministry of Education of the People's Republic of China, "Guidelines on Prevention and Management of Bullying and Violence in Primary and Secondary Schools," http://www.moe.edu.cn/srcsite/A06/s3325/201611/t20161111_288490.html.

30. "General Principles of the Civil Law of the People's Republic," January 1, 1987, https://baike.baidu.com/item/ General Principles of the Civil Law of the People's Republic /5020404?fr=aladdin.

31. Yunuo Wang, "Definition, Causes and Countermeasures of School Bullying," *Legal System and Society* 12 (2017): 243–45.

32. Qi An, "Deconstruction and Legal Resolution of the Dilemma of School Bullying: Taking American Anti-Bullying Legislation as a Reference Paradigm," *China Youth Research* 5 (2017): 112–18.

33. Lijun Xie, "Legal Responsibility and Avoidance Strategies of Schools and Teachers in School Bullying," *Management of Primary and Secondary Schools* 8 (2016): 15–18.

34. Jing Wang, "Rule of Law in School Bullying," *Law and Society* 31 (2016): 201–3.

35. "Five Underage Girls in Beijing Have Been Sentenced for School Bullying," *Sina News*, November 7, 2017, http://news.sina.com.cn/s/2017-11-07/doc-ifynmnae2595251.shtml.

36. Jiahua Zhou, "Research on the Reasons and Coping Strategies of School Bullying," *Asia-Pacific Education* 29 (2016): 103.

37. Wangyang Li, "Legal Constraints and Governing of School Bullying," *Legal World* 7 (2017): 264.

38. Chunjing Su, Shuhui Xu, and Hucheng Yang, "Analysis of the Causes and Countermeasures of School Bullying in Primary and Secondary Schools from the Perspective of Family Education," *Chinese Journal of Education* 11 (2016): 18–23.

39. Muhua Wang and Li Song, "Prevention and Intervention of School Bullying: Perspective of Family-School Cooperation," *Educational Science Research* 3 (2017): 76–80.

40. Chunguang Hu, "Bullying Behavior: Implications, Causes and Prevention Strategies," *Education Research and Experiment* 1 (2017): 76–82.

41. Xiangying Yan and Jianlong Yao, "Research on the Governance Mechanism of 'Tolerance but Not Connivance' of School Bullying: Legal Thinking on the Phenomenon of School Bullying in Primary and Secondary Schools," *Chinese Journal of Education* 1 (2017): 10–14.

42. Shiya Zhang and Fuquan Huang, "Research of School Bullying," *Global Outlook of Education* 46, no. 3 (2017): 103–17.

43. Lili Ren, Changyong Nie, Hai Yuan, and Zhiqiang Fang, "Study on School Bullying Based on the Multiple Logistic Regression Model," *Journal of Anqing Normal University* (Natural Sciences Edition) 23 (2017): 36–39.

44. Chunjin Chen and Tingjin Zhi, "The Influencing Factors of School Bullying and the Construction of Long-Term Prevention Mechanism Based on the Analysis of Behavior Measurement Data of School Bullying of Youth, 2015," *Educational Development Research* 37, no. 20 (2017): 31–41.

45. Dawei Wang, "How Does the Principal Deal with School Bullying? Comprehensive Thinking from the Perspective of Public Security and Pedagogy," *Management of Primary and Middle Schools* 8 (2016): 12–15.

46. Junjie Li, "Analysis of Basic Problems of School Bullying," *Shanghai Educational Research* 4 (2017): 5–9.

CHAPTER 6

1. Political Constitution of Colombia, 1991, Article 44.

2. Political Constitution of Colombia, 1991, Article 45.

3. Ministerio Nacional de Educación, *Ruta de acompañamiento pedagógico situado: El ambiente escolar y el mejoramiento de los aprendizajes*, 2015, https://institucioneducativ aciudaddecartago.files.wordpress.com/2015/10/1-contextualzaicic3b3n-sesic3b3n -ambiente-escolar-y-mejoramiento-de-los-aperndizajes-1.pdf.

4. Amrit Thapa, Jonathan Cohen, Shawn Guffey, and Ann Higgins-D'Alessandro, "A Review of School Climate Research," *Review of Educational Research* 83, no. 3 (2013): 357–85, doi:10.3102/0034654313483907.

5. Ibid.

6. Ley de Convivencia Escolar, https://www.mineducacion.gov.co/cvn/1665/articles -319679_archivo_pdf.

7. Decreto 1965, https://www.mineducacion.gov.co/1621/ articles-328630_archivo_pdf_Decreto_1965.pdf.

8. Código de la Infancia y la Adolescencia, https://www.oas.org/dil/esp/Codigo_de_la _Infancia_y_la_Adolescencia_Colombia.pdf.

9. "Latin America Progress Briefing 2015," Global Initiative to Put an End to All Corporal Punishment of Children, http://endcorporalpunishment.org/wp-content/uploads /regional/LA-briefing-2015-EN.pdf.

10. Sonia Eljach, "Violencia escolar en América Latina y el Caribe," 2011, https://www .unicef.org/costarica/docs/cr_pub_Violencia_escolar_America_Latina_y_Caribe.pdf.

11. "Colegios no pueden castigar con malos tratos a los alumnos: Corte," *El Tiempo*, February 13, 2018, http://www.eltiempo.com/justicia/cortes/colegios-no-pueden-castigar -a-sus-alumnos-con-maltrato-fisico-corte-constitucional-182136.

12. Felicia Knaul and Miguel Angel Ramirez, *Family Violence and Child Abuse in Latin America and the Caribbean: The Cases of Colombia and Mexico* (Washington, DC: Inter-American Development Bank, 2005); Enrique Chaux and Ana María Velásquez, "Peace Education in Colombia: The Promise of Citizenship Competencies," in *Peace Initiatives in Colombia*, ed. V. Bouvier (Washington, DC: US Institute of Peace, 2009); Cathy McIlwaine and Carolina Moser, "Violence and Social Capital in Urban Poor Communities: Perspectives from Colombia and Guatemala," *Journal of International Development* 13 (2001): 965–84.

13. Germán Darío Valencia Agudelo and Deiman Cuartas Celis, "Exclusión económica y violencia en Colombia, 1990–2008: Una revisión de la literatura," *Perfil de Coyuntura Económica* 14 (2009): 113–34.

14. Enrique Chaux, Andrés Molano, and Paola Podlesky, "Socio-Economic, Socio-Political and Socio-Emotional Variables Explaining School Bullying: A Country-Wide Multilevel Analysis," *Aggressive Behaviour* 35, no. 6 (2009): 520–29; K. A. Dodge, J. E. Bates, and G. S. Pettit, "Mechanisms in the Cycle of Violence," *Science* 250 (1990): 1678–83; Deborah Gorman-Smith, David B. Henry, and Patrick H. Tolan, "Exposure to Community Violence and Violence Perpetration: The Protective Effects of Family Functioning," *Journal of Clinical Child and Adolescent Psychology* 33, no. 3 (2004): 439–49; Nikeea Copeland-Linder, Sara Johnson, Denise L. Haynie, Shang-en Chung, and Tina L. Cheng, "Retaliatory Attitudes and Violent Behaviors Among Assault-Injured Youth," *Journal of Adolescent Health* 50, no. 3 (2012): 215–20.

15. David Schwartz and Laura J. Proctor, "Community Violence Exposure and Children's Social Adjustment in the School Peer Group: The Mediating Roles of Emotion Regulation and Social Cognition," *Journal of Consulting and Clinical Psychology* 68 (2000): 670–83; D. R. Musher-Eizenman, P. Boxer, S. Danner, E. F. Dubow, S. E. Goldstein, and D. M. L. Heretick, "Social-Cognitive Mediators of the Relation of Environmental and Emotion Regulation Factors to Children's Aggression," *Aggressive Behavior* 30 (2004): 389–408; Nancy Guerra, Rowell Huesmann, and Anja Spindler, "Community Violence Exposure, Social Cognition and Aggession Among Elementary School Children," *Child Development* 74, no. 5 (2003): 1561–76.

16. R. A. Gellman and J. L. Delucia-Waack, "Predicting School Violence: A Comparison of Violent and Nonviolent Male Students on Attitudes Toward Violence, Exposure Level to Violence, and PTSD Symptomatology," *Psychology in the Schools* 43, no. 5 (2006): 591–98; Christopher I. Eckhardt, Suhr L. Rita Samper, and Amy Holtzworth-Munroe, "Implicit Attitudes Toward Violence Among Male Perpetrators of Intimate Partner Violence," *Journal of Interpersonal Violence* 27, no. 3 (2012): 471; A. J. Goldberg, J. M. Toto, H. R. Kulp, M. E. Lloyd, J. P. Gaughana, M. J. Seamon, and S. P. Scott Charles, "An Analysis of Inner-City Students' Attitudes Towards Violence Before and After Participation in the 'Cradle to Grave' Programme," *International Journal of the Care of the Injured* 41, no. 1 (2010): 110–15.

17. Thomas W. Farmer, David Estell, Man-Chi Leung, Hollister Trott, Jennifer Bishop, and Beverly D. Cairns, "Individual Characteristics, Early Adolescent Peer Affiliations, and School Dropout: An Examination of Aggressive and Popular Group Types," *Journal of School Psychology* 41, no. 3 (2003): 217–32.

18. Ministerio de Educación Nacional, "Estándares básicos de competencias ciudadanas," https://www.mineducacion.gov.co/1759/articles-116042_archivo_pdf4.pdf.

19. Ibid., 149.

20. Decreto 1965.

21. Ministerio de Educación Nacional, "Ruta de atención integral para la convivencia escolar," https://www.mineducacion.gov.co/1759/articles-322486_archivo_pdf_ruta.pdf.

22. Decreto 1965.

23. Chaux and Velásquez, "Peace Education in Colombia."

24. Cátedra de Paz, http://www.somoscapazes.org/catedra-de-la-paz.php.

25. Luis Felipe Higuita-Gutiérrez and Jaiberth Antonio Cardona-Arias, "Validación de una escala de bullying en adolescentes de instituciones educativas de Medellín, Colombia," *Educación y Educadores* 20, no. 1 (2017): 9–23.

26. Instituto Nacional de Medicina Legal y Ciencias Forenses, "Informe de gestión 2017," http://www.medicinalegal.gov.co/documents/20143/39839/INFORME+DE+GESTION +2017+V1.pdf/ede01c18-323f-b8ed-a5ec-ca66db48b1a6.

27. Cifuentes Osorio, "Exámenes médico legales por presunto delito sexual: Colombia," 2015 http://www.medicinalegal.gov.co/documents/20143/49523/Violencia+sexual.pdf.

28. Ibid.

29. Olga Rodríguez-Jiménez and José Guillermo Martínez-Rojas, "Cinco instrumentos objetivos para medir el maltrato por abuso de poder entre pares," *Avances en Medición* 7 (2009): 129–34; Sanjay Nanwani, "Democratic Citizenship Education in Schools: Towards More Demo-Critical Teacher Practices and Classroom Climates" (PhD diss., Universidad de Los Andes, 2019).

30. "Ministerio de Educación Nacional de Colombia. Decreto 1965 (2013)." Prado et al. (2010); Paredes et al. (2006); Uribe et al. (2012); Cassiani-Miranda, Gómez-Alhach, Cubides-Munévar, and Hernández-Carrillo, "Prevalencia de bullying y factores relacionados en estudiantes de bachillerato de una institución educativa de Cali, Colombia, 2011," *Revista de Salud Pública* 16, no. 1 (2014): 14–26; Sánchez et al. (2009).

31. Cassiani-Miranda et al., "Prevalencia de bullying": 14–26; M. T. V. Paredes, L. I. Lega, H. Cabezas, M. E. Ortega, Y. Medina, and C. Vega, "Diferencias transculturales en la manifestación del bullying en estudiantes de escuela secundaria," *Revista Latinoamericana de Ciencias Sociales, Niñez y Juventud* 2, no. 9 (2011): 761–68; C. L. Mesa-Melo, C. A. Carvajal-Castillo, M. F. Soto-Godoy, and P. N. Urrea-Roa, "Factores asociados a la convivencia escolar en adolescentes," *Educación y Educadores* 16, no. 3 (2013): 383–410.

32. Ombudsman's Office, Personería de Medellín, 2013.

33. Higuita-Gutiérrez and Cardona-Arias, "Validación de una escala de bullying."

34. E. Chaux, M. Barrera, A. Molano, A. M. Velásquez, M. Castellanos, M. P. Chaparro, and A. Bustamante, "Classrooms in Peace Within Violent Contexts: Field Evaluation of Aulas en Paz in Colombia," *Prevention Science* 18, no. 7 (2017): 828–38.

35. C. Torrente and F. Kanayet, "Contribucion de las competencias ciudadanas al rompimiento de la violencia en Colombia: Un estudio a nivel nacional" (CESO Paper No. 15, Universidad de los Andes, Bogotá, 2007).

36. E. Chaux and A. M. Velásquez, "Violencia en los colegios de Bogotá: Contraste internacional y algunas recomendaciones," *Revista Colombiana de Educación* 55 (2008): 4–37.

37. "Índice Sintético de Calidad Educativa," http://aprende.colombiaaprende.edu.co/es /siemprediae/86402.

38. Ibid.

39. Ibid. (my translation).

40. S. Nanwani, "Democratic Citizenship Education in Schools."

41. Verónica Lopez, "School Violence and *Convivencia Escolar* in Chile," chapter 4 in this volume.

CHAPTER 7

1. Eric Debarbieux, *Violence à l'école: Un défi mondial* (Paris: Armand Colin 2006).

2. Anne Wuilleumier and Eric Debarbieux, "Police Programmes and Public Policies to Ensure Security at School" (report, Institut National des Hautes Etudes de la Sécurité

et de la Justice, Paris, 2016), https://inhesj.fr/sites/default/files/inhesj_files/etudes
-et-recherches/rapportfinalanr.pdf.

3. Nicolas Sarkozy, "Déclaration de M. Nicolas Sarkozy, Président de la République, sur les efforts en faveur de la sécurité des français, à Paris le 28 mai 2009," http://discours .vie-publique.fr/notices/097001581.html.

4. For example, Eric Debarbieux, "Pas de schémas simplistes pour aborder un phénomène complexe," *Le Monde*, 2010, https://www.lemonde.fr/idees/article/2010/04/02/pas-de -schemas-simplistes-pour-aborder-un-phenomene-complexe-par-eric-debarbieux _1327986_3232.html.

5. Eric Debarbieux, *A l'école des enfants heureux . . . Enfin Presque* (Paris: UNICEF, 2011).

6. For videos, see Ministry of Education, https://www.education.gouv.fr/cid55976/assises -nationales-sur-le-harcelement-a-l-ecole.html.

7. See the press kit on the official website CANOPE (a site of the French Ministry of Education), https://www.reseau-canope.fr/climatscolaire/fileadmin/user_upload/enquetes /Enqu%C3%AAte_personnels_2d_degr%C3%A9.pdf.

8. Ministry of Education, https://www.education.gouv.fr/cid102387/loi-n-2013-595-du-8-juillet-2013-d-orientation-et-de-programmation-pour-la-refondation-de-l-ecole-de -la-republique.html.

9. Ministry of National Education, "Non au harcèlement," https://www.nonauharcelement .education.gouv.fr/.

10. Ministry of Education, "Rapport d'activité de la Délégation Ministérielle," https:// www.education.gouv.fr/cid2765/climat-scolaire-et-prevention-des-violences.html

11. The Higher School of National Education is a national training center for inspectors, principals, and other educational senior executives. In each district's departmental administrative zone, a person is appointed whose role is to help with the implementation of bullying prevention policies and to assist in managing the most difficult cases.

12. Christina Salmivalli, Antti Kärnä, and Elisa Poskiparta, "Counteracting Bullying in Finland: The KiVa Program and Its Effects on Different Forms of Being Bullied," *International Journal of Behavioral Development* 35, no. 5 (2011): 405–11.

13. France takes part in two international surveys that have dimensions concerning school climate, mental health, or bullying: HBSC (Health Behaviour in School-Aged Children) and PISA (Program for International Student Assessment).

14. Eric Debarbieux, *Etat des lieux*, vol. 1: *La violence en milieu* (Paris: ESF, 1996). See also Cécile Carra and François Sicot, "Une autre perspective sur les violences scolaires: L'expérience de victimation," in *La violence à l'école: Etat des savoirs*, ed. Bernard Charlot and Jean-Claude Emin (Paris: Armand Colin, 1997).

15. I objected to this centralized approach when I was a Ministerial Delegate, preferring to form local groups and use data that would enable analysis of the schools' situation from a more contextualized perspective.

16. Debarbieux, *A l'école des enfants heureux*.

17. DEPP, "Enquête nationale de climat scolaire et de victimation auprès des collégiens 2017," *Note d'information, no. 17.30* (Paris: Ministère de l'éducation nationale).

18. Eric Debarbieux, *Ne tirez pas sur l'école* (Paris: Armand Colin, 2017).

19. Catherine Blaya, *Les ados dans le cyberspace: Prises de risque et cyberviolence* (Brussels: De Boeck, 2013).

20. Eric Debarbieux and Benjamin Moignard, "Les impasses de la punition à l'école," in *L'impasse de la punition à l'école*, ed. Eric Debarbieux (Paris: Armand Colin, 2018).

21. Ibid.
22. Russell J. Skiba, Robert S. Michael, Abra Carroll Nardo, and Reece L. Peterson, "The Color of Discipline: Sources of Racial and Gender Disproportionality in School Punishment," *Urban Review* 34, no. 4 (2002): 317–42; Jean-Paul Payet, *Collèges de banlieue: Ethnographie d'un monde scolaire* (Paris: Méridiens Klincksieck, 1995).
23. Denise C. Gottfredson, *Schools and Delinquency* (Cambridge, UK: Cambridge University Press, 2001).
24. Rami Benbenishty and Ron Astor, *School Violence in Context: Culture, Neighborhood, Family, School and Gender* (New York: Oxford University Press, 2005); Dan Olweus, *Bullying in Schools: What We Know and What We Can Do* (Oxford, UK: Blackwell, 1993).
25. Marc Van Meenen, "Sécurité publique et violence scolaire: L'apport de la science du danger," in *L'école face à la violence: Décrire, expliquer, agir*, ed. Eric Debarbieux (Paris: Armand Colin, 2016).
26. Stéphanie Rubi and Johanna Dagorn, "Genre et violences à l'école: Défaire les stéréotypes sexués à l'école," in *L'école face à la violence: Décrire, expliquer, agir*, ed. Eric Debarbieux (Paris: Armand Colin, 2016).
27. Benjamin Aguilar, Alan L. Sroufe, Byron Egeland, and Elizabeth Carlson, "Distinguishing the Early-Onset/Persistent and Adolescence-Onset Antisocial Behavior Types: From Birth to 16 Years," *Development and Psychopathology* 12, no. 2 (2000): 109–32; see also Gerald R. Patterson, John B. Reid, and Thomas J. Dishion, *Anti-Social Boys* (Eugene, OR: Castilian, 1992).
28. Denise C. Gottfredson, David B. Wilson, and Stacy S. Najaka, "The Schools," *Crime: Public Policies for Crime Control* (2002): 149–89.
29. American Psychological Association Zero Tolerance Task Force, "Are Zero Tolerance Policies Effective in the Schools? An Evidentiary Review and Recommendations," *American Psychologist* 63, no. 9: 852–62, doi:10.1037/0003-066X.63.9.852.
30. Eric Debarbieux, *Le désordre des choses*, vol. 2: *La violence en milieu scolaire* (Paris: ESF, 1999); see also Jeremy D. Finn and Timothy J. Servoss, "Misbehavior, Suspensions, and Security Measures in High School: Racial/Ethnic and Gender Differences," *Journal of Applied Research on Children: Informing Policy for Children at Risk* 5, no. 2 (2014).
31. Hill M. Walker, Elizabeth Ramsey, and Frank M. Gresham, *Antisocial Behavior in School: Evidence-Based Practices* (Belmont, CA: Wadsworth, 2004).
32. Line Massé, Nadia Desbiens, and Catherine Lanaris, *Les troubles de comportement à l'école* (Montréal: Gaëtan Morin, 2013).
33. Ibid., 231.
34. Jane Nelsen, *Positive Discipline* (New York: Ballantine Books, 2006).
35. Erling Roland and David Galloway, "Professional Cultures in Schools with High and Low Rates of Bullying," *School Effectiveness and School Improvement* 15 (2004): 241–60.
36. David Smith, J. Bradley Cousins, and Rebecca Stewart, "Antibullying Interventions in Schools: Ingredients of Effective Programs," *Canadian Journal of Education/Revue canadienne de l'éducation* 28, no. 4 (2005): 739–62.
37. Denis Jeffrey and Fou Sun, *Enseignants dans la violence* (Québec: Les Presses de l'Université Laval, 2006).
38. David Hargreaves, *Challenges for the Comprehensive School: Curriculum, Culture and Community* (London: Routledge, 1982).

39. Denise C. Gottfredson, "School-Based Crime Prevention," in *Evidence-Based Crime Prevention*, ed. Lawrence W. Sherman, David P. Farrington, and Doris L. Mackenzie (London: Routledge, 2003).

CHAPTER 8

1. Rami Benbenishty and Ron Avi Astor, *School Violence in Context: Culture, Neighborhood, Family, School, and Gender* (New York: Oxford University Press, 2005); Ron Avi Astor and Rami Benbenishty, *Bullying, School Violence, and Climate in Evolving Contexts: Culture, Organization and Time* (New York: Oxford University Press, 2019).

2. Benbenishty and Astor, *School Violence in Context*; Mona Khoury-Kassabri, Rami Benbenishty, Ron Avi Astor, and Anat Zeira, "The Contributions of Community, Family, and School Variables on Student Victimization," *American Journal of Community Psychology* 34 (2004): 187–204; Idit Fast, "Understanding Educational Policy Formation: The Case of School Violence Policies in Israel," *Sociology of Education* 89 (2016): 59–78; Yossi Shavit and Carmela Blank, "School Discipline and Achievement in Israel," in *Improving Learning Environments: School Discipline and Student Achievement in Comparative Perspective*, ed. Richard Arum and Melissa Velez (Stanford, CA: Stanford University Press, 2012), 104–36.

3. Fast, "Understanding Educational Policy Formation."

4. Astor and Benbenishty, *Bullying, School Violence, and Climate.*

5. Ron Avi Astor, Rami Benbenishty, and Joey Nuñez Estrada Jr., "School Violence and Theoretically Atypical Schools: The Principal's Centrality in Orchestrating Safe Schools," *American Educational Research Journal* 46 (2009): 423–61.

6. Ministry of Education, *The General Manager Circular: Optimal Educational Climate and Coping with Violent and Dangerous Events* (Jerusalem: Ministry of Education, 2015).

7. See http://cms.education.gov.il/NR/rdonlyres/7026D76E-AA10-491C-AE61-91 85170EF0E5/125168/matzegetkidumaklim.ppt (in Hebrew).

8. Carol D. Ryff and Burton H. Singer, "Know Thyself and Become What You Are: A Eudaimonic Approach to Psychological Well Being," *Journal of Happiness Studies* 9 (2008): 13–39.

9. See http://education.academy.ac.il/Index/Entry.aspx?nodeId=1035&entryId=21084.

10. Joseph A. Durlak, Celene E. Domitrovich, and Roger P. Weissberg, eds., *Handbook of Social and Emotional Learning: Research and Practice* (New York: Guilford Press, 2005); National Commission on Social, Emotional, & Academic Development, https://www .aspeninstitute.org/programs/national-commission-on-social-emotional-and-academic -development/.

11. See https://meyda.education.gov.il/rama-mbareshet/.

12. Ron Avi Astor, Rami Benbenishty, Amiram Vinokur, and Anat Zeira, "Arab and Jewish Elementary School Students' Perception of Fear and School Violence: Understanding the Influence of School Context," *British Journal of Educational Psychology* 76 (2006): 91–118; Mona Khoury-Kassabri, Ron Avi Astor, and Rami Benbenishty, "Middle Eastern Adolescents' Perpetration of School Violence Against Peers and Teachers: A Cross Cultural and Ecological Analysis," *Journal of Interpersonal Violence* 24 (2009): 159–82.

CHAPTER 9

1. Peter K. Smith et al., "Cyberbullying: Its Nature and Impact in Secondary School Pupils," *Journal of Child Psychology and Psychiatry* 49, no. 4 (2008): 376–85, doi:10.1111

/j.1469-7610.2007.01846.x; *Ending All Forms of Violence Against Children by 2030: The Council of Europe's Contribution to the 2030 Agenda and the Sustainable Goals*, Council of Europe, 2017, https://violenceagainstchildren.un.org/sites/violenceagainstchildren.un.org/files/2030_agenda/sdg_leaflet.pdf.pdf.

2. Robert Slonje, P. K. Smith, and A. Frisén, "The Nature of Cyberbullying, and Strategies for Prevention," *Computers in Human Behavior* 29, no. 1 (2013): 26–32, doi:10.1016/j.chb.2012.05.024.

3. Ada Fonzi, *Il bullismo in Italia: Il fenomeno delle prepotenze a scuola dal Piemonte alla Sicilia: Ricerche e prospettive d'intervento* (Florence: Giunti, 1997).

4. Maria Luisa Genta et al., "Comparative Aspects of Cyberbullying in Italy, England, and Spain: Findings from a DAPHNE Project," in *Cyberbullying in the Global Playground: Research from International Perspectives*, ed. Quing Li et al. (Chichester, UK: Wiley-Blackwell, 2012), 13–32; Annalisa Guarini et al., "Migliorare le relazioni per crescere: Percorsi di prevenzione per la scuola secondaria" (studi documenti, Ufficio Scolastico Regionale, Emilia Romagna, June 2018), http://istruzioneer.gov.it/wp-content/uploads/2018/10/Studi-e-documenti-21_4.pdf.

5. Versari, Stefano, "Sussidiarietà," In *Voci dalla scuola* (Salerno: Tecnodid, 2003), 343–50.

6. *PISA 2015 Results*, vol. 3 (Paris: OCED, 2017).

7. MIUR, *Ufficio Statistica e studi*, https://miur.gov.it/documents/20182/250189/Notiziario+Stranieri+1718.pdf/78ab53c4-dd30-0c0f-7f40-bf22bbcedfa6?version=1.1&t=1562782116429.

8. MUIR, "Piano Nazionale per l'educazione al rispetto," 2017, https://www.miur.gov.it/documents/20182/0/Piano+Nazionale+ER+4.pdf/7179ab45-5a5c-4d1a-b048-5d0b6cda4f5c?version=1.0.

9. MIUR, "Linee guida per il diritto allo studio delle alunne e degli alunni fuori dalla famiglia di origine," 2018, https://www.miur.gov.it/web/guest/-/scuola-fedeli-e-albano-firmano-le-linee-guida-per-il-diritto-allo-studio-delle-alunne-e-degli-alunni-fuori-dalla-famiglia-di-origine.

10. Eurydice/Cedefop, "Tackling Early Leaving from Education and Training in Europe: Strategies, Policies and Measures" (report, Publications Office of the European Union, Luxembourg, 2015).

11. "I diritti dell'infanzia e dell'adolescenza in Italia: Gruppo di Lavoro per la Convenzione sui diritti dell'infanzia e dell'adolescenza," Gruppo CRC, 2017–18, https://www.ausl.bologna.it/asl-bologna/dipartimenti-territoriali-1/dipartimento-di-cure-primarie/il-faro/centro-doc/centro-di-documentazione/per-i-professionisti/area-sociale/VIII rapporto%20CRC.pdf/preview_popup/file.

12. MUIR, "Linee di Orientamento per azioni di prevenzione e di contrasto al bullismo e al cyberbullismo," 2015, https://www.istruzione.it/allegati/2015/2015_04_13_16_39_29.pdf.

13. See https://www.miur.gov.it/benessere-organizzativo.

14. MUIR, "Linee di indirizzo generali ed azioni a livello nazionale per la prevenzione e la lotta al bullismo," 2007, https://archivio.pubblica.istruzione.it/normativa/2007/dir16_07.shtml.

15. Dan Olweus, "Bullying at School," in *Aggressive Behavior* (Boston: Springer, 1994), 97–130; Irene Whitney and Peter K. Smith, "A Survey of the Nature and Extent of Bullying in Junior/Middle and Secondary Schools," *Educational Research* 35, no. 1 (1993): 3–25, doi:10.1080/0013188930350101.

16. See https://www.smontailbullo.it.
17. MUIR, "Regolamento recante modifiche ed integrazioni al decreto del Presidente della Repubblica 24 giugno 1998, n. 249, concernente lo statuto delle studentesse e degli studenti della scuola secondaria," 2007, https://iostudio.pubblica.istruzione.it/documents /11039/26431/DPR_235_2007.pdf/04eb7e6a-7a0c-4d45-86e8-27eb3ef3149e.
18. MUIR, "Linee di Orientamento per azioni di prevenzione del bullismo e del cyberbullismo."
19. MUIR, "Piano Nazionale per la prevenzione del bullismo e del cyberbullismo a scuola 2016/2017," 2016, https://www.istruzione.it/allegati/2016/Piano_azioni_definitivo.pdf
20. "Formazione E-Learning per Insegnanti sulle strategie antibullismo," https://www .piattaformaelisa.it.
21. MUIR, "Legge n.71, 29 Maggio 2017, Disposizioni a tutela dei minori per la prevenzione e il contrasto del fenomeno del cyberbullismo," 2017, http://www.astrid-online.it /static/upload/legg/legge-29-maggio-2017--n.-71.pdf.
22. See https://noisiamopari.it/site/it/home-page/.
23. See https://noisiamopari.it/site/it/home-page/, p. 22.
24. MUIR, "Aggiornamento line di orientamento per la prevenzione e il contrasto del cyberbullismo," 2017, https://www.miur.gov.it/documents/20182/0/Linee+Guida +Bullismo+-+2017.pdf/4df7c320-e98f-4417-9c31-9100fd63e2be?version=1.0.
25. Anna Civita, *Bullismo e politiche di contrasto: Autonomie locali e servizi sociali* (Bologna: Mulino, 2012).
26. Ibid.
27. "I diritti dell'infanzia e dell'adolescenza in Italia."
28. CENSIS-MIUR, "Prima indagine nazionale sul bullismo per MIUR," Centro studi investimenti sociali, http://cdn1.regione.veneto.it/alfstreaming-servlet/streamer?resource Id=c3f888d1-b2cc-40db-b30e-5140bc528a08/Censis.
29. "Il bullismo in Italia: Comportamenti offensivi e violenti tra i giovanissimi," Istituto Nazionale di Statistica (ISTAT), 2014, https://www.istat.it/it/files/2015/12/Bullismo.pdf.
30. Stephen T. Russell, K. O. Sinclair, P. V. Poteat, and B. W. Koenig, "Adolescent Health and Harassment Based on Discriminatory Bias," *American Journal of Public Health* 102 (2012): 3, doi:10.2105/AJPH.2011.300430.
31. Simona C. S. Caravita, E. Donghi, A. Banfi, and F. Meneghini, "Essere immigrati come fattore di rischio per la vittimizzazione nel bullismo: Uno studio italiano su caratteristiche individuali e processi di gruppo," in *Maltrattamento e abuso all'infanzia* (Milan: FrancoAngeli, 2016).
32. *Minority gender* defines a group whose sexual identity, orientation, and practices represent a minority with respect to surrounding society. This term includes transgender, genderqueer, intersex individuals other than the more common LGBT. Luca Pietrantoni, G. Prati, and E. Saccinto, "Interventi per l'età adolescenziale et giovanile: Bullismo e omofobia," *Autonomie locali e servizi sociali* 1 (2011): 67–79.
33. Franco Cavallo et al., "Trends in Life Satisfaction in European and North American Adolescents from 2002 to 2010 in over 30 Countries," *European Journal of Public Health* 25 (2015): 2, doi:10.1093/eurpub/ckv014.
34. Alessio Vieno, M. Lenzi, G. Gini, T. Pozzoli, F. Cavallo, and M. Santinello, "Time Trends in Bullying Behavior in Italy," *Journal of School Health* 85 (2015): 441–45, doi:10.1111/josh.12269.

35. Kayleigh L. Chester et al., "Cross-National Time Trends in Bullying Victimization in 33 Countries Among Children Aged 11, 13 and 15 from 2002 to 2010," *European Journal of Public Health* 25 (2015): 2, doi:10.1093/eurpub/ckv029

36. Franco Cavallo et al., *Rapporto sui dati HBSC Italia 2014* (Turin: Dipartimento di Scienze della Sanità Pubblica e Pediatriche, 2016).

37. *PISA 2015 Results.*

38. World Health Organization, "WHO fi-006," 2018, http://www.health.fi/connect.

39. Phillip T. Slee, "The P.E.A.C.E. Pack: A Program for Reducing Bullying in Our Schools," in *The International Handbook of School Bullying*, ed. Shane R. Jimerson et al. (New York: Routledge, 1996).

40. Antonella Brighi and A. Guarini, "Turning Obstacles into Opportunities: The Effects of the SEED Program in Bullying Prevention in Preschool and Primary School" (report, European Commission, Justice Programme, Daphne III, University of Bologna, 2015).

41. Guarini et al., "Migliorare le relazioni per crescere."

42. Benedetta E. Palladino, A. Nocentini, and E. Menesini, "Evidence-Based Intervention Against Bullying and Cyberbullying: Evaluation of the NoTrap! Program in Two Independent Trials," *Aggressive Behavior* 42 (2016): 2, doi:10.1002/ab.21636.

CHAPTER 10

1. *Gekkan Seitoshidou* (January 1980); *Kyouiku Shinri* (February 1981).

2. See Mitsuru Taki, "Ijime-koui no hassei-youin ni kansuru jissyouteki kenkyu," *Kyouiku Syakaigaku Kenkyuu* 50 (1992): 366–88; Mitsuru Taki, "Relation Among Bullying, Stress and Stressor: A Follow-Up Survey Using Panel Data and a Comparative Survey Between Japan and Australia," *Japanese Society* 5 (2001):118–33; Mitsuru Taki, "Japanese School Bullying: Ijime: A Survey Analysis and an Intervention Program in School" (paper, Understanding and Preventing Bullying: An International Perspective, Queen's University, Kingston, Ontario, October 19, 2001); Mitsuru Taki, "Ijime Bullying: Characteristic, Causality and Intervention: Measures to Reduce Bullying in Schools" (paper, Oxford-Kobe Seminars, Kobe Institute, Kobe, Japan, May 21–25, 2003); Mitsuru Taki et al., "A New Definition and Scales for Indirect Aggression in Schools: Results from the Longitudinal Comparative Survey Among Five Countries," *International Journal on Violence and School* 7 (2008); Mitsuru Taki, "Relations Among Bullying, Stresses, and Stressors: A Longitudinal and Comparative Survey Among Countries," in *International Handbook of School Bullying*, ed. Shane R. Jimerson, Susan M. Swearer, and Dorothy L. Espelage (New York: Routledge, 2010).

3. Taki, "Ijime Bullying"; *The Report of International Symposium on Education 2005: Save Children from the Risk of Violence in School: Based on the Follow-Up Study and International Comparison* (Tokyo: NIER and MEXT, 2006); *Ijime tsuiseki tyousa 2004–2006: Ijime Q&A* (Tokyo: NIER, 2009); *Ijime tsuiseki tyousa 2007–2009: Ijime Q&A* (Tokyo: NIER, 2010); *Ijime tsuiseki tyousa 2010–2012: Ijime Q&A* (Tokyo: NIER, 2013); *Ijime tsuiseki tyousa 2013–2015: Ijime Q&A* (Tokyo: NIER, 2016). NIER longitudinal surveys began in 1998 and are ongoing.

4. This situation was, for the most part, the same in Canada in the 1990s and in the US in the 2000s; only serious physical violence attracted people's attention.

5. Peter-Paul Heinemann, *Mobbning: Gruppvåld bland barn och vuxna* (Stockholm: Natur och Kultur, 1972).

6. Dan Olweus, *Mobbning: Vad vi vet och vad vid kan göra* (Stockholm: Liber, 1983); Dan Olweus, *Bullying at School: What We know and What We Can Do* (Oxford, UK: Blackwell, 1993).

7. *Ijime no nai gakkou-zukuri: Gakkou ijime boushi kihon houshin sakutei Q&A* (Tokyo: NIER, 2013).

8. *Ijime no nai gakkou-zukuri 2: Cycle de susumeru seitoshidou: Tenken to minaoshi* (Tokyo: NIER, 2014).

9. Mitsuru Taki, "Fostering Social Self Efficacy by Japanese Style Peer Support Program" (paper, Dawson College and ACCC Conference, Toronto, September 29–October 1, 2011).

10. *Zenkyousyokuin ga ninshiki wo kyouyuu si syutaiteki ni torikumukoto de ijime no mizenboushi wa kanou* (Tokyo: NIER, 2018).

11. Japanese schools usually have three terms a year and a long school holiday period between terms.

12. *Syakaisei no kiso wo hagukumu "kouryuu-katsudou" "taiken-katsudou"* (Tokyo: NIER, 2004).

CHAPTER 11

1. Antoinette Hetzler, "From Anti-Bullying Legislation and Policy to Everyday School Reality," paper presented at the Swedish Network for Research on Social Policy and Welfare, November 2012, Göteborg, Sweden; Antoinette Hetzler, "Trouble in School: Law, Policy and the Dynamics of Everyday Life at School," in *Resultat Dialog 2014* (Motala, Sweden: Vetenskapsrådet, 2014), 78–87); Antoinette Hetzler, "War at Work: The Inner Dynamics of Strategic Threats and Violence in Swedish Schools" (paper presented at the American Sociology Association, Chicago, August 2015); Antoinette Hetzler, "Framing Work Injury/Sickness in a Changing Welfare State: Naming and Blaming," in *The Transformation of Work in Welfare State Organizations: New Public Management and the Institutional Diffusion of Ideas*, ed. F. Sowa, R. Staples, and S. Zapfel (London: Routledge, 2018), 223–41; Antoinette Hetzler, *Vad händer med kvinnodominerade yrken? Utsatthet inom läraryrket och socionomyrket* (Malmö, Sweden: Bokbox, 2018); Antoinette Hetzler and Colm Flahtery, "Guaranteeing Social Rights and Regulating the Public Sector," *European Journal of Cultural and Political Sociology* 4, no.1 (2017): 25–51; Antoinette Hetzler, with Mitsuru Taki, "Promoting a Positive School Climate for Less Bullying and/or Harassment" (paper, Third International Symposium on Bullying, Tokyo, 2016).

2. In addition, there were 119,076 children in the six-year-old preschool class.

3. All Swedish laws are referenced in Sverige Författningssamling (SFS) by the area of law, the year, and the number of the consecutive law in the particular year.

4. Brå, "Grövre våld i skolan," 2009, https://www.bra.se/download/18.cba82f7130f475a2 f180003129/1371914721392/2009_6_grovre_vald_skolan.pdf., pp. 14, 57.

5. Abusive behavior includes bullying. A behavior does not have to have happened more than once for it to be considered an abusive behavior. A government inquiry proposed that "the responsibility for monitoring action to combat discrimination in establishments subject to the Education Act of 2010 be transferred from the Discrimination Ombudsman to the Swedish School Inspectorate. Consequently, the provisions in the Discrimination Act pertaining to establishments subject to the Education Act of 2010 are to be coordinated with the rules against abusive behavior" ("Bättre skydd mot

diskriminering," Statens Offentliga Utredningar [SOU] 2016:87, https://www
.regeringen.se/4af295/contentassets/b42c019548304be987083fb37f73d74f/battre
-skydd-mot-diskriminering-sou-201687, p. 36). However, as of October 2019, no
decision had been taken.

6. The study targeted schools through the results of an intense review of all högstadiet
schools in two Swedish cities with more than 100 students. Eight schools from each
city were chosen according to a scale of high, middle-high, middle-low, low on a variety of variables presented by the National Agency for Education for the previous ten
years. The variables included income and education of parents, actual student grades,
expected grades, number of students of non-Swedish background, percentage of male
students. Four schools from each city participated in the research project "Conflict in
School." See endnote 1 above.

7. The revised survey was based on the survey designed by the USA School Rights Proj-
ect: Calvin Morrill, Lauren Edelman, Richard Arum, and Karolyn Tyson, "Legal
Mobilization in US Schools: How Race Conditions Students' Response to Laws and
Rights" (paper, Center for the Study of Law and Society Speakers Series, University of
California, Berkeley February 2, 2009).

8. The Swedish Institute for Education Research, founded in 2015, is still in the development phase and therefore not discussed here. The development of its profile is not
directed toward abusive behavior and school climate, although this might be incorporated into its work in the future.

9. The Education Act of 1985 replaced the Education Act of 1962 and was then replaced
by the current Education Act of 2010. The Education Act of 1985 was amended more
than seventy times. During its duration, the entire school system was reformed, and
detailed regulation of schools by the national state government was replaced by a decentralized system of local municipality and private owner responsibility for local and
private schools.

10. As of January 1, 2009, the Child and Student Protection Act (SFS 2006:67) was replaced by the Discrimination Act (SFS 2008:567), which combined and replaced seven
different laws against discrimination around gender, gender identities, ethnic belonging, religion, disability, sexual preferences, and age. The sections of the Child and Student Protection Act that referred to grounds of discrimination were transferred to the
Discrimination Act, and those that governed other abusive behavior that were not considered as caused by discrimination were written into a new section of the Education
Act of 1985 (14a kap. 15§). In this way, the law separated bullying and abusive behavior by reason of discrimination and other abusive behavior. Abusive behavior includes
the concept of bullying but is a wider concept. The rules of evidence were that a student was required to present evidence that abusive behavior had taken place, and the
school was required to present evidence that there was an investigation and that measures had been taken. The Education Act of 2010 used much of the same wording from
the amended Education of Act of 1985 (14a kap. 5§) but strengthened language around
the duty of the school so that the municipality or the legal authority for private schools
has to show that abusive behavior or reprisals against reporting other abusive behavior
did not occur. By 2016 a special investigator appointed by the government left a series
of propositions for changes in Discrimination Act and in the Education Act of 2010 in
order to make work against discrimination in Sweden even more effective and better
organized.

11. Minister of Culture Alice Bah Kuhnke proposed to transfer some parts of the monitoring responsibility for protection against discriminatory behavior in schools to the SSI and indicated that there would be a change in the wording of the Education Act of 2010 reflecting this change (effective March 2019) to "forbid discrimination and other abusive behavior." See Alice Bah Kuhnke, "Utkast till lagrådsremiss: Stärkt skydd mot diskriminering i skolan," October 2018, https://www.regeringen.se/4a3513/contentassets /54ae0a1c20d745b2841359d9f889867f/utkast-till-lagradsremiss-starkt-skydd-mot -diskriminering-i-skolan.pdf). As of October 2019, the change was still under review. The DO had objections to the suggested changes of October 2018, and the BEO also had objections to the proposed changes and sent their written objections to the Swedish government in October 2018. See https://www.do.se/om-do/vad-gor-do/remissvar /remissvar-under-2018/yttrande-over-utkast-till-lagradsremiss-starkt-skydd-mot -diskriminering-i-skolan/; https://www.regeringen.se/4a97f0/contentassets/b8aec 621b771479283bd549cf87393ad/statens-skolinspektion.pdf.

12. Anders Hamberger, Sara Carlbaum, Agneta Huylt, Lena Lindgren, and Ulf Lundström, "School Evaluation in Sweden in a Local Perspective: A Synthesis," *Education Inquiry* 7, no. 3 (2016): 349–71, doi:10.3402/edui.v7.30115; Mikael Holmgren, Olof Johansson, Elisabet Nihlfors, and Pia Skott, "Local School Governance in Sweden: Boards, Parents and Democracy," *Journal of School Public Relations* 33, no. 1 (2012): 8–28; Stig Montin and Mikael Granberg, *Moderna kommuner* (Malmö: Liber, 2007).

13. Hamberger et al, "School Evaluation in Sweden in a Local Perspective," 11; Hetzler, "From Anti-Bullying Legislation and Policy to Everyday School Reality," 4; Hetzler and Flaherty, "Guaranteeing Social Rights and Regulating the Public Sector."

14. See note 10 above.

15. OECD, "Improving Schools in Sweden: An OECD Perspective," 2015, http://www .oecd.org/edu/school/Improving-Schools-in-Sweden.pdf.

16. SSII, *Skolenkäten våren 2016: Fördupad analys om respect mellan elever och lärare*, Dnr. 2015:726, https://www.skolinspektionen.se/globalassets/publikationssok/statistikrapporter/skolenkaten/2016/skolenkaten-vt-2016-analysrapport.pdf; Skolverket, *Attityder till skolan* (Stockholm: Wolters Kluwers, 2016).

17. FOHM, *Skolbarna hälsovanor i Sverige 2013/14* (Stockholm: Folkhälsomyndigheten, 2014); Skolverket, *Attityder till skolan*, 14.

18. "Samling för skolan: Nationell strategi för kunskap och likvärdighet," SOU 2017:35.

19. Karl Grunewald, *Från idiot till medborgare: De utvecklingsstördas historia* (Stockholm: Gothia, 2009); Rolf Helldin, Helen Dwyer, and Mara Allodi Westling, eds., *Specialpedagogiska nybyggare: En historisk antologi om organisation, funktionshinder och särskilt stöd under 1900-talet* (Uppsala, Sweden: Föreningen för Svensk Undervisningshistoria, 2011), 153.

20. Skolverket, *Främja, förebygga, upptäcka och åtgärda* (Stockholm: Fritze, 2014).

21. For pupils with severe learning disabilities there is a special program that used to be the responsibility of regional counties, but since 1996 local school boards in each municipality have had full responsibility for the program. European Agency for Special Needs and Inclusive Education, "Sweden: Special Education Within the Education System," https://www.european-agency.org/country-information/sweden/national-overview /special-needs-education-within-the-education-system.

22. Malin Albinsson, Marie Back, Marie Björk, Thomas Bushby, Charlotte Jacobsson, Maria Lantz, Linda Hallberg, Anna Klemets, Christian Skoglöw, and Annette Strömbäck,

"Kartläggning av särskilt stöd och tidiga insatser: Fallstudier av internationella utbild-
ningssystem" (working paper, Specialpedagogiska Institutionen, Stockholms Universi-
tet, Stockholm, 2016), https://www.specped.su.se/polopoly_fs/1.303217.1477304552!
/menu/standard/file/Working%20_Paper_2C_2016.pdf; "Samling för skolan," 16.

23. The programs that were evaluated were Friends, SET, Lions Quest, Olweus Bullying
Prevention Program, Farsta Method, Skolkoment, Skolmedling, and Stegvis. The evaluation used both surveys and interviews and took place over three years. Ten thousand
students between ages ten and sixteen and thirty-nine different schools participated in
the study. Because none of the schools used only one method and used parts of different programs, the study evaluated the effects of particular methods that could be found
in the programs and could be used independent of the program. The study also evaluated the experiences that school personnel and students had with the eight programs.
Skolverket, *Vad fungerar? Resultat från utvärdering av metoder mot mobbning* (Stockholm: Fritze, 2011).

24. "Samling för skolan," 16.

25. Skolverket, *What Influences Educational Achievement in Swedish Schools? A Systematic
Review and Summary Analysis* (Stockholm: Fritzes, 2010), https://www.skolverket.se
/download/18.6bfaca41169863e6a6589bb/1553962125580/pdf2318.pdf; Skolverket,
Kvalitetsarbete i praktiken (Stockholm: Fritzes, 2015).

26. Skolverket, "An Assessment of the Situation in the Swedish School System: Summary
of Report 421," https://www.skolverket.se/getFile?file=3551; "Skolverkets lägebedömn-
ing 2015, Report 421," ttps://www.skolverket.se/getFile?file=3432.

27. "Samling för skolan," 16.

28. Skolverket, *Främja, förebygga, upptäcka och åtgärda*, 17.

29. Ibid., 17.

30. lverket Allmänna råd 2009 (SKOLFS 2009) *Allmänna råd och kommentarer* https://
https://www.lerum.se/globalassets/documents/forvaltningssidorna/utbildning-och
-barnomsorg/fakta-och-info/skolverkets-allmanna-rad.pdf *För att främja likabehandling
och förebygga diskriminering, trakasserier och kränkande behandling.* This was replaced
in 2012. Skolverket Allmänna råd 2012 (SKOLFS 2012:10) *Arbetet mot diskriminering
och kränkande behandling* http://www.bromstensskolan.org/dok/ref/AR_KB.pdf. English translation from Antoinette Hetzler: "To promote equal treatment and to prevent discrimination, harassment and abusive behavior." The document that replaced it
(2012)—with my English translation—is "Work against discrimination and abusive
behavior."

31. OECD, "Improving Schools in Sweden."

32. Skolverket, *Attityder till skolan*, 14.

33. Ibid.

34. BRUK stands for Bedömning, Reflektion, Utvärdering, Kvalitet (assessment, reflection, evaluation, quality).

35. Information on the quality workshop can be found at https://www.skolverket.se
/skolutveckling/kompetensutveckling/kvalitetsverkstaden.

36. SSI, "Skolenkäten våren 2019: Redovisning för Skolenkäten," https://www.skolins
pektionen.se/globalassets/0-si/05-statistik/skolenkaten/skolenkaten-vt-2019/totalrapport
-skolinspektionen-vt-2019.pdf.

37. OECD, *Improving Schools in Sweden*, 13.

38. Ibid.

39. Hamberger et al., "School Evaluation in Sweden in a Local Perspective," 11.

40. Agneta Hult and Charlotta Edström, "Teacher Ambivalence Towards School Evaluation: Promoting and Ruining Teacher Professionalism," *Education Inquiry* 7, no. 3 (2016): 305–25, doi:10.3402/edui.v7.30200.

CHAPTER 12

We are indebted to Edgar Rivera-Cash, who took a leadership role in harvesting the 2011–17 state-level policy trend findings. We are also grateful to Alberto Valido and Luz E. Robinson, who assisted in the preparation of this chapter.

1. Annette Fuentes, "A Brief History of School Violence in the United States," in *Lockdown High: When the Schoolhouse Becomes a Jailhouse* (New York: Verso Books, 2011).

2. Marieke Brock, Norma Kriger, and Ramón Miró, "School Safety Policies and Programs Administered by the US Federal Government: 1990–2016" (report, National Criminal Justice Reference Service, US Department of Justice, Washington, DC, 2017), https://www.ncjrs.gov/pdffiles1/nij/grants/251517.pdf.

3. "The Prevention of Youth Violence: A Framework for Community Action," US Department of Health and Human Services, Centers for Disease Control, National Center for Environmental Health and Injury Control Division of Injury Control, and Office of the Assistant Director for Minority Health, 1992, https://wonder.cdc.gov/wonder/prevguid/p0000026/p0000026.asp.

4. David Cantor, Scott Cantor, Carol A. Hagen, Michael J. Mason, Amy J. Siler, and Adrienne von Glatz, "A Closer Look at Drug and Violence Prevention Efforts in American Schools: Report on the Study on School Violence and Prevention" (report, US Department of Education, Washington, DC, 2001), https://books.google.com/books?id=3WLurDveCQ4C&pg=PP4&dq=A+Closer+Look+at+Drug+and+Violence+Prevention+Efforts+in+American+Schools:+Report+on+the+Study+on+School+Violence+and+Prevention,%E2%80%9D+(US+Department+of+Education,+2001&hl=en&sa=X&ved=2ahUKEwjphPOGr4_lAhURU98KHcQXB_cQ6AEwAHoECAEQAg#v=onepage&q=A%20Closer%20Look%20at%20Drug%20and%20Violence%20Prevention%20Efforts%20in%20American%20Schools%3A%20Report%20on%20the%20Study%20on%20School%20Violence%20and%20Prevention%2C%E2%80%9D%20(US%20Department%20of%20Education%2C%202001&f=false.

5. CDC, "Fatal Injury Reports: National, Regional and State," 1999–2017, https://webappa.cdc.gov/cgi-bin/broker.exe; CDC, "Nonfatal Injury Reports, 2001–2014," https://webappa.cdc.gov/sasweb/ncipc/nfirates2001.html.

6. Anlan Zhang, Ke Wang, Jizhi Zhang, and Barbara A. Oudekerk, *Indicators of School Crime and Safety: 2016* (Washington, DC: National Center for Education Statistics, 2017), https://eric.ed.gov/?id=ED574084.

7. Dewey Cornell, "The Prevention of Gun Violence in Schools and Communities Written Statement for the Forum on School Safety Hosted by Committee Democrats and Democratic Leadership House Committee on Education and the Workforce," 2018, https://curry.virginia.edu/sites/default/files/images/YVP/Cornell%20Hearing%20Statement%203-20-18.pdf; Lauren Musu-Gillette, Anlan Zhang, Ke Wang, Jizhi Zhang, and Barbara A. Oudekerk, "Indicators of School Crime and Safety" (report, NCES 2019-047/NCJ 252571, National Center for Education Statistics, US

Department of Education, and Bureau of Justice Statistics, Office of Justice Programs, US Department of Justice, Washington, DC, 2018), http:// nces.ed.gov or https://bjs.gov.

8. Associated Press–NORC Center for Public Affairs Research, University of Chicago, "School Safety and Shootings," 2019, http://www.apnorc.org/projects/Pages/School-Safety-and-Shootings—.aspx.

9. James H. Price and Jagdish Khubchandani, "School Firearm Violence Prevention Practices and Policies: Functional or Folly?" *Violence and Gender* (March 19, 2019), https://doi.org/10.1089/vio.2018.0044.

10. Mark Dynarski, Linda Clarke, Brian Cobb, Jeremy Finn, Russell Rumberger, and Jay Smink, *Dropout Prevention. IES Practice Guide* (Washington, DC: National Center for Education Evaluation and Regional Assistance, 2008), https://eric.ed.gov/?id=ED502502.

11. Aspen Institute, "From a Nation at Risk to a Nation at Hope," *A Nation at Hope* (blog), 2019, http://nationathope.org/; American Educational Research Association, *Prevention of Bullying in Schools, Colleges, and Universities: Research Report and Recommendations* (Washington, DC: American Educational Research Association, 2013); National Academies of Sciences, Engineering and Medicine, *Preventing Bullying Through Science, Policy, and Practice* (Washington, DC: National Academies Press, 2016), https://www.nap.edu/catalog/23482/preventing-bullying-through-science-policy-and-practice.

12. National Center for Education Statistics, "Elementary and Secondary Education Enrollment," 2018, https://nces.ed.gov/fastfacts/display.asp?id=372.

13. Jonathan Cohen and Edgar Rivera-Cash, "School Climate, Social Emotional Learning and Bully Prevention Policy: US State Trends, Challenges and Future Directions" (working paper, 2018).

14. Jonathan Cohen, Elizabeth M. McCabe, Nicholas M. Michelli, and Terry Pickeral, "School Climate: Research, Policy, Practice, and Teacher Education," *Teachers College Record* 111, no. 1 (2009): 180–213, http://www.tcrecord.org/Content.asp?ContentId=15220; Amrit Thapa, Jonathan Cohen, Shawn Guffey, and Ann Higgins-D'Alessandro, "A Review of School Climate Research," *American Education Research Association* 83, no. 3 (2013): 357–85, doi:10.3102/0034654313483907; Stephanie Jones and Jennifer Kahn, "The Evidence Base for How We Learn: Supporting Students' Social, Emotional, and Academic Development," Aspen Institute, 2017, https://www.aspeninstitute.org/publications/evidence-base-learn/.

15. Carolyn MacCann and Richard D. Roberts, "New Paradigms for Assessing Emotional Intelligence: Theory and Data," *Emotion (Washington, D.C.)* 8, no. 4 (2008): 540–51, doi:10.1037/a0012746; National Research Council, *Education for Life and Work: Developing Transferable Knowledge and Skills in the 21st Century* (Washington DC: National Academies Press, 2012), https://www.nap.edu/catalog/13398/education-for-life-and-work-developing-transferable-knowledge-and-skills; Paul R. Sackett and Philip T. Walmsley, "Which Personality Attributes Are Most Important in the Workplace?" *Perspectives on Psychological Science* 9, no. 5 (2014): 538–51, doi:10.1177/1745691614543972; Brenna Schroeder, Mary Morris, and Malcolm Flack, "Exploring the Relationship Between Personality and Bullying: An Investigation of Parental Perceptions," *Personality and Individual Differences* 112 (July 1, 2017): 144–49, doi:10.1016/j.paid.2017.02.066; Jonathan Cohen and Amrit Thapa, "School Climate Improvement: What Do U.S. Educators Believe, Need and Want?" *International Journal on School Climate and Violence*

Prevention 1, no. 2 (2017): 90–116; Anya Kamenetz, "Social and Emotional Skills: Everybody Loves Them, But Still Can't Define Them," *NPR*, August 14, 2017, https://www.npr.org/sections/ed/2017/08/14/542070550/social-and-emotional-skills-everybody-loves-them-but-still-cant-define-them.

16. Jonathan Cohen, "School Climate, Social Emotional Learning, and Other Prosocial 'Camps': Similarities and a Difference," *Teachers College Record* (2017), https://www.tcrecord.org/content.asp?contentid=22165.

17. Dorothy L. Espelage, "Leveraging School-Based Research to Inform Bullying Prevention and Policy," *American Psychologist* 71, no. 8 (2016): 768–75, doi:10.1037/amp0000095; Anthony A. Volk, René Veenstra, and Dorothy L. Espelage, "So You Want to Study Bullying? Recommendations to Enhance the Validity, Transparency, and Compatibility of Bullying Research," *Aggression and Violent Behavior* 36 (2017): 34–43, doi:10.1016/j.avb.2017.07.003.

18. Dorothy L. Espelage, Kathleen. C. Basile, and Merle E. Hamburger, "Bullying Perpetration and Subsequent Sexual Violence Perpetration Among Middle School Students," *Journal of Adolescent Health* 50 (2012): 60–65, doi:10.1016/j.jadohealth.2011.07.015; Dorothy L. Espelage, Kathleen C. Basile, Lisa De La Rue, and Merle E. Hamburger, "Longitudinal Associations Among Bullying, Homophobic Teasing, and Sexual Violence Perpetration Among Middle School Students," *Journal of Interpersonal Violence* 30, no. 14 (2015): 2541–61, doi:10.1177/0886260514553113; Michele L. Ybarra, Dorothy L. Espelage, Jennifer Langhinrichsen-Rohling, Josephine D. Korchmaros, and Danah Boyd , "Lifetime Prevalence Rates and Overlap of Physical, Psychological, and Sexual Dating Abuse Perpetration and Victimization in a National Sample of Youth," *Archives of Sexual Behavior* 45, no. 5 (2016): 1083–99, doi:10.1007/s10508-016-0748-9.

19. "Dear Colleague Letter: Harassment and Bullying," Letters (Correspondence), US Department of Education and Office for Civil Rights, 2010, https://www2.ed.gov/about/offices/list/ocr/docs/dcl-factsheet-201010.html; Dorothy L. Espelage and Lisa De La Rue, "Examining Predictors of Bullying and Sexual Violence Perpetration Among Middle School Female Students," in *Perceptions of Female Offenders: How Stereotypes and Social Norms Affect Criminal Justice Responses*, ed. Brenda L. Russell (New York: Springer, 2013), 25–45, doi:10.1007/978-1-4614-5871-5_3; American Association of University Women (AAUW), "Sexual Harrassment," https://www.aauw.org/.

20. Espelage, *Bullying Perpetration and Subsequent Sexual Violence.*

21. Sarah J. Rinehart and Dorothy L. Espelage, "A Multilevel Analysis of School Climate, Homophobic Name-Calling, and Sexual Harassment Victimization/Perpetration Among Middle School Youth," *Psychology of Violence* 6, no. 2 (2016): 213–22, doi:10.1037/a0039095; AAUW, "Sexual Harrassment."

22. Rinehart and Espelage, "A Multilevel Analysis of School Climate."

23. New York State Education Department, "School Safety Data Reporting"(report, NYSED-IRS, New York, 2016), http://www.p12.nysed.gov/irs/school_safety/school_safety_data_reporting.html.

24. Jonathan Cohen, Dorothy L. Espelage, Stuart W. Twemlow, Marvin W. Berkowitz, and James P. Comer, "Rethinking Effective Bully and Violence Prevention Efforts: Promoting Healthy School Climates, Positive Youth Development, and Preventing Bully-Victim-Bystander Behavior," *International Journal of Violence and Schools* 15 (2015): 2–40, https://www.researchgate.net/publication/281593701; Dorothy L. Espelage, Melissa K. Holt, and Rachael R. Henkel, "Examination of Peer-Group Contextual

Effects on Aggression During Early Adolescence," *Child Development* 74, no. 1 (2003): 205–20, doi:10.1111/1467-8624.00531; Merle E. Hamburger, Kathleen C. Basile, and A. M. Vivolo, *Measuring Bullying Victimization, Perpetration, and Bystander Experiences: A Compendium of Assessment Tools* (Atlanta: CDC, National Center for Injury Prevention and Control, 2011), https://stacks.cdc.gov/view/cdc/5994; Joshua R. Polanin, Dorothy L. Espelage, and Therese D. Pigott, "A Meta-Analysis of School-Based Bullying Prevention Programs' Effects on Bystander Intervention Behavior," *School Psychology Review* 41, no. 1 (2012): 47–65.

25. See https://www.pbis.org/.

26. Jonathan Cohen, "School Climate Policy and Practice Trends: A Paradox. A Commentary," *Teachers College Record* (2014), https://www.researchgate.net/publication/262915293_Cohen_J_2014_School_Climate_Policy_and_Practice_Trends_A_Paradox_A_Commentary_Teachers_College_Record_Date_Published_February_21_2014_http wwwtcrecordorg; Cohen et al., *Rethinking Effective Bully and Violence Prevention Efforts.*

27. Anthony S. Bryk, Louis M. Gomez, Alicia Grunow, and Paul G. LeMahiu, *Learning to Improve: How America's Schools Can Get Better at Getting Better* (Cambridge, MA: Harvard Education Press, 2015); Dean L. Fixsen, Sandra Naoom, Karen Blasé, Robert Friedman, and Frances Wallace, "Implementation Research: A Synthesis of the Literature" (report, NIRN Project Site, Tampa, FL, 2005), https://nirn.fpg.unc.edu/resources/implementation-research-synthesis-literature; Bryk et al., *Learning to Improve*; Michael Fullan, "Choosing the Wrong Drivers for Whole System Reform," *Voprosy Obrazovaniya* 4 (2011): 79–105, doi:10.17323/1814-9545-2011-4-79-105; Karen Blase, Melissa Van Dyke, and Dean Fixsen, "Implementation Drivers: Assessing Best Practices. Adapted with Permission by The State Implementation and Scaling-Up of Evidence-Based Practices Center (SISEP)" (report, National Implementation Research Network, University of North Carolina, Chapel Hill, 2013), https://nirn.fpg.unc.edu/resources/implementation-drivers-assessing-best-practices.

28. Bryk et al., *Learning to Improve.*

29. Ibid.

30. Blase et al., "Implementation Drivers"; Fixsen et al., "Implementation Research."

31. Bryk et al., *Learning to Improve*; Michael Fullan, "Choosing the Wrong Drivers for Whole System Reform"; Michael G. Fullan, *The Principal: Three Keys to Maximizing Success* (San Francisco: Jossey-Bass, 2014).

32. American Educational Research Association, *Prevention of Bullying in Schools, Colleges, and Universities: Research Report and Recommendations* (Washington, DC: AERA, 2013); Ron Avi Astor and Rami Benbenishty, *Bullying, School Violence, and Climate in Evolving Contexts: Culture, Organization, and Time* (Oxford, UK: Oxford University Press, 2019); National Academies of Sciences, "Preventing Bullying Through Science, Policy, and Practice."

33. Dorothy Espelage, Eric M. Anderman, Veda E. Brown, Abraham Jones, Kathleen L. Lane, Susan D. McMahon, Linda A. Reddy, and Cecil R. Reynolds, "Understanding and Preventing Violence Directed Against Teachers: Recommendations for a National Research, Practice, and Policy Agenda," *American Psychologist* 68, no. 2 (2013): 75–87, doi:10.1037/a0031307.

34. Aspen Institute, "From a Nation at Risk to a Nation at Hope."

35. American Psychological Association Zero Tolerance Task Force, "Are Zero Tolerance Policies Effective in the Schools? An Evidentiary Review and Recommendations,"

American Psychologist 63, no. 9 (2008): 852–62, doi:10.1037/0003-066X.63.9.852; Christopher Boccanfuso and Megan Kuhfeld, "Multiple Responses, Promising Results: Evidence-Based, Nonpunitive Alternatives to Zero Tolerance" (Research-to-Results Brief, Publication #2011-09, Child Trends, Bethesda, MD, 2011), https://www .childtrends.org/wp-content/uploads/2011/03/Child_Trends-2011_03_01_RB _AltToZeroTolerance.pdf; Anne Gregory, Dewey Cornell, Xitao Fan, Peter Sheras, Tse-Hus Shih, and Francis Huang, "Authoritative School Discipline: High School Practices Associated with Lower Bullying and Victimization," *Journal of Educational Psychology* 102, no. 2 (2010): 483–96, doi:10.1037/a0018562; Emily Morgan, Nina Salomon, Martha Plotkin, and Rebecca Cohen, "School Discipline Consensus Report: Strategies from the Field to Keep Students Engaged in School and Out of the Juvenile Justice System" (report, Models for Change: Systems Reform in Juvenile Justice, Council of State Governments Justice Center, New York, 2014), http://www.modelsfor change.net/publications/831.

36. Linda A. Dusenbury, Jessy Zadrazil Newman, Roger P. Weissberg, Paul Goren, Celene E. Domitrovich, and Amy K. Mart, "The Case for Preschool through High School State Learning Standards,"in *Handbook of Social and Emotional Learning: Research and Practice*, ed. Joseph A. Durlak, Celene E. Domitrovich, Roger P. Weissberg and Thomas P. Gullotta (New York: Guilford Press, 2015), https://www.casel.org/wp -content/uploads/2016/06/The-Case-for-PreSchool-through-High-School-SEL -Standards-Book-Chapter.pdf.

37. AERA, "Prevention of Bullying in Schools, Colleges, and Universities"; National Academies of Sciences, "Preventing Bullying Through Science, Policy, and Practice."

38. Aspen Institute, "From a Nation at Risk to a Nation at Hope."

39. James P. Comer, *School Power: Implications of an Intervention Project* (New York: Free Press, 1980); Anthony Bryk and Barbara Schneider, *Trust in Schools: A Core Resource for Improvement Educational Leadership* 60, no. 6 (2003): 40–45.

40. Susan H. McDaniel and Eduardo Salas, "The Science of Teamwork: Introduction to the Special Issue," *American Psychologist* 73, no. 4 (2018): 305–7, doi:10.1037/amp0000337.

41. Bryk et al., *Learning to Improve.*

42. AERA, *Prevention of Bullying in Schools*; National Academies of Sciences, "Preventing Bullying Through Policy and Practice"; Izabela Zych, David P. Farrington, Vicente J. Llorent, and Maria M. Ttofi, *Protecting Children Against Bullying and Its Consequences* (New York: Springer, 2017); Ruth Berkowitz, Hadass Moore, Ron Avi Astor, and Rami Benbenishty, "A Research Synthesis of the Associations Between Socioeconomic Background, Inequality, School Climate, and Academic Achievement," *Review of Educational Research* 87, no. 2 (2017): 425–69, doi:10.3102/0034654316669821; Cohen et al., "School Climate"; Aidyn Iachini, Ruth Berkowitz, Hadass Moore, Ronald Pitner, Ron A. Astor, and Rami Benbenishty, "School Climate and Social Work Practice," in *Encyclopedia of Social Work* (New York: Oxford University Press, 2017); Thapa et al., "A Review of School Climate Research."

43. Office of Safe and Drug-Free Schools, *Mobilizing for Evidence-Based Character Education* (Washington, DC: US Department of Education, 2007); CDC, *School Connectedness: Strategies for Increasing Protective Factors Among Youth* (Atlanta: US Department of Health and Human Services, 2009); M. Dynarski, L. Clarke, B. Cobb, J. Finn, R. Rumberger, and J. Smink, "Dropout Prevention: A Practice Guide" (NCEE 2008–4025, National Center for Education Evaluation and Regional Assistance,

Institute of Education Sciences, US Department of Education, Washington, DC, 2008), http://ies.ed.gov/ncee/wwc.

44. Joseph A. Durlak, Roger P. Weissberg, A. B. Taylor, and K. B Schellinger, "The Impact of Enhancing Students' Social and Emotional Learning: A Meta-Analysis of School-Based Universal Interventions," *Child Development* 82 (2011): 405–32, https://casel.org/the-impact-of-enhancing-students-social-and-emotional-learning-a-meta-analysis-of-school-based-universal-interventions.

45. Cohen and Thapa, "School Climate Improvement"; John Bridgeland, Mary Bruce, and Arya Hariharan, *The Missing Piece: A National Teacher Survey on How Social and Emotional Learning Can Empower Children and Transform Schools: A Report for CASEL* (Civic Enterprises, 2013), https://eric.ed.gov/?id=ED558068.

46. Jonathan Cohen, Amrit Thapa, and Ann Higgins-D'Alessandro, "School Climate/Social Emotional Learning Measurement Systems: Trends, Contributions, Challenges and Opportunities," *Journal of Educational Leadership and Policy* 1 (2017): 117–39.

47. See Jonathan Cohen and Dorothy L. Espelage, "Feeling Safe and Being Safe: Individual and Systemic Considerations," chapter 1 in this volume.

48. Lauren Musu-Gillette, Anlan Zhang, Ke Wang, Jizhi Zhang, Jana Kemp, Melissa Diliberti, and Barbara A. Oudekerk, *Indicators of School Crime and Safety: 2017* (Washington, DC: National Center for Education Statistics, 2018), https://nces.ed.gov/pubs2018/2018036.pdf.

49. CDC, "Preventing Sexual Violence," 2012, https://www.cdc.gov/violenceprevention/sexualviolence/index.html.

50. Laura Kann, Tim McManus, William A. Harris, Shari L. Shanklin, Katherine H. Flint, Barbara Queen, Richard Lowry, David Chyen, Lisa Whittle, Jemekia Thornton, Connie Lim, Denise Bradford, Yoshimi Yamakawa, Michelle Leon, Nancy Brener, Kathleen A. Ethier, "Youth Risk Behavior Surveillance: United States, 2017," *Morbidity and Mortality Weekly Report: Surveillance Summaries* 67, no. 8 (2018): 1–114, doi:10.15585/mmwr.ss6708a1.

51. Linda Charmaraman, Ashleigh E Jones, Nan Stein, and Dorothy L. Espelage, "Is It Bullying or Sexual Harassment? Knowledge, Attitudes, and Professional Development Experiences of Middle School Staff," *Journal of School Health* 83, no. 6 (2013): 438–44, doi:10.1111/josh.12048.

52. US Department of Education and Office for Civil Rights, "Dear Colleague Letter."

53. Tracy Evian Waasdorp, Elise T. Pas, Benjamin Zablotsky, and Catherine P. Bradshaw, "Ten-Year Trends in Bullying and Related Attitudes Among 4th- to 12th-Graders," *Pediatrics* 139, no. 6 (2017), doi:10.1542/peds.2016-2615.

54. Chad A. Rose, Lisa E. Monda-Amaya, and Dorothy L. Espelage, "Bullying Perpetration and Victimization in Special Education: A Review of the Literature," *Remedial and Special Education* 32, no. 2 (2011): 114–30, doi:10.1177/0741932510361247.

55. National Center on Safe and Supportive Learning Environments (NCSSLE), "School Climate Survey Compendium," 2019, https://safesupportivelearning.ed.gov/topic-research/school-climate-measurement/school-climate-survey-compendium.

56. Cohen et al., *School Climate/Social Emotional Learning.*

57. CASEL, "Measuring SEL," 2019, https://measuringsel.casel.org.

58. Howard S. Adelman and Linda Taylor "Expanding School Improvement Policy to Better Address Barriers to Learning and Integrate Public Health Concerns," *Policy Futures in Education* 9, no. 3 (2011): 431–46, doi:10.2304/pfie.2011.9.3.431; Futures Without

Violence, "Safe, Healthy, and Ready to Learn: Policy Recommendations to Ensure Children Thrive in Supportive Communities Free from Violence and Trauma," 2015, https://traumasensitiveschools.org/wp-content/uploads/2015/11/Safe-Healthy-and -Ready-to-Learn_Full-Report.pdf; Morgan, "School Discipline Consensus Report"; National Academies of Sciences, "Preventing Bullying Through Policy and Practice"; National Council of Juvenile and Family Court Judges, "Judicially-Led Responses to the School Pathways to the Juvenile Justice System Project: An Overview of the Lessons Learned," 2016, http://www.ncjfcj.org/School-Pathways-TAB.

59. Eva Brown Hajdukova, Garry Hornby, and Penni Cushman, "Bullying experiences of students with social, emotional and behavioral difficulties (SEBD)," *Educational Review* 68, no. 2 (2016): 207–21; Kaylee Mitchell, "Bullying in Our Schools: The Impact of the Olweus Bullying Prevention Program" (master's thesis, the College at Brockport, SUNY, 2017), https://digitalcommons.brockport.edu/ehd_theses/715/; Trish Krajniak, "Guide for Illinois Charter School Student Discipline" (report, Transforming School Discipline Collaborative, Chicago, 2017).

60. Bryk et al., *Learning to Improve.*

61. Howard S. Adelman and Linda Taylor, *The Implementation Guide to Student Learning Supports in the Classroom and Schoolwide: New Directions for Addressing Barriers to Learning* (Los Angeles: Corwin Press, 2006); Adelman, "Expanding School Improvement Policy."

62. National School Climate Center, "School Climate and Pro-Social Educational Improvement: Essential Goals and Processes That Support Student Success for All," *Teachers College Record* (May 2015), https://www.iirp.edu/wp-content/uploads/2015/05 /SC-and-Prosocial-Educational-Improvement.pdf.

63. McDaniel and Salas, "The Science of Teamwork."

64. Polanin et al., "A Meta-Analysis of School-Based Bullying Prevention Programs"; Sandra L Christenson, Amy L Reschly, and Cathy Wylie, *Handbook of Research on Student Engagement* (New York: Springer, 2012), https://www.springer.com/us/book /9781461420170; Lonnie R. Sherrod, Judith Torney-Purta, and Constance A. Flanagan, *Handbook of Research on Civic Engagement in Youth* (Hoboken, NJ: John Wiley & Sons, 2010).

65. Astor and Benbenishty, *Bullying, School Violence, and Climate*; Jerusha Conner, R. Ebby-Rosin, and A. S. Brown, "Speak Up and Speak Out: Student Voice in American Educational Policy," in *National Society for the Study of Education Yearbook* (New York: Teachers College Record, 2015); Teri Dary, Terry Pickeral, Rob Shumer, and Anderson Williams, "Weaving Student Engagement into the Core Practices of Schools: A National Dropout Prevention Center/Network" (position paper, National Dropout Prevention Center/Network, Clemson, SC, 2016); Ontario Ministry of Children and Youth Services, "Guidelines for the Development of a School Bullying Prevention and Intervention Plan (BPIP 2017-2018)," 2017, https://www.ddsb.ca/school/claremont /Claremonts%20Bullying%20Presentation%20%20Intervention%20Pla/Bullying %20Prevention%20and%20Internvention%20Plan%202017%202018.pdf.

66. National Academies of Sciences, "Preventing Bullying Through Policy and Practice"; Zych et al., *Protecting Children Against Bullying*; Astor and Benbenishty, *Bullying, School Violence, and Climates.*

67. Ron Avi Astor, Linda Jacobson, Stephanie L. Wrabel, Rami Benbenishty, and Diana Pineda, *Welcoming Practices: Creating Schools That Support Students and Families in*

Transition (Oxford, UK: Oxford University Press, 2017); National Academies of Sciences, "Preventing Bullying Through Policy and Practice"; Roger Weissberg, Joseph A. Durlak, Celene E. Domitrovich, and Thomas P. Gullotta, *Social and Emotional Learning: Past, Present, and Future* (New York: Guilford Press, 2015), https://www.research gate.net/publication/302991262_Social_and_emotional_learning_Past_present_and _future; Jones and Kahn, "The Evidence Base for How We Learn."

68. AERA, "Prevention of Bullying in Schools, Colleges, and Universities"; National Academies of Sciences, "Preventing Bullying Through Policy and Practice"; Weissberg et al., "Social and Emotional Learning"; Jones and Kahn, "The Evidence Base for How We Learn"; Ruth Berkowitz, Hadass Moore, Ron Avi Astor, and Rami Benbenishty, "A Research Synthesis of the Associations Between Socioeconomic Background, Inequality, School Climate, and Academic Achievement," *Review of Educational Research* 86, no. 10 (2016): 1–45, doi:10.3102/0034654316669821.

CHAPTER 13

1. Annelie Laas and Trynie Boezaart, "The Legislative Framework Regarding Bullying in South African Schools," *Potchefstroom Electronic Law Journal* 17, no. 6 (2014): 2667–702, http://dx.doi.org/10.4314/pelj.v1716.12.

2. Izabela Zych, Rosario Ortega-Ruiz, and Rosario del Rey, "Scientific Research on Bullying and Cyberbullying: Where Have We Been and Where Are We Going," *Aggression and Violent Behavior* 24 (2015): 188–98.

3. Michal Molcho, Wendy Craig, Pernille Due, William Pickett, Yossi Harel-Fisch, Mary D. Overpeck, and HBSC Bullying Writing Group, "Cross-National Time Trends in Bullying Behaviour 1994–2006: Findings from Europe and North America," *International Journal of Public Health* 54 (2009): S1–S10, http://springerlink.com/content /j15430j1x087r023/fulltext.pdfol; Ken Rigby and Peter K. Smith, "Is School Bullying Really on the Rise?" *Social Psychology of Education* 14, no. 4 (2011): 441–55; Tracy E. Waasdorp, Elise T. Pas, Benjamin Zablotsky, and Catherine P. Bradshaw, "Ten-Year Trends in Bullying and Related Attitudes Among 4th- to 12th-Graders," *Pediatrics* 139 (2017): e20162615.

4. Dan Olweus, "Norway," in *The Nature of School Bullying: A Cross-National Perspective,* ed. Peter K. Smith, Yohji Morita, Josiane Junger-Tas, Dan Olweus, Richard Catalano, and Phillip Slee (London: Routledge, 1999), 28–48.

5. Yuichi Toda, "Bullying (Ijime) and Related Problems in Japan: History and Research," in *School Bullying in Different Cultures: Eastern and Western Perspectives,* ed. Peter K. Smith, Keumjoo Kwak, and Yuichi Toda (Cambridge, UK: Cambridge University Press, 2016), 73–92.

6. Peter K. Smith, "Research and Practice in the Study of School Bullying," in *Blackwell Handbook of Developmental Psychology in Action*, ed. Kevin Durkin and Rudolph Schaffer (Oxford, UK: Blackwell, 2016), 290–310.

7. Ibid.

8. Dan Olweus, *Forskning om skolmobbning* (Stockholm: Almqvist & Wiksell, 1973); Dan Olweus, *Aggression in Schools: Bullies and Whipping Boys* (Washington DC: Hemisphere, 1978).

9. Antibullying Alliance, https://www.anti-bullyingalliance.org.uk/; Kidscape, https:// www.kidscape.org.uk/cyberbullying/; YouthWorks Consulting, https://www.esafety forschools.com/; Ditch the Label, https://www.ditchthelabel.org/.

10. Anne Gregory and Dewey Cornell, "'Tolerating' Adolescent Needs: Moving Beyond Zero Tolerance Policies in High School," *Theory into Practice* 48, no. 2 (2009): 106–13.

11. Dewey Cornell, Kathan Shukla, and Timothy Konold, "Peer Victimization and Authoritative School Climate: A Multilevel Approach," *Journal of Educational Psychology* 107, no. 4 (2015): 1186–1021.

12. Peter K. Smith and Sonia Sharp, "The Problem of School Bullying," in *School Bullying: Insights and Perspectives*, ed. Peter K. Smith and Sonia Sharp (London: Routledge, 1994), 1–19; Dieter Wolke and Muthanna Samara, "Bullied by Siblings: Association with Peer Victimisation and Behaviour Problems in Israeli Lower Secondary School Children," *Journal of Child Psychology and Psychiatry* 45, no. 5 (2004): 1015–29.

13. R. Matthew Gladden et al., *Bullying Surveillance Among Youths: Uniform Definitions for Public Health and Recommended Data Elements, Version 1.0.* (Atlanta: National Center for Injury Prevention and Control, CDC, 2014).

14. Olweus, "Norway"; Stuart W. Twemlow, Peter Fonagy, Frank C. Sacco, and John R. Brethour Jr., "Teachers Who Bully Students: A Hidden Trauma," *International Journal of Social Psychiatry* 52, no. 3 (2006): 187–98.

15. Wenxin Zhang, Liang Chen, and Guanghui Chen, "Research on School Bullying in Mainland China," in Smith et al., *School Bullying in Different Cultures*, 113.

16. Jun Sung Hong and Dorothy Espelage, "A Review of Research on Bullying and Victimization in School: An Ecological System Analysis," *Aggression and Violent Behavior* 176 (2012): 311–22.

17. Mark L. Hatzenbuehler, Laura Schwab-Reese, Shabbar I. Ranapurwala, Marci F. Hertz, and Marizen R. Ramirez, "Associations Between Antibullying Policies and Bullying in 25 States," *JAMA Pediatrics* 169, no. 10 (2015): e152411.

18. Marizen R. Ramirez, Patrick Ten Eyck, Corinne Peek-Asa, Angela Onwuachi-Willig, and Joseph E. Cavanaugh, "Evaluation of Iowa's Anti-Bullying Law," *Injury Epidemiology* 3, no. 1 (2016): 15.

19. Peter K. Smith, Cherise Smith, Rob Osborn, and Muthanna Samara, "A Content Analysis of School Anti-Bullying Policies: Progress and Limitations," *Educational Psychology in Practice* 24, no. 1 (2008): 1–12; Peter K. Smith, Alison Kupferberg, Joaquin A. Mora-Merchan, Muthanna Samara, Sue Bosley, and Rob Osborn, "A Content Analysis of School Anti-Bullying Policies: A Follow-Up After Six Years," *Educational Psychology in Practice* 28, no. 1 (2012): 47–70; Noel Purdy and Peter K. Smith, "A Content Analysis of School Anti-Bullying Policies in Northern Ireland," *Educational Psychology in Practice* 32, no. 3 (2016): 281–95.

20. Erik Flygare, Gun-Marie Frånberg, Peter Gill, Björn Johansson, Odd Lindberg, Christina Osbeck, and Åsa Söderström, "Evaluation of Anti-Bullying Methods" (Report 353, National Agency for Education, Stockholm, 2011), www.skolverket.se.

21. Joseph A. Durlak, Roger P. Weissberg, Allison B. Dymnicki, Rebecca D. Taylor, and Kriston B. Schellinger, "The Impact of Enhancing Students' Social and Emotional Learning: A Meta-Analysis of School-Based Universal Interventions," *Child Development* 82, no. 1 (2011): 405–32.

22. Lauren McNamara, "Recess: Supporting a Culture of Meaningful Play at School," in *The Cambridge Handbook of Play: Developmental and Disciplinary Perspectives*, ed. Peter K. Smith and Jaipaul L. Roopnarine (Cambridge, UK: Cambridge University Press, 2018), 686–703.

23. Helen Cowie and Peter K. Smith, "Peer Support as a Means of Improving School Safety and Reducing Bullying and Violence," in *Handbook of Youth Prevention Science*, ed. Beth Doll, William Pfohl, and Jina Yoon (New York: Routledge, 2010), 177–93.

24. Helen Cowie and Patti Wallace, *Peer Support in Action: From Bystanding to Standing By* (London: Sage, 2000); Joshua R. Polanin, Dorothy L. Espelage, and Therese D. Pigott, "A Meta-Analysis of School-Based Bullying Prevention Programs' Effects on Bystander Intervention Behavior," *School Psychology Review* 41, no. 1 (2012): 47–65.

25. Claire Garandeau, Elisa Poskiparta, and Christina Salmivalli, "Tackling Acute Cases of School Bullying in the KiVa Anti-Bullying Program: A Comparison of Two Approaches," *Journal of Abnormal Child Psychology* 42, no. 6 (2014): 981–91; Ken Rigby, "School Perspectives on Bullying and Preventative Strategies: An Exploratory Study," *Australian Journal of Education* 61, no. 1 (2016): 24–39.

26. Nick Axford, David P. Farrington, Suzy Clarkson, Gretchen J. Bjornstad, Zoe Wrigley, and Judy Hutchings, "Involving Parents in School-Based Programmes to Prevent and Reduce Bullying: What Effect Does It Have?" *Journal of Children's Services* 10, no. 3 (2015): 242–51.

27. Hagit Sasson and Gustavo Mesch, "Parental Mediation, Peer Norms and Risky Online Behaviors Among Adolescents," *Computers in Human Behavior* 33 (2014): 32–38.

28. Barbara Spears and Jette Kofoed, "Transgressing Research Binaries: Youth as Knowledge Brokers in Cyberbullying Research," in *Cyberbullying Through the New Media: Findings from an International Network*, ed. Peter K. Smith and Georges Steffgen (Hove, UK: Psychology Press, 2013), 201–21.

29. See https://www.ou.nl/web/blurred-lives/project.

30. Conor McGuckin and Lucie Corcoran, eds., *Bullying and Cyberbullying: Prevalence, Psychological Impacts and Intervention Strategies* (Hauppauge, NY: Nova Science, 2017).

31. Mattias Persson, Linn Wennberg, Linda Beckman, Christina Salmivalli, and Mikael Svensson, "The Cost-Effectiveness of the KiVA AntiBullying Program: Results from a Decision-Analytic Model," *Prevention Science* 19, no. 6 (2018): 728–37.

32. Peter K. Smith, *Making an Impact on School Bullying: Interventions and Recommendations* (London: Routledge, 2019).

33. Tomoyuki Kanetsuna and Yuichi Toda, "Actions Against *Ijime* and *Net-Ijime* in Japan," in Smith et al., *School Bullying in Different Cultures*, 334–49.

34. Peter K. Smith, Keumjoo Kwak, Rubina Hanif, Tomoyuki Kanetsuna, Jess Mahdavi, Siu-Fung Lin, Ragnar Olafsson, and Zehra Ucanok, "Linguistic Issues in Studying Bullying-Related Phenomena: Data from a Revised Cartoon Task," in Smith et al., *School Bullying in Different Cultures*, 280–98; Peter K. Smith, Fran Thompson, Adam Rutland, Alice Jones, Suresh Sundaram, Damanjit Sandhu, Kirandeep Kaur, Barbara A. Spears, Silvia Koller, Reda Gedutiene, Ruthaychonnee Sittichai, and Yulia Kovas, "Issues in Cross-National Comparisons and the Meaning of Words for Bullying in Different Languages," in *Bullying, Cyberbullying and Pupil Well-Being in Schools: Comparing European, Australian and Indian Perspectives*, ed. Peter K. Smith, Suresh Sundaram, Barbara A. Spears, Catherine Blaya, Mechthild Schäfer, and Damanjit Sandhu (Cambridge, UK: Cambridge University Press, 2018), 61–80.

35. Sonia Livingstone, Leslie Haddon, Anke Görzig, and Kjartan Olafsson, *Risks and Safety on the Internet: The Perspective of European Children: Full Findings* (London: EU Kids Online, London School of Economics and Political Science, 2011).

36. Geert Hofstede, Gert Jan Hofstede, and Michael Minkov, *Cultures and Organizations: Software of the Mind* (New York: McGraw-Hill, 2010).
37. Marilyn Campbell, Margaret Kettle, and Suresh Sunduram, "Societal and Cultural Considerations in Understanding Peer Bullying in India," in Smith et al., *Bullying, Cyberbullying and Pupil Well-Being in Schools*, 26–44; Peter K. Smith, Anke Görzig, and Susanne Robinson, *Issues of Cross-Cultural Variations in Cyber-Bullying Across Europe and Beyond* (WP 449, Media@LSE Working Paper Series, London School of Economics, London, 2018), 1–28.
38. Linqin Ji, Wenxin Zhang, and Kevin Jones, "Children's Experience of and Attitudes Towards Bullying and Victimization: A Cross-Cultural Comparison Between China and England," in Smith et al., *School Bullying in Different Cultures*, 170–88.
39. Peter K. Smith and Susanne Robinson, "How Does Individualism-Collectivism Relate to Bullying Victimization?" *International Journal of Bullying Prevention* 1, no. 1 (2019): 3–13.
40. Hannah Gaffney, Maria M. Ttofi, and David P. Farrington, "Evaluating the Effectiveness of School-Bullying Prevention Programs: An Updated Meta-Analytical Review," *Aggression and Violent Behavior* 45 (2019): 111–33.

CHAPTER 14

1. Craig Jerald, "The Implementation Trap: Helping Schools Overcome Barriers to Change," 2005, https://files.eric.ed.gov/fulltext/ED494092.pdf; Rodger Kessler and Russell E. Glasgow, "A Proposal to Speed Translation of Healthcare Research into Practice: Dramatic Change Is Needed," *American Journal of Preventive Medicine* 40, no. 6 (June 1, 2011): 637–44, https://doi.org/10.1016/j.amepre.2011.02.023; Harold I Perl, "Addicted to Discovery: Does the Quest for New Knowledge Hinder Practice Improvement?" *Addictive Behaviors* 36, no. 6 (2011): 590–96, https://doi.org/10.1016/j.addbeh.2011.01.027; W. Carl Sumi et al., "Implementation and Sustainability of an Evidence-Based Program," *Journal of Emotional and Behavioral Disorders* 22, no. 2 (2014): 95–106, https://doi.org/10.1177/1063426613520456.
2. Dean L. Fixsen, Sandra F. Naoom, Karen A. Blase, Robert M. Friedman, and Frances Wallace, "Implementation Research: A Synthesis of the Literature," *Louis de La Parte Florida Mental Health Institute Publication*, The National Implementation Research. Network, 2005; Dean L. Fixsen, Karen A. Blase, Sandra F. Naoom, and Frances Wallace, "Core Implementation Components," *Research on Social Work Practice* 19, no. 5 (2009): 531–40, https://doi.org/10.1177/1049731509335549; Dean L. Fixsen, Karen Blase, and Melissa Van Dyke, *Implementation Practice and Science* (Chapel Hill, NC: Active Implementation Research Network, 2019); Trisha Greenhalgh, Glenn Robert, Fraser MacFarlane, Paul Bate, and Olivia Kyriakidou, "Diffusion of Innovations in Service Organizations: Systematic Review and Recommendations," *Milbank Quarterly* 82, no. 4 (2004): 581–629, https://doi.org/10.1111/j.0887-378X.2004.00325.x; Jerald, "The Implementation Trap: Helping Schools Overcome Barriers to Change Is School Improvement"; Rachel G. Tabak, Elaine C. Khoong, David A. Chambers, and Ross C. Brownson, "Bridging Research and Practice: Models for Dissemination and Implementation Research," *American Journal of Preventive Medicine* 43, no. 3 (2012): 337–50, https://doi.org/10.1016/j.amepre.2012.05.024.
3. Fixsen et al., "Implementation Research: A Synthesis of the Literature."
4. Ibid., 40.

5. Dean L. Fixsen, Caryn Ward, Karen A. Blase, Sandra Naooom, Alison Metz, and Laura Louison, "Assessing Drivers Best Practices Active Implementation Research Network," 2018, www.activeimplementation.org; Terje Ogden, Gunnar Bjørnrbekk, John Kjøbli, Joshua Patras, Terje Christiansen, Knut Taraldsen, and Nina Tollefsen, "Measurement of Implementation Components Ten Years after a Nationwide Introduction of Empirically Supported Programs: A Pilot Study," *Implementation Science* 7, no. 1 (2012), https://doi.org/10.1186/1748-5908-7-49.

6. Caryn Ward, Kimberly St. Martin, K Horner, Robert Horner, Michelle Duda, Kimberly Ingram-West, Marick Tedesco, David Putnam, Martha Buenrostro, and Erin Chaparro, "District Capacity Assessment" (University of North Carolina at Chapel Hill, 2015), https://nirn.fpg.unc.edu/resources/district-capacity-assessment-dca.

7. Mark W. Lipsey, "The Primary Factors That Characterize Effective Interventions with Juvenile Offenders: A Meta-Analytic Overview," *Victims & Offenders* 4, no. 2 (2009): 124–47, https://doi.org/10.1080/15564880802612573.

8. Matthias J. Naleppa and John G. Cagle, "Treatment Fidelity in Social Work Intervention Research: A Review of Published Studies," *Research on Social Work Practice* 20, no. 6 (2010): 674–81, https://doi.org/10.1177/1049731509352088.

9. Peter M. Senge, *The Fifth Discipline: The Art and Practice of the Learning Organization* (New York: Doubleday, 2006); Victoria J. Marsick and Karen E. Watkins, "Demonstrating the Value of an Organization's Learning Culture: The Dimensions of the Learning Organization Questionnaire," *Advances in Developing Human Resources* 5, no. 2 (2003): 132–51, https://doi.org/10.1177/1523422303005002002.

10. Gareth Morgan and Ramirez Raphael, "Action Learning: A Holographic Metaphor for Guiding Social Change," *Human Relations* 37, no. 1 (1983): 1–28; Karl E. Weick, Kathleen M. Sutcliffe, and David Obstfeld "Organizing for High Reliability: Processes of Collective Mindfulness," *Research in Organizational Behavior* 21 (1999): 81–123; Ralph D. Stacey, *Strategic Management and Organisational Dynamics*, 3rd ed. (Harlow, UK: Prentice Hall, 2002).

11. Kevin J. Dooley, "A Complex Adaptive Systems Model of Organization Change," *Nonlinear Dynamics, Psychology, and Life Sciences* 1, no. 1 (1997): 69–97, https://doi.org/10.1023/A:1022375910940.

12. Ibid.

13. Eva Oberle, Celene E. Domitrovich, Duncan C. Meyers, and Roger. P. Weissberg, "Establishing Systemic Social and Emotional Learning Approaches in Schools: A Framework for Schoolwide Implementation," *Cambridge Journal of Education* 46, no. 3 (2016): 277–97, https://doi.org/10.1080/0305764X.2015.1125450.

CHAPTER 15

1. Michael Fullan, "The Moral Imperative Redefined," *Principal Connections* 23, no. 1 (2019): 18–21.

CHAPTER 16

1. Peter Stearns, *The Industrial Revolution in World History* (New York: Routledge, 2013), doi:10.4324/9780429494475.

2. UN General Assembly, *Convention on the Rights of the Child*, Article 19, http://wunrn.org/reference/pdf/Convention_Rights_Child.PDF1989; and http://www.ohchr.org/Documents/ProfessionalInterest/crc.pdf.

3. Amrit Thapa, Jonathan Cohen, Shawn Guffey, and Ann Higgins-D'Alessandro, "A Review of School Climate Research," *Review of Educational Research* 83, no. 3 (2013): 357–85.

4. UNESCO, *Universal Declaration on Cultural Diversity: A Vision, a Conceptual Platform, a Pool of Ideas for Implementation: A New Paradigm*, 2002. https://unesdoc.unesco.org/ark: /48223/pf0000127162; UNESCO, "The Cultural Wealth of the World Is Its Diversity," 2016, https://www.rmccaustralia.org.au/the-cultural-wealth-of-the-world-is-its -diversity-unesco/.

5. Hyojin Koo, "A Time Line of the Evolution of School Bullying in Differing Social Contexts," *Asia Pacific Education Review* 8, no. 1 (2007): 107–16; Grace Skrzypiec, Earvin Alinsug, Ulil Amri Nasiruddin, Eleni Andreou, Antonella Brighi, Eleni Didaskalou, Annalisa Guarini, et al., "Self-Reported Harm of Adolescent Peer Aggression in Three World Regions," *Child Abuse and Neglect* 85 (2018): 101–17.

6. Kayleigh. L. Chester, Mary Callaghan, Alina Cosma, Peter Donnelly, Wendy Craig, Sophie Walsh, and Michal Molcho, "Cross-National Time Trends in Bullying Victimization in 33 Countries Among Children Aged 11, 13 and 15 from 2002 to 2010," *European Journal of Public Health* 25, no. 2 (2015): 61–64.

7. Grace Skrzypiec, Mirella Wyra, and Eleni Didaskalou, "Peer Aggression and Bullying," in *A Global Perspective of Young Adolescents' Peer Aggression and Well-Being: Beyond Bullying*, ed. Grace Skrzypiec, Mirella Wyra, and Eleni Didaskalou (London: Routledge, 2019).

8. Ross Homel, "Can Police Prevent Crime?" in *Unpeeling Tradition: Contemporary Policing*, ed. Keith Bryett and Colleen Lewis (Brisbane, Australia: Macmillan, 1994), 7–34.

9. Barbara. M. Newman and Philip R. Newman, *Development Through Life: A Psychological Approach* (Belmont, CA: Wadsworth, 2012).

10. Urie Bronfenbrenner, "Ecological Systems Theory," in *Six Theories of Child Development: Revised Formulations and Current Issues*, ed. Ross Vasta (London: Jessica Kingsley, 1992), 187–249.

11. Martin Fishbein, "A Reasoned Action Approach to Health Promotion," *Medical Decision Making* 28 (2008): 842.

CHAPTER 17

1. S. D. McMahon, E. Peist, J. O. Davis, K. Bare, A. Martinez, L. A. Reddy, D. L. Espelage, and E. M. Anderman, "Physical Aggression Toward Teachers: Antecedents, Behaviors, and Consequences," *Aggressive Behavior* (forthcoming).

ACKNOWLEDGMENTS

WE THANK THE MANY INDIVIDUALS who contributed to this volume.

We are indebted to the wonderful editorial support and guidance we have received from Nancy Walser at the Harvard Education Press. Nancy has been a partner to and with us since the original conception of the book. Her thoughtful, critical, and caring assistance has made this book clearer and more accessible.

We are grateful to the important administrative support that Alberto Valido and Luz E. Robinson provided to both of us during the preparation of these chapters.

In many ways, all of our lives are a process, in part, of building on past efforts. And we are indebted to the learning and work of many of our research and practice colleagues, including Arthur Horne, Matthew Mayer, Ron Astor, Rami Benbenishty, Catherine Blaya, Eric Debarbieux, Dewey Cornell, Michael Furlong, Grace Skrzypiec, Phillip Slee, Stu Twemlow, Wendy Craig, Jun Hong, and Amanda Nickerson.

I (Jonathan Cohen) am eternally grateful to Stacey Fredericks—my wife and dear friend. Our partnership and the family we have grown together are the foundation for my learning and work.

I (Dorothy Espelage) appreciate every day the support that I receive from my life partner and biggest fan, Ray (Ray Ray) Musleh. With daily affirmations from Ray, I am able to do this challenging (yet rewarding) scholarship and translational research.

ABOUT THE EDITORS

JONATHAN COHEN is copresident of the International Observatory for School Climate and Violence Prevention and cofounder and President Emeritus of the National School Climate Center. A practicing clinical psychologist and psychoanalyst, he is also an adjunct professor in the Department of Psychology and Education (Clinical Psychology) at Teachers College, Columbia University; a member of the Council for Distinguished Scientists at the Aspen Institutes' National Commission on Social, Emotional and Academic Development; a member of the Educational Advisory Council for Character. org; and a Diplomat in Clinical Psychology with the American Board of Professional Psychology. He has also served as a consultant to the World Bank, UNICEF's Child Friendly Schools Program, and a growing number of educational ministries around the world.

Cohen is the author of more than a hundred peer-reviewed papers, book chapters, and briefs, as well as five books. Two of his books have been awarded the American Library Association's Choice for an Outstanding Academic Book Award, *Educating Minds and Hearts: Social Emotional Learning and the Passage into Adolescence* (Teachers College Press, 1999) and *Caring Classrooms/Intelligent Schools: The Social Emotional Learning of Young Children* (Teachers College Press, 2001).

DOROTHY L. ESPELAGE is the William C. Friday Distinguished Professor of Education at the University of North Carolina at Chapel Hill. A fellow of the American Psychological Science Association (APA) and the American Educational Research Association, she is the recipient of the APA's Lifetime Achievement Award in Prevention Science and the 2016 Award for Distinguished Contributions to Research in Public Policy.

Espelage has authored more than 170 peer-reviewed articles, five edited books, and seventy chapters on bullying, homophobic teasing, sexual harassment, dating violence, and gang violence. Her research focuses on translating empirical findings into prevention and intervention programming. She advises members of Congress on bully prevention legislation and conducts regular webinars for the Centers for Disease Control, National Institutes of Health (NIH), and National Institute of Justice. She authored a 2011 White House brief on bullying among LGBTQ youth and attended the White House Conference in 2011. She has also been a consultant on the stopbullying.gov website and consultant to the National Anti-Bullying Campaign, Health Resources and Services Administration in the US Department of Health and Human Services and has presented multiple times at the Federal Partnership to End Bullying Summit and Conference. Espelage is a consultant to the NIH Pathways to Prevention Initiative to address bullying and youth suicide.

ABOUT THE CONTRIBUTORS

MONISA AIJAZ is a postdoctoral research associate at the University of North Carolina (UNC) at Chapel Hill. She works with the World Health Organization Collaborating Center for Research Evidence for Sexual and Reproductive Health at UNC's Gillings School of Global Public Health to develop the implementation capacity in three low- and middle-income countries using the Active Implementation Frameworks. She also provides technical assistance to the Title X family planning program grantees in the US to build their capacity for addressing complex challenges. Aijaz earned her MD in India, where she worked in a tertiary care maternity hospital and realized the need for effective implementation of the evidence-based practices. She completed a Master's of Public Health degree at UNC with an emphasis on implementation science and its application to improve maternal and child health outcomes. Aijaz has worked on identifying the commonalities of concepts and constructs across various implementation frameworks and is currently working on the identification of implementation competencies for frontline practitioners in the interest of developing implementation strategies and measures of implementation capacity in low- and middle-income countries.

RON AVI ASTOR holds the Marjory Crump Chair Professorship in Social Welfare at the UCLA Luskin School of Public Affairs, with a joint appointment in the UCLA Graduate School of Education and Information Studies. His work examines the role of the physical, social-organizational, and cultural contexts in schools related to different kinds of school violence. His studies have included tens of thousands of students, teachers, parents and administrators, and findings from these studies have been published in more than 150 scholarly manuscripts. His most recent books, all published by Oxford

University Press, include *Bullying, School Violence, and Climate in Evolving Contexts: Culture, Organization, and Time*; *Mapping and Monitoring Bullying and Violence: Building a Safe School Slimate*; and *Welcoming Practices: Creating Schools That Support Students and Families in Transition.* Currently, Astor is creating an international model for sustainable and scalable infrastructures that support safe and welcoming schools. Astor has won numerous national research awards from the Society for Social Work and Research, American Psychological Association (APA), and the American Educational Research Association (AERA). He holds an honorary doctorate from Hebrew Union College, is a fellow of the APA, AERA, and SSWR and is an elected member of both the National Academy of Education and the American Academy of Social Work and Social Welfare.

CLAIRE BEAUMONT is a psychologist, doctor of educational psychology, and professor in the Faculty of Education, Université Laval, Québec. A school psychologist and clinical psychologist for more than twenty years, working with children with serious behavioral problems, she now holds the Research Chair in School Well-Being and Violence Prevention at Université Laval, where she focuses on training school personnel to create compassionate schools, preventing and reducing school violence, and promoting social-emotional learning, peer support systems, collaborative school practices, and positive support for students with behavioral disorders. She is the author of several hundred scientific and professional articles, has served on the scientific committees of seven world conferences on violence, has participated in various national and international research projects, and consults with various departments and governments in Canada and elsewhere. Since 2012 Beaumont has been conducting the first national longitudinal research to monitor the evolution of the various components related to violence in Quebec schools.

RAMI BENBENISHTY is Professor Emeritus at the Hebrew University of Jerusalem and at Bar Ilan University, Israel. His main area of interest is the safety, welfare, and well-being of children around the world. He studies children and youth in both community normative settings, such as schools, and in out-of-home placements, such as foster homes and residential care, and investigates and tries to improve decision processes that lead to referral to protective services, removal of children from their biological families, and eventual reunification. He developed a conceptual, methodological, and technological framework for monitoring processes and outcomes in human services that was implemented in foster care services in the US and is used to monitor school violence and climate in schools and districts and at the national level. Benbenishty consults with governments and researchers around the world. He has authored numerous papers, book chapters, books, and technical reports, and his work has been recognized and received multiple awards, including France's Chevalier des Ordre de Palmes Academique, the Society for Social Work and Research's Excellence in Research Award, Israel's Landau Prize for Research and Science, and, most recently, Israel's prestigious EMET Prize for Science, Art, and Culture.

KAREN BLASE has been a program developer, researcher, program evaluator, program director, and published author in human services for over forty-five years. She is a cofounder of, director of, and implementation scientist with the Active Implementation Research Network and is a cofounder of the National Implementation Research Network. She is Senior Scientist Emerita at the Frank Porter Graham Child Development Institute at the University of North Carolina at Chapel Hill. She served on the board of directors and as president of the Pyramid Model Consortium, which focuses on evidence-based programs and practices for social-emotional development and inclusion for young children and their families. Blase's scientist/practitioner career has included international replication of evidence-based services for children and families engaged with early childhood services, child welfare systems, juvenile justice, domestic violence and children's mental health. Her current interests include the application of implementation science to support systems for civic and voter education and voter registration and for ensuring voting rights.

ANTONELLA BRIGHI is an associate professor of developmental psychology, Faculty of Education, at the Free University of Bolzano, Italy, and an adjunct lecturer in education at Flinders University, South Australia. She is the director of the Students' Well-Being and Prevention of Violence (SWAPv-IT) Joint Research Laboratory established by Flinders University, Bologna University, Italy, and the Free University of Bolzano. Brighi's research focuses on risk and protective factors of bullying and cyberbullying as well as on intervention programs for the prevention of these phenomena and on the promotion of well-being, from childhood to adolescence, with a focus on the emotional impact of social exclusion and aggression on mental health and coping and resilience. She has been part of an international network of researchers on cyberbullying, representing Italy, and was awarded a research fellowship by the Australian Research Council in 2013. She has led several international research projects on bullying and cyberbullying in school contexts and in juvenile detention settings. She also consults with schools on the implementation of programs for the development of socioemotional competencies and on the promotion of psychological well-being.

ERIC DEBARBIEUX is a professor of educational sciences at Bordeaux University, France, and a former member of the French Educational Ministry. He has worked in education for children and adolescents in need and has led numerous research projects in Europe, South America, and Africa studying violence in schools. He cofounded the International Observatory for Violence in Schools.

AMERICA EL SHEIKH received her bachelor of science degree in psychology from the University of Florida in the fall of 2017. Since then she has worked as a full-time research assistant for Dorothy Espelage, and is applying to mental health counseling programs. Her interests include multicultural psychology and counseling, protective factors for minorities, prevention science, and understanding barriers and enablers for seeking mental health treatment and services. One of her primary goals is to be conversational in at least three languages. In her free time, she volunteers at a crisis and suicide hotline, loves to travel, dance, do yoga, cook, be in nature, and spend time with family and friends.

HE ER'LIN is a PhD candidate in education at Beijing Normal University. Her research interests are focused on students' social emotional learning, principals' instructional leadership, and school bullying. Her research activities include a study on the instructional leadership of primary and middle school principals from the perspective of Confucian democracy and a study of the impact of a social-emotional learning project on teacher professional development.

DEAN L. FIXSEN is an implementation scientist and codeveloper of the evidence-based Active Implementation Frameworks and is a director of the

Active Implementation Research Network. He has spent his career developing and implementing evidence-based programs, initiating and managing change processes in provider organizations and service delivery systems, and working with others to improve the lives of children, families, adults, and society. Fixsen has served on numerous editorial and professional boards and has advised federal, state, and local governments in the US and globally. He cofounded the National Implementation Research Network and the Global Implementation Initiative and is a research affiliate with the University of North Carolina World Health Organization Collaborating Center for Research Evidence for Sexual and Reproductive Health. He is also a member of the founding board of editors of the journal *Implementation Science*.

MICHAEL FULLAN is Professor Emeritus at the Ontario Institute for Studies in Education, University of Toronto, and president of Michael Fullan Enterprises. He serves as the global leadership director for New Pedagogies for Deep Learning. An educational researcher, he is known for his work on educational reform and has consulted with school districts, teacher groups, research institutes, and governments. Fullan is the author of forty-five books. He holds honorary doctorates from several universities from around the world.

HAGIT GLICKMAN is the general director of RAMA, an independent governmental unit within the Israeli Ministry of Education that addresses the need for professional measurement, evaluation, and assessment in the education system. She has worked on a variety of research projects in the area of education, including the design and analysis of large-scale assessments and surveys, cross-sectional and longitudinal studies, evaluations of educational programs, and development of applied statistical and psychometric methodologies.

ANTOINETTE HETZLER is Professor Emerita of Sociology at Lund University in Sweden. Her research is focused on the development of the welfare state and implementation of social reforms in the areas of health, education, and welfare. She has authored a number of books in Swedish, including *Vad händer med kvinnodominerade yrken? Utsatthet inom läraryrket och socionomyrket* (What is happening with women-dominated professions? Vulnerability within the elementary school teacher and social worker professions) (Bokbox, 2018). Her recent published work in English on Swedish elementary schools includes (with Colm Flaherty) "Guaranteeing Social Rights and Regulating the Public Sector," *European Journal of Cultural and Political Sociology* (2017), and "Framing Work Injury/Sickness in a Changing Welfare State: Naming and Blaming," in *The Transformation of Work in the Welfare State Organizations: New Public Management and the Institutional Diffusion of Ideas*, ed. Frank Sowa, Ronald Staples, and Stefan Zapfel (Routledge, 2018).

EINAV LUKE started her career as a school counselor and a trainer in charge of supporting Israeli schools in their climate improvement efforts. She oversaw the unit in charge of violence prevention and climate improvement in the Ministry of Education and heads the Department for Support and Prevention in the Psychological and Counseling Services. Among her responsibilities, she oversees development and dissemination of a wide range of programs designed to promote students' safety, social-emotional learning, and effective parental involvement in schools.

VERÓNICA LÓPEZ is a professor in the School of Psychology at Pontificia Universidad Católica de Valparaíso, Chile. She is director of the Center for Research in Inclusive Education and of the Programa de Apoyo a la Convivencia Escolar. Former editor-in-chief of the journal *Psicoperspectivas*, she is the author of more than fifty articles in peer-reviewed journals, thirty book chapters, and three books. Her research focuses on school violence, school climate, and inclusive education.

MAO YAQING is on the education faculty at Beijing Normal University. He serves as Deputy Head of the National Working Group of experts on the training of Primary and Secondary School Principals, Vice Chairman of the National Association for the training of Primary and Middle School Principals, and as director of the executive office of the joint project of UNICEF and China's Ministry of Education around school management. Mao studied as a senior visiting fellow at the University of London and at the University of Michigan. He has served on more than twenty national natural science foundation projects, Ministry of Education–UNICEF international projects, and national philosophy and social science projects. He is responsible for the research and development of Chinese national policies in basic education and has published nearly 1 hundreds papers on education research. Mao's research focuses on educational leadership and school improvement, students' social-emotional learning, and the comprehensive reform of school management.

SANJAY K. NANWANI earned his PhD at the Universidad de los Andes in Colombia. He was a Predoctoral Visiting Fellow at the Harvard Graduate School of Education and a fellow and principal investigator with Save the Children Philippines. He was also a tutor and consultant in the Advanced Programme on Child Rights, School and Classroom Management at Lund University, Sweden (sponsored by the Swedish International Development Agency), where he worked on supporting projects in Latin and Central America. His areas of interest are democratic citizenship education, peace education, classroom and school climate, and teacher development. Currently he teaches at Externado University in Colombia and conducts research in the field of education at Universidad de los Andes.

DAVID RATNER works at RAMA, the Israeli national authority for measurement and assessment in education, as a director of applied research in education. In recent years he has conducted research on subjects such as the national reform in pedagogy ("meaningful learning"), programs for gifted students, and extracurricular programs in schools. Additionally, Ratner specializes in the history and society of Ethiopia and the Jewish-Ethiopian community and has published books and articles on these subjects. He holds a PhD in sociology and anthropology from Ben Gurion University.

TAL RAZ is a senior director of surveys and program evaluation at RAMA, the Israeli national authority for measurement and assessment in education. Her fields of research and expertise include nationwide organizational and pedagogical reforms (e.g., the New Horizon reform), programs for the advancement of peripheral schools, and nationwide surveys.

SANTIAGO RINCÓN-GALLARDO is an education consultant and chief research officer at Michael Fullan Enterprises in Toronto, where he conducts research and advises leaders and educators to transform teaching and learning across entire educational systems in North America, Latin America, Europe, and Australia. As an educator and organizer, he worked for over a decade to promote grassroots educational change initiatives in Mexican public schools serving historically marginalized communities. He was the director of a small nongovernmental organization that catalyzed a movement to turn conventional classrooms into tutorial networks in thousands of schools across the country. Gallego's academic work explores how effective pedagogies for deep learning can spread at scale; it has been published in multiple academic journals, books, and book chapters. His most recent book is *Liberating Learning: Educational Change as Social Movement* (Routledge, 2019).

HILA SEGAL-ZADVIL is the head of the Unit on Optimal Climate and Violence Prevention at the Psychological and Counseling Services in the Israeli Ministry of Education. She develops educational and psychological interventions designed to promote well-being and prevent violence among students and oversees the professional preparation and training of a cadre of expert counselors who work with schools and kindergartens to help initiate and sustain optimal school climate.

HANNA SHADMI was the director of the Psychological and Counseling Services in the Israeli Ministry of Education and oversees the organizational management and professional development of twenty-eight hundred psychologists and five thousand counselors employed within the Ministry of Education. Her responsibilities include developing methods and tools to promote the wellness and mental health of students within the education system in Israel, implementing Life-Skills Programs, providing special programs for high-risk children, directing the functioning of these psychological and counseling services during national crises, and ensuring that the issues of mental health and well-being are considerations within the Ministry of Education and all other related governmental offices.

GRACE SKRZYPIEC is a psychologist and former secondary teacher. She is Co-Director of the Student Wellbeing and Prevention of Violence (SWAPv) research centre at Flinders University, South Australia, and Co-President of the International Observatory on School Climate and Violence Prevention. Her research interests include student well-being, peer aggression, anti-social behavior and adolescent offenders. She is the chief investigator for the international peer aggression and well-being study involving 12 countries and over 7000 students. In 2014 she was the recipient of the Vice-Chancellor's Award for Early Career Researchers in recognition of outstanding contributions to excellence in research. Her background includes research on adolescent health with CSIRO and with adolescent offenders at the Office of Crime Statistics and Research (OCSAR) in South Australia. At Flinders University she is a Senior Lecturer in Research Methods and Statistics in the College of Education, Psychology and Social Work.

PHILLIP T. SLEE is a Professor in Human Development, College of Education, Psychology & Social Work Flinders University, Adelaide. He is a trained teacher and registered psychologist. His areas of research interest include, child & adolescent mental health, childhood bullying/aggression, stress and teacher education. His particular interest is in the practical and policy implications of my research. He has presented his work nationally and internationally in workshops and lectures. His website is http://www.caper.com.au. He is also the Director of the Flinders Centre for 'Student Wellbeing & Prevention of Violence' (SWAPv): http://www.flinders.edu.au/ehl/educationalfutures/groups -and-centres/swapv/.

PETER K. SMITH is Emeritus Professor of Psychology at Goldsmiths, University of London. He is a fellow of the British Psychological Society, the Association of Psychological Sciences, and the Academy of Social Sciences. He served as chair of the European Cooperation in Science and Technology Cyberbullying Action (COST ACTION IS0801) 2008–12. Smith was principal investigator of the Bullying, Cyberbullying, and Pupil Safety and Wellbeing project financed by the Indian-European Research Networking in the Social Sciences initiative and co-PI of a comparative study of cyberbullying in Qatar and the UK. He was recently co-PI of the EU project Blurred Lives: A Cross-National, Co-Participatory Exploration of Cyberbullying, Young People and Socio-Economic Disadvantage. Smith's publishing credits include two hundred refereed journal articles and twenty-eight authored and edited books, including *Understanding School Bullying: Its Nature and Prevention Strategies* (Sage, 2014) and *Adolescence: A Very Short Introduction* (Oxford University Press, 2016). In 2015 he was awarded the William Thierry Preyer Award for Excellence in Research on Human Development by the European Society for Developmental Psychology.

BARBARA A. SPEARS is Professor of Education and Social Development in the School of Education, University of South Australia. She has published and presented her work nationally and internationally on youth voice, cyberbullying, sexting, mental health and wellbeing, and the role of technology in young people's social relationships. She is Chair of the Australian Universities' Anti-Bullying Research Alliance, which regularly provides evidence-informed advice to government policy development. She has a particular interest in pre-service teacher education and the translation of research to policy and practice.

MITSURU TAKI is a guest researcher with the Guidance and Counseling Center at Japan's National Institute for Educational Policy Research (NIER) in the Ministry of Education, Culture, Sports, Science and Technology (MEXT). He was formerly the head researcher of NIER and continues the cohort research targeting all students from fourth grade to ninth grade in one Japanese city since 1998. The research involves collecting the data on the experience of harassment and violence every half year. He also organized the cross-national collaborative research, based on three waves of longitudinal surveys, on harassment and violence, with Australia, Canada, Korea, and US in the 2004-2006, and with Sweden in 2014-2016.

INDEX